BACKSTORY

BACKSTORY

**Interviews with Screenwriters of
Hollywood's Golden Age**

Edited and with
an introduction by
Pat McGilligan

University of California Press
Berkeley / Los Angeles / London

University of California Press
Berkeley and Los Angeles

University of California Press, Ltd.
London, England

© 1986 by The Regents of the University of California

Library of Congress Cataloging-in-Publication Data
Main entry under title:

Backstory: interviews with screenwriters of Hollywood's
    golden age.

    Bibliography: p.
    Includes index.
    1. Screen writers—California—Los Angeles—Interviews.
2. Hollywood (Los Angeles, Calif.)—Biography.
I. McGilligan, Pat.
PN1998.A2B24 1986   812'.03'09 [B]   85-28949
ISBN 0-520-05666-3 (alk. paper)
ISBN 0-520-05689-2 (pbk. : alk. paper)

Printed in the United States of America

1 2 3 4 5 6 7 8 9

Contents

Acknowledgments

This book, a collective endeavor, was made possible by a roster of contributors who were selfless in their support and cooperation; and by the interview subjects themselves, who magnanimously allotted their time and energy, in one or two instances, literally in the final days of their lives.

The James M. Cain interview was originally published as "Tough Guy: James M. Cain Interviewed" in the May/June 1976 issue of *Film Comment.* The John Lee Mahin interview was originally published as "Bombshell Days in the Golden Age: John Lee Mahin Interviewed" in the March/April 1980 issue of *Film Comment.* The W. R. Burnett interview was originally published in the January/February 1983 issue of *Film Comment.* All three interviews are reprinted courtesy of the magazine and of their respective authors. The Mahin and Burnett pieces have been augmented for publication in this anthology.

The Donald Ogden Stewart interview was originally published in the Winter 1970 issue of *Focus on Film.* The Casey Robinson interview, prepared under the auspices of the American Film Institute History Program through the sponsorship of the Louis B. Mayer Foundation, was originally published in *Focus on Film,* no. 32 (April 1979). Both interviews are reprinted here courtesy of the magazine and their respective authors.

Filmographies were compiled by Pat McGilligan. Credit is due to the AFI researcher Dennis L. White for W. R. Burnett's screen credits and book titles; to the biographer Roy Hoopes for James M. Cain's; to Joseph McBride and Todd McCarthy for John Lee Mahin's film titles;

to Joel Greenberg and Allen Eyles for Casey Robinson's; and to Allen Eyles, again, for Donald Ogden Stewart's. In every case there were emendations by the editor.

For aid and comfort the editor is indebted to Susan Setmire for transcription, Bill Paul, Sheila Schwartz, Richard Corliss, Allen Rivkin of the Writers Guild of America—West for expert counsel, Maxine Fleckner, Catherine Turney, Ronald L. Davis of Southern Methodist University, and James V. D'Arc of the Harold B. Lee Library, Brigham Young University.

Appreciation and regrets to Vera Caspary, Sheridan Gibney, Marguerite Roberts and John Sanford, Wells Root and John Wexley for interviews omitted for reasons of space. Particular thanks to John Bright for illuminating background and perspective on the profession.

For reading the introduction and providing helpful criticism and suggestions, I am particularly grateful to the editor's editor, Jeanne Frissell, and to my longtime colleagues Joseph McBride, Gerald Peary, and David Thomson.

Photographs are courtesy of Mark Willoughby and the Collectors Bookstore in Hollywood, the Margaret Herrick Library of the Academy of Motion Picture Arts and Sciences, Allen Eyles, David Thomson, Homer Dickens, the University of Wisconsin Center for Film and Theatre Research, Ned Comstock and the University of Southern California archives, Mary Corliss and the Museum of Modern Art stills archives, Richard Maibaum, the British Film Institute, and Marc Wanamaker and the Bison Archives. The special photography is by Alison Morley.

This book is inscribed to Ken Mate, whose affection for W. R. Burnett proved contagious.

Introduction

The title of this volume, *Backstory,* is a screenwriters' term for what happens in the plot of a movie before the screen story actually unfolds. It is an apt title, I think, for a book in which fifteen old-time screenwriters from the so-called Golden Age of Hollywood—that grand epoch stretching from the last days of silent pictures, through the heyday of sound, to the collapse of the studio system with the onslaught of television—are encouraged to tell their side of the story about what happened, on and off the set, before the cameras rolled. It is especially apt, too, because the term is no longer in common usage. Most of the men and women who wrote movies in the late silent and early sound eras died long ago, and the rules and traditions that governed their work are long since arcana. This book is dedicated to their "backstory."

Nineteen-twenty-six, the year when the sound-on-disc process called Vitaphone was introduced, marked the beginning of the end of silent movies and the birth pangs of the talkies. It was a watershed year for motion pictures, one that in its array of consequences augured radical changes in the nature of screenwriting and in the lives of movie writers.

Before 1926, at least to judge by the official credits, there were no screenwriters. The expression per se scarcely existed. The profession was fragmented into specialties. The assignments and credits were dictated by the big muckamucks, then rationed out to deserving writers, to some extent arbitrarily. There were subspecies of gag-writers, continuity writers, treatment writers, scenarists, adaptors, titlists, what-have-you. The publicity and myths lionized producers and directors. If one believes the myths, there were no scripts, just disconnected bits and pieces of paper with enormous gaps allowing presumed geniuses such as DeMille, Von Stroheim, and D. W. Griffith to extemporize as they roared along.

"To this day," Philip Dunne tells us in his autobiography (*Take Two: A Life in Movies and Politics*), "screenwriters hate to be referred to as script writers or scenario writers, both designations having originated in the bad old days of total writer subservience" (p. 45). Just when the "bad old days" became the "good old days," or whether they ever did, is another matter. But from the period of the earliest one-reelers screenwriting plainly has been a much put-upon profession—riven by inequities of compensation and recognition, by internecine chauvinism and rivalries, by egomania on the one hand and self-loathing on the other. Or at least that is part of the "backstory."

Although the ditchdiggers who preceded the early sound writers have not left much of a trail in memoirs or histories, we do know they were a less homogeneous lot than today's crop of movie writers, and that they did not stream into Hollywood via the respectable isthmus of academia. After all, this was still the era of the dying frontier, and movies were scorned as legitimate entertainment (not to mention Art). It took a certain spunk, a hardiness, to "Go West, Young Writer."

Because it was the West, Westerners already had a foot in the door. Many early film personnel, not just writers, had peculiarly western backgrounds (or perhaps the first generation wore their colors more on the surface). Ex-vaudevillians, cowboys and Indian scouts, Pinkertons, circus roustabouts, dandies and pugilists, traveling salesmen, ex-cons and con artists, former Legionnaires and Lafayette Escadrille flyers, grande dame novelists and lady wits—no doubt the silent era wordsmiths were a motley crew compared to their more socialized descendants.

With sound came "additional dialogue," and the advantage was ceded to an outcropping of "talk experts" from the East. Among the newcomers were many more men than women; they probably looked different from their predecessors, with their fashionable three-piece suits and watch fobs, and talked different, with their sophisticated airs and urban slang. The influx, which began after the excitement of *The Jazz Singer* in 1927 and tapered off in the early 1940s, included scribes from every quarter—playwrights, journalists, poets, essayists, songwriters and lyricists, advertising copywriters, press agents, and refugees from radio. These arrivistes of sound debarked from the Twentieth Century Limited at Pasadena to a VIP welcome perchance, then joined a community of writers that was thrown into a tumult by the bewildering upheavals in the film business and by the irritating presence of the newcomers themselves.

If on the surface the Easterners were less variegated, if they exuded a certain sameness to the veterans, they were disparate under the skin and not necessarily comradely with one another. Before sound, there were castes and snobberies among movie writers; afterwards there were fresh neuroses and conflicts. Identifiable cliques and claques emerged—old-timers who did not mix with the young blood, originators who sniffed at adaptors, constructionists who sneered at dialogue specialists, social realists who belittled comedy writers, and so on.

As astonishing as are the number of now-famous writers who must have passed one another in the 1930s in the corridors of MGM or Warners are the anecdotes about writers who we would think surely must have known each other—W. R. Burnett and James M. Cain, for example; or Cain and Raymond Chandler—but who we discover exchanged nary a glance. The interviews in this volume illustrate how deeply rooted were the attitudes and divisions that kept screenwriters a family of strangers.

With sound, the complexion of screenwriting changed, even though the fragmentation and usurpation did not. The studio system was consolidated, and there arose new rules and superstitions regarding screenplays. Many of the old-timers did not survive the transition. The titlists, as a breed, became extinct. The genres became formulized, and the bromides of some of the dependable clichés began to show signs of fizzling out.

In the new industry the shooting script gained supremacy over the original story, widening the gulf between the initial inspiration and the final product. There developed a crucial difference between story and script and consequently between the writer of the story and the writer of the script—not always one and the same person. Even today the argument persists over whether story or script is more important, like a kind of chicken-or-the-egg argument to outsiders. In any case, the shooting script became the central need in studio filmmaking during the 1930s. Not only did it "break down" the story and systematize the continuity but also it dictated *how* and *what* was to be shot. All scheduling and budgeting came down to the shooting script; that is where the money men got their hands on the elements of the story; that is where writers, typically, were left behind.

In the early 1930s producers developed a favorite strategy for coping with the vagaries of sound. Old-timers were partnered with newcomers on the theory that the old-timer would supply "experience" while the newly arrived screenwriter would constitute a "fresh mind." The old-timer would supply the visual application, the newcomer would bubble over with up-to-date jargon. The old-timer would take care of the script mechanics; the newcomer, the story twists. If two writers couldn't crack a project, why then the body count could pile up to ten or fifteen. The newcomers had an advantage in this arrangement because they did not know the old rules and so unwittingly devised new ones. Movies became topical, tough, violent, explicit, racy. Genres such as the musical and the screwball comedy, unthinkable in a medium without the crackle of a soundtrack, were successfully inaugurated.

The early sound era screenwriters could not have been expected to give birth to a revolutionary aesthetic, nor did they. The script form had already been pioneered for silent pictures, and, to prove this point, in attics and archives there are many elaborately detailed screenplays for the classic films by DeMille, Von Stroheim, Griffith, and others. The new job was to strike a balance between visual prerogatives and the impetus for dialogue—for, as Charles Bennett puts it in this volume, the American mania for "quip, quip, quip." In other words, screenwriters had to become "screen writers"—two distinct words, as Philip Dunne stubbornly chooses to phrase it. This was not accomplished overnight; it is a process ongoing today. Yet it is interesting how many of the movies of the early 1930s are still fresh for the effort and stand up to contemporary expectations.

Within the restrictions was a tremendous opportunity to be creative. Of the primary occupational groups emigrating to Hollywood, newspapermen and (less commonly) -women seemed to fare best under the limitations. For one thing, the pay was better in screenland than in journalism. The deadlines were easier, compared with, say, an afternoon fire written up for a five-star final. And reporters accustomed to the whims of a tyrannical editor did not find producers such a terrible threat to their integrity. Newspaper people knew how to compromise. It may be, too, that their training in the who-what-why-where-when-and-how school of narrative journalism best suited the storytelling strictures of motion pictures. In any case, the metropolitan dailies yielded such durable giants of the field as Frank Nugent, Dudley Nichols, the Mankiewicz brothers (Herman and Joseph), Ben Hecht and Charles MacArthur, and Nunnally Johnson.

The Broadway carpetbaggers arrived proclaiming theatre to be a higher calling and movies a degrading pit stop, a smug conviction certain to grate. Nearly all of the first-rate playwrights of the 1930s and 1940s spent time in the film colony. Despite grumbling to the contrary, the time proved valuable—whether for playing polo, paying bills, or for long-term growth and development—for the likes of George Abbott, Sidney Howard, Robert E. Sherwood, S. N. Behrman, Marc Connelly, Moss Hart, Richard Rodgers and Oscar Hammerstein, Laurence Stallings, Maxwell Anderson, Lillian Hellman, Samson Raphael-son, George S. Kaufman, Sidney Kingsley, Clifford Odets, and John Van Druten.

If playwrights immeasurably enhanced the standard of motion pictures by their contributions, they also, by and large, scurried back to New York to mount their next productions, leaving the full-time mop-up Hollywood screenwriters feeling understandably tenuous. That, of course, is no longer the situation, with the stage exerting less impact on Hollywood trends nowadays. But the belief that any estimable playwright lowered himself by merchandising his talent in the film industry is one that has a curious echo in the prejudice of modern screenwriters against television.

Then there were the novelists—the dime-novelists, Westerners, mystery writers, and serialists, as well as the best-selling authors and the royalty of literature who passed through Hollywood in flight from Hitler or in quest of some quick, convenient money. In the hierarchy of writers the novelist may be regarded as a superior creature, but less so, according to the creed of the times, if under contract to an industry that catered to the lowest common denominator in its audience. Among novelists of stature, for example, Hemingway refused on principle to work in Hollywood as a screenwriter. His unflinching orthodoxy influenced a generation of literati. As late as 1946, Harold Ross, the erstwhile editor of *The New Yorker,* said of Nunnally Johnson, who by then had already racked up two Oscar nominations for his screenplays, "He is one of six humorists in the country. Johnson is also sickening from my standpoint, for he has been sucking around the diamond merchants of Hollywood and hasn't written anything. There is a misspent life" (Froug, 1972, p. 242).

The image of the screenwriter as a cringing hack "sucking around the diamond merchants" was certainly congenial to many producers. (That may be the way they looked at it, too.) Yet this stigma was also nurtured by the self-flagellation of writers. Certainly their guilt and paranoia about Hollywood hit some kind of peak in the 1930s, a time when many old-fashioned and perhaps pretentious people still did not appreciate the future of motion pictures. There was also an escalating cultural tug-of-war between New York City and Los Angeles, and the failures on both coasts encouraged the backbiting among screenwriters.

Not that the successes among screenwriters always felt superior. In this volume Charles Bennett, highly regarded for his screenplays for Hitchcock and DeMille, calls Hollywood "the greatest destroyer" for its carrot-on-the-stick blandishment of writers. Ben Hecht, that most agile and prolific of all screenwriters (six nominations, two Oscars—not a bad batting average), bragged in his autobiography (*A Child of the Century*) that he wrote most of his screenplays in two weeks' time, never spent more than eight weeks on a movie, and earned "tremendous sums of money for work that required no more effort than a game of pinochle" (p. 467). Hecht loved yet hated Hollywood, and he felt that he had squandered too much of his life and genius writing movies.

Still, for every serious writer who died on the vine (Hollywood and Vine, as it were), for every F. Scott Fitzgerald who stubbed his toe on the welcome mat outside Louis B. Mayer's office, another writer flourished or at least maintained equilibrium. Tom Dardis's *Some Time in the Sun* makes the refreshing point that, contrary to popular wisdom, novelists such as F. Scott Fitzgerald, William Faulkner, John O'Hara, and Nathanael "Pep" West were sustained by their Hollywood jobs when their fiction was not selling. Authors such as Burnett and Cain, as their interviews in this anthology reveal, did their best work as novelists during Hollywood residence. Cain, Niven Busch, and other novelist-screenwriters of the era were enormously affected *by* the movies, a complicated, relatively unstudied cross-fertilization that was all part of the moment.

In any event, most screenwriters of the period were not raking in "tremendous sums of money." When the author Leo Rosten surveyed salaries in the film industry in 1938 as part of his research for *Hollywood: The Movie Colony, the Movie Makers,* he determined that only seventeen studio screenwriters made $75,000 or more annually, compared with four musical directors, forty-five directors, fifty-four producers and executives, and eighty actors. (Interviews with two of those privileged seventeen, John Lee Mahin and Casey Robinson, are included here.) Although movie writers may have been earning more money per annum than the average American, the vast majority of the writers were not enjoying the fruits of Eden.

Ironically, the prestige of the craft of screenwriting actually took a dip with the heralded arrival of sound. Although writers had not enjoyed preeminence during the silent days, neither did they swiftly gain ground when dialogue became the end-all and the be-all. If anything, the profusion of credits, which represented the upper hand of producers (which was not always a bad thing), mounted. The dignity of the writer continued to be at the mercy of circumstances. The cult of the director was in ascendancy.

Especially during the early sound era, writers were low on the totem pole. Novelists were excluded from adapting their own titles. Scenarists were banished from the sets of the movies they had written (which, in many cases, were even then in the process of being rewritten).

Impersonal or hackneyed genre assignments were doled out as a form of punishment. Unbeknownst to one another, writers worked on multiple or alternative versions of the same script. Credits were withheld out of pique, jealousy, or bizarre ulterior motives. Credits were summarily awarded to in-laws or mistresses. Marathon working hours were requisite. Writers punched in on a time clock at some studios, as if they were assembling gizmos on a conveyor belt. A generation of unschooled moguls preferred the oral "pitch" to the written word.

The Screen Writers Guild materialized on the scene in the early 1930s to take stock of the situation, endeavor to improve working conditions, fight for a bigger slice of the pie, and strive to ennoble the ordinary screenwriter.* From the outset the New Deal for movie writers was impeded by a powerful faction within, led partly by some veterans from the silent days who wished to protect their cushy employment and their cosy relationships with producers. The political issues of the decade—the trial of the Scottsboro Boys, the imprisonment of Tom Mooney, the Salinas Valley lettuce strike, the organizing of the Guilds, the rise of the U.S. Communist Party, the civil war in Spain, the development of the antifascist front, and so on—heightened the split within the profession and indeed were integrated to a certain degree into the subject matter of films. There were "message" movies from the right as well as from the left.

At a gathering in 1936, a writer named Richard Schayer inveighed against the nascent Guild and pronounced screenwriting a "soft" racket incompatible with unionization, to which Dorothy Parker, in an early Guild round-robin, replied stingingly,

> Through the sweat and the tears I shed over my first script, I saw a great truth—one of those eternal, universal truths that serve to make you feel much worse than you did when you started. And that is that no writer, whether he writes from love or for money, can condescend to what he writes. You can't stoop to what you set down on paper; I don't know why you can't, but you can't. No matter what form it takes, and no matter what the result, and no matter how caustically comic you are about it afterward, what you did was your best. And to do your best is always hard going. [*Screen Guilds Magazine,* May 1936]

---

* The distinction between the Screen Writers Guild and the Writers Guild of America is a subtle one. The Screen Writers Guild was founded in 1933 in Hollywood. When, in 1954, the Guild merged with the Radio Writers Guild and the Television Writers Guild, the new organization was called the Writers Guild of America—East (or West). Motion picture awards are presented annually by the Screen Branch of the Writers Guild of America—West. The screenwriters in this volume tend to refer to the Screen Writers Guild or the Writers Guild interchangeably. Only where it is a matter of some historical concern has their phraseology been corrected.

This split between the "soft racketeers" and the "hard-liners," a logical outgrowth of the aesthetic in-fighting as well as of genuine political differences, became a bitter one.

The Guild's demands were modeled after contractual inroads made by the Dramatists Guild and the Author's League of America: not only control of credits, but royalties for story material; lease, rather than outright sale, of stories; the right to audit company books; a minimum salary; benefits. After a long, complicated struggle with the producers, the film companies, and the conservative element (which in the meantime had formed the short-lived Screen Playwrights, a house union), the Guild settled with the producers in 1941, nine years after the writers had first united. A minimum-fee scale was established; credits (and later, residuals) were surrendered to Guild jurisdiction. Often these credits would be parceled out in grievance procedures that seemed no less acrimonious than those that had been the sole domain of producers. Ownership of story rights, the real sticking point, was entirely conceded to producers. Indeed, all pre-1951 films were later bequeathed by a weakened Guild to television, with no royalties due to writers. (When *Woman of the Year* became a hit on Broadway in 1981, the MGM corporation profited from the story rights, but the writers who concocted the screenplay independently of the studio, Michael Kanin and Ring Lardner, Jr., did not share in the windfall.)

The Guild's relative impotence at key historical moments; its inability to forge meaningful alliances with other labor units in the film industry; its political vacillation and internal factionalism—these are among the reasons that the militancy of the 1930s dissipated in compromise and retreat. The full history is complex, profound, and it cannot be treated adequately here. This much can be said: the right wing of the Guild, which often sided with the producers, scorned national and international issues unrelated to the immediacies of screenwriting and saw Communists under every bedsheet. It succeeded in pushing both liberals and leftists to the right—or to the middle, as it were. The incessant discord was all the more inducement for the neutrals (of which there were plenty) to just sit it out.

As is so vividly documented in Nancy Lynn Schwartz's *The Hollywood Writers' Wars,* the Guild was in an equivocal stance when, in 1947, the House Un-American Activities Committee (HUAC) slipped into town and began ferreting out suspected Communists and "fellow travelers." "Friendly" information was provided to the government by grudge-carrying former members of the Screen Playwrights, who pointed angry fingers at Guild activists. Their very organizing was seen as a Red plot; their studio-approved, and in many cases studio-hatched, scripts boiled over with cryptic Commie propaganda, sandwiched between the lines. The by-now-moderate Guild leadership did not abjectly capitulate but instead trod a thin anti-Communist line while pursuing legal recourse on behalf of some blacklisted writers. Yet its position was historically ignoble. Screenwriting was the dominant profession of the Hollywood Ten. And many screenwriters targeted for their progressive politics had substantial careers abridged, besmirched, destroyed. Ironically, it was to be another two decades—coinciding with the return of the blacklisted generation that dovetailed with the raised voices of the anti-Vietnam War movement—before there was once again any spark of militancy and pride in the writer's branch. Sad to say, the Guild never quite recovered its initial prospects and momentum.

The minimums and conditions facing screenwriters today are a vast improvement over the past, to be sure, and writers of movies are arguably in a more powerful position than ever before. Still, the trends in the marketplace are far from ideal. The new boy network that has replaced the studio system of yore seems no more sympathetic to writers. Presently there is more of an emphasis on original scripts, fewer adaptations of plays and novels, less reliance on dialogue and a revival of the purely visual approach, generally sloppier construction ("The TV generation doesn't know how to construct a plot," is a recurrent plaint in this book), an occasional willingness to pay big bucks for scripts (at least those written by William Goldman, Robert Towne, Paul Schrader, and others), and (alas) a return to the ancient practice of enlisting multiple rewrites for an ailing screenplay. Plus ça change!

The legacy of the "bad old days," the mystique and final say-so of the director, the troubled history of the Guild—all have taken and continue to take their toll on the collective ego of screenwriters. If the interviews in this book seem particularly ironic, self-effacing, embittered, and aggrieved, this is because screenwriting, for all its genuine "progress," remains an "invisible" profession.

The plaque-givers have fallen into line. In over ten years of giving awards to directors and to venerable stars, the American Film Institute (AFI) has not seen fit to bestow its Life Achievement Award on a single screenwriter—except, in the instances of Orson Welles, John Huston, and Billy Wilder, on "hyphenates," whose work as directors has been emphasized over their merit as writers. Nor is this bias likely to be altered. The television network contract with the AFI demands that those honored have the high profile that writers customarily lack. The honorary Oscar has been conferred on make-up artists, special effects people, cartoonists, choreographers, cinematographers, stunt men, humanitarians, juveniles, and three times on Bob Hope—but only three times in sixty years has it been given to a screenwriter who was not also a director. The New York Film Critics waited over twenty years before inaugurating a category for Best Writing. The Guild's own annual awards ceremony is neither widely publicized nor telecast.

Film critics who speak so reverently of the versatility of a William Wellman or a Howard Hawks, a George Stevens or a Raoul Walsh—directors who could put across a screwball comedy, a sprawling western, or a hard-boiled gangster yarn with equal aplomb—have little or no knowledge of the scores of writers who write all such stories—the Seton I. Millers, Anthony Veillers, Sidney Buchmans, and Sonya Leviens, and so on who wrote those very movies for Wellman and Hawks, Stevens and Walsh.

The "name above the title" may well have been Frank Capra, but savored among old-time screenwriters is the apocryphal story of how Robert Riskin, the writer of *Lady for a Day, It Happened One Night, Mr. Deeds Goes to Town, Lost Horizon,* and other "Capracorn," entered the director's office in a fury, threw 120 blank pages of script on his desk, and announced, "Here! Let's see you give *that* the Capra touch!"

Books upon books upon more books are written about glamorous stars, boastful directors, and flamboyant producers. But only recently and in retrospect are we beginning to appreciate the work of leading screenwriters. This collection of interviews with screenwriters is intended as a modest valentine to the fifteen of them, all of whom are writers who came to Hollywood and of age *with* Hollywood during the sound era. While this may be an artificial unity—because the careers of some of these writers either predate sound or postdate it by a few years—it is nonetheless a unity because with sound came full maturity to the calling of "screenwriter."

The interviews that follow are with individuals of all stripes. W. R. Burnett was first and foremost a novelist. He regarded his screenplays as financial support for his fiction writing. Yet his personal stamp is on all of his work, and as fine a novelist as he was (check out the unadulterated prose of *Little Caesar, High Sierra,* or *The Asphalt Jungle*), his influence as a screenwriter on motion pictures is arguably as important as that of any single American writer. The bleak fatalism of his stories reflects his philosophy of life: "You're born, you're gonna have trouble, and you're gonna die."

James M. Cain, too, was more of a novelist and less of a screenwriter in that he had few formal credits to flaunt for his seventeen years of servitude in Hollywood. He began as a journalist and honed his imagination in Hollywood; Cain's tales—spider's nests of sex, intrigue, duplicity, and murder—are still rich fodder for remakes.

The third novelist in our company, Niven Busch, is an opposite example. Also a newspaperman who apprenticed in Hollywood, Busch learned the rules of dramaturgy and then transferred his "story craft" to the arena of fiction with notable success. Characteristically, Busch writes on the grand scale with Freudian implications, seeing psychological dimensions to the West that titillated this Easterner.

As mentioned, the theatre supplied Hollywood with many top-flight writers. One of these is Charles Bennett, a displaced Englishman whose second play, *Blackmail,* generated an association with Alfred Hitchcock and was the springboard for Bennett's half-century-long career. While Bennett chose to subordinate himself to great directors, his work shows a pattern of interest in themes of mistaken identity, jaunty romance, improbable adventure, and dubious history.

Frances Goodrich and Albert Hackett, a married couple, were thespians before they were playwrights. At MGM they became one of Hollywood's most admired screenwriting teams—four Oscar nominations, four Writers Guild awards, and a catalog of credits that range from their adaptation of Dashiell Hammett's *The Thin Man* to the Nelson Eddy–Jeanette MacDonald musicals to their Pulitzer Prize–winning play and film script of *The Diary of Anne Frank.* In addition to bristling wit and sexual repartee, their signature is usually a guarantee of elevated tone.

From Broadway by way of Amherst and Oxford came Allan Scott and his propensity for effete comedy, put to fine effect in six Astaire-Rogers musicals. Although he harbored a nagging social conscience and worked effectively in suspense and melodrama, it may be that musical comedies and the picaresque romance best reflected his ebullient personality and a lifelong commitment to popular entertainment.

Also interviewed here is the lesser-known Richard Maibaum, a young and nervy social-consciousness playwright who sojourned in Hollywood in the 1930s and who is still going strong writing the James Bond canvases in the 1980s. As a boy Maibaum devoured the heroic tales of Alexandre Dumas, and his adult writing career has been largely given over to comic-book variations on Dumas's themes.

Interviewed as well is Norman Krasna, a former newspaper copy boy: Krasna came to Hollywood as a press agent for Warner Brothers, went to New York to write a Broadway play in his off hours, and returned to Hollywood as a junior writer. He is a good illustration of the writer who managed to balance two prosperous careers, one on Broadway and one in Hollywood. Said to have been one of the models for Budd Schulberg's Sammy Glick (Jerry Wald was another), Krasna built his reputation on a role-reversal conceit that had deeply personal roots.

Then there are those writers impossible to categorize: Donald Ogden Stewart is one. Famed as a humorist, he was also something of a novelist, something of a playwright, and an actor (briefly on Broadway and in movies). Stewart was a confidant of Hemingway's (and is said to have provided a model for one of the characters in *The Sun Also Rises*) and a social activist in Hollywood, where he was later blacklisted. A celebrated bon vivant in his own right, Stewart was mostly content to enlist his gadfly intelligence in the service of other people's stories.

Likewise from a patchwork background is John Lee Mahin, a former repertory actor, newshound, and film critic, whose friendship with Ben Hecht and Charles MacArthur led to his summons to Hollywood and to a career at MGM as one of the film industry's best adaptors. He found his niche writing racy comedies and stories of manly derring-do, but he seemed infinitely versatile. An unreconstructed rightist, he is a spokesman in this volume for the Screen Playwrights and the wing of conservatives in Hollywood who knowingly fostered the blacklist.

A trio of other great adaptors were coincidentally all ensconced at Warner Brothers for a spell: Lenore Coffee, who came to Hollywood in 1919, became a fixer-upper of movie scripts, and later, in the 1940s, one of the vaunted screenwriters for Bette Davis and Joan Crawford vehicles. The unhappiness of her own life is the subtext of her screenplays. The former press agent Julius J. Epstein, in partnership with his identical twin brother Philip G. Epstein, also commenced as a fixer-upper, stayed on in Hollywood for fifty years, and carved out a vocation as a high-comedy specialist. The brothers Epstein were particularly noted for their facility with hit Broadway plays (or, in the case of *Casablanca,* flop plays). But as Julius J. Epstein correctly points out in his interview, if the urbane urban comedy became his trademark, this did not preclude his eventful forays into other genres.

Casey Robinson, a former high school teacher of English, had the reputation of being able to take any novel, no matter how long-winded or unwieldy, and condense it into a dramatic screenplay. Not a "moonlighting" playwright, newsman, novelist, or professional writer-for-any-occasion, Robinson was instead one of the latter-day school of screenwriters whose life was devoted to writing movies and only movies.

In this category is Philip Dunne, son of the essayist and humorist Finley Peter Dunne. Philip Dunne, along with the writers Lamar Trotti and Nunnally Johnson, was one of the mainstays of Twentieth Century–Fox. But, despite two Academy Award nominations, the Writers Guild Laurel Award for Achievement over a lifetime, and over forty impressive screen credits as a writer, director, and producer, he says of himself that he functioned as little more than a "good cabinetmaker" when adapting someone else's story into one of his screenplays. This comment, like Henry Fonda's remark that he wanted to be remembered simply as a "good actor," ought not to be taken at face value.

Taken together, these interviews comprise an affectionate group portrait of the movie writers of a bygone era—of their lives and lifestyles, of their vast body of work, of their differing approaches to the challenge of writing motion pictures. This book is not meant to be a scholarly or historical work, a purely factual study, or even a complete representation of the profession. Names and faces are missing. It would take six hundred such interviews to reflect the diversity of writers who wrote our favorite movies. The selection of writers was limited, obviously, to those who survived into the late 1970s and early 1980s. (Even so, it has been a race against time. Samson Raphaelson, the playwright who collaborated so closely with Ernst Lubitsch, agreed to an in-depth interview. Lillian Hellman, who cut a swath in Hollywood as well as in stage circles, also evinced willingness. Both died before the interviews could be arranged.)

What do these people have in common? Everything and nothing. To a certain extent, it can be said that they are all unsung. Only Coffee (in England), Dunne, and Stewart have published autobiographies. Despite scattered nominations in the group, only three are Oscar winners, whereas seven are recipients of the Writers Guild Laurel Award for Achievement that represents the testimonial of peers.

However, it is a reasonably indicative group and includes writers who tackled every genre, who specialized in one distinct genre, who worked for one studio or every studio, or who freelanced from producer to producer. The group also includes those who swear Twentieth Century–Fox was superior to MGM, or vice versa, as well as defenders and detractors of producers Goldwyn, Selznick, Wallis, Zanuck, and others. It is a group that includes self-described right wingers, left wingers, middle-of-the-roaders, and iconoclasts.

Their reminiscences, taken singly or en masse, contain both complementary and conflicting accounts of authorship, Guild politics and Hollywood lore, polar appraisals of other writers and of specific scripts. (In this book there are at least two irreconcilable versions of how *Casablanca* came into being, and likewise two for *Scarface;* also we can boast the "constructionist" and two uncredited contributors to the screenplay of *Foreign Correspondent.*)

No overblown claims are advanced in these screenwriters' names and no hyperbole about their credits (which ought to speak for themselves). These writers have this in common—pride in having been writers and of having written stories for movies that mirror their own ideas and person-alities. They are the authors of their movies if not exactly the *auteurs*, the dominant figures of the filmmaking process. They are not enamored of *auteur* theory as it applies to directors, for they know that, even in Hollywood, in the beginning is the word. These are the people who were indeed there in the beginning, when directors—and movies—were fumbling for words. This is their "backstory."

A Note on Credits

It is not a simple job to compile the filmography of a screenwriter, for as Richard Corliss has written in his indispensable book, *Talking Pictures,* "A writer may be given screen credit for work he didn't do (as with Sidney Buchman on *Holiday*), or be denied credit for work he did do (as with Sidney Buchman on *The Awful Truth*)." Which is to say, there are irresolvable gaps in the best sources.

The American Film Institute's Catalog of Feature Films (1921–1930, 1961–1970) is incomplete for the years that are missing and not always reliable for the years that are covered. The joint project of the Academy of Motion Picture Arts and Sciences and the Writers Guild of America—West, *Who Wrote the Movie (And What Else Did He Write)? (1936–1969),* is less than authoritative. It overlooks movies written before the inception of the Guild and toes the official Guild line of accreditation thereafter. Consequently, excluded are many famous and not-so-famous instances of uncredited complicity; in the case of *Yankee Doodle Dandy,* for instance, there is no mention of the Epstein brothers, who were publicly thanked for their script by the Cagneys in Hollywood trade papers at the time of the film's release. The blacklist years are riddled with aliases and omissions. And the Guild maintains rules (disallowing screen credit to any director who has not contributed at least 50 percent of the dialogue, for example) that, while they may protect screenwriters, do not promote a full accounting of the screenplay.

The credits for this book were cross-referenced from several sources— those cited above, *The New York Times* and *Variety* film reviews, *Interna-*

tional Motion Picture Almanac and *Motion Picture Daily* yearbooks, *A Guide to American Screenwriters: The Sound Era, 1929–1982* by Larry Langman (New York and London: Garland Publishing, 1984) and the *Film Encyclopedia* by Ephraim Katz (New York: Perigree Books, 1979). In individual cases there was additional spadework by the original inter- viewers and by *Film Comment* and *Focus on Film* magazines. As a final resort, whenever possible, the interview subjects were confronted with the results of research and asked to add to or subtract from the list. This is not to say that memories are not convenient or forgetful. In the cases of Charles Bennett and Lenore Coffee, movie titles materialized for which there was no backup proof of existence in reference sources—*Shadow of the Wing* and *Branded Woman,* respectively. They are mentioned on the generous assumption that these pictures may have been photographed but not released or that they were independent, low-budget productions somehow lost in the cinema shuffle.

As to specific claims and counterclaims as to who wrote exactly what, there is another kind of cross-referencing to be done. The oral historian cannot always separate fact from factoid or opinion from the ax-to-grind. Likely there is much in this collection of reminiscences that contradicts, or is contradicted by, material in other books. Partly, such conflicting tales are to be expected of a branch of the film indus- try that has been relatively untapped for its perspective, where egos and careers have been so trampled. And partly such differences issue inevitably from individual points of view on a group enterprise.

Charles Bennett:
First-Class
Constructionist

Interview by Pat McGilligan

*The newly arrived Charles Bennett would appear
wreathed in scarves, draped in a dashing blazer, or
dustily booted, fresh from a polo match. He flew
planes, rode like a Cossack, and could on occasion
come dangerously near stealing scenes from the
Boss [Cecil B. DeMille], who had always been second to none in "office performances."*

Jesse L. Lasky, Jr.,
Whatever Happened to Hollywood?

Safe it is to say of Charles Bennett that his life, his career, would
have turned out very differently if the movies—and Hollywood—had
not happened along. In Great Britain his roots were in legitimate
theatre. His mother had squandered the family fortune, such as it was,
producing flop plays. A Shakespearean and Shavian actor of some
repute in his youth, Bennett once played in a Stratford-Upon-Avon
production of *Othello* top-billed over John Gielgud. (A poster of that
occasion hung in his study in Beverly Hills, and he delighted in point-
ing it out to visitors.) He was a budding playwright with a bright future
when a man named Alfred Hitchcock purchased his second mounted
play and turned it into England's first full-length, "all-talkies" motion
picture.

The vitality of Great Britain's theatre scene was ebbing away even
as the motion picture industry was busy being born. Bennett found
steady work churning out "B" scenarios but, more important, he
found distinction as the writer or co-writer of seven of the early Hitchcock films regarded by many critics as the cornerstone of the director's
oeuvre—*Blackmail* (1929), *The Man Who Knew Too Much* (1934),
The Thirty-Nine Steps (1935), *The Secret Agent* (1936), *Sabotage*
(1936), *Young and Innocent* (1937), and (later in the United States)

17

Charles Bennett in Beverly Hills, 1984. (Photo: Alison Morley)

Foreign Correspondent (1940). Only Eliot Stannard (who wrote the scenarios for *The Pleasure Garden* in 1925, *The Mountain Eagle* and *The Lodger* in 1926, *Downhill* and *Easy Virtue* in 1927, *Champagne* in 1928, and *The Manxman* in 1929, all silent pictures) collaborated as a

writer with Hitchcock to such an extent—Stannard, that is, and Hitchcock's wife, Alma Reville, whose recurrent credit as a screenwriter
Bennett respectfully disputes in this interview.

Part of the wave of foreign talent lured to Hollywood prior to World
War II, Bennett was brought over by Universal in 1937—and promptly
relegated to a piece of romantic kitsch, not the perfect assignment for
one of the world's premiere dramatic constructionists. A series of similar misadventures followed; only after he was summoned by Hitchcock
(himself brought to Hollywood by David O. Selznick upon Bennett's
advice) as co-writer of *Foreign Correspondent* did he establish his foot-
ing in the United States. Inexplicably, after the success of that movie, he
was cut off by Hitchcock, who was terribly insecure about writers and
about his own mystique and who never gave writers much credit where
it might otherwise shine on "Hitch." Auteurist film critics have fawned
over Hitchcock but overlooked such writers as Stannard, Bennett, and
John Michael Hayes (who wrote a quartet of superior Hitchcock films in
the 1950s), who were instrumental in embroidering the Hitchcock
themes. You can look hard in François Truffaut's *Hitchcock,* Donald
Spoto's *The Art of Alfred Hitchcock,* Raymond Durgnat's *The Strange
Case of Alfred Hitchcock,* or Robin Wood's *Hitchcock*—to name four of
the essential texts—without finding any expansive or complimentary
mention of Bennett.

It is not hard to understand Bennett's consequent loyalty to Cecil B.
DeMille, who would seem to be Hitchcock's antithesis as a filmmaker
in so many ways. DeMille took Bennett under his wing, enlisted him in
undercover right-wing political activities, and utilized him in three key
films in the twilight of DeMille's long career. From there Bennett went
on to carve out solid credits as writer (and occasional director) of in-
tricately plotted mystery, suspense, horror, adventure, and film noir. If
he fell under the spell of the producer Irwin Allen in the 1950s, to his
everlasting unhappiness, at least the opportunity arose to adapt such
old masters as Arthur Conan Doyle, Jules Verne, and Edgar Allan
Poe.

When I met Bennett, he was in his eighties and working on his second
novel. The first remained unpublished, though H. N. ("Swanie") Swanson (the legendary Hollywood literary agent for Burnett, Cain, Faulkner,
and others), himself an octogenarian, was handling the prospects. Bennett's desk was strewn with out-of-sequence notes for the work-in-
progress. The walls of his hacienda were decorated with his collection of
nineteenth-century playbills, a cherished link to his theatrical past.

The wine flowed freely, and so did the conversation. In the words of
his lifelong friend Robert Nathan, the nonagenarian author of *Portrait
of Jennie* and other works, Bennett had the qualities of "an aging elf,"

for he was as pixieish and melodious a man as you would ever be fortunate enough to meet. How handsome and persuasively charming he must have been in his prime! Blunt in his opinions, direct in his anecdotes—long will his rich baritone purr (the English accent intact) ring in my ears. Our sessions together ended on a somewhat melancholy note as Bennett was forced to concede, upon reflection, his deep regret at ever having been enticed to Hollywood.

1929   *Blackmail* (Alfred Hitchcock).* Play basis, co-scenario.

1930   *The Last Hour* (Walter Forde). Play basis.

1931   *Two Way Street* (George King). Co-story.
        Deadlock (George King). Co-story.
        Number Please (George King). Co-story.

1932   *Partners Please* (Lloyd Richards). Script.

1933   *Mannequin* (George A. Cooper). Script.
        Paris Plane (John Paddy Carstairs). Script.
        Hawleys of High Street (Thomas Bentley). Co-script.
        The House of Trent (Norman Walker). Co-script.
        Matinee Idol (George King). Script.

1934   *The Secret of the Loch* (Milton Rosmer). Co-script.
        Gay Love (Leslie Hiscott). Co-script.
        Warn London (T. Hayes Hunter). Co-script.
        The Man Who Knew Too Much (Alfred Hitchcock). Co-theme, co-script.

1935   *Night Mail* (Herbert Smith). Co-script.
        Blue Smoke (Ralph Ince). Story.
        The Thirty-Nine Steps (Alfred Hitchcock). Co-scenario, co-adaptation.
        The Clairvoyant (Maurice Elvey). Co-script.
        King of the Damned (Walter Forde). Co-script.

1936   *The Secret Agent* (Alfred Hitchcock). Script.
        Sabotage (a.k.a. *A Woman Alone*) (Alfred Hitchcock). Script.

1937   *Young and Innocent* (a.k.a. *A Girl Was Young*) (Alfred Hitchcock). Co-script.
        King Solomon's Mines (Robert Stevenson). Co-scenario, co-dialogue.

* In the filmographies in this volume, the directors' names appear in parentheses following the titles.

1938   *The Adventures of Marco Polo* (Archie Mayo). Uncredited contribution.
The Young in Heart (Richard Wallace). Adaptation.

1939   *Hidden Power* (Lewis D. Collins). Uncredited contribution.
Balalaika (Reinhold Schunzel). Co-script.

1940   *Foreign Correspondent* (Alfred Hitchcock). Co-story, co-script.

1941   *They Dare Not Love* (James Whale). Co-script.
Reap the Wild Wind (Cecil B. DeMille). Co-script.

1942   *Saboteur* (Alfred Hitchcock). Uncredited contribution.
Joan of Paris (Robert Stevenson). Script.

1944   *Forever and a Day* (Multiple directors). Co-script.
The Story of Dr. Wassell (Cecil B. DeMille). Co-script.

1947   *Ivy* (Sam Wood). Script.
Unconquered (Cecil B. DeMille). Co-script.

1948   *The Sign of the Ram* (John Sturges). Script.

1949   *Madness of the Heart* (Charles Bennett). Script, director.
Black Magic (Gregory Ratoff). Script.

1950   *Where Danger Lives* (John Farrow). Script.
No Escape (Charles Bennett). Script, director.

1951   *Kind Lady* (John Sturges). Co-script.

1952   *The Green Glove* (Rudolph Mate). Story, script.

1954   *Dangerous Mission* (Louis King). Co-script.

1956   *The Man Who Knew Too Much* (Alfred Hitchcock). Co-screen story of remake.

1957   *The Story of Mankind* (Irwin Allen). Co-script.

1958   *Curse of the Demon* (Jacques Tourneur). Co-script.

1959   *The Big Circus* (Joseph M. Newman). Co-script.

1960   *The Lost World* (Irwin Allen). Co-script.

1961   *Voyage to the Bottom of the Sea* (Irwin Allen). Co-script.

1962   *Five Weeks in a Balloon* (Irwin Allen). Co-script.

1965   *War Gods of the Deep* (a.k.a. *The City Under the Sea*) (Jacques Tourneur). Co-script.

Produced plays include *The Return, Blackmail, The Last Hour, Sensation, Big Business, Midnight, The Danger Line* (collaboration), and *Page from a Diary.*

Television work includes writing and directing episodes of "Schlitz Playhouse of the Stars," "Four Star Playhouse," "Cavalcade of America," and so on.

Academy Awards include a nomination in 1940 for co-writing the original screenplay of *Foreign Correspondent* in collaboration with Joan Harrison.

What writers inspired you as a boy?

Oh, Christ, that's a difficult one. Let me give it some thought. My favorite writer, of course, was H. Rider Haggard, who wrote *King Solomon's Mines, Allan Quatermain,* things like that. My second favorite writer was H. G. Wells, who wrote *The War of the Worlds.* As regards my third favorite writer . . . I can't remember. (*Laughs*)

Was there a point in your life at which you decided to become a writer, or was it a gradual development?

Let's put it this way. I had acted before I went into the army. And when I came out of World War I at the age of nineteen, I went back into acting. At first I was a terrible actor. I used to get jobs and be fired from them; but gradually I learned to act.

At the age of twenty-three I played Romeo, sometimes twice-nightly by the way. In those days there were theatres that would have two performances a night. For example, I remember coming in to the Alexandra Theatre in Birmingham for a two-week season. I was the juvenile lead at the age of twenty-two or twenty-three. One afternoon I played Marc Antony with his famous speech in the afternoon, and Romeo twice that evening. A pretty hard day's work, you must admit! Somehow, out of all this, I became a reasonably good actor. In fact, at the end of '23 or at the beginning of '24, I went to the Bristol Little Theatre, doing a play a week, playing most of the important parts. And during that time I think I really learned to act.

Then I became Ben Greet's juvenile leading man for Ben Greet's Shakespearean company, which took me to Paris. There I became quite a hit at the English Theatre. I went back there in '25 and '26 as the star of the theatre! Also, by that time, I was still hankering after being a writer, because acting wasn't enough. I wasn't making enough money. Does that sound reasonable?

You weren't being gratified artistically?

It was enough artistically, but it wasn't enough financially, let's put it that way. So I sort of gradually began to write plays. I had always been writing, ever since the age of about twelve, without ever quite realizing it. I think I wrote my first play at the age of thirteen, a three-act thing. I don't know what it was about, and I wish to God I had it now. The fact remains that I never really gave up writing. I edited the school magazine when I was fourteen and wrote the serial in it—that kind of stuff. So I suppose I was always, after a fashion, a writer—not necessarily good, but a writer.

When I was in Paris in 1925, I wrote my first play, *The Return,* and as we were doing a new play every two weeks and rehearsing most of the days, how the hell I had time to write anything at all I don't know. I haven't the faintest idea. Anyway, I wanted to be a writer, and so I wrote my first play, which wasn't produced until the spring of 1927 at the Everyman Theatre. It was an artistic success that didn't make any money. Somehow, at the same time, while I was still with Ben Greet, I wrote *Blackmail,* which Tallulah Bankhead eventually played in London early in 1928. And this was reasonably successful—in fact, so successful that Hitchcock made it into the first British talking picture.

Blackmail (1929) and The Man Who Knew Too Much (1934)

When did you first become aware of motion pictures?

Film? When Hitchcock made *Blackmail* into the first talking picture [in England], I began to realize that there were such things as motion pictures. Until then, I had only been interested in theatre. Before the end of the year I had a tremendous success in the theatre called *The Last Hour,* which was a melodrama. It was a big year for me—1928. *The Last Hour* was also made into a movie [in 1929], and by that time I found myself somehow in the film industry.*

In 1929 I was making an immense amount of money, and I was happy. I had six plays touring the country. Then, talkies were really beginning to hit, and the theatres were beginning to go to hell. You see, every town in those days had a Theatre Royale or an Opera

---

* One might endlessly argue the precise year of film releases. A U.S. film often has a British release a year or two later—but not always. A British film might have a U.S. release a year or two later—or never. A U.S. film might officially premiere in New York or Los Angeles weeks apart, and thus fall into a separate calendar year, depending on one's reference point. Some sources list the year of production, while most sources prefer the calendar year of release. Here, as elsewhere throughout this volume, the editor has attempted to reconcile these discrepancies for which, alas, there is no international tribunal. In parentheses is listed the *release* year, as is *indicated* by the text of the specific interview. But nothing in this area is writ in stone.

House or something. Every little town! But they were all dying, dying, dying, and we were left with a thriving and growing film industry.

At that time, British International Pictures, which was the top British company, put me under contract for a couple of years to come and write for them. I had just got married and I was perfectly happy with enough to get along on. There I wrote a thing called *The Hawleys of High Street* [1933], a comedy—which I don't know how the hell I wrote, because I am not a comedy writer.

I was under contract to British International from 1929 to 1930. Then I started to write rather cheaper pictures. I wrote a thing called *The Secret of the Loch* [1934], because the Loch Ness monster had been sighted, and I went up to the Scottish highlands and searched out Loch Ness. I never met the monster, but I found a wonderful Scotch whiskey, by the way. I wrote about ten movies during that period, I suppose. I'd write the damned things in a month or less and be paid about 300 pounds for them, which wasn't bad in those days.

All for different companies?

There were quite a few for a guy named George King, who was the world's worst director. And other studios used to grab these stories of mine and make them. So I was very happy. I was living rather comfortably; I had a lovely flat in West Arlington Dover, overlooking Belgrave Square—it's the best part of London. Nothing wrong with that.

Before 1928 and Blackmail, *had you seen many films?*

Of course I had.

What was your attitude toward them?

Contempt. (*Laughs.*)

What were the precise circumstances of your first meeting with Hitchcock?

In early 1928, when he was making *Blackmail,* I was invited up to Elystree, where the picture was shooting. Hitch was extremely friendly. We got to know each other. We went up to the Plough, which was the local pub on a hill, and had a lot of drinks together. And we became very, very good friends. The result was, when I did eventually sign up with British International, I had a good relationship with him, and was asked, "Why don't you work with Hitchcock?"

I thought you received a co-screenwriting credit on Blackmail.

No. I haven't got a co-screenwriting credit on *Blackmail.* There is *no* screenwriting credit on *Blackmail.* It is only "from the play by Charles Bennett." (*Points.*) You can see it on the original poster over there on the wall if you want to, by the way. I didn't actually work on the screenplay, but I'm not kidding myself about that—the film was my play.

After *Blackmail,* Mycroft [Walter Mycroft], the story editor at British International, said, "Charles, why don't you work with Hitch? We own the rights to *Bulldog Drummond* [the novel and many sequels by Cyril McNeile, writing under the pen name of Sapper]. We'd like you to write a story about Bulldog Drummond, which Hitchcock will direct."

So I wrote a story called "Bulldog Drummond's Baby"—and this was a story about Bulldog Drummond's baby being stolen in Switzerland in order to force Bulldog Drummond into a horrible situation. The picture wasn't made by British International. But the following year Hitch moved over to Gaumont-British and took the rights with him and changed the title. I was called in later, and this story became *The Man Who Knew Too Much*. Which has been made twice [by Hitchcock], let's face it.

Now let me get this straight: The Man Who Knew Too Much *was an original story of yours based on the character of Bulldog Drummond . . .*

It was an original story I wrote, taking the character of Bulldog Drummond, and writing an original story about what happened to him.

Then why does the original credit line read "based on an original theme by Charles Bennett and D. B. Wyndham Lewis"?

D. B. never had anything to do with it. He was a very lovely guy. D. B. Wyndham Lewis was brought in while we were working on "Bulldog Drummond's Baby" to write some dialogue, which was never used, but since he had been brought in, it was eventually decided to give him a story credit. In those days there was no such thing as the Writers Guild to dictate who wrote what. It was the producer who decided who wrote what. So he got a story credit, which he was never entitled to. A very lovely guy. He's dead now, I'm afraid.

Why are so many other people credited on the screen with dialogue— A. R. Rawlinson, Edwin Greenwood, Emlyn Williams?

Because that was typical of the period. Typical of the period! (*Laughs.*) In those days, a picture would be going into production, and then someone would say, "Oh, let's alter this scene or that scene." Then you'd get all sorts of screenwriters working on it. In the case of *The Man Who Knew Too Much*, I wouldn't know; they kept calling in people to alter scenes—not necessarily *construction*—but *scenes*. It was a very weird world we lived in, in those days, but a very amusing and exciting world.

So when "Bulldog Drummond's Baby" became The Man Who Knew Too Much, *what happened to your initial dialogue?*

My dialogue was considerably altered.

I have often wondered why, years later, Hitchcock would care to remake one of his own greatest successes.

Because it was a terribly good story. I asked him myself why he did it, many times, and he always admitted one should never remake a classic. Perfectly true. *The Thirty-Nine Steps* [1935] has been remade twice—and flopped each time. Gilliat and Launder's *The Lady Vanishes* has been made again—and flopped. One should never remake a classic. It's absurd, mmm?

Did Hitchcock ever explain his reasons for doing it?

Only his own regrets for doing it.

The Constructionist

When did you become associated, full-time, with Hitchcock?

In 1932 or 1933 Hitchcock asked me to come over to Gaumont-British, where *The Man Who Knew Too Much* was by that time being made, and he wanted to get ahead with John Buchan's story *The Thirty-Nine Steps*. He wanted me to construct the damned thing. Possibly, I suppose, I was the best-known constructionist in the world at that time. I'm not being conceited, but I was awfully bloody good. I was a first-class constructionist. I'm not saying I was the best dialogue writer in the world. Sometimes we had to bring in dialogue writers—for example, on *The Thirty-Nine Steps* we brought in Ian Hay, who wrote some lovely dialogue. But the important thing—and Hitch always knew this—is construction. Get your story, get your architecture right, and you can always add your dialogue afterwards. That was always the Hitchcock attitude, up till the day of his death.

Define construction for me.

Construction is: a story starts at the beginning, it develops, it works itself out, and it works up to its finale. The great essence of construction is to know your end before you know your beginning; to know exactly what you're working up to; and then to work up to that end. To just start off and wander on the way isn't any good whatever . . . because you're wallowing.

Was it your background as an actor and a playwright that gave you such a knack for construction?

No, I think it was just an instinctive thing. I think playwrighting comes into construction, because you can't write a play unless you know about construction, but I think I was born as a good constructionist. It's as simple as that.

Do you feel that you have a weakness at dialogue?

I've been told that—by my wife particularly. (*Laughs.*) I don't believe it, quite frankly. What I will say is, I know I am a tremendous constructionist. I will say also that I don't consider myself Noel Coward as regards writing dialogue, let's put it that way. That is, I don't compare myself to Noel Coward or Charlie Brackett, who was a great dialogue writer, but I consider myself a better constructionist.

I am interested in the fact that on The Thirty-Nine Steps, The Secret Agent *[1936],* Sabotage *[1936], and* Young and Innocent *[1937], Hitchcock's wife, Alma Reville, receives a co-adaptation credit.*

She doesn't. She never did a damned thing. She gets "continuity." I'll tell you exactly why. I don't want to say anything against Alma. I adored Alma. She was one of the most wonderful people in the world. But Hitchcock had an arrangement with the companies he worked for that said that Alma would write continuity for a certain amount of money every week. Well, of course, she never did a damned thing, because continuity was really Hitchcock saying, "I'll shoot it this way or that way." Hitchcock was remarkable in that respect, let's face it. When it came to shooting a picture, he knew exactly what shots he wanted. He'd shoot the damned thing in such a way that it couldn't be cut any way except the way he shot it. And that's continuity. Alma got money for that alleged continuity. Well dammit, why not? Hitchcock was perfectly right to get more money that way. I don't remember seeing Alma at all during the writing. Except at the end of the day, perhaps, when we'd go home for a drink at Hitchcock's apartment. Hitch served up very good cocktails. I'll always remember that.

All this foolery with credits didn't bother you in those days?

Nothing bothered me in those days. I was young and very good looking.

Then, are the scenarios for The Thirty-Nine Steps, The Secret Agent, Sabotage, *and* Young and Innocent *entirely yours?*

Alma had nothing to do with *The Thirty-Nine Steps* at all. As regards *Young and Innocent,* that becomes a problem. I remember, Hitch and I went to Switzerland together, to the Palace Hotel at St. Moritz, where I was writing *Young and Innocent*—not the script so much as the construction of the script; working out the scenes. At the same time I received this offer from Universal Pictures to come over to the United States, so I never quite finished it. By the time I came to America, Hitchcock somehow finished it, but I wasn't there for the end of the production, so I don't know who did the writing. It couldn't have been Alma. Our favorite haunt for work was the Palace Hotel in St. Moritz. Hitch and I went there three or four years in a row. I would ski and he would sit in the hotel. Alma would ski with me, by the way.

Hence, her co-credit?

(*Laughs.*)

In the case of The Thirty-Nine Steps, *what was the relationship between the film and John Buchan's novel?*

It came from the novel. Not that the novel had anything to do with our film. The novel doesn't even have a woman in it.

How did you and Hitchcock develop the changes from the novel into the story of the film?

Hitch and I would sit down together and discuss it a lot. Gradually, out of all of it, we—I suppose, *I*—evolved the structure of the screenplay. All sorts of things in *The Thirty-Nine Steps*—like the famous scene with the farmer's wife and things like that—none of this was in the novel. In fact, very little of it was in the novel.

Was Mr. Memory in the novel?

No.

An invention of yours or Hitchcock's?

Mine. The point is, what we were faced with is the fundamental idea—which is tremendously good—of a guy who hasn't done anything but is on the run for murder, with not only the cops but the villains after him. Now, that has been used a thousand times since, but I think we were the first to use it to such an extent. And that idea is what we got from Buchan. A helluva good idea. What's wrong with it?

Let's move on to The Secret Agent. *What is the relationship there between the Somerset Maugham source material and the film?*

They were short stories by Maugham about a British spy, and what I had to do as constructionist was to take the stories and turn them into one consistent story. It was as simple as that.

What about the contribution of Jesse Lasky, Jr.?

He wrote a few lines and that is all. He got an "additional dialogue" credit.

Hitchcock often said that your next collaboration, Sabotage, *which is based on* The Secret Agent *by Joseph Conrad, didn't quite work for a number of reasons. Do you share his misgivings?*

Yes. I think the main trepidation is that we wanted Robert Donat and Robert Donat was suffering terribly from asthma and we had to get John Loder instead. Loder was a delightful character, a great friend of mine—a member of my cavalry troop out here [in Hollywood] when I was running one—but John was not a good actor. He wasn't Robert Donat. I think that made a 100 percent difference to the movie.

Hitchcock also said that the boy getting killed by a bomb—and the fact that the audience anticipated the boy's death—was ultimately a mistake in storytelling. Do you agree with that assessment?

No. This is what the story is about. Conrad's whole story is about a kid who gets killed. Dammit, this is based on Conrad! I remember the critic of *The Observer*, C. A. Lejeune, at a party after the first showing—she came up to me and said, "Charles, you should be ashamed of yourself for killing that child." And I said, "What the hell are you

"A helluva good idea": Robert Donat on the Lam in The Thirty-Nine Steps. *Charles Bennett wrote the script; Ian Hay contributed "lovely dialogue."*

talking about? Read Conrad's *Secret Agent* and see for yourself. Blame Conrad for it!" Save the life of the kid? Where's your story? If you're writing Conrad's *Secret Agent,* you have to be faithful to it. If you're doing *Secret Agent*—later called *Sabotage*—you're doing *Secret Agent;* it's as simple as that.

Excluding, for the moment, Foreign Correspondent, *which of the early stories directed by Hitchcock—from the British period—do you feel most fond of and most proprietary?*

It's a very hard question to answer. But I imagine it has to be one of the best stories I think I ever wrote in my life—and I wrote it, let's face it, and nobody else—*The Man Who Knew Too Much.* It was a helluva good story.

Collaborating with Hitchcock

Have you ever read Hitchcock *(New York: Simon & Schuster, 1966), Hitchcock's published conversations with François Truffaut?*

No.

In the transcript, Hitchcock often says, in speaking of this scene or that scene, "I thought of this detail, I thought of that detail."

Oh, Hitchcock thinks of *everything!*

Do you mean that ironically?

I mean it ironically. I was reading Donald Spoto's book [*The Dark Side of Genius: The Life of Alfred Hitchcock.* Boston: Little, Brown, 1983] the other day, and I noticed in speaking of the remake of *The Man Who Knew Too Much* that it is called Hitchcock's story. It wasn't Hitchcock's story at all. It was my story! (*Laughs.*)

For example, Hitchcock tells Truffaut that to properly exploit the locale of Switzerland in the storytelling, one had to utilize familiar details that were commonly associated with that country—milk chocolate, the Alps, the lakes, village dances. All of this, it is implied, was part of his conception for The Secret Agent.

(*No reply.*)

Well . . .?

(*Laughs.*) You see, everything Hitchcock says is always his conception. The one thing Hitch has never allowed for is for any writer to have any real credit. It always has to be Hitch. It always has to be Hitch.

Hitchcock always seems to be saying to Truffaut, "my idea," "my story."

Completely untrue. Hitchcock was never a constructionist, never a storyteller. Hitch had good ideas, and the problem of the writer— always too often, by the way—and [Sidney] Gilliat and [Frank] Launder [collaborators on Hitchcock's *The Lady Vanishes* and *Jamaica Inn*] could tell you the same thing—was how the hell to get it into the story.

Where did you, as the writer, leave off and Hitchcock pick up?

In general, without me in the pictures I worked on with Hitch, there wouldn't have been any story. I think it's as simple as that. I would take a story and turn it into something good. After that, Hitch and I would turn it into a screenplay, and then, as often as not, we'd call in certain people to write dialogue for it. I never worked with anyone else in my life in quite that way; I've always written my own dialogue. So, basically, the picture would be mine; he would bring in the dialogue writers after I had left the picture.

Can you describe a typical story session with Hitchcock in the mid-thirties?

Well, for a long time I used to pick him up in the morning—he lived on Cromwell Road, and I lived overlooking Belgrave Square, very superior—and we'd drive to the studio together, where we'd chat. I would have had ideas that I wanted to discuss as regards construction.

He would listen, agree or disagree. Then we would go to lunch. Lunch would be extremely good—probably at the Mayfair Hotel—for which, goddammit, usually he used to pay, which delighted my heart. Then we'd come back to the studio, where he'd go to sleep. I would do a little work and presently he would wake up and say, "What are we doing now, Charles?" So we'd talk a little more, then we'd go back to his flat, where we'd have a few cocktails and just enjoy the evening. That was a very pleasant way of working, by the way.

Would you have to go home and sort it all out? Would the real writing occur, therefore, when he was not around?

I would say so, yes. Dammit, that's the only way to work.

Would you write visually, or would you say that Hitchcock had his greatest influence in the visual application of your ideas, however mutually arrived at?

I do write visually, of course. I think any screenwriter writes visually, don't you think? But I'm not talking about camera technology, no. I have nothing to do with camera technology whatsoever. But if I'm writing a story, the big people are *happening* and they're *there* and they're doing the *things* and they're *saying* the things I think they should be saying; and I can *see* them doing it.

Would you always include instructions for close-ups and so on?

Oh, yes. But not with Hitchcock. For the simple reason that you knew damned well that any suggestion of anybody's would never be taken. Hitch would shoot it exactly the way he wanted to shoot it when he went on the set. He was the great director, let's face it.

Let's take a specific scene. The famous Albert Hall scene in The Man Who Knew Too Much. *How did you write it versus how he filmed it?*

That originally I wrote, of course, for "Bulldog Drummond's Baby" . . . What do you mean, how did he film it? He filmed it magnificently. But I wrote it—with the clash of the cymbals and all that kind of stuff.

So he would give it the visual application?

The *camera* application, not the visual application, which is the writer's.

The fact that Hitchcock did not allow any writer to receive real credit—is that a character flaw?

Yes, very much a character flaw. And a very ungenerous character flaw, actually, because as I said, he is totally incapable of creating a story or developing a story. He has got good ideas—but he will never give credit to anyone but himself.

Did Hitchcock ever sit down at the typewriter?

No.

Was he a literate man?

Yes, literate to the extent of reading. Yes, but I must admit his form of reading was he liked to read the dirtiest parts of *Ulysses* and things like that.

He scorned dialogue in the process of construction?

No interest in dialogue whatsoever.

What about characters and characterizations?

Well, I suppose character grows out of construction, not out of dialogue. First of all, a dialogue writer has to have someone he's writing about, otherwise he can't write dialogue. So character has to come out of construction.

Many of the minor characters in Hitchcock's movies are so piquant, so memorable. Did he have many ideas in this regard? Who took the lead in developing these characters?

One would say, "Here's the milkman coming in *The Thirty-Nine Steps,* and it's a little part but a good part—and the situation is important—so let's get a bloody good actor to act it." I frequently used to come up with the actors, I must admit. Take the milkman, for example. There was a beautiful actor named Frederick Piper, who had been with me in the days of Ben Greet, and he was the milkman in *The Thirty-Nine Steps* who, when the guy says there is a spy upstairs, says, "Oh, yeah." I'd been an actor myself for so long, and I knew actors as well or better than Hitchcock.

Hitchcock was always very complimentary toward himself as regards casting.

So am I. (*Laughs.*)

At one point in their conversations, Hitchcock told Truffaut that he was greatly affected by the stylization of American films in the 1930s. Is that true?

That's true. He was. I wasn't, particularly. I wasn't convinced that the American style of film was exactly what we needed in England. I felt we had something to offer that Hollywood didn't—and I think I was right, by the way. It was a strange period, the beginning of sound. Everybody in America believed that the story didn't mean a damned thing; the only thing that mattered was sound—dialogue, dialogue, dialogue. The result was that, in the middle-thirties, in American films, a horrible thing happened; every line had to be a quip of some sort. Every damned line. Like someone would say, "I won't forget you," and someone else would reply, "I've forgotten you already." That kind of dialogue. Which, to me, was so bloody revolting. I couldn't stand it. That sort of dialogue had nothing to do with story development. That was the great fault in American pictures at the time.

Could Hitchcock have been talking about visual stylization as well?

When you are talking about visual stylization, you are talking out of my reach. Hitch was the visual character; I was the constructionist, the developer, the writer.

What was it about the British film industry at the time that was so different from what was going on in Hollywood?

I think that we, over there, at that time in the 1930s, were more interested in telling a good story. It's as simple as that.

Whereas, Hollywood was more interested in . . .

Dialogue, dialogue, dialogue! Quip, quip, quip! That sort of crap. Even in the great American films of that period, like those of Robert Riskin, you'll find the same thing—you had to have the quick reply.

Riskin did it well.

Of course. He did it brilliantly. But that, to me, isn't the answer to storytelling. I've never gone in for the immediate quip as an answer to dialogue. To me, dialogue has to be what a guy should say under given circumstances. Does this make sense?

In other words, not all dialogue needs to be memorable. Often dialogue can be, or should be, quite mundane.

Exactly. Why not?

Coming to Hollywood

After I'd written *Blackmail, The Man Who Knew Too Much, The Thirty-Nine Steps*—with a lot of lovely dialogue by Ian Hay—*Sabotage, The Secret Agent,* and *Young and Innocent,* one way or another Hollywood wanted me. I was getting sixty pounds a week from Gaumont-British at that time, which was considered reasonable money in England. But Universal in Hollywood came through with $1,000 a week, which was two hundred pounds a week, so naturally I had to accept it.

When I came over here, I was a complete flop, by the way. They immediately decided they couldn't afford to use me and they loaned me out at a profit—which irritated me immensely—to Goldwyn. I worked on a picture about Marco Polo [*The Adventures of Marco Polo,* 1938], written by Robert E. Sherwood. I was put on to alter his material, but dammit, his writing was so good I could do nothing to better it, so I was rather a flop, I'm afraid, with Goldwyn. I suppose I worked on it for about four weeks.

Then I went back to Universal. Well, goddammit, I was one of the top drama and suspense writers in England, so they put me on some stupid comedy about some poor French girl. I couldn't do a damned thing with it. I didn't have the faintest idea what to do with it. So eventually, after about six months, Universal dropped my contract.

I said to [my agent] Myron Selznick, "What the hell do I do next?" He put me on to David O. Selznick, and I wrote *The Young in Heart* [1938]. I should have got the full credit—because I constructed the whole damned thing—but they brought in Paul Osborn to write more dialogue, and he got the credit and I got the adaptation credit.

I liked Selznick, by the way. He was a strange character, a most bewildering character to work for, horrible to work for. You could spend all day working on the screenplay, and then he'd say, "Oh, Charles, I'd like to have a little chat after dinner. I'll have some food sent in from the Brown Derby." So you'd come back and eat some food from the Brown Derby, and then you'd have your chat—along with Bill Wright [production associate William Wright] and a lot of Selznick's top directors, such as [Lewis] "Millie" Milestone. People like that, all under contract to him, who were part of his "team," would be sitting around. You'd sit all night. I'd come home at dawn, dead tired. And as I was leaving, he'd say, "By the way, Charles, do you think we could have what we were talking about on paper by the time I come in at noon tomorrow?" Incredible! Impossible! But I liked him very much. I found him extremely intelligent. Very productive. Very creative. And a wonderful person. As regards working for him, I never wanted to again.

Were you instrumental in bringing Hitchcock to his attention?

Selznick said to me one night—I suppose it was at two in the morning—"I'm faced with the fact of bringing over two British directors, one or the other. There's Alfred Hitchcock, whom you've worked with. And there's Robert Stevenson, whom you probably know." (And of course, I knew him—he had been at Gaumont-British with me for many years. I did some work on *King Solomon's Mines* [1937]. Somehow or other, I got a credit on it, which I don't think I probably deserved.)

I said, "Well, bring them both over. They're awfully good, both of them." He said, "Do you really think so, Charles?" I said, "Yes, they are both tremendously good." He said, "Fine." And he did—he brought them both over on my advice. I should have got 10 percent of Hitchcock. My God!

Tell me about working on Balalaika *[1939] at MGM.*

Do you want to hear a funny story? Swanson [the literary agent H. N. Swanson] sold me to Larry Weingarten, who was a top producer at MGM, married to Irving Thalberg's sister [Sylvia Thalberg]—always a help. They brought me in to work on a story, which was my type of story, a thing by Eric Ambler. But it didn't work as far as I was concerned. All Larry had been interested in was the first few pages, but after that there was no particular story, and I was supposed to provide the story. I worked on it for about four weeks, but I was getting no place. And I was getting very unhappy because I knew if I failed on this and Larry Weingarten and I parted company, it wouldn't do me any good in Hollywood.

One day he sent me a small scene—about five or six pages—and asked me if I could do anything with it. He said they had sixty writers working on it and no one had been able to come up with anything. And this was *Balalaika*—which, by the way, was from a play by one of my closest, oldest friends in the world, Eric Maschwitz.

So I read the scene, and I sat down and wrote my own version of the scene, which I thought was pretty good. Then, I went into Larry's office with these five or six pages and said, "Here's the scene you asked for." Larry said, "Very interesting, let's have a look at it." So he started to read the scene; but after about three pages, he threw it aside and said, "I don't understand what this is about at all. I don't understand what you're aiming at," and he threw it on the floor.

At which point I saw a guy who was lying on a couch in the corner, and he was also reading a copy of it. I said, "Wait a minute! Let's see what this fellow has to say." This was Reinhold Schunzel, a German director of importance, who had been brought over by MGM. Presently, very slowly—even though Larry kept saying, "What are you waiting for? What are you waiting for?"—he said, "Zis is a scene." Larry said, "What?" He said, "Zis is a scene. Zis is the first scene I have been presented with for the direction of zis movie." I said to Larry, "Read it again." So Larry picked it up and read it again and said, "This is a scene."

Except for that director, I would have been finished in Hollywood. The result was, I was immediately transferred from the Ambler story I was working on and put on *Balalaika,* which I worked on very successfully and got a credit.

Foreign Correspondent (1940)

Looking back, I think, with *Foreign Correspondent,* Hitch summoned back—again—his best constructionist, as he knew me to be.
Joan Harrison shares the scenario credit with you.
We started out there with a treatment written by someone called "Inside Europe" [based on *Personal History* by Vincent Sheean]—or something like that. Walter Wanger bought the rights, but it wasn't a story at all, in no sense. So Hitchcock was asked to make it, and he called me in. From the word go, I had to write a story, which was *Foreign Correspondent.* Hitchcock was extremely helpful, as he always

was, except, as I told you, Hitch would come up with wonderful ideas, and once you'd get your storyline straight, your bewilderment was in how to get his ideas embodied in the storyline.

As regards Joan, Joan was our secretary, but she happened to be Hitchcock's protégée at that time, and he asked me as a favor if I'd mind letting her name be on the picture. She had only been his secretary. She had never come up with a solitary idea or a solitary thought. I thought, "I'm so bloody important, what the hell does it matter?" So I said yes.

How is it that you and Hitchcock never worked together again?

I think there was a love and hate thing that went on between us over the years. I think, for a great many years, Hitch objected to the fact that I'd been so successful and such a part of his beginnings, and he loathed anybody getting any credit whatsoever. I think this really was a part of him, this resentment. You'll find that no writer ever gets any credit from Hitch. I think that since I had written seven of his top movies, for a while he resented me, and then he became my friend again.

I used to go to lunch with him at Universal [years later] and on one weekend I went up to Santa Cruz with him and stayed a lovely night with him. He said, "This is a business-recreation trip, Charles. Let's talk business!" We never talked business at all! For the rest of my life he remained my friend and my enemy. What the hell can you say about a thing like that? Hitch was like that. He could write you a wonderful letter saying, "My love to you always," and the next one could be signed, "Yours very truly."

In the Spoto book, he is depicted as unhappy and partly sadistic. If he was a character in a film, would it be possible to convey him?

Impossible to convey him. As you know, I'm cited in the Spoto book very heavily. But I would say this was such a weird character that it would be very, very hard to spot it or to put it down in any plain form. Don't you agree, mmm?

It sounds as if his mood or his personality could turn on a dime.

He could be the kindest guy in the world. He could bend over backwards to be kind! He could bend over backwards to be sadistic and horrible. That was Hitch. Like with poor Dickie Beville, his assistant for so many years. My God, poor Dickie never knew where he was with Hitch. On one occasion, Dickie (who was a delightful character) and his wife, Molly (who was very beautiful) had arranged to go to the opera at Covent Garden that night. She had got a special evening dress for the occasion, and Dickie was going in full tails. Leaving the studio, Hitch said, "I'll ride you back to London." Said Dickie Beville, "Oh, thank you, that's very kind of you, Hitch." They started out, but Dickie found out that they were not going the usual way into London at all. Dickie said, "What's going on?" Hitch said, "Don't worry about it, everything will be alright." They ended up at Shamley Green [where Hitchcock had a country house], about thirty miles south of London, near Guildford. The result was that Dickie couldn't get back to London so that he and his wife could go to the opera. Pure sadism on Hitch's part. Just to say, "You s.o.b., you'll do anything I want you to do." In other words, if Dickie had objected on the way, Hitch would have said, "You're no longer my assistant director."

World War II and Cecil B. DeMille

After I finished *Balalaika* and *Foreign Correspondent,* Swanie got me involved in something at Columbia [*They Dare Not Love,* 1941] that starred George Brent. Columbia was utterly ridiculous, the whole thing. You had this office down on a patio. On your first day there, you were invited to lunch with Harry Cohn in the executive dining room. When you came in, there were all the top people of Columbia sitting around. You sat down. Harry Cohn said, "How wonderful to see you, Charles. Welcome!" At which point he pressed a button, and the chair under you collapsed—and you fell on your ass. And everybody laughed, laughed, laughed. This was evidently the greatest joke in the world, that Harry Cohn could collapse a chair under his latest writer. (*Laughs.*) This was true! So I never went into the executive dining room again.

Did you work closely with the director James Whale at all?

James Whale was fired after the first week because they decided he was not doing a good job. Which was utterly ridiculous, because James Whale was a magnificent director. Charlie Vidor was brought on. Why the hell Harry Cohn fired James Whale, I don't know—it must have been a personal thing because Harry Cohn was like that.

I finished *They Dare Not Love,* and by this time I was working on *Reap the Wild Wind* [1941] for DeMille down the canyon. One night I went to a huge party at [producer] Stephen Ames's—a multi-, multi-, multi-millionaire—a magnificent party up at Holmby Hills. At the party, at the bar, there was Harry Cohn. And Harry Cohn said, "Charles, how wonderful to see you! Tomorrow we go into production on your movie." I said, "Oh, lovely! Good luck." He said, "Oh, we won't need it. We love you dearly . . ." I was his closest friend in the world.

The following day, I said to Alan LeMay, "My new picture is starting today, up at Columbia; let's go on the set." We came up to the

Columbia gate, and the guy at the door, who knew me perfectly well, said, "Yes, Mr. Bennett, what do you want?" I said, "I want to go on my set. My picture is shooting for the first time today." He said, "Oh, wait a minute. I have to ask Mr. Cohn's permission for anyone to go on the set." I said, "Oh, that'll be alright. Mr. Cohn is my friend. We talked at a party just last night." So he got on the phone to Cohn and I could hear Cohn on the phone, "Do you think I'd let that stupid s.o.b. of an Englishman on the set! Tell him to go away!" What the hell can you do with people like that? One night I was his closest friend, the next day I was a stupid s.o.b. of an Englishman.

Is it true that you served in the Secret Service during World War II?

I wouldn't say I was ever completely recognized. I was *used,* it's better to put it that way.

Can you elaborate?

It's awfully difficult to elaborate on a thing like the Secret Service. I'm terribly sorry about that. I'd like to, but I can only tell you one thing, which nobody has ever known, which is that for a long time in this town the top meetings, with Richard B. Hood, head of the FBI [in Los Angeles] and people like that, took place in the private office of Cecil B. DeMille. Mmmm, a naughty one, eh?

Why were you involved?

You tell me. I would get a call from DeMille's secretary, saying—in a nasal voice—"Mr. Bennett, Mr. DeMille would like you to come across to his office." I would say to Alan LeMay, "Excuse me, but Mr. DeMille wants to see me . . ." I would go across the hall, and there would be Richard B. Hood of the FBI [L.A. bureau], the head of naval intelligence, people like that. And I would be asked to do certain jobs.

So, in a sense, you were drafted.

Yes.

Did this secret work have to do with World War II or domestic security?

It had to do with World War II—we were anti-Nazi at the time, naturally. But, strangely enough, a lot of it was anti- our own ally— Communist Russia.

Why do you say "strangely enough"? Did that bother you?

Well, I was asked to do things that were anti-Soviet. I remember all sorts of idiot things—like going down to San Pedro . . . I won't go into details. But there were all sorts of jobs I had to do, and some of them were anti-Soviet, and the Soviets were our allies at the time. It was only because it was known, even then, that these would be our eventual enemies. This was after Hitler had invaded Russia, you know.

Were you on DeMille's payroll during all this, or the government's?

On DeMille's payroll. $1,500 a week. Not bad!

Did you feel you had to do this because of DeMille? Were you conflicted at all?

I didn't feel conflicted at all. They were asking me to do a job, and it was as simple as that. Very few people in the world ever knew about it. Very few people in the world knew that DeMille was mixed up in the Secret Service.

How long did it go on?

I don't know. Eventually, I went back to England to write. My country was at war. It was bloody hard to get back to England at that time. Again and again I had been told, "No, your better job is to stay in Hollywood and write anti-fascist, anti-Nazi pictures," which, let's face it, I was doing.

Who told you this?

Ian Hay—who became General Ian Hay, head of British intelligence. He wrote me a letter saying, "Charles, stay over there. You're doing a better job there than you could ever do carrying a rifle over here." That made sense, in a way, but it irritated me.

Eventually, I managed to persuade the British Ministry of Information to allow me to come back and write for them. To do that, you had to get special permission to cross the Atlantic. You'd wait for a month and then you'd be told to appear at so-and-so pier in New York, and then you'd be in a convoy for twenty-three days chased all the way by a German sub. I crossed the Atlantic in the beginning of 1944. I remember very well that around that time the bombing of Britain was starting—not the great bombing, but the V-bombs. The doodlebugs.

As my train pulled into London, a V-bomb hit about a quarter of a mile away from the station. Everyone was running in every goddamned direction. My lovely ex-wife, Maggie, who was an officer in England, flying with the Air Transport Auxiliary, came up to London to meet me. We stayed at the Savoy Hotel overlooking the Thames. Every night you could see these damned things coming up over London—they had red tails—and the interesting thing about them was you never had to worry until the sound of the engine cut out. The moment the engine cut out, the bloody thing would turn and perhaps come back at you. I remember, Maggie and I didn't give a goddamn. We would sit at this huge, picture window looking across the Thames and watch these things coming up in the light. It was fun! (*Laughs.*)

How long did you remain in England, and what did you do there?

I was writing propaganda films for the Ministry. At the same time, I must admit, I did a job on the side—Two Cities Pictures [Two Cities Films, a leading production unit of the Rank Organization] asked me to write a movie about the murderous Madeleine Smith. I wrote it and I loved it; it was very good, I think. And they paid me about four thousand pounds, which helped me along, because I was working for nothing for the Ministry—except for expenses.

It was decided that I would direct the picture—according to the contract. I was very happy about this because I loved my screenplay. When the war finished, the contract still existed. Then, suddenly, I got a telegram from Sir John [Sir John Davis, who succeeded Lord Arthur Rank as head of the Rank empire], the number two man at Rank, which had taken over Two Cities, saying, I couldn't direct the picture because David Lean wanted to make a version of it with his own wife [the actress Ann Todd] starring. There was nothing I could do about it. Instead, he said, we will switch you to another movie.

The other movie [*Madness of the Heart* in 1949] was such a horrible thing that I didn't even read it until I was on my way back across the Atlantic to direct it, and then I wanted to throw up. But I had to make it. Margaret Lockwood was my star—a very good actress. And I had a fifty-five-day shooting schedule. Everything was right about it except the story, which was awful.

At this point, in Hollywood, you were in the unusual position of being a freelancer, rarely under contract to a single studio or for more than one film. What were the advantages and the disadvantages?

The advantages of being a freelancer were, you could move from studio to studio and you could increase your salary, if necessary. The disadvantages were that if you happened to run into a couple of flops, you might get your option dropped and find yourself on your ass. For example, MGM, at that time, was full of contract writers—I should think about sixty of them—and they were all desperate for the next credit they could get in order to ensure that they got their option taken up. Most of them went around with daggers behind their backs trying to stab any writer who got in their way. It was a fight to the finish.

Did you always keep regular hours as a writer?

I suppose I kept some sort of schedule. But I never bothered particularly about keeping hours. I think much more important than keeping hours is what happens in the evening when you *think* . . . when you suddenly say to yourself, "Wait a minute . . ."

For example, DeMille, when he was looking for an ending to *Reap the Wild Wind,* said to me and Alan LeMay, "This is no good. For God's sake, we've got to find an ending." I knew it was true. We had no ending. And in my bath, in the morning of the following day, I said to myself, "What's wrong with a giant squid?" I thought about John Wayne and Ray Milland fighting this giant squid under the sea, and it struck me that this would be a very good ending. The following day, I came in and I acted out the entire sequence for DeMille. "Here's John Wayne and Ray Milland out to kill each other . . . and here comes the giant squid!" I played the giant squid. At the end of it, DeMille sat there, completely mesmerized. Then he just nodded and said, "Charles. Wonderful. In *Technicolor.*" He was sold. It cost a quarter of a million dollars to shoot, but it is the one thing most people remember about *Reap the Wild Wind.*

You ask, when and how often do you work? I don't know. You work at all times. A writer never stops working. How can you stop thinking? If you have a thing running through your mind, how can you stop thinking about it?

You wrote one picture for Cecil B. DeMille before the onset of American involvement in World War II, and then two others later on. I would guess that someone like DeMille would have to be the very opposite of someone like Hitchcock.

I would say DeMille was in every way as literate, in many ways as sophisticated, but in most ways kinder. I adored DeMille. He was a very, very kind man—in spite of all that crap you hear about him being a bully. I don't know; he may have been tough on the set now and then, but who isn't? Dammit, I always found DeMille to be the kindest, gentlest person I knew. I loved him dearly.

Which of your DeMille pictures are you most fond of?

From a construction point of view, *Reap the Wild Wind* was my favorite. That was my construction—and thank God, because they were in a goddamned mess when I was brought in on it.

Unconquered [1947]—that was me alone, except for Fredric Frank, a lovely guy but he couldn't write his own name.

As regards *The Story of Dr. Wassell* [1944], I was really the constructionist, but I will say that as it was American dialogue, and particularly American navy dialogue, Alan LeMay subscribed an immense amount to it. His strength was that type of tough American dialogue, at which he was awful bloody good.

Jesse Lasky, Jr., is mentioned in the credits to Reap the Wild Wind *and* Unconquered—*what did he contribute?*

Nothing. (*Laughs.*) Jesse was adorable, but all Jesse used to do was, after we had finished our screenplay, sit down in DeMille's office with DeMille and make one or two minor alterations. That's all he ever did. Jesse is a delightful character and I think he's a good writer, by the way. But as regards the DeMille pictures, no.

How about Jeannie MacPherson—who is credited in Writers Guild records with an uncredited contribution to Reap the Wild Wind *and* The Story of Dr. Wassell?

Nothing. She had been a friend of DeMille's many years earlier, and he kept her on the payroll for that reason. Never. She never subscribed a thing. Never.

Yes, Mr. DeMille (from left to right): Eddie Jones, the writer-producer Sidney Biddell, Cecil B. DeMille, Charles Bennett, the screenwriter Alan LeMay, the field secretary (as opposed to "stationary" secretary) Berenice Mosk, Marion Crist. (Photo: Academy of Motion Picture Arts and Sciences, Cecil B. DeMille Collection)

What I meant partly was, I don't think DeMille was as good a director as Hitchcock—and there must have been some adjustments for you, as the writer.

I'll tell you about DeMille as a director. He was a tremendous visionary as regards the peak thing, the immense thing. But when it came to the actual scenes, no, he had a dialogue director whose job it was to put the actors through rehearsals and to tell the actors how to play the scenes. So DeMille took over the vastness of the production, while his assistant brought in the dialogue. If DeMille objected, that was a different matter. Otherwise, he would accept it.

Let me give you a specific example. The attitude toward the Indians in Unconquered—*I'm thinking of the scene where Paulette Goddard is roped to a stake and surrounded by a tribe of savages. At best, the attitude behind that scene seems archaic and absurd today. Where did that come from?*

I have a horrible idea it came from me.

It doesn't seem like a very modern view of Indians, even for that period.

Well . . . Boris Karloff! (*Laughs.*)

Were there limitations in writing for Gary Cooper?

Yes! Yes! My God there were! When I was first loaned out to Goldwyn and working on *Marco Polo*, I wrote a scene for Cooper, and then I was confronted by one of the top management people. "What the hell are you doing?" he said. "You've written a scene here for Gary Cooper that he couldn't speak in a million years." I said, "You mean I should stick to 'yep' and 'nope?'" He said, "Exactly." Not "yep" and "nope" exactly, but shorter dialogue. You were really up against it with Gary Cooper. He wasn't a great actor. He was a personality.

Worse, even, I remember, with Victor Mature. This idiot character, he would refuse to learn a scene because he'd say, "I don't have time to learn it. Let's cut it." You put words into the mouths of these personalities and only hope that they deliver them.

I'm sorry. I haven't asked you about Joan of Paris *[1942]—one of the best anti-fascist, anti-Nazi pictures.*

I loved it. It's my favorite picture of all the pictures I've ever been connected with. Because it was more human, more in touch with my hatred of Germany, with my love of my country and my feeling for France. It was a sad, beautiful story of a girl who dies in the cause against the Nazis—I simply loved *Joan of Paris*. To me, the tragedy of it is, due to the fact that it wasn't played by proper stars—it should have been played by Cary Grant and people like that—it didn't make any money. But it was a helluva good picture and acclaimed by critics as one of the best pictures of its year.

The Great Destroyer

I want to ask you about a number of other films you worked on. Ivy *[1947], directed by Sam Wood?*

I liked *Ivy*, but it wasn't very successful. I think Sam Wood didn't do a very good job on it. Sam Wood was a strange director . . . there were a lot of great directors in those days who weren't really great. They were *dependent*. First on the writers, second on their art directors and people like that. Sam, in particular, was dependent on his art directors and *Ivy* is a good example of that.

I will never forget the horrible ending to *Ivy*—where the girl falls down the thing and boom! I remember my son watching it one day on the telly and saying, "Oh, that's a sudden end." I said, "That's not the way I wrote it." The ending, as far as I was concerned at least, was Sir Cedric Hardwicke, as the detective, giving some sort of reasoning for what had happened. But no, not a bit of it. Boom! Desperately sudden.

And Black Magic *[1949]?*

I think it was a helluva good script ruined by Orson Welles and Gregory Ratoff, who were given their complete freedom to do so. Eddie Small, who was backing the picture, was afraid to cross the Atlantic by air; crossing the Atlantic by boat took two or three weeks. Ratoff, who was directing, and Welles, who was acting the lead, had a free hand in Rome, so they decided to rewrite all sorts of stuff. The result was, when the picture came back, it couldn't even be cut. It was so dreadful, what they had done with it, that I spent four nights directing little scenes in order to make it cutable at all. The result was that I was against the movie at the time. But I think it was a pretty good movie really.

No Escape *[1950]? Your second directing job.*

That was awful. Forget it. I was broke.

Then answer this for me: Why is it that nearly every screenwriter in Hollywood sooner or later succumbs to the temptation to become a director?

Power! There's nothing in the world gives you the power of being a director. It's like being a general, a commander-in-chief.

The Green Glove *[1952]? Your story and screenplay.*

I loved it. But the disaster of *The Green Glove* was the fact that we had to shoot it in France, and the French unions were only allowed to have five or six English-speaking actors. Rudy Mate, unfortunately—a delightful director, a delightful person—had, I think, seven backgrounds. He had been born as a Czech [actually—in Cracow, Poland], and had been through so many countries and so many changes that he didn't know what he was; he spoke eight or nine languages, but none of them well. With the result that, when these guys who were French spoke bad English with French accents, to him it was perfectly logical. A lot of the picture, as far as I am concerned, was unintelligible. Oh well, I had a helluva good time. They took me over to Paris for three or four months at their expense, which was fun, and then in the South of France for about two or three months. I was being paid well. I shouldn't complain.

And Dangerous Mission *[1954]?*

That was the most ghastly mess. W. R. Burnett and Irwin Allen had worked on this script, and it didn't make any sense whatsoever. Louis King, the director, came to me after they had already been shooting for two weeks and said, "For God's sakes, Charles, see if you can help us straighten this out." So I was brought in at two thousand dollars a week, and what I had to do was at least make some sense out of the script. I made sense of it, eventually, but it was bloody difficult, particularly because Victor Mature strongly objected to playing a dialogue scene that wasn't in the script, which had to be there eventually in order to make sense of the story. Irwin, who was frightened to death of Mature, would say, "Leave it to Victor," and I would have to fight like a bloody hyena.

Curse of the Demon *[1958]? A cult favorite—I would think you'd like it.*

No. Because of the script I wrote, which was infinitely better than what was shot. I had bought the rights myself [to "Casting the Runes," a short story by Montague R. James], then I wrote the bloody screenplay. Dick Powell—and all sorts of people—were crazy about it, wanted to do it. But nobody quite came up with the deal.

I was over in England directing a series for television. The day before I was coming back from England, a guy by the name of Hal Chester turned up and said, "Would you sign this contract for *Demon*? Because I can set it up with Columbia—but I'll need your signature." So I was in a hurry to catch the goddamned plane, I said yes.

When I got back to America, I learned to my surprise that Dick Powell's right-hand man had set it up for me to shoot the picture at RKO—with me as director. That was exactly what I wanted but, goddammit, I had signed this letter of intent before leaving England. So . . . this guy, [the producer] Hal Chester, messed up the screenplay quite a bit. It was so good, the screenplay, that it couldn't be completely destroyed, only half destroyed. It's still considered a good movie.

I think the job [the director] Jacques Tourneur did with what Hal Chester gave him was awfully good. Hal Chester, as far as I'm concerned, if he walked up my driveway right now, I'd shoot him dead.

You spent most of the fifties and the early part of the sixties working for Irwin Allen, not the classiest filmmaker in Hollywood. How did you ever get mixed up with such a character?

God knows! I had written *The Sign of the Ram* [1948], which Irving Cummings, Jr., had produced with his father. Then Irving Cummings, Jr., asked me to write *Where Danger Lives* [1950]. That was the beginning of my association, God help me, with Irwin Allen. From that moment on, I must admit, I wish to God I'd been dead. He is the *end*! Irving Cummings was the real producer of *Where Danger Lives*. But due to the fact that Irwin Allen knew somebody who was important with the Hughes organization, he was allowed to be a co-producer. He had nothing at the time.

The Story of Mankind *[1957] was Allen's first full-blown attempt at writing, directing, and producing.*

That was dreadful. Because Irwin desperately wanted to have the first credit on the story, so everything I wrote he wanted to cut out. (*Laughs.*) I hated everything to do with that picture.

What about The Big Circus *[1959]?*

I had been directing for Eddie Small in England—the Monte Christo series, the Charlie Chan series, for television. I got a cable in Rome asking me to come back and write for Irwin, and I said no. But when I came back, there was Irwin in a horrible mess with this guy, who is the greatest, bloody, successful ham writer in the world—Irving Wallace. Their script was awful. It had reached the stage that Columbia had told Irwin to get the hell out. They had $90,000 in it—which wasn't very much in those days, let's face it. But they had said, "We're not interested anymore."

Then I came back from England. After two or three weeks, Irwin Allen approached me and said, "Charles, won't you try and help?" I said, "What will I get out of it?" He said, "If we can straighten out the script, we can get the finishing money." I straightened it out in a couple of weeks; I was always good at that sort of thing. Then I wrote the screenplay, which of course he naturally had to take credit on, which he didn't deserve.

Did he do any actual writing?

No. Irwin was never a writer. He was always a promoter. A bloody good promoter, by the way.

That was *The Big Circus*—which made little money for me but an immense amount of money for Victor Mature. I shall never forget Victor Mature. George Jason, a wonderful agent, was at that point with MCA—and Victor Mature was an MCA client. Victor Mature said, "I am not satisfied with the script. There are things I want altered." So Irwin, who was frightened to death of Victor Mature, said to me, "Charles, please, you go talk to George Jason and Victor Mature and straighten this matter out."

So I came up to a house on the hills above Hollywood with George Jason and an assistant—two top MCA agents—and Victor Mature. I said, "Well, what's the problem?" George Jason said, "Charles, the problem is that you have Gilbert Roland walking the tightrope across Niagara; and Victor thinks that, since it is he who is the star of the picture, it is he who should be walking the tightrope across Niagara." I said, "Wait a minute. Roland is playing a wire-walker; Victor isn't, he's playing the promoter of the circus." Jason said, "Can't you alter the picture so that Victor Mature walks across Niagara?" Can you believe this? (*Laughs.*)

It went on like this with the utter, ridiculous, idiot demands that only Victor Mature could come up with—and naturally he was backed up by MCA. Eventually I managed to say no. "Get out of the picture if you don't like it," I said. When I told Irwin, he was shaking with fright. "I said 'no,'" I told him, "Victor Mature is not going to walk across Niagara."

Do you like any of the pictures you made in association with Irwin Allen?

No.

Voyage to the Bottom of the Sea [1961]? Five Weeks in a Balloon [1962]?

Uh-uh. They were all jobs that I did well, let's put it that way. Let's not think in terms of something that I will carry down to my grave as things that I am proud of.

Why did you stick with Irwin Allen for so long?

Money. I shouldn't have, I agree with you. I should have said, "To hell with you!" and I should have been doing other things. But money is hard to resist in this world.

Particularly in Hollywood.

Particularly in Hollywood.

Why, in the 1950s when you were at your peak and able to sell stories and write movies on the basis of your reputation, why weren't you writing stories that were particularly meaningful to you? Stories with characters and ideas that had some personal significance?

Let's say I should have been, but I'm not sure I was. I should have turned into a novelist at that time.

You say that to me with what seems to be very sincere regret.

Very sincere regret, yes.

Why?

Well, dammit, I could have made much more money that way. (*Laughs.*)

Is it only the money?

No . . . I'd like to have had a certain amount more fame, I suppose. Why not?

Money and fame—we're still talking in terms of superficialities. Are you only interested in the money and fame?

Personal enjoyment, mmm?

It seems to me that you had only a few entirely pleasant experiences as a screenwriter in Hollywood and that in most cases everything you felt was worthwhile in a script was taken out.

I think if you ask most Hollywood screenwriters that question, you'll find that the answer is exactly what I'm saying now: very few. Yes, exactly.

So why did you keep at it for nearly fifty years?

Money! (*Laughs.*)

Does Hollywood extract more than your life's blood?

Yes, I think of course it does. I think Hollywood is the greatest destroyer that a writer can ever meet with. I think the greatest thing that can ever happen to a writer—like my dear friends, Sidney Gilliat and Frank Launder—is the fact that they never came to Hollywood. The worst thing in the world for a writer is to come to Hollywood. It destroys you.

When did you start writing novels?

Two years ago. (*Laughs.*)

Why have you turned to fiction at such a late point in your life?

Because I'm too old. Philosophically I've decided I want to do what I want to do.

W. R. Burnett:
The Outsider

Interview by Ken Mate and Pat McGilligan

More good movies have been made from W. R.
Burnett's novels than from Fyodor Dostoyevsky's.

Andrew Sarris

When William Riley Burnett died in April of 1982 at the age of eighty-two, he left behind a career that spanned a prolific half century: sixty screenwriting credits, at least thirty-six published novels, fifteen serialized stories in magazines such as *Redbook* and *Collier's,* over a hundred songs, some twenty plays, and (crafted in the last year of his life as a "literary exercise") more than twenty short stories. If his name is unfamiliar, the titles of his pictures may ring familiar bells: *Little Caesar* (1930), *High Sierra* (1941), *Yellow Sky* (1948), *The Asphalt Jungle* (1950) (all based on his novels), or his last major effort, *The Great Escape* (1963). Twenty-nine movies are based on either his novels or his magazine stories; many of them he also adapted for Hollywood; some (such as *Iron Man, Law and Order, High Sierra,* and *The Asphalt Jungle*) were remade not once but several times. Burnett is one of the American authors whose work was most often adapted to the screen within his lifetime.

Fully half his books, and the movies that were made from them, dealt with gangsters or criminals. Burnett was neither. He was a gentle man, whimsical, big and shambling (he had been a football player briefly at Ohio State in his youth); although he was among the first at the scene of the St. Valentine's Day Massacre, he refused to view the bloody aftermath. Burnett had the Irishman's gift of gab and a natural wit that was to stand him in good stead in Hollywood, as well as a certain way of looking at the world: realistic, pragmatic, and hard-bitten.

W. R. Burnett was born on Thanksgiving Day, 1899, in Springfield, Ohio, of mixed Welsh-Irish ancestry (he preferred to emphasize the Irish), the scion of a family of Ohio political bosses. His grandfather had been mayor of Columbus; his father was Governor James Cox's right-hand man. Burnett himself worked on Cox's 1920 presidential campaign. That year saw Burnett married, supporting his young wife on his earnings as a statistician for the state of Ohio while embarking on his literary career. He read indiscriminately, though with a predilection for the French, especially Balzac and Prosper Mérimée. He went to the public library on his lunch hour and after work wrote into the wee hours of the morning, a discipline he maintained until his dying day. Bored and isolated in Ohio, he "escaped to Chicago" in 1927, settling into the Northmere Hotel as a desk clerk to soak up the atmosphere of the big city and to experience life. Two years later he wrote *Little Caesar,* and his writing career was launched.

Little Caesar was a literary sensation and a runaway bestseller, and Warner Brothers quickly snapped it up for motion pictures. (Burnett always held that Jack Warner told him he bought the book not on its merits as literature but because its main character hailed from Youngstown, Ohio—the brothers Warner were the sons of a Youngstown butcher.) The film version was a big hit; a New York stage actor named Edward G. Robinson became a movie star. Burnett followed his novel to Hollywood and never left.

Ironically, Burnett's inexhaustible virtuosity may have reduced his critical stature. Had he stuck to writing crime novels, he might now have a reputation similar to those of James M. Cain, Raymond Chandler, and Dashiell Hammett. Writes Dennis L. White, who researched Burnett extensively for the American Film Institute: "As Burnett's gangster novels and films are not restricted to any narrow or conventional definition of the genre, his career as a whole ranges beyond one genre. He is the preeminent underworld writer, but he is also more. His second novel is about boxing, his third a political western, his fourth about dog racing. Several of his novels are set in Ireland; several more are about politics; two are about a composer and the agony of artistic creation; one is a first-person narrative from the point of view of a woman. In addition to the realistic crime story, Burnett is, for example, also the master of the equally authentic story of the Old West." His 1930 "political western," *Saint Johnson,* is one of the first tellings of the legend of Wyatt Earp, Doc Holliday, and the shootout at the OK Corral.

Throughout the thirties Burnett wrote novels and serialized stories, for the most part shunning screenwriting. He preferred to sell

W. R. Burnett in Los Angeles, 1981. (Courtesy: W. R. Burnett)

Hollywood his stories to subsidize his literary efforts. A plunge into bankruptcy, brought on by one day too many at the track, forced Burnett into a more active screenwriting career. His first major assignment: to adapt his own novel, *High Sierra*, to the screen. His collaborator was John Huston, who has called Burnett "one of the most neglected American writers. There are moments of reality in his books that are quite overpowering. More than once they've had me breaking into a sweat" (Huston, 1980, p. 78).

High Sierra broke so many conventions of the gangster genre that the Production Code office sent Jack Warner a memo with forty-three annotated objections to the script. In a memo of his own, Huston cautioned the producer Hal Wallis against sanitizing Burnett's novel: "Take the spirit out of Burnett, the strange sense of inevitability that comes with our deepening understanding of his characters and the forces that motivate them, and only the husk of the story remains." Although Burnett and Huston were forced to compromise somewhat, the film version of *High Sierra* still carried a wallop—one that reverberated through the decades, up to *Bonnie and Clyde* (1967) and the outlaw pictures of the seventies.

With *High Sierra*, Burnett vaulted into the ranks of Hollywood's most proficient and highly paid screenwriters. He turned out original screen stories (*Wake Island*, 1942; *Crash Dive*, 1943; *San Antonio*, 1945) and his novels remained popular as source material for successful films. In 1946 Warner Brothers paid him twelve weeks' salary to write a novel, *Nobody Lives Forever*, and then kept him on salary to write the screenplay. Burnett was equally adept at salvage and polish work (on such films as *The Westerner* in 1940 and *Background to Danger* in 1943) and was a frequent collaborator with other top Hollywood screenwriters of the day. Occasionally, this fierce anti-Communist shared writing chores with such Party members as Albert Maltz (on *This Gun for Hire* in 1942) and John Howard Lawson (on *Action in the North Atlantic* in 1943)—Hollywood's strategy for balancing the political scales.

In 1950 Burnett's *The Asphalt Jungle* was picked up by MGM's Dore Schary, who, after a period of failure and frustration, wanted to do a movie with "shooting and fucking," according to Burnett. John Huston co-wrote his third script from a Burnett novel, Marilyn Monroe had her first featured role, and Sam Jaffe won the Best Actor prize at Venice for his portrayal of a master criminal. In his literary and screen-work in the fifties, Burnett continued to explore the dark side of the American Dream. His last major screenwriting stint was on *The Great Escape*. Steve McQueen incarnated a last variation on the classic Burnett anti-hero: an imprisoned man for whom there was no escape, either to freedom or to the vainglorious deaths of *Little Caesar*'s Rico or *High Sierra*'s Roy Earle—only a rubber ball bounced endlessly against the wall of a cell.

When we met Burnett, he was a near-Joycean figure: wielding his putter against would-be muggers as he walked his dog near his "crackerbox" in Marina del Rey, where he moved after fire had gutted his Bel Air home a number of years before. His eyes were hooded behind thick-lensed spectacles that he traded for a magnifying glass when working far into the night on his continuing literary endeavors. At the time of his death, he had five full-length books in various stages of completion.

To the end, he was like one of the central figures in a Burnett novel—still an outsider. Although his novels are widely available in England, France, Germany, and Italy, they are largely out of print in the United States. No Oscar adorned his mantelpiece, no special Writers Guild Laurel Award for Achievement, no American Film Institute Life Achievement Award. He was reconciled to his obscurity—indeed, he was proud of it—and when he died, his obituary was buried on page twelve of the *Daily Variety*.

1930   *Little Caesar* (Mervyn LeRoy). From Burnett's novel.

1931   *The Finger Points* (John Francis Dillon). Co-story.
        Iron Man (Tod Browning). Novel basis.

1932   *Law and Order* (Edward L. Cahn). From his novel *Saint Johnson*. Uncredited contribution.
        Beast of the City (Charles Brabin). Story.
        Scarface: Shame of a Nation (Howard Hawks). Co-script.

1934   *Dark Hazard* (Alfred E. Green). Novel basis.

1935   *The Whole Town's Talking* (John Ford). From his short story "Jail Break." Uncredited contribution.
        Dr. Socrates (William Dieterle). From his short story.

1936   *Thirty-Six Hours to Kill* (Eugene Forde). From his short story "Across the Aisle."

1937   *Wine, Women, and Horses* (Louis King). From his novel *Dark Hazard*.
        Wild West Days (Ford Beebe, Cliff Smith). Thirteen-part serial from his novel *Saint Johnson*.
        Some Blondes Are Dangerous/Blonde Dynamite (Milton Carruth). From his novel *Iron Man*.

1939   *King of the Underworld* (Lewis Seiler). From his short story "Dr. Socrates."

1940   *The Westerner* (William Wyler). Uncredited contribution.
The Dark Command (Raoul Walsh). From his novel.
Law and Order (Ray Taylor). From his novel *Saint Johnson*.

1941   *High Sierra* (Raoul Walsh). Novel basis, co-script.
The Get-Away (Edward Buzzell, J. Walter Rubin). Co-script.
Dance Hall (Irving Pichel). From his novel *The Giant Swing*.

1942   *This Gun for Hire* (Frank Tuttle). Co-script.
Bullet Scars (D. Ross Lederman). Uncredited remake of "Dr. Socrates."
Wake Island (John Farrow). Co-story, co-script.

1943   *Crash Dive* (Archie Mayo). Story.
Action in the North Atlantic (Lloyd Bacon, Byron Haskin). Adaptation.
Background to Danger (Raoul Walsh). Script.

1945   *San Antonio* (David Butler). Co-story, co-script.

1946   *Nobody Lives Forever* (Jean Negulesco). Novel basis, script.
The Man I Love (Raoul Walsh). Uncredited contribution.

1948   *The Walls of Jericho* (John M. Stahl). Uncredited contribution.
Belle Starr's Daughter (Lesley Selander). Story, script.
Yellow Sky (William A. Wellman). Novel basis.

1949   *Colorado Territory* (Raoul Walsh). Uncredited remake of *High Sierra*.

1950   *The Asphalt Jungle* (John Huston). Novel basis, uncredited contribution.

1951   *Iron Man* (Joseph Pevney). Novel basis.
The Racket (John Cromwell). Co-script.
Vendetta (Mel Ferrer). Script.

1953   *Law and Order* (Nathan Juran). From his novel *Saint Johnson*.
Arrowhead/Adobe Walls (Charles Marquis Warren). Novel basis.

1954   *Dangerous Mission* (Louis King). Co-script.
Night People (Nunnally Johnson). Uncredited contribution.

1955   *Captain Lightfoot* (Douglas Sirk). Novel basis, co-script.
Illegal (Lewis Allen). Co-script.

1956   *I Died a Thousand Times* (Stuart Heisler). From his novel *High Sierra*. Script.

1957   *Accused of Murder* (Joe Kane). From his novel *Vanity Row*. Co-script.
        Short Cut to Hell (James Cagney). Remake of *This Gun for Hire*.

1958   *The Badlanders* (Delmar Daves). From his novel *The Asphalt Jungle*.

1959   *The Hangman* (Delmar Daves). Uncredited contribution.

1960   *September Storm* (Byron Haskin). Script.
        The Lawbreakers (Joseph M. Newman). Script.

1962   *Sergeants Three* (John Sturges). Story, script.

1963   *Cairo* (Wolf Rilla). From his novel *The Asphalt Jungle*.
        The Great Escape (John Sturges). Co-script.
        Four for Texas (Robert Aldrich). Uncredited contribution.

1967   *The Jackals* (Robert D. Webb). Remake of *Yellow Sky*.

1968   *Ice Station Zebra* (John Sturges). Uncredited contribution.

1969   *Stiletto* (Bernard Kowalski). Uncredited contribution.

1972   *Cool Breeze* (Barry Pollack). From his novel *The Asphalt Jungle*.

1974   *Thunderbolt and Lightfoot* (Michael Cimino). Uncredited remake of *Captain Lightfoot*.

Novels include *Little Caesar, Iron Man, Saint Johnson, The Silver Eagle, The Giant Swing, Dark Hazard, The Goodhues of Sinking Creek, Goodbye to the Past: Scenes from the Life of William Meadows, King Cole, The Dark Command: A Kansas Iliad, High Sierra, The Quick Brown Fox, Nobody Lives Forever, Tomorrow's Another Day, Romelle, The Asphalt Jungle, Stetch Dawson* (a.k.a. *Yellow Sky*), *Little Men, Big World, Vanity Row, Adobe Walls: A Story of the Last Apache Rising, Big Stan* (written under the pseudonym John Monahan), *Captain Lightfoot, Pale Moon, It's Always Four O'Clock* (written under the pseudonym James Updyke), *Underdog, Bitter Ground, Mi Amigo: A Novel of the Southwest, Conant, Round the Clock at Volari's, The Goldseekers, Sergeants Three* (novelization of Burnett's script), *The Widow Barony, The Abilene Samson, The Roar of the Crowd, The Winning of Mickey Free, The Cool Man, The Loop,* and *Goodbye Chicago*.

Academy Awards associated with Burnett's work include an Oscar nomination in 1930–31 for the screenwriters Francis E. Faragoh and Robert N. Lee for adapting *Little Caesar;* a nomination for Burnett in 1942 for co-writing the original screenplay of *Wake Island* with Frank Butler; and a nomination in 1950 for the screenwriters Ben Maddow and John Huston for adapting *The Asphalt Jungle.*

Writers Guild awards include Best Written American Western in 1949 for *Yellow Sky* (Lamar Trotti's screenplay based on Burnett's novel).

When did you decide to become a writer?
After I got married. Before that I was interested in athletics. I played freshman football at Ohio State until I realized I was out of my class. I quit school and got married at twenty-one. My wife stayed home, you know, and I couldn't run around. So I got interested in reading and writing. I read everything I could get my hands on. Absolutely indiscriminately. I'd read Joseph Conrad on the one hand and *The Amateur Gentleman* [by Jeffery Farnol] on the other. I didn't know good from bad. Little by little I made up my taste.

I started out to write plays. If I had done what I wanted, I would have eventually gotten into the theatrical side of music, musicals—or jazz, writing songs. But by the time I went to Chicago in 1928, I had written five novels. I didn't have an agent, I didn't know from nothing. I'd just write 'em and send 'em away. The fifth novel I sent to Scribner's. Some reader at Scribner's recommended it to Maxwell Perkins, who was *the* editor in those days. He wrote me about it. He wanted me to rewrite it. But by that time I was thinking about something else. I don't rewrite on order anyway (*laughs*), so I put it aside.

Little Caesar (1930)

The city of Chicago appalled me. The contrast between Columbus, Ohio, for God's sake, and Chicago—why, you could be run over by a bus in Chicago and nobody would even look at you. It was a great thing for a writer, because it hit me with such impact. There was so much about it that I couldn't figure out—and, little by little, I figured it out.

I didn't know anything about gangsters, but I read the newspapers. Then I met an Italian guy who went by the name of Barber. He was very cautious with me because he thought I was a newspaper writer. Then he found out I was writing books about, as he put it, things that never happened; he thought that was ridiculous. He couldn't understand why anybody would want to write or read a novel. So he began to talk to me.

What I got from him was a viewpoint. I'm not a gangster; he really was. I had the old-fashioned Ohio ideas about right and wrong, remorse and all that stuff, which to him was utter nonsense. I'd ask him, after he'd kill guys, leave 'em on the street, how did he feel? And he said, "How do soldiers feel?" To him it was a war. He was the pay-off man for Terry Druggan on the North Side. Druggan was Bugs Moran's second-in-command.

One time we went to a prizefight on the West Side of Chicago, and there were two guys who sat up above us; and every time I looked at them, they were looking down at us or him. Finally we drove home and those guys followed us, and I could see myself getting killed for nothing. I never did understand what that was all about, because when we got close to the hotel, they rolled up beside us, looked at us, and moved on.

One Fourth of July I went up on the roof of the hotel to look at fireworks. He came up with his girl. He was drunk and he had a gun—boom, boom, shooting all over the place. That bothered me, but I didn't want to run or anything.

What was his girl like?

A prostitute. Quiet. She better be quiet. I went to the St. Valentine's Day Massacre with John Kelley of *The Trib,* but I couldn't go inside. I saw it, I just saw it. It was a slaughterhouse—blood all over the wall and guys lying around on the floor. I got one look at it and I said, "uh, uh." I didn't want any of that.

What were you striving for in the character of Rico?

I was reaching for a gutter Macbeth—a composite figure that would indicate how men could rise to prominence or money under the most hazardous conditions, but not much more hazardous than the men of the Renaissance. Nobody understood what I meant by the quotation from Machiavelli at the front of *Little Caesar:* "The first law of every being is to preserve itself and live. You sow hemlock and expect to see ears of corn ripen." It meant, if you have this type of society, it will produce such men. That's what I was looking for, a type. Rico was doomed from the first. If he had a tragic flaw, it was over-impulsive action. But he is the picture of overriding ambition.

Where did you pick up your style of dialogue?

I had a literary theory about dialogue. This was in the twenties. Novels were all written in a certain way, with literary language and so much description. Well, I dumped all that out; I just threw it away. It was a revolt, a literary revolt. That was my object. I wanted to develop a style of writing based on the way American people spoke—not literary English. Of course, the fact that the Chicago slang was all around me made it easy to pick up.

Ultimately, what made *Little Caesar* the enormous success it was, the smack in the face it was, was the fact that it was the world seen completely through the eyes of a gangster. It's a commonplace now, but it had never been done before then. You had crime stories but always seen through the eyes of society. The criminal was just some son-of-a-bitch who'd killed somebody and then you go get 'em. I treated 'em as human beings. Well, what else are they?

Where did the plot come from?

There isn't any plot. I don't have any plot in my books. Just life. And the relationship of characters and what happens to them.

Why do you take such exception to the word "plot"?

Because, in the motion picture business, the plot takes the place of everything else. The plot's all there is, and the characters are names. Anything that doesn't advance the plot is cut out.

Did you observe the filming of Little Caesar?

I was on the set and talked to [the director Mervyn] LeRoy, but I didn't know what he was doing. LeRoy threw out Rowland Lee's script because it wasn't any good. It didn't follow the book. LeRoy was twenty-eight at the time, Darryl Zanuck was twenty-seven, I was twenty-eight, and Eddie Robinson was thirty. LeRoy stood up to the rest of them and threw the script out. Francis Faragoh rewrote it. It was not a good script, although he did get the important thing in, which is the character of Rico. Otherwise, the script is taken straight out of the book, except for the ending, in which Rico dies in a flophouse.

I was disappointed in the film because they conventionalized it. In my book, the guy who starts after Rico, the Irish detective, he never gets him. He just fades out of the picture like he naturally would. Then that stuff about Rico in a flophouse—try to imagine Rico in a flophouse! It's the last place he'd ever be. And in the movie version, the fence, the old woman, she turns against Rico and tells him off. Hell, he would have killed her. Amazing! What made the movie is Robinson and the fact that Rico came out as he did in the book. That casting! It's an Italian picture, and not an Italian in it. Stanley Fields, William Collier Jr., Doug Fairbanks, Jr.—isn't that ridiculous? It drove me crazy!

When they opened *Little Caesar* at the Strand Theatre in New York, they opened it cold, yet they had to get out the mounted police and run it twenty-four hours a day. Then, I'll never forget the premiere out here [in Los Angeles]. They had every goddamned person on stage—the actors, the director, the cameraman—and when they were finished

Gutter Macbeth: Edward G. Robinson, W. R. Burnett, and Mervyn LeRoy on the set of Little Caesar.

introducing all of them, Ben Lyon, the emcee, finally says, "Oh yes, the *writer*. There always has to be a *writer*." Can you imagine that? He introduced me and I said, "Screw you." I wouldn't stand up for him. That was typical of Hollywood. That's one of the things that made it very tough for me when I came to Hollywood. I realized what the status of the writer was.

Scarface (1932) and Howard Hughes

You worked for Howard Hughes on Scarface. *How did that come about?*

His agent called me up and told me he wanted me to work on *Scarface*. He paid me $2,000 a week. Hughes was very stand-offish. He always had six or seven men between him and you. I did *Scarface* and he liked what I did; and then I didn't hear from him for twenty years.

How many writers were on the project before you came along?
About twelve.
Who worked on it after you—just Ben Hecht?
That's right.
What was your principal contribution?
I wrote a whole script.
You rewrote a whole script?
I *wrote* a whole script. I don't say my script was very good. I don't
say anybody could write a good script under those circumstances. It
was a mess. Nobody really knew what the hell they were doing—
except for Howard Hawks apparently. But I never got along with
Hawks, and I didn't work for Hawks when I was working for Hughes.
I went in and talked to Hughes, and he gave me an office down the
hall, and they started bringing in scripts. Pretty soon I had twelve
scripts piled on my desk, until I said, "What the hell's all this?"

The basis for the story was a book written by this guy named Armitage Trail. He was lucky to have four dollars in his pocket at any given
time. He got $25,000 for the book because Hughes wanted to use the
title and some of the material. The book was an awful piece of crap—
pulp. Armitage Trail never drew another sober breath, and in about
two years he died of a heart attack in Grauman's Chinese Theater.

Hughes had the book as a sort of skeleton—with an incest theme. I
don't know what it was with Hughes and incest. So I wrote a whole
script, and after I finished it, Hughes set a starting date. But Hawks
didn't like my script. So they brought Ben Hecht in ten days before
shooting. And Ben said, "I'll give you a shootable script in ten days for
a thousand dollars a day." He was really a brilliant guy. He was his
own worst enemy. All that money he made went right through his
fingers. I think Hecht was responsible for getting that picture made.
He tightened it all up. He was an absolute pro, when he wanted to be.
And he managed to tell the story, such as it was. Ben is a lot better
writer than he gets credit for.
Yes, he's a wonderful screenwriter.
No, not screenwriter. *Writer.*
So then you didn't hear from Hughes for twenty years? Was that on
Vendetta *[1951]?*
Yes, I got a call from Stuart Heisler, who was scared stiff of
Hughes. "I got a strange request from Howard Hughes," he told me.
"Will you look at a film called *Vendetta* with me and see what you
could do with it?" There was a million dollars worth of film shot,
which was a lot then, and it was terrible. I don't know what had
happened to [the writer-director] Preston Sturges, who was a brilliant
guy—whether he was sore at Hughes and it was an act of sabotage, or

whether he had gone nuts. It was a story of Corsican incest and revenge that never should have been made in the first place. During one scene I literally fell on the floor laughing. There are Corsicans hiding behind some bushes with big hats on. Bang! They shoot at each other. Bang! Their hats fly off. It was like a comedy in which the broad walks by the comic and wiggles and his hat goes up in the air.

I said, "This is impossible. You don't expect me to work on a bunch of shit like this, do you?" Heisler said, "Well, there go our jobs." So we called Hughes and Heisler told him, in the opinion of both of us, that we could not salvage anything. He said, "Okay, start over." So I wrote a new script, and Heisler shot the movie. But we were stuck with the story. He had promised Faith Domergue a picture and *Vendetta* was it.

Did Hughes have any idea of how a story should be told?

Oh, yeah! One day Hughes called me up from Washington, D.C. My wife picked up the phone and said, "My God, it's Howard Hughes on the phone." I said, "Okay, I'll talk to him." An hour and a half. Did you ever talk on the phone for an hour and a half? I never talk on the phone for too long if I can help it. I practically fell asleep. My wife was bringing me coffee. Hughes went over the whole *Vendetta* script. But then he said, "In this speech of so-and-so's, don't you think this should be a colon instead of a semicolon?" That threw me.

One time Heisler and I met him to talk about *Vendetta* at the Sunset Towers at two o'clock in the morning. Pretty soon a beat-up, junky Chevrolet pulls up and Hughes gets out. He had on tennis shoes, no coat, a dirty looking shirt, kind of crummy looking pants. When we went up in the elevator, I could see dirt on the inside of his collar. His suite looked like the anteroom of a doctor's office. And that's where we had our meeting. I don't know why we had to meet that way, but that was Hughes. Conspiracy, you know.

The damnedest thing that happened to me regarding Hughes was on a Sunday in 1953 when I got a call from RKO Studios. It was about a picture called *Dangerous Mission* [1954]. The script was already written. Irwin Allen was producing it—one of his first credits. Horace McCoy wrote the script. And they were on location in Montana with seven expensive actors when they called me.

Howard wouldn't read the script; he wouldn't pay attention to anyone, so the head of the studio just went ahead with it. Then, Hughes got hold of the script and stopped it while they had these people sitting on their asses at high salaries in Montana. So I went over to Irwin Allen and said, "For chrissakes, what the hell do you want me to do?" It was a terrible script. I couldn't believe Horace wrote it—he must have been drunk—and Irwin didn't know what was wrong with it. So in four weeks I got him a shooting script, but what it cost for those four weeks! And funny enough, it's not a bad picture.

The book *Empire: The Life, Legend, and Madness of Howard Hughes* [by Donald L. Barlett and James B. Steele. New York: Norton, 1979] gives the impression that Hughes mismanaged RKO. Hughes didn't mismanage RKO. He didn't manage it at all. He didn't care. It was a write-off. He was always cordial to me. I remember one time when he really surprised me. He had a funny look on his face and his hands behind him. Then he came out with a book, a novel of mine called *Goodbye to the Past*. And he said, "Would you mind autographing this for me?" Kind of shy, you know. Like a kid coming up to you.

Beast of the City (1932)

There were never any good Capone pictures, as far as I know, but I think my *Beast of the City,* with Walter Huston, Jean Harlow, and Jean Hersholt as Capone, is one of the best crime pictures of all. Hersholt was a greasy, offensive Capone. Really good.

Who directed that?

Charles Brabin, an Englishman. Everything about it was wrong. Making an American hoodlum picture, giving it to an Englishman. We'd have a story conference, and he'd go to sleep right in your face.

But Brabin did a good job of directing?

Strangely enough, he did.

Law and Order (1932)

Your book Saint Johnson *was the basis for* Law and Order, *one of the first tellings of the shootout at the OK Corral.*

I had read a very fine biography about Wyatt Earp and saw the possibilities of a fine western novel. I had never written a western novel. So everybody said to me, "Burnett, are you out of your mind? Let Zane Grey write the westerns, for chrissakes!" Well, you know me. I read about this "Hell Dorado" celebration in Tombstone, Arizona, where they recreate the fight at the OK Corral. So I took a train down there, and just like Chicago it hit me.

What hit you?

Everything. Tombstone. The Mogollon Mountains in the distance, where the Apaches used to hide. The whole thing. So I called my wife on the phone and told her I was gonna stay there a little while, and I started to write in the hotel. An old rickety hotel—I was the only one in it. At night the coyotes would come into town and knock the garbage cans over in the back of the place.

I got the complete feel of the town because it was practically preserved. I got a great feel for the country. That's what really makes the book. This was in the 1930s, but I talked to three different ranchers, in their sixties or seventies, who were still hashing over the feud, which was very interesting. It was not an historical thing for them, it was something that had happened yesterday, and they were still on different sides. That's what I mean when I say I got the real feel of the men and the countryside.

One night, we got drunk, and we went up at midnight and recreated the OK Corral shootout. Bang. I got the idea it was kind of a political thing—Republicans versus Democrats. The Earps were Republicans, and the sheriff and the other gang were all Democrats. Mrs. Earp was much younger than Wyatt, you know, and she was greatly in love with him. When he died, she objected very strenuously to the publication of my book. She came out to Universal Studios to try to stop them from filming it. So I talked to her for an afternoon, and she turned out to be a very nice woman. She realized I felt very strongly that Earp was a hero, a western hero, and we became friends.

Some of my best books, in my opinion, are westerns. I got interested in the Southwest because of the multiple culture: the Indian, the Latin, and the Anglo. I tend to think in trilogies, and my western trilogy [of books] is *Adobe Walls*, *Pale Moon*, and *Mi Amigo*. It takes the Southwest from the last Apache uprising to the coming of the carpetbaggers and the railroad in the third volume. I think *Adobe Walls* would probably be among my four or five top books.

The Whole Town's Talking (1935)

Was John Ford in on the story sessions?

Yeah, but he didn't say anything. Usually he rules them; *you* don't say a thing. Because *he* does the talking. I don't even know why he took the picture. I never could figure out John. One day, I had a big beef with [the producer] Sam Briskin. I'm half-Irish—at least—and Ford is all-Irish, and he didn't say a word, but I could see he was absolutely delighted when Briskin jumped on me; and I jumped all over Briskin in a loud and raucous voice, which wasn't done at Columbia. Briskin said, "Why don't you write a story that's got a good finish on it?" I said, "Why did you buy it? I didn't make you buy it." And we got into it. I never did take any of that crap from Hollywood. You know, John was a big spender, he could have been broke, he might have needed the money. It's not really a Ford picture, although it's beautifully directed.

So you only came in for a couple of days and helped figure out the ending for them?

Yeah, I helped them. But they had it so screwed up it was a little hard to straighten out. We did the best we could. And it turned out to be a hell of a good picture.

John Huston

John Huston wrote the script for the first version of Law and Order. *Later, you and he collaborated on other films.*

We got along fine. But we didn't work well together, because I work fast on the typewriter and he dictates. He likes to sit down and completely talk out a scene, which would take a day and wear me out. I can't work that way. Then, he'd go into his office and dictate it, which took another day, just for a lousy little scene. John isn't really a writer. John is a director. And he writes that way, which make his scripts no good for ordinary reading.

You know what happened on *High Sierra,* don't you? John, who belted the grape a little now and then, was at one of those big Holly-wood cocktail parties with Paul Muni, and he didn't like Muni. Warners had bought the book for Muni. John got a little loaded and told Muni what he thought of him as an actor. So Muni waited until the script came to him, and he turned it down because Huston was the writer. So Jack Warner said to Huston, "Get Burnett. Get Burnett and let him work on the script with you, and if Muni comes up with any objections, we'll say, 'For chrissakes, what do you want? We got the author on it.'"

Well, I never had so much fun in my life, John and I working together. We laughed most of the time; we could hardly get any work done. Anyway, we got a fine script and gave it to Muni, and Muni turned it down again. You know what happened? Warner fired him. I thought the studio was going to collapse that day. Everybody went around saying, "For chrissakes, they fired *Muni.* He's getting five thousand a week. You can't fire the star."

Then George Raft refused it.

Bogie talked him out of it.

I thought it was because Raft didn't want to die at the end of another picture.

Nah, that's bullshit. Bogie talked Raft out of it and got the part himself.

The conspirators: Sam Jaffe (back to camera), Sterling Hayden, James Whitmore, and Marc Lawrence in W. R. Burnett's The Asphalt Jungle, *screenplay by John Huston and Ben Maddow, directed by Huston.*

What was Bogie's logic?
That the part didn't suit Raft at all. Which it didn't.
Did you ever have any working disagreements with Huston?
I'd argue with him now and then, but he was really a tough customer. It was really hard to win arguments with him. If Huston really likes a property, there's no person who can put it on the screen better. But if he is not entirely sold on the thing he is doing, he can make a bomb.

I had a bad argument with him over a project that I had with [the producer] Sid Luft called "Man o' War." It was going to be the next project at Warners after *A Star Is Born* [1954]. I said to Sid, "How about John Huston to direct?" and sent him the script. One of the leading characters was a Negro—someone who grew up with the Man o' War and never left it. I had lunch with John at Romanoff's to talk about the script, and he got a little snotty about the Negro character. He said, "I don't want to do a picture in which we've got a fucking

Uncle Tom." That black activist stuff was the very thing I wanted to keep out of the picture. I treated this man as a man, not as a racial symbol. A man, just like any other man. Why should I want to falsify him into something fashionable? We had quite an argument. Then we wound up laughing.

Was Huston more liberal than you?

I don't think so. Huston was *like* me, a rebel. Do you know what a rebel is? People confuse a revolutionary with a rebel. A revolutionary is a politician who is out of office. And a rebel is a guy who is suspicious of all authority, left or right. So Huston's like me. I know he was criticized for his casting in *The Asphalt Jungle*. Sterling Hayden was a Communist. Marc Lawrence was a Communist. So was Sam Jaffe. That's three. But so what? The object is to get a movie. And he certainly did—beautifully cast. He didn't destroy the novel, he stuck to it. Character by character, step by step. That made for a good picture.

High Sierra (1941)

Let's talk about High Sierra. *I understand that the character Roy Earle was drawn partly from [John] Dillinger. Where did the idea come from?*

A friend of mine and his wife, and my wife and I, went up to June Lake trout fishing. I got to thinking what a wonderful hideaway that would be for hoodlums. Who would ever look for them up there? It's a beautiful lake, remote, on a good road, but nobody went there in those days except fishermen. I understand it's a tourist spot now, where the fishermen stand on each other's feet. Also, there was a dog there. The dog didn't seem to belong to anybody, and he went from house to house and he took to me. The colored guy up there said he brought bad luck to people. So I used the dog, and the colored guy, in the story. Little things like that began to occur to me, you know.

Charley Blake, who was the ace Dillinger reporter, had done a lot of work with me on a Dillinger movie for Warners. Charley and I worked for six weeks researching Dillinger, and then Warners began to get worried about the project, began to say we shouldn't do it. There was a lot of resistance in those days from certain associations. When they put out the publicity that we—the author of *Little Caesar* and the ace Dillinger reporter—were going to make *Dillinger,* boy, did that get a reaction! Telephone calls and letters of protest. So Jack Warner said, "Forget it." He just called it off. But I still had the research, and I had also had the luck to sit down and talk to Charley Blake, who went to the morgue in the wagon with Dillinger.

So you had the setting, the dog, the Negro character, your research on Dillinger . . . then what?

The rest wrote itself practically.

Was there a replay of frontier themes in Roy Earle's heading West?

Maybe, maybe. I had the same idea in *Dark Hazard* [1934], you know. A gambler who winds up in California. You see, there's a confusion here: Dillinger and Roy Earle, such men are not gangsters, organized crime, mafioso. They were a reversion to the western bandit. They had nothing in common with the Italian, Irish, or Polish hoodlums in Chicago. An entirely different breed, and Roy Earle was a perfect example.

Earle's a man who is out of his element.

You've got it. There are plenty of those symbolic characters in my books. Arky in *Little Men, Big World* is one of them. Dix in *The Asphalt Jungle.* And there's also a country boy, in one of my best books called *Babylon,* which is not published yet.

What are they symbolic of?

Old America, rural America and a simpler time.

In High Sierra, *what do Babe and Red and Marie represent—counterpoint? She's there to show what amateurs they are and as someone for them to fight over?*

No, no, no. That's plot again. She's there because they picked her up in a dance hall. That's just the kind of broad they would pick up. It was stupid of them to bring her along when they're planning a big robbery.

That's plot.

I don't call it plot. "B" movies are *all* plot. That's plot at its worst. What's the plot of *Macbeth?*

There's no plot. It's jealousy and rivalry and . . .

Now you're talking. The plot of *The Asphalt Jungle* is that a bunch of guys get together and rob a place.

What are the parts of High Sierra, *the film, that you don't like?*

Well, John and I had to fight [the producer Mark] Hellinger. Hellinger was a swell guy, don't misunderstand me. I liked him. But he was a sentimentalist. We got into an awful struggle about the character of the lame girl with him. He just couldn't take it, after Roy had her foot fixed, that she turned against Roy . . . that was too much for Hellinger. So we had to give a little on a couple of scenes like that. The main point wasn't as strong as it should have been. I corrected that in the remake, *I Died A Thousand Times* [1956]. The remake is a better picture. Except we had two repulsive people in it—Jack Palance and Shelley Winters.

Why do you say it's a better picture?

A reversion to the western bandit: Roy Earle (Humphrey Bogart) makes his last stand in High Sierra. *W. R. Burnett adapted his own novel in collaboration with John Huston.*

I think the script's much better. I cleaned up the script. I had a free hand. Willis Goldbeck [the producer] and I made the picture for Warners. I cut it down, shortened it. A lot of that dialogue [in the first version] was in as a result of Hellinger. He'd say, "Bill, I don't understand that, I don't understand that . . . line." Huston would look up at the ceiling and say [*Sing-song*], "Got to have another line in here so he'll understand that line." In the remake I took all that bullshit out.

And did you clean up the sentimentality too?

Oh, believe me! It's a much better picture, script-wise, although not pictorially, because Raoul Walsh did a hell of a job. Stuart Heisler is also a fine director; he never gets the credit he deserves. But those people! Who gives a damn what happens to Shelley Winters? Or Jack Palance, for that matter?

The Westerner (1940)

You have an uncredited contribution on The Westerner.

Well, all I did was sit and talk.

To whom?

Sam Goldwyn and William Wyler. Sam called me in because I'd done quite a bit of work for him before. But I never got anything on the screen with Sam. They were having a lot of trouble straightening out the script. I remember I suggested one thing that helped. They had two cities, they only needed one. I remember I said, "What do you need two cities for?" and everybody just sat there and looked at each other blankly. Nobody had ever thought of that. That can happen. You can get messed up in a script.

George Raft

You know that coin thing in *Scarface*? It's one of the things that made the damned picture. That was Raft's idea. He realized he wasn't a good actor, which he wasn't. But he knew if he *reacted* to what other people said, he was effective. So I went over his scripts with him sometimes, him saying, "I don't need this line, I don't need this line . . ." Sometimes I wouldn't take the lines out because they were absolutely necessary to what came later, which never occurs to an actor, you know.

Would Raft sit in on story sessions?

You had to get rid of Raft. They'd lie to him, tell him they weren't having a conference, anything to get rid of him. Look at *Background to Danger* [1943]! I was always afraid that I'd have to face Eric Ambler after what we did to that. The point of *Background to Danger* was that this man was a salesman, an outsider, and suddenly things begin to happen to him that he can't understand. And he gets involved in all this espionage. But Raft wouldn't do it unless he was an FBI man. The whole story went out the window.

Why didn't the original story make sense to Raft?

He said he didn't want to be any ribbon salesman. I think he wanted to be on the side of the law for a change.

San Antonio (1945)

Raoul Walsh was going to direct *San Antonio* originally. Then David Butler was assigned to direct it. That scared the hell out of us because he had never made anything but musicals. But he got a good picture out of it. Ever see *San Antonio?* You'd be surprised.

How I wrote it is a very funny story. Max Brand—his real name was Frederick Faust—had so much money he didn't know what to do with it, but he kept on writing. Warner or somebody had the bright idea to do a big Errol Flynn picture and to hire "Heinie" Faust to write it. They gave him carte blanche, which they never did, because of his enormous reputation. He used to come in every day which a briefcase and go out every night with a briefcase. This irritated the hell out of all the other writers—you know, because we thought this guy was showing off or something, taking his work home. We found out later he brought in two quarts of gin every day and drank them up—took the empties out.

A few months later I get a quick-hurry-up call from Jim Geller, who was boss of the story department. He said, "Boy, have we got trouble." I said, "What's the matter?" He said, "We have a color commitment, we have a shooting date, we have [Errol] Flynn. And 'Heinie' Faust has come up with a very original idea for us. A western in which there's no action." I muttered, "Oh, boy"—by that time I knew about those two quarts of gin. He said, "Go over and talk to [the writer-producer] Bob Buckner"—the guy who was supposed to produce it and was about to hang himself—"and see what you guys can come up with."

So I wrote a screenplay in three weeks. Then I rewrote it. First, I came up with the idea that really floored everybody. Do a picture with Flynn and Marlene Dietrich. How about that? Now that's a combination. Jack Warner called me and said, "That's the best idea we've had at this studio in a long time . . ." Then he wouldn't pay Dietrich the money. We were up in his office talking about it, and he pulled a desk drawer out, and said, "Look at all these contracts in here. All these no good sons-of-bitches sitting around on their asses, earning $1,500 a week, $2,000 a week. Why should I go out and get Dietrich?" So he gave it to Alexis Smith. She was alright.

Writers and Screenwriters

You said Ben Hecht was one of the best screenwriters in Hollywood.
Who else would you consider to be among the top four or five?
Dudley Nichols was the best. No argument.
How about Billy Wilder?
Pretty good. Eccentric, but clever.
How about Preston Sturges?
Preston Sturges was one of the best, but crazy, a little nutty. He had
a big desk and a horn on it that honked. Honk, honk. He thought it
was goddamned funny.
Did you know William Faulkner?
I knew Bill well. Absolute southern gentleman, precisely dressed,
when he was sober. Faulkner really looked like Poe. I would cast
Faulkner as Poe. I really liked him. I had a weakness for Faulkner.
And I never could finish one of his books, except *Sanctuary.*
What was his attitude toward Hollywood?
I don't know. He never had much to say about anything. He was very
quiet. One time, when I was standing outside the studio, Bill came out
smoking his pipe, and we stood there for a few minutes, exchanging a
couple of words. On the lot we had one of those overnight geniuses—a
woman—someone who had published a book about her family or some
goddamned silly thing and is suddenly a national celebrity and then you
never hear of them again. They were making her movie at the time, and
she was throwing her weight around the studio. Oh, she was a most
unpleasant person. She began to raise hell with Faulkner because of his
terrible influence on American writing. Faulkner smoked his pipe and
looked at her. People who were passing by looked embarrassed. I just
stood there, what else could I do? He never said a word, never said a
word, not to me, not to her. Just smoked his pipe.
Did you know Raymond Chandler, James M. Cain, or Dashiell
Hammett well when they were in Hollywood?
I never knew Chandler at all. I was never friendly with Cain, but I
used to run into him quite often at the Swanson office, sitting in the
outer office. He'd bother me because he wouldn't look at you except
with sort of a sidelong glance. Big guy. Kind of a messed-up face.
Irishman, I guess. Hammett I only met once—he looked like a university professor. Tall and slender, beautifully dressed, elegantly dressed,
quite a gentleman, you know.
The mystery novel never attracted me, though. It's just a trick.
Once you find out who did it, so what? That's it. Forget it. Nobody
will ever want to read it again. Of course, there are some masters—
[Arthur] Conan Doyle was one of the best writers of his time. He

doesn't get credit for it but he was. He had a prophetic view of London, and he selected just the right style; the Sherlock Holmes and Watson books are masterpieces, in my opinion. And then there's [Georges] Simenon. He's the closest in merit to Conan Doyle—sort of a poor man's Balzac. Simenon didn't write mysteries at all—they're police procedure novels. Simenon is so good, and so painful.

The French take mysteries a lot more seriously. They appreciated Chandler before any American critics did. But Chandler is not in the same class as Simenon. There's just no comparison. Simenon is a first-class novelist and Chandler isn't. Simenon gives you the poor man's Paris. A wonderful descriptive writer—and he can set a scene or show you a picture in a sentence, two sentences.

What about Horace McCoy? He wrote a few good novels and then his career seemed to dissipate. What happened?

That's a good question. He was a very unhappy guy in many ways, and I never could figure him out. I liked him personally. He told me that he was working as a newspaperman in the South, trying to write, and someone gave him *Little Caesar* to read. After he read it, he said, "That's it." That's what started him writing.

I think *They Shoot Horses, Don't They?* is a helluva fine book, but I don't really care much about his other books. He wrote a Hollywood book I didn't like, and then he wrote *Scalpel,* which I made the mistake of reviewing for the *Saturday Review of Literature.* I didn't like it and I said so. Then I ran into McCoy in a bookstore. If I hadn't been a friend of his, he'd have flattened me. He was a great big guy, you know, about six-foot-four. He would have been a championship tennis player if he hadn't damaged his knee to such an extent that it was useless.

Last I saw of Horace that I remember, I was working at Warners in the 1950s, when it was Death Valley. There were only three or four or five of us screenwriters on contract. There was a writer there—who I will not name because he is famous now as a novelist—who bugged the hell out of us. McCoy and I just wanted to talk about sports at lunch, and we couldn't shake this guy. Every day at lunch he followed us to the lunchroom, until finally Horace and I had to go off the lot for lunch. Horace was a car nut, and he knew of a place in the valley where they had every kind of car. So we used to go have lunch over there someplace and then go see the cars together.

The Screen Writers Guild

Were you involved in the formation of the Guild at all?

Hell no, I didn't even want to join. Agent said you better join, so I joined. I didn't want to bother with any union. I was doing alright. I didn't *need* any union, but the studio wanted you to join. Warners wanted you to join.

Because it made it easier to deal with the entity?

I think so. Closed shop, which is wrong, but . . . I'm absolutely for unions. I'm just not for the way they've become—a nuisance.

Were you at Warners in the forties when the writers were asked to respect the picket lines set up by the Conference of Studio Unions?

I can't remember. I know I crossed a picket line. I think I was at Metro when that happened.

Yet you collaborated on scripts with several Guild activists, writers who were also members of the Communist Party. John Howard Lawson on Action in the North Atlantic. *Albert Maltz on* This Gun for Hire.

That's right. They were Commies.

Were you aware of their political views when you were working with them?

Oh, are you kidding? We were loaded with card-holders in Hollywood. I'm very anti-Communist, due to the fact that I'm a rebel. I couldn't possibly live under such a Communist government. I'd get killed; I'd be shot. The least government suits me, and that's what we've got. We've got democracy in this country that verges on anarchy. And that's the ideal government for me. So I'm satisfied.

So how did you collaborate with them?

Well, I liked Albert Maltz. He was a really nice fellow. Lawson I didn't like at all; he was a big jerk. He was commissar, boss of the Commie writers. At that time the Communists controlled the Screen Writers Guild, and one day he came to me and said, "Bill, I need credits, you don't need credits. Let me have all the credits on *Action in the North Atlantic.*" Can you imagine such crust as that? So for the first time I arbitrated. And lost. Because "the boys" were in and I was in trouble. Lawson got one of the top credits for *Action in the North Atlantic,* which he didn't deserve at all. I wrote every action scene in that picture step by step; the director didn't have to do anything except read his script. That's what Jerry Wald, the producer, said.

Some of the Communists were no-good bastards, and some of them were alright, just like everybody. Gordon Kahn was a kick! What a funny guy! A little short guy, he wore a monocle. He was a very good investigative reporter. A long time ago, before other people were into it, he experimented with every kind of drug. He used to sit in my office and tell me about the effects of all the various drugs he was taking. He wrote articles about drug-taking that were definitive for the time. He was interesting. I used to sit and look at him and wonder, what the hell does he want to be a Communist for? Some of the others were dumb clods, you could understand it.

You worked with Lester Cole, too—or at least he wrote the screenplay

for the second version of Iron Man, *called* Some Blondes Are Dangerous *[1937].*

I liked Lester. I didn't really work with him, but I liked him. He was
a nice guy. A lot of those Commies were friends of mine. I liked them.

Did you feel sorry for them during the period of blacklisting?

Why should I feel sorry for them? They were all card-holding Communists. What's the big deal?

Didn't you think they should be allowed to work?

I am not exactly in favor of people who advocate the overthrow of
the government by violence.

*But because you collaborated with them you knew what little actual
effect they had in Hollywood.*

Yes, but still, that's what they were *for.*

What is the difference between the message of a picture like The
Public Enemy—*co-scripted by John Bright, who was blacklisted—and*
Little Caesar?

I'm not talking about messages. I'm talking about what those guys
stood for. They didn't get much message into those pictures. They
were always trying to recruit me. Oh God, that was funny! You see,
we had an underground of anti-Communists in the writer's building—
me, Jack Moffitt, Tom Reed, Graham Baker. Alvah Bessie was always
trying to recruit me. He was trying to make me understand that if I
were a writer in Russia I'd have enormous status. What a lot of bullshit! But I just let him talk. He was a pretty good guy.

Why was Jack Warner so tolerant of Communists on his payroll?

He didn't even know what was going on. Jack was a Democrat, but
really I'd say Jack was non-political.

*Did you remain friendly with any of your former colleagues who
were Communists during the McCarthy era?*

A friend of mine, Frank Capra, came up and gave me a long pitch,
trying to get me to sign petitions in their favor. I chased him out of the
house. Why should I sign? If they want to be Communists and overthrow the government, let them take what they've got coming. I never
did anything actively either way. We had some right wing organizations too, but they were a little hard to stomach. At Metro they tried
to get me to join, but I wouldn't.

Warner Brothers

*Did you have any sense of how the writers' group at Warners com-
pared with the other studios in town? Did Warners value writers more or
less?*

I don't think any of the studios valued writers very much. If the writer could fit the Warners system, it was far and away the best place to be. And I wrote everyplace. Metro—you might as well be out in the middle of the desert. Nobody even knew you were there. You could sit there for four weeks and draw your pay and not say anything and you never heard from anybody. Paramount was always hit-or-miss—they had people coming in and out. It wasn't a well-run place, ever. Columbia was a tight ship. Harry Cohn was tough, real tough. Republic was a joke. And Fox, I would say, was very well run under [Darryl] Zanuck. Very well run.

Zanuck appreciated writers?

Yes, he did. He was a writer himself. Or at least he claimed he was. I never saw anything he wrote. To me, there was no comparison. Warners was far and away the best studio in town. Of course, I'm going more on my own experience. Jack Warner could be a bastard to anybody—directors, actors, or writers.

What about Jack's brother Harry? Did he exercise any creative leadership?

I don't think "creative" is a word you could apply to Harry! The biggest bore who's ever lived in the history of the world! He used to sit next to me when I'd visit the executive dining room. I guess nobody else would listen to him. All he talked about was his charities and his horses. I don't know how two brothers could be so different. Jack got around pretty good, and Harry was a puritan. Certain writers in the writers' building would give the secretaries a pretty bad time. Not at Warners. All the girl had to do was complain to the madam—the woman in charge—and if there was any further trouble, she'd tell Harry Warner and he'd say, "Fire him."

Did Jack Warner involve himself artistically—buying properties, deciding that such-and-such a story was something Warners ought to make?

Oh, absolutely. With the story boss, Jim Geller, or whoever it happened to be at that time. Geller, that Scotsman, was there for years. He had a lot to say about what was bought.

What was your experience—comparatively—at MGM?

I'm trying to think. Louis B. Mayer ran the studio, and later Dore Schary.

Schary has a good reputation as a producer.

He wasn't good for anything, as far as I'm concerned. He almost wrecked RKO, so they put him in charge at Metro.

What was his problem?

His problem was he didn't know what to make. He came into Metro and made *Plymouth Adventure* [1952]. It went out and died. Then he made two or three more, and every one of them died. He had done the same thing at RKO. But they still thought he was a genius. Then Schary got mad and said, "Okay, I'm going to make a picture in which there is some shooting and fucking," so he bought *The Asphalt Jungle*. (*Laughs.*) It's true. They paid $100,000 for it.

Was Zanuck a creative producer?

Zanuck's fault was, he wasn't interested in women. He was interested in women personally, God knows, but not artistically, let's put it that way. He did much better with men's pictures. He was very autocratic, even more so than Hal Wallis. Wallis was quiet, he wouldn't yell. Zanuck would yell.

One of the best producers was Hal Wallis. I wouldn't call him a particularly creative man, but he knew what he wanted to see up on the screen. The producer's really in charge, you know. And if he doesn't know what the hell he's doing he screws everything up. Like my pal Jerry Wald. Now Jerry made some pretty good pictures— *Mildred Pierce* [1945], for example. But he couldn't make up his mind for five minutes. He'd drive you crazy. If he'd seen a movie he liked the night before, he'd want to steal it. I'd say, "Jerry, it doesn't have anything to do with what we're doing."

You haven't been through this—you don't realize the things I've been through with the producer sitting there and having no idea what the fuck he is doing. He doesn't know whether to go this way, that way, down the middle, or what. And he's the one who has to say it. The writer can't say it. I mean, I *can* say it, but I don't have the authority. In those days, most directors didn't have the authority either.

Is that why someone like Michael Curtiz did his best work at Warner Brothers—because of the supervising producers?

Curtiz needed somebody to sit on him. He didn't have any judgment about what to make.

How did he compare to Raoul Walsh in that regard?

Technically, Mike may have been as good, but Walsh was much smarter, much cleverer. Walsh didn't need anybody. If he'd have wanted to, which he didn't, he could have produced *and* directed. It's true Walsh is not much interested in complexities. He's interested in making a certain kind of picture, mostly action. Which is the *motion* picture.

The Fifties

When I have something to say and I can't say it in one book, I do a trilogy. I don't know why. The first one was *The Asphalt Jungle; Little Men, Big World; Vanity Row*. That was a study of corruption of a whole city in three stages: status quo, imbalance, and anarchy.

The last time I read *Vanity Row,* I could hardly believe it. I had completely forgotten about it, it was so many books and years ago. It sounded just like things are right now: wiretapping, Watergate, you name it. Anyway, *Vanity Row* has what in Hollywood is called a good gimmick. One of the pillars of the city is murdered on the streets; it looks like he's been killed by hoodlums or something like that. What people don't know is, there's a big struggle going on in the city over the wire service. You control the wire service, you control the gambling, and this pillar of the republic is a front man with the administration for dealing with the Chicago hoodlums.

The lead character is Roy Hargis, a perfect Bogart part, a hatchet man for the administration. His job is to find a patsy. So he finds this guy's girlfriend, and he begins to build a case against this girl. The hatchet man becomes fascinated by this broad. She is absolutely a no-good bum, but a beauty. And the gimmick is: she killed him. Now that he's got her hooked, he's got to get her off.

It was a very unusual book, and nobody was more surprised than I was when Republic bought it. You know Republic? Formerly Repulsive. Herbert Yates ran a cheap operation, and they paid me a lot of money for it. They also paid me to write the script. The director, Joe Kane, was a very nice fellow; we got along fine, and all he said to me was, "Write it." So I wrote the script just like the book; I got my money and left. Well, Yates was married to Vera Hruba Ralston. She was a Czechoslovakian champion ice skater. And he decided to put her in the picture [*Accused of Murder* in 1957] in the girl's part. Well, the wife of the head of the studio couldn't be guilty, so he made her innocent. The whole goddamned show went out the window.

Did you know about it?

Not until it came out.

They didn't consult you?

Of course not. Swanson, my agent, loved it! Can you imagine such stupidity? I've run into a lot of pretty stupid things in Hollywood, but that's the stupidest. They buy the book because it has such a very unusual story, and then they throw the whole story out.

Captain Lightfoot (1955)

Did you work with Douglas Sirk on the original Captain Lightfoot?

Douglas Sirk was a German, a very bright man who had done a lot of very good intellectual stuff in Europe. When he found out I knew about Alban Berg, the composer, he could hardly ever get on the subject of *Lightfoot.* All he wanted to talk about was his early experience in the German theatre in the 1920s, when he staged Frank Wedekind's *Earth Spirit,* which was the basis for *Lulu.* But Sirk was a very bad job of miscasting. He had no sense of humor. And *Captain Lightfoot* is a light piece, full of humor.

Captain Lightfoot *was more or less remade as* Thunderbolt and Lightfoot *[1974] by the director Michael Cimino.*

He stole it. Son-of-a-bitch. I called the studio law department and said, "What the fuck is going on here?" They didn't do a thing.

He even kept the same names.

I know it. That son-of-a-bitch. I'm glad *Heaven's Gate* flopped.

Sergeants Three (1962)

You spend a lot of time in your career working on the set, rewriting films as they were being shot.

I got to doing that so much for Jack Warner, I got out of Warners. I got to be Warner's troubleshooter and that was bad. Because people start thinking you're a company man. That way, you wind up without any credits either.

Were any of your scripts filmed just as you wrote them?

In all my time in Hollywood, I only got one script through untouched. Needless to say, it's one of my pet pictures: *Sergeants Three.* I got a call from "Swanie" to go to Columbia to have lunch with Frank Sinatra, which I did. Frank said he had an idea to take *Gunga Din* [1939] and kid it. Good idea. But Frank didn't know what to do with it. So I went home and thought about it and figured out a way to do it. I put it out West with this fanatical tribe of Indians, and that's *Sergeants Three.*

I wrote a treatment and gave it to Howard W. Koch, the producer. Howard read it and said, "This is swell, but I've got to give it to Frank." Frank was in Las Vegas. So Howard Koch went there and stayed for three days and never got him to read it. Finally he got him on the phone and said, "Frank, what do you want us to do?" Frank said, "Write the script." I said, "I wrote it." Frank said, "Howard, what do you think?" Howard said, "I think it's swell." I don't think Koch ever read it. I don't think Frank ever read it. So they shot my first draft. Scared the hell out of me, you know. John Sturges directed it—back-to-back he directed two of the best pictures I ever did, *Sergeants Three* and *The Great Escape. The Great Escape* has to be the best picture I ever worked on.

The Great Escape (1963)

James Clavell has a co-screenwriting credit on The Great Escape.
Clavell came on the set when we were shooting. I don't want to minimize what he did because he went through hell so he deserves the credit. Here's what happened. I worked on the script for a year. I was still working on it while John was shooting another picture in Japan. Then he came back and we went to work. I had 225 pages, which was way too long. So we spent one whole day cutting it and wound up with 250 pages! (*Laughs.*) We'd find stuff to put back in, when we thought we were taking stuff out. Finally, he went with that script.

The story came from a book?
It was a factual account by a British officer [Paul Brickhill] who had been in a prisoner-of-war camp. Good material. The problem was, you had so much to tell, so many characters. If your continuity wasn't perfect, you were going to wind up with a mess. I did the continuity before I wrote the script.

Most screenwriting, especially nowadays, doesn't have continuity. The script is never quite sure where it's going or why. So when I write a continuity for myself, I start out with scene one and explain who's in it and what happens to them. I do that with every scene in the whole picture. So all you have to do is read my continuity and you know the whole damned thing from start to finish. I have never written a novel yet without knowing the finish first. That's continuity.

When I went on *The Great Escape*, there were no Americans in it. I told John, "We're making this for the American public, so there have to be Americans." The Jim Garner character and the Steve McQueen character are mine. All that baseball stuff, the guy sitting in jail—that's all mine. It never would have been the same if it were all British without those two characters. It was all shot in Germany, you know. And McQueen was an impossible bastard. A third of the way through the picture, McQueen took charge. I had to rewrite his scenes and rearrange them . . . oh, he drove you crazy. He wanted changes all the time. So they got Clavell, and Clavell worked through the whole picture in Germany, making little changes here and there, trying to pacify McQueen. I've done that and that's no bed of roses. I think he deserved his credit.

Writing for Film

Was there a point in your career at which you were writing novels with the notion of turning them into movies?
I never had any idea of turning them into movies. Some of them just

fell into movies, and some of them didn't. I sold seventeen of them. But it was just the reverse for me—I worked in pictures to subsidize novel writing. Novel writing was what I was interested in—not pictures, for chrissakes. What happened to so many good American novelists when they came out here didn't happen to me. They got into the big money and quit writing novels. I published some thirty-five novels. I was actually subsidizing myself so I could write novels.

Films I never took seriously as an artistic endeavor, but I always did the best possible work I could do; I never brushed it off or anything. Under the circumstances, which are never any good; the circumstances are mostly poor, because writers have no control whatsoever. Screenwriting consists of rewriting and I don't rewrite. I don't *have* to rewrite. I know what I'm writing when I write.

When I first came out to Hollywood, I couldn't even *read* a script. I said, "What are all those numbers—those scene numbers?" Little by little, I picked it up. Johnny Monk Saunders helped me the most, I think, and then a cutter, Jim Newcombe. Jim and I would go down to the projection room or to a theatre and sit away from everybody so we didn't bother them, and he'd tell me about every shot, every cut, why it was cut that way, why it was done this way. Little by little, I got a good grasp of film writing.

The trouble with most film writing is that too many writers have no feel for film. They're writing stories, they're writing plays, they're not writing for film. There's far too much dialogue written—you don't need it. You can tell so much with the camera—with a cut or with a reaction. I had one thing to my advantage, which was I had a very good sense of structure, as my novels proved. Once you have a structure, you've got the whole picture.

What is the relationship between structure and plot?

Structure is not plot. You can have a lousy plot and a good structure in the same picture. The structure or continuity is how you tell the story, in what form and in what order. You can tell it backwards. I have. I wrote a novel backwards that drove my publisher crazy. *Goodbye to the Past*—some people think it is my best book. It goes from 1929 to 1865—backwards. I am very good at structure.

They would call you in sometimes when they had a plot but problems with the structure?

They called me in when they didn't have *anything*. When I did *Wake Island*, all we had was a blank page and a title—*Wake Island*. Wake Island hadn't even fallen yet when I started to write the story.

So in that case they wanted plot and structure from you?

Yes, I did that quite a lot. Then what happens around the studio is, say, there's two months in which they don't shoot; then they've got an *old script.* Then they need what in Hollywood is called a "fresh mind." Well, there's no such thing as a fresh mind in Hollywood. (*Laughs.*) Then there's a rewrite of some kind, and that's the reason why I have so few solo credits—because I was one person who could originate. The people who could originate were few and far between in Hollywood. You give 'em a blank piece of paper, they go nowhere. They've got to have something to write a script about; they can't make it up.

Did your novels become more cinematic as time went on?

No. I think they were always dramatic. More dramatic than most novels. Because I started out as a playwright, that was my first impulse. So many novels are narrative—they don't show, they tell. So it's harder for the screenwriter because he has to do all the work. With my novels, you don't have to work as hard; just chop them up and use the dialogue.

Did you draw your characters mostly from real life?

There is practically no way you can put a real person down [on paper] because the simplest person is too complex for books. Has to be simplified. So I take traits from people I've met and develop a character from them. You can only approximate a human being. Some writers can do that better than others, of course. Most books I read now, the people aren't people, they're just names. They don't have any individuality or even any humanity, for that matter. And there's so much obsession with sex novels nowadays. Just a small biological function that has become an obsession for reasons unknown to me. That's a sign of emotional immaturity in a writer, I would say.

Writers were restricted in the early days of Hollywood in what they could do with sex and romance.

Oh yes, you couldn't do just anything. That's not necessarily bad. People don't understand that. Sometimes limitations on a writer are better than total freedom. It gives you a framework, what you can and what you can't do.

Can you give an example of how you resolved the problem of suggesting a romance or sex in one of your scripts?

In *High Sierra* we had a girl living with two guys and we got away with it—in 1940! We had twenty-seven pages of objection from the Johnston office. We had to rewrite the script and send it to them. We had [the Motion Picture Code official] Geoff Shurlock from the Johnston office on the set with us practically every day, trying to change things. But we got 'em through.

Did you win on every point?

No, we had to give on some.

How did you win on the main point?

Just by yelling. Our argument was that it was an absolutely integral part of the drama, which it was.

Philosophy of Life

Did you ever consciously try to express your philosophy of life in a novel or in a picture?

No.

Suppose a producer had said to you, "We need a happy ending here."

Nobody ever said anything like that to me. I'm the only writer who's ever got away with one downbeat picture after another.

Does that express your point of view about life?

It certainly does.

Which is . . .

It stinks. (*Laughs.*) But it's fun.

But in stories like High Sierra *and* The Great Escape *you do express a little hope at the end as well.*

Yes. Well, I don't know. I don't want to express hope at the end, but there is hope alright. Life is a pretty absurd thing.

Your point of view about life seems ingrained from your earliest upbringing.

Well, we were a political family. My grandfather was a political boss in Clark County, Ohio, for about thirty-five years. My father dabbled in politics all his life. From the age of six years up, I heard what they thought of the people who were running our destinies. And they were right.

Did that turn you into a Democrat?

My father was a Democrat. I voted for Roosevelt three times, and then I didn't like the socialistic direction of the country. But I'm not a Republican. Those stuffed shirts—how can you be a Republican? I guess I don't know what you'd call me. An independent, a rebel or something.

So even though you'd never attempt to inject your philosophical point of view into a story, it's there, regardless.

It's implied in every book I wrote. But it is not explicit.

Would it be fair to call you fatalistic?

Absolutely. That was natural to me. My father was that way too.

Did you ever read any of the existentialists?

No, I couldn't stand Sartre.

Camus?

I liked *The Plague*, but I didn't like Camus.

Cain? He had aspects of being an existentialist.

Yes, Cain did. Cain was a weirdo.

Did these writers seem at all consonant with your own thinking when you read them?

No. I'm too Irish. I have always had to struggle to keep from being a comic writer.

If someone asked you about the themes in your work, in your career, what would you say?

I'd say, let *them* analyze my themes. You have to understand, I've gotten some very good reviews. But in the United States, you have a literary snobbery. If it's a gangster novel, it can't be literary. If it's a western, it can't be literary. That's partly why my work has not been regarded seriously here.

Also, my work does not exude liberalism. It's not *anti*-liberal, it's not anything—it's the way I see the world. But it's not liberal. And almost all novels are written from the liberal viewpoint. To me, that's why they're so boring.

But are there consistent themes in your work?

Don't make life hard on me! You see, I write instinctively—that's the reason I write so fast. My primary purpose was always the same as Balzac's: to give the most realistic picture of the world around me that I could possibly do.

So you consider yourself a realist?

Yes.

Yet you really didn't have a lot of contact with gangsters.

I had enough. Enough for my purposes. I didn't have to go out and shoot at people. That's the Hemingway idea. You'd have to go out and shoot somebody before you know how it feels to shoot someone. That's nonliterary. Hemingway made me mad when Willa Cather wrote a war novel—*One of Ours*—and he jumped all over her because she didn't know what it was like to get shot at. That's a lot of nonsense.

A writer has to have an imagination—that's what makes a writer. He has to be able to put himself imaginatively in the position of whatever character he selects. And I have a very good grip on reality, which I inherited from my father, so I pretty much know the limitations of humanity and the possibilities in life, which aren't very great for anybody. You're born, you're gonna have trouble, and you're gonna die. That you know. There's not much else you know.

So why were you drawn to gangster and outlaw characters?

One reason is, because I found I could give a picture of the world as I saw it and not shock the hell out of everybody. That's the way criminals and gangsters were expected to act, you know.

So you saw the world similarly to the way your characters saw it?

Very little difference.

That seems to be the way you felt toward the Communist writers in Hollywood, too. They carried the card, they should be prepared to pay the price.

That's right. You have to pay for things in life. It's no bed of roses. It's like my father said: "The Irish cry at what others laugh at, laugh at what others cry at."

Did you ever write your father into a story as a character?

I never could. But I finally got him into disguise in *Captain Lightfoot*. He's Captain Thunderbolt.

We have talked about why gangsters attracted you. Why did westerns?

Well, I think I'm attracted by outlaws, for one thing. That is, outsiders.

Do you see yourself as an outsider?

Oh, definitely.

Outside the literary establishment?

Outside everything.

Were you always outside the critical community?

I got very fine reviews. I've been very lucky, actually. Until the 1960s. Then the world changed. Obviously, there was a revolution—in manners, morals, you name it.

It's hard to be an outsider now.

Everybody's an outsider now. It's a different world, believe me.

Do you think a novel like High Sierra *or* The Asphalt Jungle, *novels about people living outside the mainstream, could be written today?*

No, because there isn't as much to play against. When everybody is screwing everybody, what do you got? You don't have any morality, you certainly don't have love.

Is that why the narrative structure in films has degenerated, too, because there is no longer any social framework?

There's no doubt about it in my estimation. *Everything* is falling apart.

Niven Busch:
A Doer of Things

Interview by David Thomson

This interview was conducted in the summer of 1983, not long after a dinner party at the Washington Square Bar and Grill at which the honoree easily outlasted his friends and admirers—no matter that the dinner was marking his eightieth birthday. I suppose that is a way of saying Niven Busch does not act his age; he seems like a robust, merry, wicked, chuckling doer of things, not so very different from Walter Huston, say, in *The Furies* (1950). But he is so well seasoned, so much the old pro, the ex-rancher, the lifelong sportsman, that I always had trouble imagining Niven as *young*—that is, until this interview, and the old man's rapturous conjuring up of the roast chickens you could get at a New York rotisserie around 1914.

He lives in San Francisco now, where his top-floor study looks out on the Golden Gate Bridge, the water, and the hills of Marin. It is not the study of a retired writer. In 1983 and 1984 Niven was working on a new novel (his fourteenth, I think) that promised to be as expansive, energetic, and compelling as the previous one, *Continent's Edge,* published in 1980, which begins: "We lived, then, in an age of heroes. One war had just ended and another stirred its muscles, over the horizon, but in the space between the two we turned for assurance to the doers of great deeds, we pelted them with flowers and money, we asked of them only that they confirm, with so much in flux, the notion that the individual could still prevail."

When you are in Niven's company, that spirit still prevails. His physical gusto is not just energy; it is optimism and confidence transformed into action. The man is open, generous, and forthright. He loves golf and fishing as much as ever. He writes, reads, and reviews; he has great friendships and many stories to tell. He has recently been a very active board member of the San Francisco Film Festival and the host for excellent on-stage interviews with "old buddies" Robert Mitchum and Ginger Rogers.

He has a heroic presence, an epic perspective, and an undimmed capacity for doing things. From an early age he wanted to write, but he had such a facility that he was never quite sure which medium suited him best. The novel has lasted longest. But he was a journalist first, writing profiles and reporting sports for *Time* and *The New Yorker.* Then he became a screenwriter and story editor for Goldwyn. But his scripts suffered in the hands of others, and he became a producer so that at least once the picture would come out as he intended. That movie is *Pursued* (1947)—unique, beautiful, and influential. It is also a story in which energy does not hide uneasiness, guilt, and doubt.

In other words, it is too easy to see Niven Busch as just an example of prevailing gusto. He has a capacity, too, for reflection and sadness. He has had several wives (one, actress Teresa Wright, the star of *Pursued* and *The Capture*) and children, and there has been unhappiness in his life as well as joy. The best measure of his optimism and his physical bravura is his abiding openness to doubt. Hollywood veterans, especially the sportsmen, sometimes become monolithic, vain, and macho. The muscle in Niven Busch has never allowed him to abandon irony or humor, and there was nothing as touching to me in our interview as his 1983 realization, half amused, half bereft, that he still wasn't sure whether his going to Hollywood had been for the best. Such doubt about a fine past can only mean that Niven Busch is still not sure what the future holds.

1932   *Alias the Doctor* (Lloyd Bacon). Uncredited contribution.
The Crowd Roars (Howard Hawks). Actor, co-script.
Scarlet Dawn (William Dieterle). Co-script, co-dialogue.
Miss Pinkerton (Lloyd Bacon). Co-script, co-dialogue.

1933   *College Coach* (William A. Wellman). Co-script.

1934   *Babbitt* (William Keighley). Co-adaptation.
The Man With Two Faces (Archie Mayo). Co-script.
He Was Her Man (Lloyd Bacon). Co-script.
The Big Shakedown (John Francis Dillon). Co-script.

1935   *Three Kids and a Queen* (Edward Ludwig). Uncredited contribution.
Lady Tubbs (Alan Crosland). Uncredited contribution.

Niven Busch on the streets of San Francisco, 1984. (Photo: David Thomson)

1938	*In Old Chicago* (Henry King). From his story, "We the O'Leary's."
1939	*Off the Record* (James Flood). Co-script. *Angels Wash Their Faces* (Ray Enright). Co-script.
1940	*The Westerner* (William Wyler). Co-script.
1941	*Belle Starr* (Irving Cummings). Story.
1946	*The Postman Always Rings Twice* (Tay Garnett). Co-script. *Till the End of Time* (Edward Dmytryk). From his novel *They Dream of Home.*
1947	*Duel in the Sun* (King Vidor). From his novel. *Moss Rose* (Gregory Ratoff). Script. *Pursued* (Raoul Walsh). Story, script.
1950	*The Furies* (Anthony Mann). From his novel. *The Capture* (John Sturges). From his novel, script, producer.
1951	*Distant Drums* (Raoul Walsh). Story.
1953	*The Man from the Alamo* (Budd Boetticher). Co-script. *The Moonlighter* (Roy Rowland). Story, script.
1955	*The Treasure of Pancho Villa* (George Sherman). Story, script.

Nonfiction includes *Twenty-One Americans.*

Novels include *The Carrington Incident, Duel in the Sun, They Dream of Home, Day of the Conquerors, The Furies, The Hate Merchant, The Actor, California Street, The San Franciscans, The Gentleman from California, The Takeover, No Place for a Hero,* and *Continent's Edge.*

Academy Awards include an Oscar nomination in 1939 for the original story of *In Old Chicago.*

How early was it as a kid that you had a sense of what the film business was?

That is really going back. I had a sense the film business was a terrific business when I was eight years old. Or seven, because my sister hadn't been born yet, and that had to be about 1910—right at the beginning. And soon after that, I guess it was about 1916 or '15, I was going to school in New York, and I saw the big sign in Time Square, "Selznick Pictures Bring Happy Hours." And that was [the company of] Lewis J. Selznick. My father was treasurer of the company.

A group of Wall Street risk-money entrepreneurs had put my father in to watch their investment. I think he must have spent most of his time looking under the rug, because it was very hard to track old Lewis J. down. Lewis J. Selznick was an extraordinary man. Had a wizard brain—I think he was much more intelligent than his peers, like Jesse Lasky, Louis B. Mayer, Joe Schenck. But the trouble was he was so smart he met himself coming around the corner. He was crookeder than a dog's hind leg. And eventually Lewis J. was put out of business.

My father had gone broke on Wall Street. Because his firm had gone broke he could not be a member of the Exchange or trade there for five years. So he had to put in five years in Siberia—that was the film business. After his failure we had really gone through a lot of distress. His position now, with a big salary as treasurer of this well-financed company, was a boon to us, and he put me through a good, elite preparatory school.

But when you ask how it began . . . my mother, in the early days, was typing scenarios—not scripts, but the kind of continuity that was done then, which is more like a treatment today. It consisted of de-scriptions of shots. There was no dialogue. Every once in awhile you would put in a superimposed title. But even the titles were generally written by title experts. So she just put [in] the word "title." I remem-ber my poor mother, she not only had to learn to write continuity—because she had gone through hard times—but she had to learn to type! And she taught me to type. Still no good, but anyway, I type fast.

So "Selznick Pictures Bring Happy Hours" was the family theme, and the pictures did for a while. Then things didn't go quite so well, and my mother used to look at that sign and say, "But not for me." Anyway, I used to go down sometimes to the office of the World Film Corporation at 46th Street to have lunch or dinner with my Dad, and we'd eat in this marvelous chicken rotisserie—God, those chickens were the best I've ever eaten! Anyway, David [Selznick] was kind of the gofer and errand boy. He was like fifteen and I was eleven. So once in a while he'd let me sweep out a cutting room. And that was a big treat because of the smell of the film, for chrissake!

Myron, his older brother who later became my agent, was a director already. A tough little, slant-hatted, ready-fisted Jewish boy from the East Side. And he was directing people like Clara Kimball Young, Olive Thomas, Thomas Meighan, and so on. My father, who was a dandy and a big dress-up guy, was setting the style then because he had been once voted the best-dressed man on Wall Street. They were all copying him, and mother was very proud of such a man as George O'Brien imitating my father's waistcoat.

Anyway, so now I am at the good school, and my father sends me the Selznick house organ that describes the doings of the film people. I'm the only kid in the school who gets such a crazy document; and I read this and I'm fascinated. I was already interested in writing. I was writing poetry, stories; I was writing skits and I was editor of our school paper, which was a wonderful thing because it was a school honor. I was really kind of a flop at all team sports. I wasn't big enough.

Still, the main thing was getting out the paper, and I did the same [sort of thing] when I got into Princeton. I was on the papers and all that stuff. But the only place I can room at Princeton is right over the movie house. So at night I hear the piano grinding and I'm trying to study! I do the studying as quick as I can, I do my writing, and then I go downstairs for the second show; I get in free because I'm a resident, and I see all the films.

I had a cousin then who was rich and he lived in Princeton, but he wasn't old enough to go to college; he'd come in a big Cadillac, and we'd go for rides down to the speakeasies in Trenton. He was utterly fascinated by movies, while I was only peripherally fascinated. Writing was my thing, but he said, "Niven, don't you want to go to Hollywood? And write for films?" That was the first time anyone had put this notion in my head.

So we roll through a few years, and I'm writing for *Time.* I'm writing for *The New Yorker.* I'm publishing some short stories. I'm, among other things, the movie editor of *Time,* and I have five other jobs going. I'm twenty-four years old, and I didn't ever graduate from Princeton because the money ran out again, but I'm making $10,000 a year. By the time I'm twenty-five I'm making $15,000. And this is the Depression. So I knew I'd reached the end of the road as far as journalism was concerned. In New York I thought, I've got to go on doing these things because there's no place else I can do more. When one night I get a break, I jump on it. I'll tell you what the break was.

I was going out at that time with a Jewish girl, a very pretty girl, and I had tickets to a long-running show. And she said, "Oh, I don't want to go there, let's go to George White's Scandals. They're opening tonight." I said, "I don't think we can get in." She said, "Let's give it a pitch, because you know the press agent," and so on. So we go and the agent is standing at the door; he sees us and he says, "OK, you kids, go in. But don't try to go downstairs; sit upstairs, sit on the carpet somewhere, because the place is sold out."

In the intermission we mingle with the real people, and somebody taps me on the shoulder and I see this little squatty guy. He says, "Remember me? I'm Myron Selznick." I said, "How are you, Myron?" I knew by this time he was an important agent. In fact, he was the first important agent in Hollywood, and he turned everything around. Garbo was working for $75 a week and he got her $7,500. So he said, "I've been seeing your stuff in the magazines. You're doing fine." I said, "Thank you very much." He said, "How'd you like to go to Hollywood?" I said, "I'd love it." As a matter of fact, I'd been writing letters to friends of mine in Hollywood already, seeing if they could get me a job.

Two weeks later I get a telegram—"You're under contract to Warners. Report to the New York office. Get your ticket. Hit the road." Which I did. This is now the fall of 1931. I'm twenty-eight. And I'm real stuck-up. I've got a girl with me; I've got everything going. Warners isn't going to pay me more than I'm making already, to tell you the truth. But it's a chance, and I wanted to make a change. So I go to Hollywood.

Did you have any inkling that David Selznick was going to go as far as he did when you knew him as a kid?

I *was* rather in awe of David. He was precociously mature. He was more sophisticated than I was. He was going to bed with girls when I was buggering off, you know. And he was a very bright fellow. Now, later, he tried to write film reviews for *Time,* and the *Time* people liked him but they couldn't print his reviews. They were impossible [to read], and sometimes they'd give them to me and say, "Look, see if you can use any of this." But there was very seldom anything I could use. So I thought this man has no talent as a writer, but he's quite a goer. Then I watched from a distance when I got to Hollywood, because Selznick was not big when I got there. His older brother was the big noise. Much bigger; and actually his brother was smarter and tougher.

In her book [A Private View *(New York: Knopf, 1983)], Irene Selznick says she thought Myron was a tragic case because he had enormous talent and he got into being an agent when he could have done something more challenging.*

I think that could be true, and I think there was a very intense sibling rivalry between them. Myron was drinking too much quite early on. He had several other clients among the writers at Warners, and one chap said to me, "You know, when Myron drops in—it's probably because you have an option coming up—it's a good idea to have a bottle of bourbon in the bottom drawer, because before he goes upstairs to see the brass, he'll want a slug." So I kept one, and he'd take a couple of fingers. But I never saw him smashed in the daytime. I do think he was a tragic case, although really he had more influence on the business than David himself.

He told me once, "You know something, Niven, never get swell-headed about the reason you're in Hollywood. I'll tell you how it happened. I went to Zanuck one day on a routine sales call, and he said to me, 'Myron, I want some writers now, and I don't want you selling me any cheap young writers. I want master writers; I want the authors of prize-winning plays and best-selling novels. That's what we'll stick to, and I'll pay 'em whatever they're worth.'" And Myron said, "I looked at my list and I picked out you. Because you were the *least* known person I had on it, you were getting the *least* money, and I was ready to sell you for the least money. But I couldn't have Zanuck tell me my business, so I told him I'm going to sell you Niven Busch today, and he'll work for $300 a week." Mind you, this was the Depression, and I was willing to work for the bottom of the scale. Any kid today would start at $300 a week, and that's about one-tenth of what it was worth then.

Now, I jump to my first story conference. I'm in Hollywood, I have a car, and I have a contract—it's a three-month option and then a nine-month option. To me, there's absolutely no doubt in my mind that they're going to take up this three-month option. Two days after getting there I report to this first conference. They didn't let you sit around because they had a huge product.

The conference personnel on this night—and it was night because it was a conference with Zanuck (the earliest you ever started with Zanuck was about 9, usually 10 P.M.)—was Mike Curtiz, the director; Richard Barthelmess; and a Warners producer named Ray Griffith, who had had his voice box removed and talked in a hissed whisper, with gestures. He had been a famous silent comedian. So we have a man with a lost voice box and Zanuck, walking up and down and twirling a sawed-off polo stick; Mike Curtiz, who spoke in a very Hungarian accent; and Richard Barthelmess, a great star but fading because talkies had come in and he had not yet made a talking picture. Barthelmess had had a face-lift, which reduced his facial expressions to one: a lowering look of bewildered menace. His face was frozen, which is very impressive under the right circumstances—which do not arrive in every scene.

I was awed. I had been writing reviews about these people, you understand. I'm sitting there; I'm the only one in custom-made clothes (because I was a dandy, too), and I think these people look very crude. But the way they bandy about ideas that stream out, they all seem like instant whiz-kid brains. They have ideas about every situation. I'm accustomed to sitting and thinking a long time before I have an idea. Like doping out a two-thousand-word short story might take me all week. But these guys—story ideas, plot, construction, motivation is the grist of their everyday lives.

Anyway, as the story progresses I get an idea. Now, the story was about a man who has no medical degree but masquerades as a doctor; it was called *Alias the Doctor* [1932]. I don't remember ever seeing it, but I think it was made. I had an idea for introducing suspense in a scene in an operating theatre, in which this doctor, who has always been successful, knows the patient now on the table is going to die. Or the audience knows it. I've forgotten. So everybody is saying, "What do we do about this?" Now, I start to talk; I do it with misgivings, but I say, "Look, suppose there is an old autopsy surgeon in the hospital, and he has some kind of hideous instinct about death in the operating room. And we establish that when the black angel is hovering over the establishment, he feels it and gets up from his lonely little niche and goes into the operating room to see what's going on."

I don't know if it was really an original idea or if I got it out of something I'd read. But Zanuck looked at me, and he kind of tilted up his cigar and said, "I like that. Good." He had a girl named Dorothy Hecklinger who took notes, and he said, "Make a note of that." Next day, his daytime secretary comes to me and says, "I think you're in." I said, "What do you mean? I've only been to one conference." She said, "Yeah, but he [Zanuck] liked it." In those days, you didn't have too many shots. If I'd struck out—forget it. There were too many other people at the gates.

So, I don't hear any more about *Alias the Doctor*—nothing—but I get an assignment: report to Howard Hawks at the Ascot racetrack. They'd given him three scripts, and he'd already had [Kubec] Glasmon, [John] Bright, and Seton I. Miller on the story. And Zanuck was sick of sending him screenwriters. But he sent me with a very flattering note, saying, "Busch, from *The New Yorker,* is a brilliant dialogue writer, and I feel he can give you what you want for *The Crowd Roars* [1932]." I'd never written a line of dialogue, and I saw this memo on Hawk's desk; Hawks regarded it with no welcoming thoughts because he probably wanted one of the well-established top writers.

Anyway, now I'm in with Hawks, and I'm going to tell you, I was not really in awe of him. Although he had great prestige, I sort of felt he was covering up something. When he discussed the story with me, he seemed to be drawing on some source outside himself, and I wasn't sure what this was. Well, we would have a conference every evening after the day's shooting; I had to be on the set all day, so we were tired at night. But we made the effort. I'd go to his house on Bedford Drive in Beverly Hills, and he'd say, "Alright, Niven, tomorrow we're going to shoot such-and-such a scene, and I think it ought to go like this." Then with unerring accuracy he would describe how the scene should go. I'd make rough notes, and then I'd go back to my apartment in

Hollywood; with my memory fresh, I'd write the scene, which would take me till after midnight.

Then I'd go to bed, get up, and get down on the set and give the people the pages—Jimmy Cagney, Ann Dvorak (I developed a big crush on her, which got me nowhere), and Joan Blondell. They were very liberal with criticism, believe me; Jimmy would say, "Jesus Christ, Niven, what kind of shit is this? I can't say this stuff." I'd say, "What do you want to say, Jimmy?" And he'd say, "Well, look, I think I ought to go in and say, 'Fuck off!'" And he'd give me this obscene dialogue, which I'd translate back into some kind of passable English. Once I'd got it, he always liked it. And Hawks said to me, "You know, Niven, you're doing a good job," after about a week of it. So I was happy.

All the dialogue on that picture was mine, although those other three guys had credit. Now I'm getting complimented. The picture's rolling along. We're burning up Duesenbergs, crashing these $20,000 cars. Hawks got a free Duesenberg out of it because we used so many in the picture. But they didn't have car crashing down to a science, and when one stunt man was badly hurt, they got conservative. Finally, we made the car crashes with miniatures. We had two Indianapolis winners who were doing stunts; I even drove a race car for a couple of laps. I acted in that film, too. A guy walks up to Cagney who's supposed to be a gambler—that's me—and I exchange a few lines with him, but we ad-libbed.

So now I'm getting confident, and I think I know something about this. I'm an instant screenwriter. I'm at Hawk's house one night, and he's telling me how the scene ought to go. I said, "Howard, if you will permit me, I don't think it should go like that." He gave me his reptilian glare. The man had ice-cold blue eyes and the coldest of manners. He was like that with everyone—women, men, whatever. He was remote; he came from outer space. He wore beautiful clothes. He spoke slowly in a deep voice. He looked at you with these frozen eyes. You did what he said, and he usually damned well knew.

He said, "Niven, we have no time to waste. I want to explain something to you. What we're writing and shooting is my adaptation of a play by Kenyon Nicholson called *The Barker*. It played on Broadway for two years. I have taken it out of a carnival setting and put it on the racetrack. It's working very well. Nobody is going to understand its source. Now, here is *The Barker*." And he pulls out of his back pocket a tattered, coverless Samuel French play edition. He opens it and he says, "Here is the scene we're shooting tomorrow. Write it the way it is here, but don't use the same words!"

I didn't say anything then. I just did what he told me. But later on, one day when he seemed relaxed, I said, "Mr. Hawks, don't you think you could possibly be in danger of a plagiarism suit?" He gave me the glacial stare. He said, "Niven, I could be, under other circumstances. You understand this is now an original story by me? I sold *The Crowd Roars* to Warner Brothers. I am not in danger of any suit because they already own *The Barker*." Not bad. That's the way he went.

Warner Brothers would throw a lot of writers on a film. What was the community of screenwriters like at that time? Was getting credits handled amicably, or was it difficult sometimes?

It was difficult sometimes, but on the whole it was done with a good deal of cooperation. Fraternal commitment. You nearly always collaborated, because they thought two minds were better than one unless you had really proven yourself to be superior. And even if you turned in a very good screenplay, sometimes they'd hand it to somebody else just to mess around with.

Did that hurt you?

It was hard in this respect; you had come from a place where, if you were doing journalism, you had control—except that your editor could ask you for changes. You were about in the same situation with a producer. Working with a collaborator, you had to see more or less eye-to-eye. Sometimes each wrote his own version, and then you put them together. And it always involved a certain amount of stress. I don't know if it was successful or not; on the whole, it was very good for me, because I was with Hawks on my very first picture. Later, I had various other collaborators on rather mediocre pictures, not one of which I thought was worth a shit. The collaboration system was something you wanted to get away from, but you had to put up with it. I had at least one collaborator, named Tom Reed, with whom I wrote what was supposed to be the screenplay for *Babbitt* [1934]; he was a delightful guy. Reed had a fiendish sense of humor and originated some practical jokes. In those days you could stop for a week and design a practical joke! It was a fairly relaxed business.

Your boss at Warners was Zanuck?

Zanuck was my main boss for my first two years. Then I got closed out; the Depression really hit home. Nineteen thirty-four—it took a long time for the Depression to catch up with Hollywood, but when it did it was devastating. Early on, people would take their unemployment checks and cash them at the theatres, not for groceries; they were always ready to spend that quarter for the movies. Later on, the studios fired a lot of people, and they made others take salary cuts. I didn't take the cut; they just fired me because I was in one of the younger echelons. But then about six months later they called me up and asked if I wanted to come back at half salary. So I came back at $200 and made some more pictures.

I didn't mind the collaboration. What I did mind, after I got important and got some single-writing credits, was people messing up my scripts—like in the case of *The Postman Always Rings Twice* [1946]. I wrote a good screenplay, but the producer had a cousin of his, Harry Ruskin, messing up my dialogue so that he could get a credit. Then, sometimes you wrote a good film, and the producer messed it up by miscasting it. But I always loved language, and now the producer messed it up by miscasting it. But I always loved language, and now I was learning a lot about story in a truly entrepreneurial way. Instead of being alone for six months to plot something out, you might work on three stories in a week. You'd hear a shoeshine boy who'd been to the preview the night before say, "Well, sir, I thought the third act was weak—wasn't really enough motivation." What you thought was your craftsmanship coming from the forehead of Minerva was only the rules of the game.

Were you happier in Hollywood?

David, I have never known. I have never known. When I made the move, there were terrible adjustments to be made. I don't know to this day if I did the right thing. I might have been an entirely different kind of writer—might have been a better recognized writer, might have been a more literary writer. I was on the scene from '31 to '51 when I got my ranch. And in that time I guess I had my name on about twenty pictures. Of which I'm maybe proud of five. And of the five, I had collaborators on two. So the ones I could really claim as my own were the ones I not only wrote but produced, and then there were the few that were made from novels of mine. And all I ever really wanted to do was get hold of my material and control it.

Now, it might have been that without the Hollywood training I had I might never have been able to make a living—certainly not as good a living. Of course, I wrote quite a string of novels, all of which were successful. Some were praised by critics, some were denounced; but every goddamned one was a good story, and every one sold. And *Duel in the Sun* [1947] and some of the others were very big. The story craft I learned and put into them, I learned at the screenwriter's bench.

Once I had become accustomed to Hollywood, I was very happy. Happier than I had been in New York. But I was doing the drudgery, and I had the insecurity and the loneliness. A writer at that time was not an important person; you went from your little apartment to the studio, and you worked like a son-of-a-bitch. You didn't have time for much social life. You didn't meet many women. In my second year, I began to play polo because I was a good horseman. And polo was very fashionable. Horses were cheap and I could afford it. We had learned as kids to play polo on bicycles. That was my great relaxation. I played polo every day for ten years. I don't think it helped me hugely in my career, but it did afford me some good companionship.

Was it easy to make friends with actors? With Cagney, for example?

Well, with Cagney I made another picture called *He Was Her Man* [1934], with Joan Blondell. It was one of the pictures I did that I liked. But actors lived in their own world, and you lived in yours. I had some actors that were good friends—Joel [McCrea] was a good friend and so was Gene Kelly (only because he lived next to my brother-in-law); and Mitchum was a good friend because I think he thought I was lucky for him—I put him in the two pictures that really made him a star. But he was always busy, so I didn't see him very much. You were good friends while you were making a picture with them, but after that you were on another picture and you didn't see 'em any more. That's the kind of Hollywood contact that happens.

The only way I was friendly with Cagney was that *The Crowd Roars* was one of his early pictures, so I'd see him around the lot. I'd have lunch with him in the executive dining room, and once in a while we'd go off the lot. But I never saw him away from work. He never indulged in any of the sports I did. He never was on a horse—he hated horses. He even hated automobiles. He used to drive about eleven m.p.h. I thought we'd get rear-ended. I was terrified to ride with him.

Did you make many friends in Hollywood?

No, I did not make many; a person does not make many friends in Hollywood. I don't think you do even now. I made some. I had one very good producer friend, Robert Lord. He was the guy who brought me back to Warner Brothers. C. S. Forester was a very good friend. He had written a very successful play, *Payment Deferred*. He was not very outgoing, but he was so brilliant; and he encouraged me very much. I told him I had always wanted to be a novelist, and he said, "Niven, you shouldn't have any doubts. You already know three times more about plot construction than the average novelist will ever learn. You write very well, so what are you worried about?" I said, "I'm worried about being paid. I've always been paid. When I worked for magazines, it came on Friday; when I worked for studios, it came on Wednesday. They put the check on my desk—nobody's putting anything on my desk now." He said, "Don't worry, I'll fix that."

So a publisher's rep was coming out, and he said, "Call her and tell her you've got a good story, and she'll give you a contract." At this time I had great facility. I could give you a knock-down on a story, and you'd buy it. So I told her the story. She said "That's fine" and gave me a $500 advance. I was making twice that a week by that time. But it was a contract! So, no matter what happened, I wrote that novel. I took nine months, but I was also working on a film—two films—and

I'd put in a couple of hours in the morning. That [the novel] was called *The Carrington Incident.* It didn't do badly—sold best in India! I don't know why. I guess those chaps sitting around in the damp would read anything.

The next one I wrote was *Duel in the Sun.* And that was really a gimmick, because I had already written—in collaboration, mind you, I came on as a troubleshooter—*The Westerner* [1940], with Gary Cooper. That's a film I've always been proud of. The whole plot structure of that is mine. The background to that was that Goldwyn had bought a sketchy ten-page treatment with an idea about Roy Bean, the "hanging judge." Then he hired Jo Swerling, who was a good dialogue writer, a musical librettist, and a very amusing guy. But Swerling had no idea about plot. And he had no idea about the West. So Goldwyn was looking for a writer who could set him straight, and I had written a very big hit that was an original story—*In Old Chicago* [1938], for which I was nominated [for an Oscar]. So I straightened out the plot. Swerling and I had a very productive collaboration. He really didn't like me, but we worked together great. Walter Brennan came along with some good ideas; if I was stuck I ran down to Cooper's dressing room, and he would put me right. Cooper was such a fund of information about the West.

I had always liked westerns. So I decided to go and roam around for a few months in the West. Get some lore and write a really good western. I thought I could write one better than *The Westerner.* I knew a fellow who had a ranch in Arizona, and I went up there. Then I went by myself down the Panhandle, and I found some great old manuscripts and documents. I got the idea there for *Duel in the Sun.* The idea was, simply, instead of writing about two guys and wondering how to get a girl in, to write about a girl and let the guys come in as they happened. Having a woman was new, especially a very sexy woman in a family consisting entirely of men. It was dynamite—like the whore and the lighthouse. It had great success right off. Stanley Walker in the *Herald* gave it a great review, and the headline was "Melodrama Becomes Literature." It was a huge bestseller in paperback.

How did you come to work for Goldwyn?

Goldwyn dated back from the old days. When I told him the story of *The Westerner,* I told him the mistakes I thought they had made and how it should be changed. He bought that. Then he looked at me and he said, "Did you have a father called Burton Busch?" I said, "Yes, that's my father." He said, "I knew him! He was with Lewis J. Selznick. Why, Niven, that's wonderful." He would always give you that old schmaltz. He said, "I'm glad to have your father's son near me," so he used that as an excuse for not giving me more money. He said to

Melodrama becomes literature: Gregory Peck and Jennifer Jones in Duel in the Sun. *Niven Busch's second novel became David O. Selznick's extravaganza.*

my agent, "Don't worry about this boy. I am like his uncle!" He never gave me a raise.

But the first time I went to Goldwyn was when Sidney Howard had been writing a submarine story for Ronald Colman. Goldwyn liked the idea of King Vidor directing it. Sidney had sold him a ten-page original that he had written in two and a half days for a lot of money. But he didn't want to write the screenplay, and he had suggested to Goldwyn that some young writer be brought in. I'm fresh from Warners at this time. So I get to interview Sidney and Goldwyn. (William Goldman's so funny in his new book [*Adventures in the Screen Trade*] about interviews—he says you should have an almost irrepressible enthusiasm! I had it.) Sidney told Goldwyn to hire me. I was fatter then and I had a short haircut; Vidor looked at me and said, "You're German." I said, "Sure, German and Irish." He said, "You're going to be the lieutenant on the U-boat." So here was my big acting opportunity coming up. Well, the picture never got made, because halfway through Goldwyn said we got to have a girl—Anna Sten, he said. Well, there's no way you can have Anna Sten on a U-boat. Anyway, I got six months' employment out of it. And made friends with Vidor—later, he directed *Duel in the Sun.*

Then, after *The Westerner* I came back to Goldwyn as story editor and associate producer. I wanted to become a producer, you see, so I could have control of my own material, and also so I wouldn't have to write all the time and would have more time for my own writing. I didn't mind telling writers what to write, because I could think of that in a minute. I'd see the rushes with Goldwyn, I'd go and do my screenwork, and then I'd lock my door and do writing. It worked out very well. I couldn't work those long hours any more. I got along well with Goldwyn. He had much more ability than Selznick.

I was story editor on *The Little Foxes* [1941]. Lillian Hellman had written a big sprawly script, and I said, "Listen, I'd like to cut this." "Well," Goldwyn said, "Lillian Hellman says it's alright. Wyler loves it." But I cut the shit out of it. And Goldwyn loved the cuts—they saved him a lot of money. He called Wyler in, and he said, "Niven has some cuts." So I read the cuts to Wyler, and he's giving me this snarly Hungarian look; but he had to take the cuts.

Goldwyn was not very smart on stories because he couldn't really envisage them. But he had a gut feeling about it. So he'd try this person's reaction about it and then that person's. He'd even get his comptroller, Reeves Espy, in there and he'd ask him. Somehow he'd precipitate a good judgment. And once he saw film he was absolutely infallible. He knew what the audience was going to buy. I got to like him, but he was a tough old Jew. I used to walk home with him from the studio to his house. He lived just behind the Beverly Hills Hotel—Shadow Hill Way. We used to walk along the bridle paths and his car would follow about two blocks behind. It was about two and a half to three miles. We'd do it almost every night. Mrs. Goldwyn was always trying to match me up with different girls. She didn't match me up with Teresa [Wright]—Goldwyn didn't like that at all. He felt I'd have more influence on her than he did. Goldwyn was very shrewd; he never kidded himself.

Selznick used to kid himself. He took the gaspipe after he got a little power. Once, just as I was getting a fair name as a writer, I sent him word that I wanted to see him. I made an appointment to see him. I wanted to tell him to make *War and Peace,* and I thought I knew how to get a good screen adaptation out of it—leave Pierre out and just stick with the war and the two romances. Selznick was slopping around—even then he was getting kind of sloppy. He sees me at his home about ten in the morning; he's taking a shower and he's getting dressed. He'd get to the office about twelve and stay there till midnight. But he was beginning to get sloppy in his habits. He said, "How much are you getting now?" I told him and he said, "Jesus Christ, you're overpaid." I said, "You're a shitty asshole—you're making four times as much as me." So our boyhood friendship never did me a bit of good, but it led me to Myron. Then later, after David split up with Irene, my wife and I used to double date with her and Sidney Kingsley. But of the two producers, Goldwyn and Selznick, the most knowledgeable and the most disciplined was Goldwyn.

How did they compare with Zanuck?

Zanuck was a different ball of wax. He acted as not an intellectual. Goldwyn was a natural, intuitive intellectual. Selznick was a pretender and a great entrepreneur—a plastic intellectual who read a few books and liked the companionship of authors. Zanuck liked physical challenge, hunting trips, polo; he liked guys who were themselves geared toward action. He always kept his word. He was very supportive of young talent. He was the first to discover how to make pictures out of headlines. He'd take a situation in the papers, and he'd get a writer to write a story about it. The idea of writing a story about the Chicago fire was not mine, it was his. Several writers had taken a shot, and they hadn't done it. I got the assignment and I thought it was great. Then when he filmed it he gave me a credit—"based on a novel by Niven Busch"—but it wasn't a novel at all, it was a forty-page story to his idea. And he loved the way I treated it. Gene Fowler, who was a prestigious writer at that time, came in with a hell of a lot of suggestions. Zanuck was walking around the room, and he said, "Gene, thanks for everything you've said, but I'm going to relieve you of this assignment. I don't think we ought to do any of these things. I think we should make it just the way Niven wrote it." Lamar Trotti wrote the screenplay. Zanuck thought I was strictly a guy for original stories. That's what I scored on.

What about directors?

Hawks really knew the language of the camera. But Raoul Walsh was a much nicer guy. I liked Raoul immensely. He put you at ease; he was your comrade. Hawks was always your boss. But I think Hawks had great ability. I was amazed by the man's control of that spool, and he always knew where to put the camera. He always knew, looking at a scene, if anything was wrong. Some of those good action scenes he shot were shot by his assistant [Richard] Rosson. Hawks also had a good feeling for casting—what people could do, what they couldn't do. And the reason he was slow was he didn't want to make any mistakes.

Let's talk about The Postman Always Rings Twice.

Oh, I go way back on that. You see, [James M.] Cain was managing editor of department text at *The New Yorker*. And he was my boss. I had four different sports columns that I wrote for him. One day I went

Niven Busch on a publicity tour with Teresa Wright before their marriage in 1942.

in and I said, "Listen, Jim, I'm going to write next week's golf column and that's going to be it, because I'm going to Hollywood." Well, he got up from behind his desk and said, "Congratulations, Niven, wonderful; I think it's just great. Get away from this madhouse and from Ross [the editor Harold Ross]. You won't have to write this baby talk anymore."

So I go to Hollywood, and I walk into Musso & Frank's restaurant; who's sitting in the front table but James M. Cain? I said, "You son-of-a-bitch!" He said, "I couldn't tell you; I didn't want to give notice." So we dissolve: He's working for Paramount, I'm working for Warners. They close him out before they close me out. He's been out of work quite a while. Then I get out of work. We're still friends, and we see each other occasionally. He invites me over to his house, and he says someone's given him two pairs of ducks. He's married this Hungarian, and I said, "What are you doing, Jim?" "Well, I've been writing a novel." I said, "What's it about?" He said, "It's about the insurance business." I thought, "Jesus! Here's a guy out of work, he's living in Burbank, he can only give a dinner when someone gives him some ducks, and he's writing a novel about the insurance business! How hopeless can things get?" So anyway, I said, "Congratulations, how long is it?" "Oh," he said, "it's short. I wrote it first about 150,000 words, and I knocked 70,000 words out of it." Even worse, you know!

So he tells me the story and I flipped. I said, "That's the greatest goddamned thing I ever heard. It'll be a bestseller." Thank God I said that because, of course, it was. But at the same time the Johnston Office put their finger on it and said you can never film this horrible sexual thing.* Anyway, in '46 they finally begin to loosen up on some of these things. They let out that they can make it [*Double Indemnity*]. I was very hot then as a screenwriter. I'd sold novels; Selznick was making two of mine. My Christ, I'm being offered $100,000 jobs. I turned down a couple I never should have. One was *The Time of Your Life* [1948] by [William] Saroyan with Jimmy Cagney. But if I got on a novel, I wouldn't break off to do a screenplay.

---

* In 1922, as a result of mounting pressures to clean up the morality of movies, the Motion Picture Producers and Distributors of America was established. The first president of the organization was Will Hays, chairman of the Republican National Committee and postmaster general of the Harding administration. Hence, it became known as the "Hays Office." Hays's successor, from 1945 to 1961, was Eric Johnston, a business executive and prominent Republican, who served as a foreign diplomat under Eisenhower. Hence, the "Johnston Office."

In 1930, with the consent of Hays, a Production Code was drawn up by the Catholic layman Martin Quigley, publisher of the influential *Motion Picture Herald*, with the aid of Father Daniel A. Lord, a dramatics teacher at St. Louis University. The Hollywood producers accepted the Code in March 1930. Strong-minded Joseph I. Breen, a former newspaperman, became enforcer of a Production Code Administration until 1954, when he was succeeded by an Englishman, Geoffrey Shurlock, who reigned until 1968. In all, the Production Code was dominant for a quarter of a century without revision; then it began the dissolution and collapse into the present ratings system.

In this volume, screenwriters speak of the "Hays Office" and the "Johnston Office" and the "Breen Office" somewhat interchangeably, depending on chronology.

So, MGM gets to my agent, and he says the guy that should write this is Niven Busch. The producer said, "OK, let's have him." So we made a deal. I made a condition: I wanted to work at home. I took the book and I did my best with it. They cut out a lot of good stuff I had because the Johnston Office objected. Then they had Harry Ruskin, a real nonwriting gag-writer, put in a few lines. I protested his credit, and I had an arbitration on it; but the Guild felt he'd got enough of his stuff in the script.

I never really liked the picture that much. We had a sensational cast and a good mood; but there was a lot of explicit sex in the book, and they put their thumbs down. They did the same thing with *Duel in the Sun*. They said there was a horrible rape. I said, "There's no rape in it." They said, "It's statutory rape if you've got a girl fourteen years old." I said, "How old do you want her to be?" They said, "Well, twenty-five." I said, "OK." So they allowed that, but they made other little changes.

With *The Postman* they didn't want to make the disagreeable Greek a slovenly unwashed guy because then they wouldn't get an export license for Greece. So they made him an ineffectual English guy— Cecil Kellaway. He was terrible. Then the whole murder thing—you couldn't show that. It was really a bloody, terrible thing [in the book], with his voice coming back on that echo—what a great touch!

How did Duel in the Sun *get set up?*

A very complicated situation. I got RKO to buy it, because I was following my determination to be a producer—write my books and have other people write my screenplays. So I get Oliver H. P. Garrett to write the screenplay for me and RKO, and I'm the producer. The studio owns the property. We had John Wayne because the studio had a previous commitment from him. He was going to play Lewt. I don't think Wayne would have been as good as Peck, but he might have. He was a better actor than a lot of people thought. We had trouble getting a girl. I said get Veronica Lake and dye her hair. Then we tried to get Hedy Lamarr, and she gets pregnant. And Teresa didn't want it because she didn't think it suited her. I think she could have done it, but I wasn't going to pressure her. So then we negotiated for Jennifer Jones. But Selznick sends over these memos demanding this, demanding that. Charles Koerner [the production chief] at RKO says, "Look, David, these are impossible conditions—but maybe *you'd* like to do this?"

Selznick had probably been gunning for that all the time. He said, "Well, I would." Koerner sells it to him for a good big profit. And now Selznick begins to invite me over to his house simply because I'm getting some recognition and I'm married to an actress. We really aren't on very close terms. He tells me, "You'd really be surprised what I'm doing with this book, how much better I'm making it." Such bullshit! Vidor says to me, "Come on the set because I want to show you something." And he shows me how he's got the book marked and is putting the dialogue back. Selznick is looking at the rushes, and he's accepting it. Then, Vidor shows me the pages Selznick is sending down. He must have had fifteen writers on it, rewriting it. Then he's taking a little piece of each one and cribbing it out and making it as if he'd written it. The only trouble was he could never use three words if ten would suffice. Long, long speeches you wouldn't believe. Vidor took them all out.

Had Selznick deteriorated?

He had deteriorated a lot. He was taking sleeping pills at night and benzedrine by day. And he was beginning to get very sloppy and very arrogant. Then he tried to hoist Vidor out of there. I think Vidor got so disgusted—I don't know if he walked off, or if Selznick got so insulting, or if he said, "David, you'd better finish it yourself." I think David did finish it; and he tried to get credit and get Vidor's name off it. Goldwyn would never have done anything like that. He would have wanted all the honor possible for his directors. Selznick wanted all those titles.

I went to his house one night for a party. And he wasn't there. There were twenty people walking around—nice group—and we said, "Where's David?" "He's in his room asleep." About ten o'clock we ate, and we enjoyed the eating. But we hadn't seen the host, so we're all leaving. Now, the butler has gone in to wake him at a certain time, predetermined, and is giving him a shot to wake him up, which apparently is a routine. Now he comes running out in his pajamas, and he's saying, "Fellows, why are you going? Come back! I'm here now." A few people went back. I said, "Well, thanks David, I'm sorry we didn't see you more." He was living that kind of a life. I think it affected his decision making. He made bad decisions, and he kept on remaking things. Ordinarily he was very decisive. He had had good training.

What do you think of the film of Duel in the Sun?

Well, of course it was great showmanship. It had a few good scenes, and it had a big expansive canvas. It wasn't the way I would have made the picture. But I took the money and ran. It sold a lot of books for me, so why should I complain? It was an extravaganza rather than realistic. There were more people in the charge down to the railroad than there were in Texas at that time. But what a grand piece of panorama. It did not have the quality of *Gone with the Wind,* but it had the same kind of scope.

At much the same time you did Pursued.

I had absolute control over that. And I was very, very happy with the result. I had a marvelous cast, a terrific crew, and the best camera-man in the world [James Wong Howe]. I was very proud of the story; it has kind of Greek overtones—incest feeling, and all that—which the West was like. Greece in the ancient days must have been very much like the West. Passions were powerful and arms were at hand.

The story came from the time I had spent in Arizona and Texas. In El Paso I read a newspaper story about a feud and how a boy, who was the only survivor of the feud, had been brought up by the feuding family that had eliminated the other. His life had been saved because he was put in a steel bathtub by the people defending the house. The bathtub was pitted with bullets. I thought, "Jesus, what was the fate of that little boy? He's going into a family that has killed all his parents and his relatives." Seemed like a wonderful classic springboard.

How did the opportunity for control come along?

I was in a good position. That was when everything was running my way. This was at a time when the old studio system was just beginning to break down—the system of contracts, when nobody got a piece of the profits except the studios. Now, a few stars had broken loose from that, and I was trying to get a star to do *Pursued;* and I found I really couldn't do it unless I went to a major studio. I had Teresa on loan-out for one picture. I had to get a man. Robert Taylor wanted to do it. He was kind of a profile-type actor, but I would have taken him. He called me and said, "I want to do this thing." Joel McCrea had sent him a copy of it. I was ready to take Joel, but he *was* too old. I wanted to set it up at MGM. Really, I could have made a very good deal there. They would have given me a great big hunk of money up front. I wasn't hip to the Warner Brothers double bookkeeping. Nobody came out with a sizeable profit from doing any deal with Warners. They had the most foolproof, plate-steel accounting system in the world. I still don't know, and I don't think anybody else does, how they do it.

There's a great story about [John] Wayne and Warners. Wayne went to Warners, and he *never* made failures, but here he was in red ink! It was kind of a put-down to him. He knew there was skullduggery, so he wouldn't speak to Jack Warner. He said, "Don't even mention his name!" For a couple of years if he saw Warner at a benefit, he'd walk out. He wouldn't speak to him in a parking lot. Finally at some party Warner corners Wayne. He sticks out his hand and says, "Duke, you've been avoiding me." Wayne says, "That's right." "What happened, Duke? What went wrong?" Duke says, "Jack, it's very simple; you screwed me." Warner says, "Duke, I know, but that would have happened anyway. And we're your friends."

How did Mitchum come to be the guy in Pursued?

Well, he'd been in *Till the End of Time* [1946]. He was not a star at the time, but they thought he could be made one. Now, I had given up on my MGM deal, and Paramount wouldn't give me the kind of participation I wanted. But Warner's son-in-law, Milton Sperling, had a company called United States Pictures—my company was called Hemisphere Pictures—and Warners had a deal with Sperling whereby he kept a piece of the profits—because he was a relative! So he was going to split his piece with me. And still I'd get a hunk up front. I could get $150,000 and 30 percent of the net. I didn't know there wasn't going to be net. So I go to Sperling, he takes the package into Warners, and now we begin.

We're looking for a leading man. You wouldn't believe the people we tried out. Montgomery Clift had never been in a film. He comes out from New York. He reads the story, and he comes to test. It was very pitiful. He was such a good actor, and Teresa had known him and liked him. He came in completely green. He just goes on raw nerve and talent. He comes in for the test, and they throw some western clothes on him and give him two great big guns. He's a little, skinny guy, and when he comes in with these guns he looks like he's got two broken hips. He really made a very bad test. Sperling and I saw it and we said, "He'll never do."

Kirk Douglas is coming up and he's got this low-rent thing [*Champion*, 1949] that's going to hit. I liked him; he was very good-looking—manly and everything. So we get some film and Jack Warner said, "I don't like that dimple in his chin." So he said, "Let's see it again." So we ran it and I said, "Jesus, what a performance he's giving." Jack said, "I know, but that dimple in his chin." Of course, we get Mitchum and he's got one too. So we talked about Mitchum, and I wasn't too much in favor of using him. But when we tested him he looked so great. I loved his performance.

You weren't much involved on The Furies *[1950], were you?*

Nothing at all. I sold it to Hal Wallis. I saw it once, and I didn't think it had the intensity that I wanted. I thought it was a good book, and I thought the story was as good as *Pursued*, really. It had that great character of the father. I thought Stanwyck should have been better directed. And I thought the outdoor sequences should have been much better handled. They put Stanwyck on a miserable, fat-assed palomino that could hardly waddle. They were afraid she would get tossed off or something. They could have put her on a really good horse; she was a good horsewoman. I thought Gilbert Roland was good. I thought the fight up in the Pinnacles was good. But Wendell Corey was very insipid. They needed a very vital guy for that. That was a major weakness. And I think Stanwyck was disappointed. She was later in another western I did—which I've never seen—called *The Moonlighter* [1953].

You are often credited with having pioneered the "psychological western." How did that come about?

Well, I never really tried to inject a Freudian context into any of those films. My objective was to make the people real and to give them three dimensions in terms of modern culture. People in westerns weren't often like that. And maybe some of my characters *are* more modern in psychological terms than people of that period really were. Certainly their actions were self-revealing. But the Freudian element is one we impose, like a surface coating. It was not my intention. It came from the eyes of the viewers. And the movies that had this were *Pursued, The Furies, The Capture* [1950], and *The Man from the Alamo* [1953]. Now, of course, let's face it; I'd had some psychoanalysis—not a huge amount, but some. So I may have been influenced; I don't know. Really and truly, if you look at any of the masterpieces of literature, not that I'm putting myself in that class, there's a Freudian level. You could say that Shakespeare and Dostoevski prefigure Freud and Wagner—even Balzac and Stendhal. So if I'm accused of initiating the Freudian picture—it's a good label, but it wasn't intentional.

Why was it that around 1951 that you moved away from Los Angeles and movies?

Well, I was getting very worried about finances, because I knew either I was going to quit writing novels or only write occasional novels and settle down in a studio to make money and be a producer. I had very good offers there; I had cracked the barrier. Henry Ginsberg at Paramount [the Paramount production chief, formerly associated with Selznick] offered me a tremendous deal. He said, "Niven, you can do anything you want. Tell me how much you want. You can write, you can direct." I said, "Listen, Henry, what's the good? I've got a wife who makes $150,000 a year. I'm making $150,000 a year." At the end of the year—because in those days taxes were much more than now—they could take 80 percent, and we had a stupid accountant who didn't give us tax shelters.

Teresa was getting restless. She did some career things that I objected to. We were having a little trouble. We'd been married ten years, and we really got along well. I hated to see the marriage break up. The only thing I thought was: if we get away from this goddamned ratrace, if we have a ranch. I know enough about ranching now that I can run a successful ranch and have a little money. And she'll stick to the ranch—we'll be alright. She won't break it up. At least we won't go broke. So she was up on the ranch, coming and going, for a year and a half. Then she split off—and that was that.

Then again, I'd really made the decision that it was stupid to depend on films when I was getting to where I could make a living out of my books. This is what I had really wanted to do. It was too hard to ride two horses. Like with *Pursued:* it took me about six weeks to write the story; and it took me another six weeks to write the screenplay; but it took me a whole year to get the thing together. So, really, what I can do well, I'm not doing. I've been having to learn a whole new thing. [The director Stanley] Kramer and [the producer] Sam Spiegel—they do it better than I can. But they can't write books.

And the ranch thing worked out. I was happy. I married again. I raised my kids there. My kids stayed with me. I was happy on the ranch—got boring sometimes, but I could leave. I could go to Carmel, San Francisco. I still kept my foot in. I wrote several films. In the last sixteen or seventeen years I've sold about seven properties. And they're never made. I sold an original screenplay based on the San Francisco earthquake to [the producer] Joe Levine; he was going to make it a $7 million production in '66. Then, two years ago I sold Warners a racetrack story called *The Jocks.* Huston loved it. But I can't get anything made. Look at the way these major studios dissolve. They don't stay long enough to get a thing made. Right now, I don't think I'd even write a movie.

James M. Cain: Tough Guy

**Interview by Peter Brunette
and Gerald Peary**

*He was a man of music. Almost every paragraph
of his was the complex product of an orchestral
inner ear. Nobody, in my opinion, wrote quite as
well as did Jamie when he was going good, and
thank God that it is all there, in one book after
another, forever, to be found and refound.*

Samson Raphaelson,
eulogy to James M. Cain

We left Washington, D.C., behind for an unfamiliar sector of Maryland and reached it by strict attention to our road map. As we drove down darkened and angular suburban roads that were shrouded from the main highway, our minds turned inevitably to melodrama. It was the perfect setting for a prime James M. Cain murder story. That poor, unsuspecting husband in *Double Indemnity* was struck down in circumstances like these—an innocent country spin—assassinated from back of a limousine moving through the night.

We felt giddy and conspiratorial like those doomed killers, Phyllis and Walter, in *Double Indemnity*. Had we "thought of everything?" We went over our interview strategies for the tenth time, checked out the precarious tape recording set-up, and wondered how we should react if James M. Cain, tough-guy novelist par excellence and one-time journeyman screenwriter, proved put off by his eager, not-too-stoical intruders.

We arrived at 7:30 P.M. on the dot for our appointment. As he had promised in an earlier telephone conversation, Cain had the porch light on, and a cardboard box from the supermarket was placed on his frontstep. This was to distinguish his two-story wooden frame home from the dwellings of his neighbors. We parked the car, breathed deeply, and walked up to the house.

James Cain, who had been a resident in this house since 1947, opened the screen door and immediately invited us into the living room. Conversation flowed, our edginess dissipated, and our *film noir* fantasies during the drive seemed faraway and utterly silly. Even the erratic tape recorder clicked obediently along as we settled down for four hours of earnest conversation.

And Cain? He was most friendly, courteous, and respectful of the fact-finding task of fellow journalists. As he talked, the colorful vernacular of his prose flowed freely, his famous informal, "artless" style came through. While witty and profane in recounting the particulars of his varicolored career, Cain was never flippant. Happily for the interviewers, he gave his half-century-long calling—professional writing—the hard thought it deserves.

Postscript: Ironically, Cain's death in 1977 at the age of eighty-five rekindled interest in his work. Vintage Books published handsome paperback editions of his fiction. Hollywood optioned several of his novels, and two that "romped" to the screen were a dubious version of *The Butterfly* starring Pia Zadora and an either-you-love-it-or-you-hate-it remake of *The Postman Always Rings Twice* with Jack Nicholson and Jessica Lange (screenplay by David Mamet, directed by Bob Rafelson). In 1982, the fellow journalist Roy Hoopes published his exhaustive biography of "the poet of the tabloids" called *Cain*.

In his lifetime Cain was an influence on and favorite of a host of eminent authors, including Rebecca West, André Gide, Albert Camus, Jean-Paul Sartre, and Ross MacDonald. A legion of hard-boiled screenwriters took their cue from him and evolved the scurrilous genre of *film noir*. Although Cain himself had few screenplays produced, he remains very much a movie writer—that is, one whose work was forged *and* tainted by Hollywood experience as well as one whose stories will be forever enshrined as film classics.

As the biographer Roy Hoopes wrote: "It is a long time before a writer's place in his country's literature is decided, and Cain's is still undetermined. He was undeniably one of the most provocative and popular novelists America ever produced. . . . But some critics still consider him little more than a commercial phenomenon, corrupted by Hollywood, whose only contribution to our literature was to give us a glimpse of life and morality among an unattractive and insignificant class of Americans. Others feel Cain is a major American writer whose place in literature is secure" (p. xiii).

1932   *Hot Saturday* (William Seiter). Uncredited contribution.

1934   *She Made Her Bed* (Ralph Murphy). From his short story, "The Baby in the Icebox."

James M. Cain in Hollywood, mid-1940's. (Photo: Culver Pictures, Inc.)

1935   *Dr. Socrates* (William Dieterle). Uncredited contribution.

1938   *Algiers* (John Cromwell). Co-script.

1939   *Stand Up and Fight* (W. S. Van Dyke). Co-script.
        Wife, Husband, and Friend (Gregory Ratoff). From his
        novelette, "Career in C Major."
        When Tomorrow Comes (John M. Stahl). From his magazine
        serial (never sold), published in 1951 as *The Root of His
        Evil.*

1940   *Money and the Woman* (William K. Howard). From his
        magazine serial published under the title "The Embez-

zler" in *Three of a Kind*. Uncredited contribution to script.

1941   *Shanghai Gesture* (Josef Von Sternberg). Uncredited contribution.

1942   *Ossessione* (Luchino Visconti). Unauthorized Italian version of his novel *The Postman Always Rings Twice*.

1943   *The Bridge of San Luis Rey* (Rowland V. Lee). Uncredited contribution.

1944   *Gypsy Wildcat* (Roy William Neill). Co-script.
Double Indemnity (Billy Wilder). From his magazine serial, included in *Three of a Kind*.

1945   *Mildred Pierce* (Michael Curtiz). From his novel.

1946   *The Postman Always Rings Twice* (Tay Garnett). From his novel.

1949   *Everybody Does It* (Edmund Goulding). Remake of *Wife, Husband and Friend*.

1956   *Serenade* (Anthony Mann). From his novel.
Slightly Scarlet (Allan Dwan). From his novel *Love's Lovely Counterfeit*.

1957   *Interlude* (Douglas Sirk). Remake of *When Tomorrow Comes*.

1973   *Double Indemnity* (Jack Smight). From his novel.

1981   *The Postman Always Rings Twice* (Bob Rafelson). From his novel.

1982   *The Butterfly* (Matt Cimber). From his novel.

Produced plays include *Crashing the Gate, The Postman Always Rings Twice,* and *7–11*.

Nonfiction includes *Our Government*.

Novels include *The Postman Always Rings Twice, Serenade, Mildred Pierce, Love's Lovely Counterfeit, Three of a Kind* ("Career in C Major," "The Embezzler," and "Double Indemnity"), *Past All Dishonor, Sinful Woman, The Butterfly, The Moth, Jealous Woman, The Root of His Evil, Galatea, Mignon, The Magician's Wife, Rainbow's End, The Institute,* and *The Baby in the Icebox and Other Short Fiction*.

Academy Awards based on Cain's work include an Oscar nomination in 1945 for Ranald MacDougall's screenplay of *Mildred Pierce*.

To many persons, "hardboiled fiction" in America means you, Horace McCoy, Hammett, and Chandler. Do you feel the affinity?

No. To tell you the truth, I never read but ten pages of Chandler's books, if that. I never read one word of Horace McCoy. I read twenty pages of Hammett in Greenwich, Connecticut, when I worked for *The New Yorker* in 1931. I was managing editor and had to go out there every Sunday to the printer and put *The New Yorker* to bed. The make-up man needed my OK. Lying around there was this book, *The Glass Key*. I would pick this thing up and try to read it, and at the end of four or five Sundays when I'd only read about twenty pages, I said forget this goddamned book. And that's my total knowledge of Hammett.

I'm always bracketed with these guys, and I'm supposed to belong to the tough-guy school or something of that kind. I don't belong to any school, and I don't try to write tough. I suppose what they're talking about is that I write colloquial, easy, everyday speech in my books—most of my books are in the first person—and I'll have a character speak as he would talk into a tape recorder. Anyway, I suppose to these critics, whose minds are distinctly literary, this simple, somewhat intimate way of talking strikes them as tough. They always bracket me with the 1930s. I don't know what I've got to do with the 1930s. I have no consciousness of a kinship with that era. But, you know, these fellows that do criticisms have got two characteristics: one—infallibility, omniscience; the other—they got to put you in schools, hang labels on you.

Do you have a closer connection with Hemingway?

The first thing I ever read of Hemingway was "Fifty Grand," which came out toward the end of the 1920s. By that time I had written quite a few short stories and dramatic dialogues for Henry Mencken's *American Mercury*. My style was well along to being developed. These dialogues later came out in a book for Knopf called *Our Government* [New York: Alfred A. Knopf, 1930], which purported to show how inanely government is carried out at a poorhouse near Baltimore. People were being cremated, just burned up in the furnace to save the cost of digging graves. This made quite a stink around Baltimore. My conversations involved the chairman of the county commissioners, the superintendent of the almshouse, the janitor of the almshouse, and the inmate who did the talking. They had a postmortem on this stuff coming out in the papers, and it came off pretty funny. Then I did a lot of others. Some of them got very well known and were performed by little theatres. All of this came before I ever read a word of Hemingway. After "Fifty Grand" I didn't read any Hemingway until this story about the guy and the girl in the war—*A Farewell to Arms*. That was very fine. Now then, I also read "The Undefeated" and "The Short

Happy Life of Francis Macomber," which is not too good a story. "The Killers," though, is a very craggy thing. It's a thing that sticks with you.

You became a successful literary stylist without need of contemporary literary models. But do you write effortlessly, without any major problems?

My difficulty in writing a story is not in *writing* a story or in thinking of something to write a story about but in finding a *reason* this character in the first person would tell it. That's *my* problem. It doesn't have to be a very important reason; it can be the most special, cockeyed reason in the world that wraps up in a sentence or two. But just the same, I have to have that or I can't tell the story. In my stories there's usually stuff that you wouldn't think any human being would tell at all. Now I've just finished a book called *The Cocktail Waitress*, where the girl tells her story, and there's some pretty intimate stuff. This girl, like most women, is very reticent about some things—you know, the sex scenes, where she spent the night with a guy. I had her tell enough so that what happened was clear and at the same time not go into details. Once she lingered with a sex scene as if she *wanted* to tell it. *The Cocktail Waitress* is about the tenth book I've started in the third person, half wrote in the third person, then realized it wasn't right, and went back and rewrote in the first person.

It is interesting that you are utilizing a female narrator in your new novel. Which of your works do women like best?

I haven't the faintest idea. I don't know if *any* of them like my books. I wouldn't say that they are the type that women, more than anyone else would particularly go for.

Aren't there glimmerings of a women's liberation theme in Mildred Pierce?

Some, I guess, but that's not the theme of it. She is independent because she has to go and make a living for those kids. She's also a little conceited.

Before your literary fame with The Postman Always Rings Twice *in 1934, you were employed in Hollywood as a screenwriter. How did you begin?*

I came to Paramount in November 1931, when I quit *The New Yorker.* My first assignment was to remake *The Ten Commandments*, believe it or not. I was teamed with a guy named Sam Mintz, a very nice guy, and both of us were utterly appalled. We had no idea what to do with it. We'd sit around and we'd go to lunch and we'd come back and talk. By the end of a couple of weeks we got summoned to a story conference to give a report on where we were at. Where we were at was nowhere. Three or four of these guys that don't have any faces and who always sit in story conferences, the director, and a supervisor all were there. So I knocked them out of their seats with an account of where we were at on this story. I had them all but cheering. Sam and I walked back to our offices on the third floor of the writers' building at Paramount. Sam told me how proud he was of me, that he hadn't any idea I was so far along. He was so admiring. I said, "What did I tell them?" He said, "I don't know. What *did* you tell them?" I said, "I haven't the faintest idea." You can't get away with that kind of thing for long, though. They finally got our number, and we were closed out of the picture.

And afterward at Paramount?

I didn't have any assignment for four or five months. I would come in and do nothing all day—get my mail, see if there were any calls, go out or not go out, sit in my office and read *The Saturday Evening Post*—a somewhat unnerving and demoralizing life. In the last three weeks of my option I suddenly was assigned to a thing called *Hot Saturday* [1932], I think, by Harvey Fergusson. A guy I had never heard of, George Raft, was supposed to play in it. I can't remember much about that picture. I was closed out, and they made it anyway. My six-month option was not taken up. That was the end of it. But my wife liked it out there and my stepchildren did too, so we decided to stay. I didn't have the faintest idea how I was going to make the money to eat. I spent six months writing magazine articles. Then I got a job early the following year working at Columbia, although I had to take a cut in pay.

Did you meet Harry Cohn?

I was very good friends with Harry Cohn. He was always very courtly with Elina, my wife at the time. He had a side that few people ever saw; but she saw it and I saw it. He could be the most elegant, gracious guy you could imagine. He could also be a rotten, dirty son-of-a-bitch, and he often was. But he seemed to be putting on a kind of an act. His son-of-a-bitchery never quite hurt as much as it should have. He could growl or raise hell, and yet the writer or actor or whoever could get along with him.

What are your personal memories of the Columbia lot?

I used to eat lunch every day in the executive dining room—I don't know who asked me up there—and there were about twelve of us. The only thing that anybody ever ate was salami embedded in fried eggs. One day Lowell Sherman came by. He had just finished directing a picture at Paramount, *She Done Him Wrong* [1933], with a girl named Mae West. He was telling us Mae's capers. The studio censors made her raise her corsage two inches to cover up her cleavage. She went around holding up these beautiful things to people, saying, "What's the matter? Aren't they alright?" Sam Briskin, the general manager of Columbia, asked Sherman if he'd taken a bite. "No, Sam," said Lowell, "I was chewing gum at the time." The stuff you heard on picture lots!

How did you leave Columbia?

The same way. I had six weeks there. I worked for a man who later became a very close friend, Jim McGuinness. We'd both been on *The New Yorker,* and we had plenty of things to talk about. McGuinness and I were trying to cook up a story to follow a story that they had. They wanted another one with the same actor, but why it didn't pan out I don't know. To tell you the truth, I think McGuinness was just looking for someone to blow lunch on. He wasn't upset about whether we were getting anywhere or not.

Weren't you becoming discouraged by your lack of artistic success as a screenwriter?

No, I don't remember anything like that. They paid you amounts of money that didn't seem real, they were so big. If you began grieving over that kind of money, you'd go nuts, get yourself a complex. Some people secretly did, and that would account for some of the wacky, weird things out there in Hollywood. But I have to say that when I walked out of my office after being closed out, I just washed out my mind. Soon I didn't get closed out very often. I would complete an assignment and pleasantly be told goodbye by the producer. I always say I flopped in pictures, and I did at first. But toward the end, I did fairly well. After all, there ain't many of them, in Hollywood or elsewhere, that write better dialogue than I do. It's just something I naturally do well.

Did you ever encounter F. Scott Fitzgerald while in Hollywood—the classic case of the literary man who flopped in movies?

I had contact with him once. In 1937 I was sold over to Metro, and I checked in at the picture lot on time. I figured I'm paid to work, so I work. When I got there my name was only half lettered in on my door. The secretary hadn't checked in yet. I scarcely had pulled my swivel-chair out from behind my desk when there came a tap on the door. This rather good-looking youngish guy came in and said, "Mr. Cain?" I said yes. He said, "I'm Scott Fitzgerald. I just wanted to welcome you to the lot, since I heard you were here." I just said, "Well, yes, hmm, well, thanks." He wasn't there more than thirty seconds. He kind of tiptoed out in a very deferential way. "Well now," I said to myself, "that's a hell of a way to treat Scott Fitzgerald." That was a nice thing for him to do. I kept thinking all morning of something I could do to sort of carry it a step further. I decided to ask him to go to lunch with me. I went down to his office, tapped on his door, and he said, "Come in." Now, you can always tell when a writer is assigned. He wasn't assigned. He was walking around smoking. There was no secretary there. I asked him if he was going to lunch; right away he put his cigarette down and fell into step beside me. We walked over to lunch. Now, I had been talking away about something when it occurred to me suddenly that this guy had not said one word. Five minutes later it occurred to me that he was not *going* to say anything either. "What the hell is this anyhow?" I thought. "A guy sits there for forty minutes, he says not a goddamned word." Finally I said, "Well, nice seeing you," and got up, paid my check, and left. That's my encounter with Scott Fitzgerald.

How do you explain it?

It made no sense. I mentioned this incident to somebody—maybe John O'Hara—who knew him, and he told me that Scott probably thought I asked him to lunch because I pitied him for being a has-been. That's why he didn't say anything. Fitzgerald was known for doing crazy things like that. I can't say it was exactly a pleasant encounter.

What group did you associate with in Hollywood?

I didn't really hang out with anybody. But I must have done considerable "eating around," as they say. The producer Robert Bassler once told someone that he didn't hang around with movie stars. He had them under contract, worked with them, but didn't associate with them. I guess that would cover me too.

You are credited with doing the adaptation for Algiers *[1938]. Is that accurate?*

I did the first part, a twenty-minute preliminary bit with Casbah gangster types. They cast a girl I thought was the most beautiful creature I had ever seen—Hedy Lamarr. I understand that when she wrote herself up in some kind of autobiography, she mentioned with great pride that I did part of the dialogue. But the part of the picture I wrote was before she came in. I've forgotten why I was closed out. The director John Cromwell got John Howard Lawson in. He had a certain gift, but it was a very solemn and humorless gift. There were a lot of laughs in the section I dialogued but not one laugh after that. I took some little satisfaction in that.

In research, did you watch Algiers' *predecessor, the 1936 French film,* Pépé le Moko, *by Julien Duvivier?*

I probably did—that was with Jean Gabin, wasn't it? Do you know what moko means? It means maquereau, which is the French word for pimp. Pépé the pimp, we would say! And nobody knew!

You are credited on a shared screenplay with Jane Murfin and Harvey Fergusson on MGM's Stand Up and Fight *[1939], a historical drama set in nineteenth-century Maryland. What do you recall of this?*

That was with Charles Bickford, [Wallace] Beery, Robert Taylor. The first part of the script satisfied everyone, but the rest needed work. I barely remember why I was brought in, but the picture had quite an effect on my screenwriting. The producer, Jack Rubin, really instructed me. "I know you hate this picture lingo," he said. "You feel that it's very special and cinematic and celluloid, but the production company must have this stuff." I had to remember to number each shot and indicate something like: "exterior—street—medium shot—day." My script would be read by twenty guys who had something different to do with it. It would set them nuts not to know where they were at. When I got that into my head, suddenly my scripts began to be workable.

What did you contribute to the script of The Bridge of San Luis Rey *[1943]?*

I worked on it for about a month for an independent producer, but I can't remember anything about it. I had met Thornton Wilder not long after that thing was published. We were both sons of '84—our fathers graduated from the same class of 1884 at Yale. He was at one of the reunion lunches that I ran up to New York to attend. We became pretty good friends. Anyway, nobody seemed to get a script out of that book. It was a very tough assignment.

Here's a final screen credit—for Gypsy Wildcat *[Universal, 1944], shared with James Hogan and Gene Lewis.*

Let me tell you about that picture. Universal guaranteed me two weeks, so I went. I was supposed to write for an actress named Maria Montez. They showed me a film so I would know what kind of a creature I was writing for. Well, when she came on screen, I suddenly realized that I knew this girl personally. Her voice and every gesture were completely familiar to me. But I have *yet* to figure out where I met this girl. I think she must have checked hats some place in Hollywood.

The script they handed me was simply *weird*. It was a horrible pipe dream—a director's script. It was full of "interior—stage coach—medium shot—day" intercut with "exterior—castle—full shot—night." Chirst, there was more cinematic gobbledygook—eight different sequences intercutting each other at the same time. But this was after the Jack Rubin seminar, so I knew what to do. I took this script and worked on it day and night, got order into the story, and simplified it. I turned in the script and thought, "I've done something that makes sense." My last day I walked over to the producer's office to thank ["B" writer-director-producer] George Waggner and say goodbye. I saw him in there *rewriting* my script! I shook his hand and told him I was sorry he didn't like it. "Jim," he said, "I'm delighted with what you've done. But *she* couldn't play your dialogue. It has to be translated into the kind of baby talk she can handle." He told me, "I'm pinching myself for the wonderful thing you've done with this bad dream I threw at you. Now I can put this thing in front of a camera."

That was the beginning of a new phase of my picture career. After that I was a professional at the business; after that, I did alright. I worked mainly at Metro and to some extent at Twentieth Century–Fox for about five more years. I don't think I got any more credits after that picture. I must have done well, though, because my agent kept getting the price up.

Weren't you ever concerned by your lack of screen credits?

One producer asked me why I would work anonymously on his "B" picture. I told him it made no difference if the story interested me. I wasn't doing anything for a few weeks, and I didn't mind picking up some money—we always allow for that. I also didn't have to rely on pictures for my public recognition. I got plenty of that. I'd go to Europe and be interviewed, and not for being a picture writer. Nobody ever heard of who wrote a picture east of Pasadena. But they'd all heard of me. I told him; and so I could work on a "B" picture if it interested me. That seemed to be quite an eye-opener to that producer.

Could you talk about the American Authors' Authority that you started in Hollywood in 1946?

What I was trying to do was set up an authors' organization like ASCAP [American Society of Composers, Authors, and Publishers]. Composers, authors, and publishers assign the performing rights to ASCAP, and then royalties and a license fee are collected from everybody using members' compositions. I wanted writers to assign the whole copyright to an authors' authority, although authority was a bad word. It gave people the idea—especially [the journalist] Dorothy Thompson—that I was trying to control what people wrote. The capacity of some people to misrepresent what you are doing is almost infinite. Anyway, the idea was to protect writers who, acting singly and without an authors' guild, were forced into disadvantageous contracts. They were victims of the gypping practices of publishers. The Screen Writers Guild was almost unanimously shouting for it because it saw the power it could give writers over their properties. But the screenwriters themselves didn't have properties whose copyrights could be assigned. I gave my plan a fair run. I propagandized for it, made speeches, wrote pamphlets and brochures and things, and circulated them. When I found it wasn't going over, I just stepped off it and that was the end. It's a dead issue, and I don't know why you bring the subject up.

Did you get opposition from management at MGM, Louis B. Mayer or others?

Mayer was always very agreeable to me. He had a way of taking you by the hand and holding on to you in a very affectionate and friendly way. Also very nice to me was Eddie Mannix, the right-hand man to Louis B. Now, Irving Thalberg—he was one of the most unpleasant guys. A few years earlier, I was ushered into the "Presence." This pale guy sat there; whether he was listening or not was hard to say. He got us picture writers in there at the time the Screen Writers Guild was being organized. He was practically telling Metro writers, "You can't join this thing." He was very offensive about it, assembling us all there to make a speech to us. Then he up and dies. There's a building on the Metro lot named after him, also known as the "Iron Lung." My office was in the "Iron Lung."

Did you know Samuel Goldwyn?

Let me tell you, he wasn't the clown or ignoramus that the Goldwyn stories would indicate. Once I had some idea that I wanted to do a picture that would be a sequel to his picture, *The Hurricane* [1937]. My agent got me over there to talk. Goldwyn gave me an hour, and he cut his calls. Now, the big producers cut their calls so they're not interrupted. It's the little bastards that you couldn't talk to more than a minute before the phone would ring and, "Oh, hiya Clark, long time no see! How ya been, fella?" Oh, for chrissake! But Goldwyn cut his calls. He talked with the greatest intelligence. I didn't have to talk down to him. Usually when a writer talks to another writer, he makes it short and sweet; but with someone else he uses a slightly different vocabulary, and he elaborates a bit. With Goldwyn I didn't have to put it into words of one syllable at all. He was with it all the way and very interested, obviously.

Now somewhere along the way it occurred to me: what became of the "mucus of a good idea"? What became of "include me out"? What became of the "Accent"? He talked as any other sharp, intelligent man would talk and with only a slight trace of an accent. Suddenly a male secretary knifed into the room. "Mr. Goldwyn, you said you weren't to be disturbed unless (mentioning some agent) called, and he's on the wire now." Goldwyn said, "OK, I'll talk to him." And then: "At 500 you *haf* a deal, at 750 I vill not pay, I *vill not pay!*" he said. I thought to myself, I found out something. Who would argue with this accent? Goldwyn got an accent whenever it paid!

Weren't you still in Hollywood at the beginning of the Hollywood Ten agitation?

I knew these guys, most of them, and they made no sense to me. Why should they be Communists? You understand, all of these guys were highly-paid and successful. Ring Lardner, Jr., for example, was one of the best picture writers that was ever in Hollywood and very much in demand. He was very deft and skillful; his dialogue was feathery, you know, and light and warm. Why Ring Lardner, Jr., should have been practically a Communist, I don't know. I think all those guys were. I got up at a meeting one time and said to Albert Maltz, "Mr. Maltz, are you or are you not a Communist?" I was booed down. I said, "My political affiliation is on the record books down here, on the voting lists." I repeated my question. "Mr. Maltz, are you or are you not a Communist?" He didn't answer me, and he hasn't answered me yet. When he didn't answer me, I took it that he was.

Why did you feel you had a right to this information?

It was becoming a public issue. I thought to myself, goddammit, why can't he say? I can say I'm registered as a Democrat. I'm not entitled to know how he votes. I simply asked if he's a Communist.

But wouldn't the writers be drummed out of Hollywood if they admitted being Communists?

Well, *I* wouldn't drum anybody out of Hollywood for saying he was a Communist or for *being* a Communist. I don't think they refused to say whether they were Communists on that account. I think that the Party line said you may not declare yourself, and that being the case, they had to refuse to say. It was as simple as that. Now *why* they were not permitted to say they were Communists, I don't know. That's my theory. I can't prove it. I didn't directly know much, and yet all of us knew a great deal by hearsay and inference. We knew these Communists; they were *friends*—guys you saw all the time and got along with and liked, most of the time. Some you found very hugger-mugger and queer and, you felt, dishonest. You wouldn't trust them. That was a very bad thing out there, this blacklist business. But that was during the McCarthy era, when the whole country was suspicious and making a trap-door melodrama of the whole thing. I don't think we'll see anything like that anymore, not for a while.

We would like to know about your various writings turned into films. Could you begin with When Tomorrow Comes *[1939] from a Cain short story?*

Much earlier, an editor at *Collier's* almost curdled my blood the first interview I had with him. He told me that he wanted "a Cinderella story with a modern twist," and I thought, "Oh Christ, what a formula." Then I thought, "Why don't you write a story that tells what really happens when the waitress marries the Harvard man?" Ten years later, I wrote the story, and then *Collier's* didn't buy it. I wrote about this Harvard guy who falls for this girl and marries her and about how his sisters treated her. It was a fairly good story, I have to say. It finally published as *The Root of His Evil,* although its working title was *The Modern Cinderella.* It was put out by Avon and sold by my agent to Universal for a nice price. They cast the Harvard man with the guy in Hollywood who could not play a Harvard man, Charles Boyer; and the girl was Irene Dunne, who had it in her contract that she had to sing at least one number. *When Tomorrow Comes* had a waitress who sings as good as Irene Dunne sings, and they made *him* a French pianist. This movie bore no relation to the original story. That's how they mangle things up.

We got into a lawsuit over that picture. They put the couple in a church overnight. In my book, *Serenade,* the couple spends three or four days in a church. One day the writer [identified in *Cain* by Roy Hoopes as Dwight Taylor] of *When Tomorrow Comes* sat down beside me and apologized. He told me that John Stahl, the director, had assembled the various people working on this story and told them that Universal had paid me a good round sum for this story and that he felt that if there was anything in *any* of my other books that would help them out, to go ahead and see what could be taken! I went home and thought to myself, "If you won't sue on that, when *will* you sue? You owe it not only to yourself but to other writers." So I did sue. Stahl and the producers gave depositions. Stahl denied everything. At this point I said to my lawyer, "I'm getting very disturbed about this thing. Practically everything in the record corresponds with what Stahl says. Practically nothing corresponds with the story the writer told me." My lawyer said that, since we had filed the suit already, we might as well go ahead.

And the court case?

John Stahl took the witness stand. And here is what I am leading to: the contrast of an honest man, wrongly accused, with Watergate and Nixon. My lawyer fired a pretty sharp question at him, and Stahl's lawyer objected, saying, "Irrelevant and immaterial." "Sustained," said the judge. But Stahl, who kind of had a Brooklyn way of talking, said, "Your Honor, I'd like to thank the court for giving me the benefit of the law. Yet since Mr. Cain made his charge in good faith, this is my *one* chance to clear my name. I will answer any question, and I don't care how irrelevant or immaterial or how plain silly."

There went my case. He convinced me, and I hardly heard the rest of it. My lawyer still gave him a pretty hot ride and asked him who thought of having the scene in the church. "I don't remember," Stahl answered, "but if it helps any, *I* did." Now you contrast that with the shifty, cover-everything-up stonewalling of Nixon and his people.

But why did the writer fabricate the story?

Someone suggested that he had a guilt complex and was always accusing himself of something, always beating his chest. I'd been to the little boys' room when I met him in the hall. I said, "Why did you tell me this goddamned cock-and-bull story? There's not a word of truth in it." He stammered, and he said that I didn't understand him correctly. He had this mea culpa complex. Also he was one of those literary guys who was much hipped on my book, *Serenade,* and he'd rather say he was directed to steal from *Serenade* than be caught snooping around my literary pants. *Serenade* deals with a theme [homosexuality] he probably flinched from admitting. There were people who used to come up to the house in *pairs* thinking I was a "brother." Well, I'm not. A psychiatrist once told me about *Serenade,* "You found one that Krafft-Ebing missed: the effect that the homo element in a man has on his singing voice. That was a very sharp observation." In *Serenade* the Mexican girl alludes to it. She says, "The voice has no *toro* in it."

What happened to the homosexuality theme in the 1956 film version of Serenade?

I think *Serenade* was bought for $35,000 around 1942, but there was trouble with the script because of the homo element. Finally I said to Jerry Wald, "Make the homo a woman instead of a man. Make this woman a sort of wine fancier and the hero have a weakness for liquor—so in some way this woman is bad for him." Wald bought it on this basis, and they went with the idea I had suggested, which was just no good. It had no moxie in it.

Was it wise casting Mario Lanza in the Serenade *lead?*

He drank and was always overweight and he had to be dieted down. A guy on a diet is cranky and disagreeable. Another thing, he was convinced that Mario Lanza was the greatest singer who ever lived. All Lanza was interested in was song cues. I never saw much of the film version. It began coming in one night on television. My wife was an opera singer and liked this guy's voice. I suspected him. I did not think that Mario Lanza did the intricate cadenzas. I thought they were dubbed. I said, "Do you mind if we cut this *ghastly* thing off? God, did you ever see any such fantastically horrible thing?" We cut it off, but I think she was annoyed with me. My wife knew nothing about dubbing, so she doted on his voice.

Who would you have liked in the role?

I had no interest. People think that, as the author, I lie awake nights worrying about what *they* did to my story, as I wrote it. As far as a picture goes, they're entitled to do whatever they want because they paid me the money.

In 1957, Interlude *was made from a Cain short story. Do you know this Douglas Sirk picture?*

Interlude was a remake of that picture with the lawsuit, *When Tomorrow Comes.* The only thing I know about *Interlude* utterly baffles me. Every six months I get a check for $3.45 or something like that from the Writers Guild. Why, I don't know. If eight or ten of my pictures paid me $3.45 each, then I'd be picking up a little money.

What of Wife, Husband, and Friend *[1939] from your serial, "Career in C Major"?*

There were two movies from that book. *Wife, Husband, and Friend* was the first version. Nunnally Johnson did the script. In 1949 Twentieth was looking for some place to put this actor, Paul Douglas, because he had just made a big hit on Broadway and was a hot property. Nunnally Johnson used the same script for *Everybody Does It* [1949]. I can't remember if I saw the second version. I didn't much care for *Wife, Husband, and Friend.* I was rather bored by it, although it didn't make much difference to me. My friend [the writer] Vincent Lawrence was very bitter about the movie, and he was savagely annoyed that I wasn't getting worked up over it. Zanuck had put in some sure-fire laughs about this fellow trying to be an opera singer who does all this slapstick. I said, "Well, what the hell, they're laughing." "Yes," said Lawrence, "and *every* one of those laughs was at the expense of the character. They made a clown out of him." That's what Lawrence had to say: never make a clown out of your leading man.

Do you have a stronger affection for Double Indemnity *[1944]?*

I had to see *Double Indemnity* probably half a dozen times in various connections, and I was never bored. I must say Billy Wilder did a terrific job. It's the only picture I ever saw made from my books that had things in it I wish I had thought of. Wilder's ending was much better than my ending, and his device for letting the guy tell the story by taking out the office dictating machine—I would have done it if I had thought of it.

There are situations in the movie that can make your hands get wet, you get so nervous—like the place where Eddie Robinson comes in to talk to Fred MacMurray. Robinson is working close to what the murder explanation is—connecting MacMurray and Barbara Stanwyck. And *she* comes and is about to rap on MacMurray's door when she hears something and pulls back; the door opens and Eddie Robinson comes out with MacMurray, and she's hiding behind the door. I tell you, there for a minute, it is just beautiful. I wish I had thought of something like it.

But my story was done very slapdash and very quick—I had to have money. I had made a lot of money, but I had to pay it all out to liquidate something I had hanging over my head. I was flat broke. To make money quick I thought, well, you can do a serial for *Liberty,* and the idea for this thing popped into my head. At the end I had the problem of how he and the woman could go off the deep end at the

Vintage Cain: Fred MacMurray and Barbara Stanwyck in Billy Wilder's inter-pretation of Double Indemnity. *It was Cain's favorite of the various adaptations of his novels.*

same time and he would leave an account of it in a diary or something. But the end was not done over enough. All endings to a novel have to be done over and over and over. Christ Almighty! You get sick of that last twenty pages!

In the novel Phyllis is fixated on a "death trip," but that is not translated to the movie.

No, they didn't make any effort to. I don't know whether it *can* be translated. In any case Barbara Stanwyck was about as good as they come as an actress, and at the same time she was reasonably young and appetizing. Stanwyck is also a very wonderful and likable person. We had an easy, informal acquaintanceship.

There seems to be a father-son relationship between Robinson and MacMurray in the movie.

I think there's a hint of that in the book, isn't there? But it was extended in the movie. When Eddie is told at the end that all the time the killer was right across the desk from him, Eddie says, "Closer than that, Walter." It was a nice moment, right at the end where you want a nice moment.

Why did Raymond Chandler co-author the script and not you?

They didn't ask me to write the script. I don't know. I never met Chandler until the day we had a story conference. Wilder wanted to explain to me why they weren't using more of my "deathless dialogue." He fell for the dialogue in my book, and he was annoyed that Chandler wasn't putting more of it in the script. To try and prove his point he got three contract people up, and they ran through these scenes with my dialogue. But to Wilder's astonishment, he found out it *wouldn't* play. Chandler said, "I tried to tell him, Jim," with that easy familiarity they have out in Hollywood; even first meeting me he called me by my first name. "Jim, that dialogue of yours is to the *eye.*" I said I knew my book is to the eye, although I *could* write to the ear. Chandler said, "I tried to explain it to Billy."

A thing was said at this story conference—and not by Chandler—that made even more of an impression on me. A young guy named Joe Sistrom was Paramount's producer on the picture. He was bothered that in the script and to some extent in the book this guy hit on the scheme for the perfect murder much too quickly and easily. I said that it was implied that he had been subconsciously meditating this for years. Well, this didn't satisfy Joe Sistrom. He sat there unhappily in a sulk and then suddenly said, "All characters in 'B' pictures are too smart." I never forgot it. It was a curious observation, putting into words—vivid, rememberable words—a principle that when a character is too smart and convenient to the author's purposes, everything begins getting awfully slack and slick in the story. Slack is one fault and slick is another. Both are bad faults in a story.

Why did it take so long to film Double Indemnity *after it was written in the mid-thirties?*

Because of the Hays Office, which cost me hundreds of thousands of dollars. When I originally wrote that story, I had it mimeographed and then sent over to my agent. The next day I was lunching with him in the Vine Street Derby, and he seemed gloomy. He was afraid he had priced my book too low. "I did a real snow job on it yesterday. I've already had five calls on it this morning. I've never had such a reaction to a story before." He had priced it at $25,000, and he would have to let it go there or be out of business. I told him that $25,000 wasn't hay. That afternoon the Hays Office report came in, and it started off: "Under no circumstances," and it ended up, ". . . way, shape, or form." My agent asked if I wanted to hear what was in between, and I told him I could guess.

Now skip ten years. "Double Indemnity" was to come out in *Three of a Kind,* along with "The Embezzler" and "Career in C Major," both of which already had sold to pictures. My new agent, H. N. Swanson, sent it again to eight studios. Well, one day Billy Wilder couldn't find his secretary. The relief girl said, "Well, Mr. Wilder, I think she's still in the ladies' room reading that story." Wilder said, "What story?" About this time she came out with *Double Indemnity* pressed to her bosom—she'd just finished it and had this ga-ga look on her face—and Wilder snatched the book from her and took it home and read it. The next day I had an offer—$15,000. Now there's $10,000 the Hays Office cost me on one book. Wilder made a perfectly decent picture with no trouble about it. Well, there was a little trouble caused by this fat girl, Kate Smith, who carried on propaganda asking people to stay away from this picture. Her advertisement probably put a million dollars on its gross.

What are the events behind Mildred Pierce?

Jim McGuinness, my old producer friend at Columbia, once made a remark that led to *Mildred Pierce.* Out in Hollywood all they talk about is *story*—secretaries, everybody—*story.* Well, one day we were going to lunch, talking about stories, when he said, "There's one that's never failed yet, and that's the story of a woman who uses men to gain her ends." I thought, well, if it's never failed yet that sounds like a pretty good story to me.

Secretly, then, I began to try to adjust this formula. For a while I had the woman as an airline stewardess. Then she was a girl who won a beauty contest and came to Hollywood. Neither of these came to life, so I thought, maybe it makes some difference *what* ends. I suddenly thought it might help if her children were the ends she used men for, and naturally it would be better if it focused on one child. But I had to have another child in there so it wouldn't seem so pat and easy.

Then I made her not a femme fatale at all, just a housewife, but she had that instinct to use men. Every time I had trouble with that book I thought, "My friend, you've forgotten what your story is about. This is not the story of a woman who is devoted to her daughter and is nuts about her; it's a story about a woman who uses men to gain her ends." Every time I'd remember that and reinstate that theme in the book, it would go.

No reviewer or anybody who read it ever detected that that's what the book is about. I didn't highlight it enough. I don't take much pride in *Mildred Pierce,* I have to confess to you. It's not my kind of book. I made some egregious mistakes in it, especially right at the end, which is a very costly place to make mistakes.

And the movie?

Mildred Pierce was loused up by the idea that Monty [Zachary

Scott] had died. Mark Hellinger, the first to get interested in *Mildred,* proclaimed that they would have this melodrama. Veda [Ann Blyth] would be held for murdering Monty, the guy that Mildred, her mother, was sleeping with. Jesus Christ! What kind of a fantastic superimposition was that; it had no bearing whatsoever on the theme! It made no sense to me, so I was never really able to praise *Mildred Pierce.*

I always praised Joan Crawford's performance, which was OK, and that kind of sounded like I was praising the picture. I heard her on the Merv Griffin television show one night, and he asked what her greatest moment in pictures was. Without any hesitation she said it was when she got the Oscar for *Mildred Pierce.* I interviewed her one time for some picture magazine, and every now and then I exchanged a letter with her. I guess I liked her alright. But the one time I had personal contact with her, she was wanting to put across certain things she hoped I'd put in the article. She pretended she didn't mean to push at me, and that's OK, you expect that, but I did not have the pleasant association I had with Stanwyck and with one or two others out there. Gladys George, who lived in the same hotel I did, I knew very well. She was a beautiful actress.

Was The Postman Always Rings Twice *your most successful book?*

It was not the most successful of my books in hardcover. That was *Past All Dishonor.* But in total sales, yes, it's this *Postman.* I got a little kangaroo from Pocket Books when the book had sold a million copies. That must have been around 1950, because Eisenhower was on the train going up to New York. There was someone else getting a *gold* kangaroo up there for selling ten million copies—Dale Carnegie. Hovering over him was this very good-looking number in her early thirties, very smartly dressed, very likeable. She was shooing people away from him so he didn't have to talk to anybody. He was so uncertain and bored, this guy who wrote *How to Win Friends and Influence People,* that she had to go with to kind of mother him. This struck me as very funny. As far as Hollywood, the same thing happened with *Postman* as with *Double Indemnity.* Metro bought it, and the Hays Office turned it down. After *Double Indemnity* was made, Breen [the Production Code official Joseph Breen] at the Hays Office—it was now technically the Breen Office—finally okayed the script.

Is it true that you never saw the film Postman *until recently—thirty years after?*

One of my friends took me to see it the other night. I was surprised that it was no worse than it was. It was a passably viewable picture the first time I ever actually saw the release form. After the "sneak" in Glendale in 1946, I went up the aisle on my hands and knees for fear I would run into Carey Wilson, the producer. The rough-cut they showed at this preview was just so utterly ghastly. I thought, "Jesus Christ." But when I saw it the other night, the stuff that made my blood curdle out in Glendale had been cut out. There's a place in the book where he runs off with a girl who had a cat act, and he takes her somewhere to Mexico. Well, in the first version I saw, they had this girl's cat act in the picture—leopards and pumas and lions and everything rolling around with each other—and it had no more relationship with the story than the man in the moon.

Shortly after the picture was released, I was having dinner alone in Murphy's, a corned beef and cabbage kind of place with wonderful food, and I looked up and saw Harry Ruskin, the guy who did the script, standing in front of me. He was standing with his hands on his hips in a very belligerent way, and he said, "Well, why don't you say it? It *stinks.*" I told him I didn't think it stunk any worse than most of them do. I was moderately friendly, although I didn't exactly praise the picture. He told me that he had Lana Turner dressed in white so that the public understood that the girl's pure. She may be playing around with the guy, but she's not taking her pants off for him. Ruskin had asked Carey Wilson, "Is this girl shacking this guy into bed? I know we don't put it on the screen, but *I* have to know." But Wilson couldn't make up his mind whether Lana was screwing Garfield. "Jim," Ruskin said, "he didn't know then, and he doesn't know *now.* That's why the central part of the thing is so fuzzy and shaky and squashy." I thought of that while looking at the movie the other night. It didn't seem to make much of a difference.

Have you seen the French version of Postman *called* Le Dernier Tournant? *Or the Luchino Visconti Italian version,* Ossessione?

You know, *Ossessione* was a pirated version. This fellow in Italy just went ahead and did it without buying any rights. I'm told that it was just released in this country, but I don't know how it could be. Whether they sued or had him arrested, I don't know. I didn't do anything about it because I didn't own the rights.

The French version was on the up-and-up. The rights were bought at the time the American adaptation was under the Hays Office ban, before Carey Wilson got into the act. I haven't seen either version. As I told you, I just don't look at my pictures. When my neighbor took me down to look at this *Postman* thing, she was all excited about it. I went down because I like to go places with her—the picture was secondary to me having a nice evening. She has a nice car, and she and her husband are good friends of mine.

You have stated elsewhere that the first time you went to see a film you really couldn't believe that people were entertained.

Cain's most successful book: Jack Nicholson and Jessica Lange in the 1980 remake of The Postman Always Rings Twice, *adapted by David Mamet.*

When we were boys a friend and I walked downtown to this nickelodeon. On his way to buy tickets, my friend said, "I don't say it's good entertainment. It's the best entertainment the town affords." Inside we laughed ourselves into stitches, not at how good the jokes were but at how awful they were. John Bunny was one of the comedians. The feature was *The Great Train Robbery* [1903]. I had no idea that this was moving picture history. To us it was utterly beyond belief, it was so lousy. We came out agreeing it was *not* good entertainment, but it passed the time. Movies pretty much affect me this way now.

Recently I did see a revival of the Harold Lloyd picture, *Girl Shy* [1924]. I have to confess this one picture out of hundreds of pictures I've seen did entertain me. It was very adroitly done, this silent picture. The audience was in the aisles. The next week I went down to see Harold Lloyd again in another picture. It was talking, and it was just Christ-awful. This time the audience sat there in glum, bitter silence. Only when Lloyd began hanging by his fingernails over the street twenty stories below did they come to life a little but never as they had the other night.

What is the last movie you saw at the time it was released?

The Exorcist [1973]. The picture interested me in one respect: it was the most beautifully lit thing I ever saw. The story itself was nauseating. They overtold it. The place where the ghost was supposed to shake the girl in bed—God, they had to make the bed dance up and down and do tricks and all but turn over on her. But I expected the story to stink. I didn't mind that, but the lighting was incomparable.

Have you seen other pictures in recent years?

I can tell you all the movies I've seen since coming back East in 1947. I saw *High Noon* [1952], *Come Back Little Sheba* [1952], *Kon-Tiki* [1951], and two others I can't remember. I don't even look at them on TV for free. Most pictures aren't worth seeing. Let's face it, the moving picture never did lick reality. Pictures don't go deep. If a girl has a pretty face, that's as far as the camera can look.

Lenore Coffee:
Easy Smiler, Easy Weeper

Interview by Pat McGilligan

> *At times he [Irving Thalberg] seemed to hate his very dependence on writers and his frustration that he could not perform their functions. During one heated script session he said almost contemptuously, "What's all this business about being a writer? It's just putting one word after another."*
>
> *Lenore Coffee corrected him: "Pardon me, Mr. Thalberg; it's putting one* right *word after another."*
>
> Bob Thomas,
> *Thalberg: Life and Legend*

More than a glimmer of the grande dame of screenwriters that she must have been remained in the feeble, elderly woman in the sick ward of the Motion Picture Home. From her earliest apprenticeship as a fixer-upper and titlist, Lenore Coffee went on to become (among other things) a confidante of Cecil B. DeMille and Irving Thalberg. In the sound era she flourished as an adaptor of popular women's fiction written by authors such as Lloyd C. Douglas, Fannie Hurst, Stephen Longstreet, Gwen Bristow, and Margaret Echard. She prospered as one of the favored writers of Joan Crawford and Bette Davis vehicles. And she reigned as a maharani over her Mandeville Canyon estate in the days when lady screenwriters were the toast of Hollywood.

Now she called herself Lenore Cowen (after her husband) and would only admit to being eighty-five, because she had made a promise to herself to stop counting birthdays after eighty-five. My letters to her went to England and then back to the United States, where she was confined to the industry rest home for the penniless and the alone-in-life. An ardent Anglophile, she had resettled in Great Britain in 1959 at the behest of her beloved husband, the sporadic novelist, screenwriter, and director William Joyce Cowen. After forty years as a top screenwriter, she relinquished her sprawling estate—replete with horses and stables, a beekeeper and hives, vintage wine cellar, and all the amenities for a steady stream of guests—and turned her back on movies. She had hopes of nurturing a second career as a playwright and novelist until her husband died shortly after her move to Great Britain. So, too, it seems, did her will to work. It was twenty years later—years of living in hotels and of relative stasis—before creeping poverty and advancing age brought her back to an utterly changed Hollywood.

Like her better-known silent-era colleagues, Anita Loos and Frances Marion, Coffee was a native Californian, born and reared in San Francisco. By 1983, when I interviewed her, she had outlived most of her contemporaries. Norma Shearer, whom Coffee had once championed to Irving Thalberg (who had subsequently enthroned Shearer as a star and married her), was on the grounds of the Motion Picture Home. But the old acquaintances were in wings isolated from each other, and Coffee made the strenuous effort to see Shearer only once. There was a glint of recognition in the aged actress's eyes, and she stammered, "C-C-C-offee." Shearer, once-queen of Metro, died later that year.

Coffee took pride in her sharp eyesight (no need of eyeglasses); she continued to read avidly (mostly romantic paperbacks), to talk of writing (although her hands were not up to it), and to be witty and sharp-tongued. The afternoon visit with her was memorable for its bon mots, its rambling panorama of Hollywood life, and the sly, sexual innuendo so surprising in a woman whose storytelling roots were essentially Victorian (and Roman Catholic). One could detect a sense of what a feisty and inventive writer the young Lenore Coffee must have been fresh off the train in 1919; what a formidable presence she must have been in a roomful of male studio executives.

In 1973, Coffee wrote her memoirs, which were published exclusively in England. The wistful, somewhat free-form autobiography, *Storyline,* concentrates nearly entirely on the silent era, which Coffee always harked back to as the golden time of her life. She reached her zenith as a screenwriter in the 1930s and 1940s as a fixer-upper but primarily as an in-demand contract writer for sentimental or melodramatic women's pictures at MGM and Warners.

1919   *The Better Wife* (William P. S. Earle). Story.

1920   *For the Soul of Rafael* (Harry Garson). Uncredited contribution.

The Fighting Shepherdess (Edward Jose). Uncredited contribution.

The Forbidden Woman (Harry Garson). Story.

1921   *Alias Ladyfingers* (Bayard Veiller). Adaptation.

Hush (Harry Garson). Uncredited contribution.

1922   *The Face Between* (Bayard Veiller). Adaptation.

Lenore Coffee and her daughter, publicity shot, circa 1930. (Photo: University of Southern California)

The Right That Failed (Bayard Veiller). Adaptation.
Sherlock Brown (Bayard Veiller). Scenario.
The Dangerous Age (John M. Stahl). Uncredited contribution.

1923   *The Age of Desire* (Director unknown). Titles.
Daytime Wives (Emile Chautard). Co-story.
The Six-Fifty (Nat Ross). Co-script.
Temptation (Edward J. LeSaint). Story.
Thundering Dawn (Harry Garson). Co-script.
Wandering Daughters (James Young). Titles.
Strangers of the Night (Fred Niblo). Uncredited contribution.

1924   *Bread* (Victor Schertzinger). Adaptation.
Fools' Highway (Irving Cummings). Co-script.
The Rose of Paris (Director unknown). Adaptation.

1925   *East Lynne* (Emmett Flynn). Co-adaptation.
Hell's Highroad (Rupert Julian). Co-adaptation.
Graustark (Dimitri Buchowetzki). Uncredited contribution.
The Great Divide (Reginald Barker). Uncredited contribution.
The Swan (Dimitri Buchowetzki). Uncredited contribution.

1926   *For Alimony Only* (William DeMille). Story contribution.
        The Volga Boatman (Cecil B. DeMille). Adaptation.
        The Winning of Barbara Worth (Henry King). Uncredited contribution.

1927   *The Angel of Broadway* (Lois Weber). Story, scenarist.
        Chicago (Frank Urson). Adaptation, scenario.
        Lonesome Ladies (Joseph Henaberry). Story.
        The Night of Love (George Fitzmaurice). Adaptation, scenario.
        The Love of Sunya (a.k.a. *Eyes of Youth*) (Albert Parker). Uncredited contribution.

1929   *Desert Nights* (William Nigh). Co-script.
        Ned McCobb's Daughter (William J. Cowen). Uncredited contribution.

1930   *The Bishop Murder Case* (Nick Grinde). Adaptation, dialogue, scenario.
        Mother's Cry! (Hobart Henley). Adaptation, additional dialogue.
        Street of Chance (John Cromwell). Dialogue.

1931   *Possessed* (Clarence Brown). Adaptation, dialogue contribution.
        The Squaw Man (Cecil B. DeMille). Co-script.

1932   *Arsene Lupin* (Jack Conway). Co-dialogue.
        Night Court (W. S. Van Dyke). Co-script.
        Downstairs (Monta Bell). Script.
        Rasputin and the Empress (Richard Boleslawsky). Uncredited contribution.

1933   *Torch Singer* (Alexander Hall, George Somnes). Co-script.

1934   *All Men Are Enemies* (George Fitzmaurice). Co-script, co-dialogue.
        Four Frightened People (Cecile B. DeMille). Co-script.
        Such Women Are Dangerous (James Flood). Additional dialogue.
        Evelyn Prentice (William K. Howard). Script.

1935   *Vanessa: Her Love Story* (William K. Howard). Adaptation.
        David Copperfield (George Cukor). Uncredited contribution.
        The Age of Indiscretion (Edward Ludwig). Story.

1936   *Suzy* (George Fitzmaurice). Co-script.

1937   *Parnell* (John M. Stahl). Uncredited contribution.

1938   *White Banners* (Edmund Goulding). Co-script.
        Four Daughters (Michael Curtiz). Co-script.

1939   *Good Girls Go to Paris* (Alexander Hall). Co-story.

1940   *The Way of All Flesh* (Louis King). Script.
        My Son, My Son! (Charles Vidor). Script.

1941   *The Great Lie* (Edmund Goulding). Script.

1942   *We Were Dancing* (Robert Z. Leonard). Uncredited contribution.
        The Gay Sisters (Irving Rapper). Script.

1943   *Old Acquaintance* (Vincent Sherman). Co-script.

1944   *Till We Meet Again* (Frank Borzage). Script.
        Marriage Is a Private Affair (Robert Z. Leonard). Co-story, co-script.

1946   *Tomorrow Is Forever* (Irving Pichel). Script.
        The Guilt of Janet Ames (Henry Levin). Screen story.

1947   *Escape Me Never* (Peter Godfrey). Uncredited contribution.

1949   *Beyond the Forest* (King Vidor). Script.

1951   *Lightning Strikes Twice* (King Vidor). Script.
        Branded Woman (a.k.a. *Rebound*) (Director unknown, possibly not released).

1952   *Sudden Fear* (David Miller). Co-script.

1954   *Young at Heart* (Gordon Douglas). Remake of *Four Daughters*.

1955   *The End of the Affair* (Edward Dmytryk). Script.
        Footsteps in the Fog (Arthur Lubin). Co-script.

1958   *Another Time, Another Place* (Lewis Allen). Novel basis.
        Cash McCall (Joseph Pevney). Co-script.

Novels include *Weep No More* (a.k.a. *Another Time, Another Place*).

Produced plays include *Family Portrait*.

Academy Awards include an Oscar nomination in 1938 for co-writing the screenplay with Julius J. Epstein of *Four Daughters*.

Although I had two excessively handsome parents, I was not excessively handsome—but I was clever. My mother swears I said this once:

someone said, "She's not very p-r-e-t-t-y, is she?" and I said, "But she's very b-r-i-g-h-t." This is as I am today. I was a very, very precocious child. I could read by the time I was four. No one knows how. My father said, "This child has to go to school." My mother said, "She can't, she's only four years old." So they lied about my age and got me into a kindergarten.

I ran away from home when I was fourteen. My plot sense was already developed because it took them two days to find me. My parents asked me why I did it. I said I was unhappy. Why? Because I had nothing to do all day. My father said, "What do you want to do?" I said, "I don't know." Then a voice broke in my ear, "Ask to be sent to a convent." That was a punishment in those days.

I went to two different convents—two different orders. The first order were French nuns, very strict; they would back out of a room, as you do with royalty. The other order were the Dominicans in San Rafael. I was so happy in both convents. I became a Catholic, and I was baptized in a convent chapel in my graduation dress. I specialized in Latin because I thought it would be an unusual thing to be in America: a Latin scholar.

How did you get to Hollywood?

I was writing advertising copy for a paper company that sold paper to the Orient when someone said, "There's a vacancy for an assistant at the Emporium"—which was the largest department store in San Francisco. I was only at the store for ten days when they asked me to write the copy for a full-page Sunday ad. The head of the department said, "Use your judgment," which I did. I built the ad on the premise of how to dress well on a medium salary. I started out by saying, "How would you like to buy a full wardrobe at the Emporium for $300? You'd think: Hopeless! And so it would be if it weren't for the Emporium . . ." I used an example that has always worked for me: a navy-blue suit, which you can wear one of two ways. You can wear it with a shirtwaist and a felt hat and polished brown shoes, or you can wear it with a white-lace jabot, a little toe-hat, patent leather shoes, and a patent leather bag. The same suit can serve two purposes.

Well, the ad was a sensation. When the store owner came in on Monday morning, he could barely get into his own store. The police were holding people back. He said, "You've made advertising history. Do you know what I'm going to do? I'm going to give you a three week holiday out of my own pocket—because it's going to take three weeks to replenish our stock. Can you go somewhere for $20 a week for three weeks?" "Oh, yes," I said. Then, to myself, I said, "I'll write a story." So, living rather luxuriously, I wrote a story for [the actress] Clara Kimball Young. I sent it in the post, and it was bought by the

Garson Studio by return post for a $100 check. That was nothing, but $100 in 1919 when I was only twenty years old!—that was quite nice. So I thought: I won't cash the check, I'll send a telegram. I sent a telegram that said, "Offer accepted—providing I am given proper screen recognition." That's called "screen credit." So I had my name on a picture [*The Better Wife* in 1919]. I couldn't have done a better thing.

Harry Garson came to San Francisco on another job, and I went to the St. Francis Hotel to meet him. The bellman looked in his box and said, "His key is here so he is out somewhere, but he'll be back." I saw the long, legal-sized envelopes waiting for him, and I knew the man he handed those to would be Harry Garson. I sat in the lobby, getting cross-eyed watching two entrances, and finally a very handsome man came in and got the letters.

I skidded over to him. "Are you Harry Garson?" "Yes." "I'm Lenore Coffee." "Are you the girl who wrote the story? Where did you learn to write so well for the movies?" "I didn't know I did." "You wrote a perfect, professional script. Where did you learn how?" he asked. I said, "Seeing pictures." He said, "You must come to Hollywood." I said, "I can't afford to. I have myself and my mother to support." He said, "Well, I have hunches and sometimes they're right. I think you're going to go a long way in this business. I'll pay your fare and your mother's fare to Hollywood. I'll give you $50 a week on a year's contract with one provision: that you don't write for anyone else." And that's how I got to Hollywood.

How long was that first story you wrote?

Twelve pages.

What happened next?

I'll tell you what happened when we arrived. It's very funny. As my mother and I went from the train to the hotel, we saw a billboard advertising a farewell ball for Clara Kimball Young. I found out she and Harry Garson had left for New York, and I was stranded. I didn't know what to do. I remembered my father had a banker friend, so I went to him. He said, "Well, we have a man who just opened an account here. He used to have a moviehouse, but he is going into producing pictures. His name is Louis B. Mayer. I'll give you a letter of introduction to him." So Louis B. Mayer was the first person I worked for. I told him I had a picture released already with Clara Kimball Young. I could say I was a professional writer. He gave me a job. He said, "I can't pay you $50, but I'll pay you $30." I said, "Yes."

Anita Stewart was one of his stars. I was there only a few weeks, working on one of her pictures, when the telephone rang and I answered it—because there was no staff there in those days. It was

Harry Garson. He said, "Where the hell have you been? I've got $400 back salary for you. You'd better come and get it." I said, "Where do I come to?" He gave me the address—it was right near the studio of the Keystone Cops. So I was still under contract to Harry Garson. When I reported this to Louis B. Mayer, he called me ungrateful, and it made him into an enemy of mine. But everybody fought with Louis B. Mayer, sooner or later.

After a period of time Clara and Harry decided to close down the studio, and Harry Garson said to me, "What will you do?" I said, "I am going to go out and edit and title pictures and charge $1,000 a picture." Harry said, "Do you think you'll get it?" Clara, bless her heart, said, "She'll get it." And I did just that for about two years at the Buster Keaton studio. Then I got a call from Irving Thalberg. When Irving Thalberg first came out to Hollywood—Carl Laemmle brought him out to Universal—he was not yet twenty-one. He couldn't [legally] sign contracts. He was very Italian-looking. Put him in Italian Renaissance clothes, and he would look like an Italian prince. A genius—I don't use the word lightly. He was enormously dignified—always addressed us as "ladies and gentlemen."

On a Saturday when he was just new, Thalberg sent for me. He said, "Miss Coffee, I understand you're very accomplished at tightening and editing and titling. How would you like to come here and be a writer?" I said, "Mr. Thalberg, I have titled and I have written original stories, but I have never written a script. I think you ought to know that." He said, "Oh, heck, you title well, and if you write originals you can write a script." I said, "I'm not sure. Can I think about it until Monday?" And I could see he was quite surprised.

When I got back to where I was editing and titling a picture, there was a note from Bayard Veiller at Metro, whom I had met briefly and who wanted to see me straightaway. I went to see him that afternoon. He made me the same offer—only with more money. I said, "It's odd, but I just had the same offer today—from Irving Thalberg. But I think at this stage of my career I'm better off with a playwright than a producer, however clever." So I took the Veiller offer. The money didn't really interest me. I knew talking pictures were coming, and I wanted to learn how to write dialogue. So I rang Mr. Thalberg on Monday morning and told him my decision. I don't think he ever quite forgave me. Well, I worked with Bayard Veiller for two years and had a marvelous time. I learned to write dialogue. I learned to write a *play*. Then we split up because Bayard went back to New York and wrote *The Trial of Mary Dugan*, which was a big success.

Cecil B. DeMille

Everybody called him Chief or CB. I never called him anything but Mr. DeMille. I loved working with him. It was very stimulating. Mr. DeMille was regarded as the writer of sexy comedies, but his older brother William was five times worse. Mr. DeMille did write a few stories that were sexy, but he wasn't that kind of man really. He was very religious, deeply religious.

Mr. DeMille came to me and said, "I have a very tough assignment for you—called *The Volga Boatman* [1926]. Someone [Konrad Bercovici] had done a skeleton treatment. After I read it, I said, "Mr. DeMille, I have never worked for you, and I don't know how you attack a picture. But when you have a story like this, founded on capitalism and communism, you have to *prove* something." He said, "What do you think we have to prove?" I said, "I think you have to prove both behave equally badly when they are in power." He got very excited and said, "That's wonderful! How will you do it?" We did it very easily. In one scene when the capitalists attack a boat, the Bolsheviks put the nobility to the oars—women in jewels put to the oars. It was a good idea, and it proved something.

While I was working on *The Volga Boatman,* Mr. DeMille was preparing *King of Kings* [1927], a very elaborate story about Jesus Christ. He wanted me to work on it, we were getting along so well. I said, "No, Mr. DeMille, it's not for me. H. B. Warner's not my idea of Christ; he's getting on to sixty. Jesus Christ was a young man in his thirties, a carpenter. If Harry Warner picked up a hammer, he'd drop it on his toes." So I didn't do it. Instead, Jeannie MacPherson wrote it. She always called herself "Janie," although she spelled it Jeannie. That was a love affair—at least in the beginning. Or if it wasn't love, it was propinquity. I liked her. I thought she was a very good writer. And I think she knew what Mr. DeMille wanted.

Years later [in 1939], my husband and I—who had never collaborated before—wrote a very simple story about Jesus Christ called *Family Portrait.* It was a play about Jesus and his family—Joseph, his foster father; Mary, his mother; and Mary Magdalene. It had a wonderful scene of Mary, who was so eager for news of her son that she listened breathlessly to Mary Magdalene telling her stories of him. It played on Broadway [originally in 1939, with at least two subsequent revivals], but the Church didn't like it very much. Mr. DeMille happened to be in New York and saw it, and I got a telegram from him: "I have seen *Family Portrait.* I went into the theatre with a chip on my shoulder and came out on my knees." Isn't that wonderful? It shows the generous nature he had.

The Fixer-Upper

During these years I became known as a fixer-upper. I always had a flair for finding what was wrong with a film or the first cut. Once, Sam Goldwyn had shot the ending for a film and didn't know why the ending had happened—why the girl was kidnapped by bandits in her wedding dress. I was working on *The Volga Boatman* with Mr. DeMille at the time. Mr. Goldwyn rang Mr. DeMille, and said, "I understand Miss Coffee is very good when one has such problems." Mr. DeMille said, "That's not what she's doing for me, but she is very good at that; she has lots of ideas." So Mr. Goldwyn telephoned me at the hillside house I had rented and told me he had all these people under contract and the film underway, and he described the problem. I don't know why, but I suddenly got an idea. I jumped. "Of course! Of course! The right of the first night!" Goldwyn said, "What is that?" I said, "This is a story about a Spanish duke, correct? Well, there was a law in those days that if a nobleman saw an attractive bride, he had the right of the first night. It's called *le droit de seigneur.*"

I don't know why George Fitzmaurice, the director, who was half French and half Irish, didn't think of it first. When Mr. Goldwyn brought him over, I said, "Mr. Fitzmaurice, you're half French—why didn't you think of *le droit du seigneur?*" He jumped up and said "My God!" and waltzed me up and down the room, kissing me and saying, "She's done it, Sam, she's done it!" Very excited. Sam said, "I don't believe you." I said, "Let's ring up a library or a museum." We did just that, and Mr. Goldwyn asked the librarian, "What do you have on *le droit du seigneur?*" The librarian said, "Oh, I think we've got about nine or ten books." That settled that.

Irving Thalberg used to call me in quite often. When MGM was doing *Rasputin* [*Rasputin and the Empress,* 1932], he asked me to read the script. He said, "What do you think?" I said, "Mr. Thalberg, it's so obvious, I'm surprised you didn't think of it yourself. Rasputin didn't succeed because he was so clever. It was because they were all so damned stupid." "Oh," he said, "as usual, you've put your finger on it." I did have a flair for that. It didn't make me particularly intelligent. It was instinct, like having an ear for music.

How often did you do something like that without receiving credit?

Oh, I got credit sometimes. Additional dialogue, they would call it. One day a man rang me up and said, "Miss Coffee, if they put your name on my picture, they'll think you wrote it." "Well, I didn't write it," I said, "I just wrote some dialogue." He said, "Everybody'll think that's what made the picture." I said, "Are you asking me to give you my credit?" He said, "Yes." I said, "I've heard the age of chivalry is gone, and now I believe it." And I hung up.

With or without credit, how many pictures did you work on during the silent era?

I suppose, eighty to eighty-five.

What happened to your career when talking pictures arrived?

I flourished.

Why?

I'm not sure, but I'll tell you something interesting. A silent film was like writing a novel, and a script was like writing a play. That's why women dropped out. Women had been good novelists, but in talking pictures women were not predominant. You can't tell me the name of one good woman dramatist.

Lillian Hellman.

That's what I was going to say. She was the only one.

What was the difference between the form of a silent script and a talking script?

Very little. You wrote much more description in a silent film, much more business—"He goes and closes the window," and so on.

Did you sell many stories just by telling them verbally?

I sold many stories just by telling them. I was a good actress and would have become an actress if my parents were not opposed to it when I was young. For example: when I was young, contraceptives were unheard of. Birth control was something you did after, not before. In those days there was a very popular item advertised called a "whirling spray," a form of douche. I was so good at selling stories that one day, when I was telling a story to a producer, a man walked by and said, "Don't listen. You'll find yourself buying it. She could sell a whirling spray to a nun."

I had a lot of things to overcome—a dreadful speech impediment, bad eyesight before I had my cataract operation. And I woke up stone deaf in one ear one morning after being thrown from a horse Christmas Eve day and have never heard in it since. Also, I suffered from a nervous disease. I used to excuse myself from meetings at the studio, slip out to the bathroom, and shoot myself in the arm with a hypodermic of medicine. I was very good with a needle, as they say.

After a while did you begin to specialize in women's stories?

Yes. Joan Crawford and Bette Davis. Irving Thalberg called me in one day and said, "I'm going to give you a very tough assignment but I think you can do it. Joan Crawford has done all these flapper stories, and she's getting on to twenty-five. I've got to get a new personality for her. So I want you to write something that will give her a new personality."

The three Lane sisters (Rosemary, Lola, and Priscilla) and Gale Page in a pose from Four Daughters. *For her screenplay, Lenore Coffee shared an Oscar nomination with Julius J. Epstein—although they never worked together.*

Her co-star was going to be Clark Gable. When I was working on *Chicago* [1927] for Mr. DeMille, Clark Gable turned up in the road company in Los Angeles. He was perfect for the part of the reporter; I knew how to pick people. I begged Mr. DeMille to take a look at him in the play because Mr. DeMille had never made a male star, and this man, I told him, was going to be big. After the show had moved on, I rang him up, and Mr. DeMille said, "I was editing *The King of Kings;* I wasn't in the mood." Mr. DeMille never went to the theatre. I said, "Mr. DeMille, you wouldn't take that excuse from me." It was the only time we ever had words.

Now in this movie, which was called *Possessed* [1931], Gable played the leading man; and I gave Joan Crawford a whole new personality. It was a very successful picture. Thalberg said to me once, "The only trouble is, she's been playing it [the same character] ever since."

Incidentally, Clarence Brown was a wonderful director. He had never tasted liquor. His mother was a ferocious teetotaler, so he didn't even know what liquor tasted like. He'd say, "My cocktail is to go to the barbershop and to get a wet hotpack on my face."

I met him one day coming out of Louis B. Mayer's office, and he told me Mr. Mayer had just been telling him how much he liked the picture we had done. Mr. Brown said, "I told him, 'Give me writers like Lenore Coffee, and I'll give you stuff like that all the time.'" I put my hand on his shoulder, and I said, "Goodbye, Clarence." He said, "What do you mean?" I said, "I'll never work for you again. This is a producer's studio. They don't like teams of writers-directors." And I never worked for him again.

You were still called in as a fixer-upper now and then?

Yes. Eddie Mannix [an MGM executive producer], who always liked my work, called me in after Cary Grant had refused to do a picture called *Suzy* [1936]. This was in the days of block-booking, when they sold the pictures before they were made. This picture was supposed to be with Jean Harlow—only Cary wouldn't play it. So I was called in; I was often called in on people who were having trouble.

Cary was one of the handsomest men you'd ever seen in your life—very chocolate-brown eyes, handsome beyond belief, marvelous personality. But he looked rigid; he wasn't going to play the part. So I said, "Mr. Grant, this is Saturday. Do you have any plans for the afternoon?" He said, "No." I said, "Well, will you do this? I will get someone to give us a room. You will have a script, and I will have a script. We will go through it one page at a time, and you will tell me what you won't do under any conditions and what you might do, and I'll make suggestions."

He got up and I thought, "My God, he's leaving!" No—he said, "Where's the room?" So we went through the script page by page. I always do this, by the way; it's a fabulous way to work. I'd say, "Suppose he did this? I could do that. Couldn't we turn it this way? That speech doesn't belong here. Why don't we put it somewhere else?" Cary rather enjoyed it. About two hours later he said, "I think we're getting somewhere—although we wouldn't be without your help." We finished and he signed the contract. I should have gotten a very big bonus, but I was under contract, on salary, so I got nothing.

Eddie Mannix called me in and said, "You produced this picture, you know. You were on the set at least half a dozen times a day. You saw the dailies, you saw the first cut. How would you like to be a producer here?" I said, "Eddie, you like my work, don't you? That's because I come fresh to it every morning. If I spent the night before in the back of those gangster Cadillacs full of cigar smoke, I wouldn't come fresh to it. I think it is more important that I preserve the quality of my work than flatter my vanity by being a producer."

Ultimately, why did you leave MGM?

I had written a very good story called "The Stepmother," which the studio wanted to buy. But I had written it on my own time. I said, "I want $5,000." Louis B. Mayer sent for me and flew into a rage and said, "You'll take something or other or get the hell out of this studio." A very violent scene. I said, "Mr. Mayer, please control yourself. This is not a family meeting. I understand you do this with your family, but you cannot do it with me." He said, "You are just what I always thought you were—a cold-blooded, mercenary woman." And I left the studio. Once, long afterwards at a preview, I met him, and he said, "You weren't gray then!" And I said, "Nor were you!"

Charles Vidor

I had a very wonderful experience with [director] Charlie Vidor. Eddie Small [a producer] was a rather ignorant man, but he had inklings and hunches. "I think something's wrong here," he would say, "you know?" I liked him very much. He had a hunch about *My Son, My Son!* [1940], and he bought it. He had never bought an elegant story before. And he asked me to write the script. Charlie Vidor worked with me on the script; some directors do. Then he discovered I was not going to be on the set throughout the shooting. He had thought I was going to be holding his hand all the way through. He practically had hysteria. I said, "Look Charlie, I'm not going to Siam, I'm just going to Warner Brothers."

It was his first important picture. Brian Aherne was playing the lead. "I need you!" he told me, "What am I going to do without you?" I said, "I'll tell you what I'm going to do. I'm going back to the studio. But I'll keep a copy of *My Son, My Son!* on my desk, and I'll put another binder on it so no one sees what it is. If you have any problem, go to your secretary, and she will ring me and say, 'Turn to page such-and-such, Miss Coffee. Mr. Aherne can't get out of the room on that long speech.' Then give me five minutes and I'll ring you back." We did that through the whole picture. Charlie Vidor sent me a huge box of flowers when the picture opened, and Brian Aherne, for the first time ever, sent me a telegram, "I hope my performance will be worthy of your script."

Warner Brothers

When you worked at Warner Brothers, did you work at the studio or at home?

Always at home. I had an office where I went occasionally to dictate, but I usually worked at home. At first they told me I couldn't work at home, I had to work at the studio, so I played a little trick. I wrote the first twenty pages of my first script very, very quickly and turned them in. Then I let some time pass and turned in six pages. They said, "Where's the rest?" I said, "I can't work away from home. Let's call it off." They liked the first pages I sent so much that they told me I could work at home. In those days I did a good deal of longhand. Right after breakfast, I used to sit in a comfortable chair and write in longhand.

Did you have a choice of the stories you wanted to write?

They'd ask me if I approved of a story or liked it or wanted to do it. I didn't do anything I didn't want to do. If I wanted to do it, they had to talk to my agent. I got paid quite a lot of money. You'd get pictures that they thought were up your street. They'd say, "This would be a good Coffee script. She'd be good on that." One man would say, "Who's working on the script?" Another, "Coffee." Another would say, "Good, she knows box office." I got along very well at Warner Brothers because of a producer named Henry Blanke, who always called me "Coffee darling." He would say, "We are in trouble, what do we do now, Coffee darling?"

Were there many other women writers at Warner Brothers?

They did not have women writers at Warners. They were *a-ginst.*

Was that difficult for you—working primarily with men?

No. I'm not afraid of men.

How about the writers you collaborated with? Julius J. Epstein [on Four Daughters *in 1938]?*

I don't believe I've ever met Mr. Epstein.

John Van Druten? Your collaborator on Old Acquaintance *[in 1943]?*

He wrote the play. I never worked with him directly. After a certain point in my career, I rarely collaborated. Bayard Veiller urged me never to collaborate. He said, "You will pick up the other writer's style too quickly and spoil your own style." When I was working with him, he told me once, "Now that's the best goddamned Bayard Veiller speech ever written—but I didn't write it, you did." So I tried not to collaborate.

Why do you think you wrote so well for Bette Davis and Joan Crawford?

I knew them very well. I knew their temperaments. Bette was very intelligent, well-educated; Joan was not. Bette came from a good family and was a trained theatre actress. Joan had taught herself to speak; and she spoke very well. I had great admiration for her.

Were they wholly interchangeable as actresses? Could you write the same story for either of them?

Oh, I could, but I didn't.

What was the difference in how you would alter the stories?

The difference was entirely in the dialogue. Bette spits out her words, Joan doesn't. I gave Bette short sentences, short speeches.

How about their characterizations?

Not exactly alike but very similar.

How would you distinguish between them?

I think Joan would be more susceptible. I think Bette could be pretty tough.

Were they equally skilled as actresses?

In different ways.

At this point in your career—you were so successful—why didn't you break away and write other plays?

After *Family Portrait* I wanted to. In the 1940s I wrote a play at night and wanted very badly to do it on Broadway. Ruth Gordon read the play and agreed to do it. The Theatre Guild wanted to do it. But I had just gotten an extension of my contract, and my agent said, "You can't get an extension of your contract one day and ask for a leave of absence the next." And [the director] Eddie Goulding was making a picture, and he wanted me on it. So I had to return to Warners. Sometimes your friends can be your enemies.

Graham Greene

I like Graham Greene very much. He's a convert to Catholicism, too. He said something once that I will always remember, "I wouldn't want a God I could understand." I have never forgotten that. That's rather true. *The End of the Affair* [1955] is a very good book. I wrote a beautiful script; but they got somebody in England to rewrite it, and it wasn't an improvement. I opened with the ending, the separation—after they had already stopped seeing each other—and then I backtracked to show what led to the separation. I reversed the order of the novel. Later, I met Graham Greene in England—only once. I said to him, "I had the dubious pleasure of writing the script for one of your films." He laughed and said, "Dubious pleasure! I like that very much."

Weep No More

My first book was very good. It was called *Weep No More*—after an old poem, "Weep no more, sad fountains . . ." In America, they changed the title to *Another Time, Another Place* [1958], if you can make any sense out of that. It was about a clever woman columnist—called "Sara Scott Says"—and they got that sexpot Lana Turner to play the lead in the movie. It stunk. It was just dreadful.

Looking Back

Did being a Catholic influence your writing?

I don't know. I was nearly twenty when I converted. I'm not really religious. I'm *attracted* to religion. I think my own life influenced me more.

Did certain writers influence you as a young girl?

To show you how irreligious I was, the Elsie Dinsmore books [a series of children's books written by Martha Finley under the pen name of Martha Farquharson] were my favorites. My daughter found a copy of one once and told me, "Mother, you couldn't possibly have taken these seriously." But I did. I won $500 in a lottery on a ten-cent ticket, and the first thing I did was to buy a set of Elsie books. I read the Alcott books and boy's books—written for boys. I didn't read a lot of books because I was easily made unhappy. I still can cry at a movie. I have an emotional nature. I am easily moved. They say, "Easy smiler, easy weeper." And that's true. I also smile very easily.

Would you write to make other people cry?

No. I wrote the way I felt, and the way I felt is an easy way to cry.

Why were you so good, particularly, at women's stories?

Because I am a woman and I knew women.

Did you put something characteristic of you into each story?

I made them [the heroines] suffer a little.

Then, what?

Well, it depends. If it's a man that's making them suffer, I might make the man rather noble and have him admit he was wrong. It's hard to say what I might do. I've never analyzed myself very much, really.

What kind of an ending did you strive for?

Oh, happy endings—always.

Why is that?

I don't do it purposely. I tend to want things to end happily. Things did not always happen happily for me in real life.

Yes. The more you tell me about your own life, the more I realize that there are aspects in it of disappointment, soap opera, and tragedy.

Yes. I'm sorry.

Why did you leave Hollywood at the end of the 1950s?

I wanted to live in England. I was going to write plays and novels. Then my husband died.

That was over twenty years ago. Why did you not return until now?

I didn't have the courage to go back alone to where I'd been so happy, so I just stayed on in England for the better of twenty years.

How do you look back on your time in Hollywood?

I look back on my forty years in Hollywood with nothing but pleasure. If you can work forty years in Hollywood without getting your throat cut, you can count yourself lucky.

Philip Dunne:
Fine Cabinetmaker

Interview by Tina Daniell

Careless usage has bled the word *gentleman* of nearly all distinguished connotations. But in the old-fashioned and best sense of the word, there is no more appropriate way to describe Philip Dunne.

I first made Dunne's acquaintance at a belated tribute to the Twentieth Century–Fox studio chief Darryl Zanuck, which was held at the University of Southern California more than a year after Zanuck's death. The affair was overlong and surprisingly ill planned. Clips of films that Zanuck supervised were shown without identification and in ragged condition. Many of the people rounded up to pay tribute to the colorful executive confessed that they had not known him intimately, although actor John Payne did admit to having followed Zanuck into a men's bathroom on the Fox lot to make a pitch for a role in *Sentimental Journey*. (He got it.)

Dunne's presence on the dais rescued the evening from the realm of the absurd. Having spent almost his entire professional life as a screenwriter and, eventually, a director at Fox, Dunne knew Zanuck well. He offered up a rich selection of anecdotes that revealed both liking and respect for the cigar-chomping mogul from Wahoo, Nebraska.

Even though Dunne shares most of his screenplay credits with other writers, he usually wrote alone. In a sense Zanuck was his true collaborator. Except for a few blind spots—casting was one, Dunne says—Zanuck had good filmmaking instincts, and Dunne thrived in a business he loved under Zanuck's guidance.

When Dunne entered the world of motion pictures, filmwriting was still a faintly disreputable line of work for someone of his East Coast literary credentials—his father was the well-known humorist Finley Peter Dunne, creator of the political pundit Mr. Dooley—but Dunne took to the field with great zest. During his half century in Hollywood, he never won an Oscar. But he did work on a variety of notable films such as *The Rains Came* (1939), *Stanley and Livingstone* (1939), *How Green Was My Valley* (1941), *The Ghost and Mrs. Muir* (1947), *Pinky* (1949), and *Ten North Frederick* (1958) that were influential as well as popular. Almost all of his work involved adaptation of one sort or another—a limitation he acknowledges and one that undoubtedly contributes to his oft-stated view that screenwriting is a *craft,* not an art.

In the years immediately following Zanuck's 1956 ouster by Fox's New York executives, Dunne stayed on at the studio, writing, directing, and producing. In 1965 he moved to Universal, where he performed in similar capacities. Then, in 1972, Dunne took a break from moviemaking activity to nurse his wife, the former actress Amanda Duff, back to health after a serious illness. He never returned to screenwriting.

A lifelong liberal activist (he was a volunteer speech writer for a number of Democratic candidates, including Adlai Stevenson and JFK, and he was a principal organizer of the anti-blacklist Committee for the First Amendment), Dunne continues to write for newspapers and magazines on the subject of politics. His wide-ranging interests take him afield at times. Not long ago, in *Harvard Magazine* (Dunne is an alumnus), he published a defense of empiricism that was also a critique of Ronald Reagan's political and religious dogmatism. The day I interviewed Dunne, he had just finished a remembrance of fighter Jack Dempsey for his column for *The Los Angeles Herald Examiner.*

Astronomy is another avocation. Dunne has a large telescope set up at his Malibu residence, a modernistic house that he and his wife helped design, which is situated on the bluffs overlooking the Pacific Ocean. On the night of the Academy Awards, one is as likely to find Dunne gazing at the stars through his telescope as at their counterfeits on television.

1934   *The Count of Monte Cristo* (Rowland V. Lee). Co-script.
        Student Tour (Charles F. Riesner). Co-script.

1935   *Helldorado* (James Cruze). Uncredited contribution.
        The Melody Lingers On (David Burton). Co-script, co-dialogue.

1936   *The Last of the Mohicans* (George B. Seitz). Script.

1937   *Breezing Home* (Milton Carruth). Screen story.
        Lancer Spy (Gregory Ratoff). Script.

Philip Dunne in Malibu, 1984. (Photo: Alison Morley)

1938   *Suez* (Allan Dwan). Co-script.

1939   *Stanley and Livingstone* (Henry King). Co-script.
The Rains Came (Clarence Brown). Co-script.
Swanee River (Sidney Lanfield). Co-script.

1940   *Johnny Apollo* (Henry Hathaway). Co-script.

1941   *How Green Was My Valley* (John Ford). Script.

1942   *Son of Fury* (John Cromwell). Script.

1947   *The Late George Apley* (Joseph Mankiewicz). Script.
The Ghost and Mrs. Muir (Joseph Mankiewicz). Script.
Forever Amber (Otto Preminger). Co-script.

1948   *Escape* (Joseph Mankiewicz). Script.
The Luck of the Irish (Henry Koster). Script.

1949   *Pinky* (Elia Kazan). Co-script.

1951   *David and Bathsheba* (Henry King). Screen story, script.
Anne of the Indies (Jacques Tourneur). Co-script.

1952   *Lydia Bailey* (Jean Negulesco). Co-script.
Way of a Gaucho (Jacques Tourneur). Script, producer.

1953	*The Robe* (Henry Koster). Script.
1954	*Demetrius and the Gladiators* (Delmer Daves). Story, script. *The Egyptian* (Michael Curtiz). Co-script.
1955	*Prince of Players* (Philip Dunne). Director, producer. *The View from Pompey's Head* (Philip Dunne). Script, director, producer.
1956	*Hilda Crane* (Philip Dunne). Script, director.
1957	*Three Brave Men* (Philip Dunne). Script, director.
1958	*Ten North Frederick* (Philip Dunne). Script, director. *In Love and War* (Philip Dunne). Director.
1959	*Blue Denim* (Philip Dunne). Co-script, director.
1961	*Wild in the Country* (Philip Dunne). Director.
1962	*Lisa* (Philip Dunne). Director.
1965	*The Agony and the Ecstasy* (Carol Reed). Screen story, script.
1966	*Blindfold* (Philip Dunne). Co-script, director.

Nonfiction includes: *Mr. Dooley Remembers* and (autobiography) *Take Two*.

Academy Awards include an Oscar nomination in 1941 for the screenplay of *How Green Was My Valley* and a nomination in 1951 for the story and screenplay of *David and Bathsheba*.

Writers Guild Awards include the Laurel Award for Achievement in 1961.

Before coming to Hollywood you never really thought of writing as a career. Why is that?

Well, I have a confession. I'm not very inventive. My father used to complain about modern authors, saying they didn't make things up. Neither did he, really, because he was a satirist. He took what was there, happening in the world, and satirized it. He made things up, wonderful things, but he didn't make up stories with plots and characters. And I'm not good at that either. So the movies were just perfect for me because usually I was adapting. Even my original screenplays were based on something, like say *David and Bathsheba* [1951], which was based on one paragraph in the Old Testament. It's a two-hour movie, so I had to make up a lot but not the basic story.

I never thought I could make a living as a writer. Neither did my father, who knew how tough it was, and he was the most highly paid writer of his time. He knew writing wasn't for everybody, and he probably thought none of his sons, the three of us, had any chance to make it as a writer. I was more or less pitchforked into it by the Depression. I had to have a job of some sort; it happened to be as a reader at Fox, and then, of course, it was a natural progression.

But you had moved out to Los Angeles with the idea of getting a job?

Not necessarily in the movies. I moved out here because I had sinusitis, and the doctor recommended a warm climate, either Dallas or Los Angeles. Well, we knew more people in Los Angeles. The people I knew here were the people I played polo with in the East before the Crash. I was unhorsed by the Crash. Actually, I tried to get a job in a bank or with an oil company, anything. But, of course, in 1930 there was nothing. I also had letters to studio heads. I had a letter from [the Broadway impresario] Florenz Ziegfeld and one from Quinn Martin, who had been the movie critic at the old *New York World* where my brother worked. The letter from Quinn Martin was to [the West Coast studio executive] Winnie Sheehan at Fox, and Winnie gave me a job as a reader at $35 a week. I thought it was good pay.

Had you thought much about movies before you came to Los Angeles?

No, not at all. I liked to go to the movies. I liked to take a girl to the movies on Sunday. It was just something you did. But I thought movies were quite frivolous. The older generation of my time had no feeling of respect for movies. You have to pay respect now; it's an art. But to my parents and their friends, the movies were low-down popular entertainment. They didn't care much for movies.

The only time I had movies treated seriously was when a Harvard professor of mine, a fine arts professor, took his class of six—it was a class in Renaissance sculpture of all things—to see *Flesh and the Devil* [1927] at the Paramount Theatre in Boston so we could look on Garbo as a perfect classical face. Very interesting. It was the first I could imagine a professor being interested in the movies. It had never occurred to me.

How did you make the transition from reader to writer?

Well, I was unemployed, and an unemployed reader couldn't do much of anything. I had a lot of help from different people—there's a tremendous increment of luck in it. You have to be in the right place at the right time, meet the right person. I had a lot of luck, and one stroke of luck was that [the pioneer mogul and producer] Jesse Lasky liked my stuff. He gave me the first real boost. And Rowland Lee, the director, gave me the second one when he pulled me in on *The Count of Monte Cristo* [1934].

Was that the first real writing you had done?

Well, I had been editor of my school paper, so I had that. But I really hadn't tried writing anything. I was interested in about everything else except doing anything useful up to that point.

What did being a reader teach you about being a screenwriter?

A great deal. I hate to admit this, but we got nothing but the worst stuff; all the good books and plays went through the New York readers' department. We got the pathetic originals written by out-of-work screenwriters. I kept seeing ways that I thought I could improve them. I'd write a synopsis, and I'd make it better. I couldn't help it. It would be an obvious thing that the guy had missed. And when you learn to synopsize a story, you learn to construct it. At the same time, I was moonlighting writing short stories, so all these things came together.

You wrote in your autobiography that you never read The Count of Monte Cristo *before writing the screenplay.*

Still haven't. *The Count of Monte Cristo* was a going thing when I was taken on, and Rowland Lee was really the lead writer as well as the director. We'd block out scenes, and then I'd write them or, in some cases, he did. I was put into the straitjacket of his treatment—a good straitjacket—but there it was, and there was no way to go around it.

What was the most important thing you learned from Rowland Lee?

Never leave a scene by the same door you came in. Every scene should advance the story. The other thing, which I already knew really, was to let the characters tell the story. Don't try and make the characters fit into a preconceived idea. Rather, see how the characters develop the story. The thing he didn't teach me was to be brief, because he always wanted things to be longer.

How much of your work in Hollywood was adaptation?

I had four original screenplays. One was *David and Bathsheba*. One was *The Agony and the Ecstasy* [1965], because I used nothing of the book [by Irving Stone] at all. My idea was not one man but two, the Pope and the artist. I called it Quirt and Flagg in the Sistine Chapel. One was *Demetrius and the Gladiators* [1954], where we had a lot of sets, costumes, and actors left over from *The Robe* [1953], so we cooked up a sequel. And one was *Breezing Home* [1937].

You rarely collaborated.

The collaborations I had were with Julien Josephson on three pictures: *Suez* [1938], *Stanley and Livingstone* [1939], and *The Rains Came* [1939]. Then, over my dead body, they let Julien go. I tried to dissuade Zanuck, but he said, "No, you can do it by yourself." It was very sad because Julien had been there a long time. Then, with Ring

Lardner, Jr., I collaborated on the final script of *Forever Amber* [1947], which I prefer not to mention. The last time was with Edith Somers on *Blue Denim* [1959], which I also directed. That was [the writer-producer] Charlie Brackett's idea. She had just done a play in New York, *A Roomful of Roses*, about teenagers, and he thought she had a good eye and ear for it. Those were the only real collaborations.

How did you become partners with Julien Josephson?

Zanuck. He teamed us. See, Julien had been a silent writer for Charles Ray, and he had been doing Shirley Temple and George Arliss pictures. Zanuck's idea was that I was green but probably could do something, and Julien would be the steadying hand. That was the set-up. So there was some logic in Zanuck letting Julien go when he did. At that point he said I didn't need a gyroscope anymore. Julien was a delightful fellow. He came from Roseburg, Oregon. He was almost a perfect small-town puritan. I remember Darryl saying to him once, "You can't always be right, Julien. Sometimes I have to be right." Julien was like a bulldog, very stubborn, and he would not deviate from what he thought was correct. I found that his taste was excellent. If he didn't like a scene, I never fought very hard for it. I knew there was something wrong.

What was the difference between collaboration and writing on your own?

It depends on whom I was collaborating with. We might spend a week just talking about one thing, making notes. A long novel like *The Rains Came*, for example—we had to drop a lot of material. We had to decide, first of all, what we were going to zero in on. It's usually true in adapting a novel that you discard something like 90 percent of what the author wrote unless you're talking about a thing like *The Ghost and Mrs. Muir* [1947], which is a very short novel. I had to expand it. With Julien I used to do all the first writing, and then he would act as editor and condenser and put in ideas of his own. I would lead and he would follow; then we'd get together and work out a final draft. One or the other of us would be working on a pad. I never did learn to use a typewriter, so I wrote in longhand. I still do.

Longhand on a yellow legal pad?

The only taste I share with Richard M. Nixon. Then, with Edith Somers, since I was directing, we would work out the scene together— we were working from a play so we didn't have to do an awful lot of writing. Then she would be the one who blocked it out, and I would act as the editor. With Ring, I really forget how we worked. We both had great distaste for the material. I think we divided it up because the steam was on. They had stopped the picture, and they wanted to get it restarted as soon as possible.

Did you ever work with the author of the original piece on an adaptation? For example, John O'Hara?

Yes. I sent him my script [for *Ten North Frederick,* 1958], and he approved of it. We were friends—I had known O'Hara for many years, since the 1930s—so maybe he was predisposed. John at that time was trying to catch on as a screenwriter, but he never did crack it. His métier was elsewhere. He hated *Butterfield 8* [1960] and *From the Terrace* [1960], the other two [movies adapted from his books]. So did I. But he really liked *Ten North Frederick,* although he didn't like Geraldine Fitzgerald in the part [of the wife, Edith Chapin] because he thought she was too beautiful, and he believed that people who were ugly outside were ugly inside. Crazy idea.

I thought it was O'Hara's best novel. I thought it had great compassion in it. I looked at the book and decided the key to the thing—only a few pages in the four-hundred-page novel—was Joe Chapin's affair with his daughter's roommate. That's what the story's about. Everything has to build to that and then flow away from it. So I made that the centerpiece. The most difficult aspect of adapting is to stay with the original author's style, and when you're dealing with a real stylist like O'Hara or the King James Old Testament, that's tough.

In adapting a novel did you usually attempt to pull out the dramatic focus?

You had to because a novel is such a big sprawling thing. *How Green Was My Valley* [1941] is a case in point. There I had no way of making a solid dramatic first act, second act, third act. It had to be an episodic picture. There was no way for it not to be. I prefer to work in acts if I can.

Is How Green Was My Valley *your favorite script?*

It has to be *How Green Was My Valley,* not only because of the result, but because it was a happy picture from the beginning. I felt it was all mine. There had been other writers on it, but I didn't use their stuff.

You've said it is as much William Wyler's picture as John Ford's. Why?

Well, Jack was a replacement director. Willy Wyler had been on until the New York office killed the project. For example, the decision to tell the story in flashback was made two years before Jack had ever heard of the project. Jack did a marvelous job, but he didn't think that up. Willy did half the director's job, and Ford did the other half. Ford did the actual shooting of a script that Willy had prepared. Again, Willy made very few changes in the script that was first sent to him. Willy was such a perfectionist, though, that we'd spend a week on a line.

Donald Crisp, Roddy McDowall, and Walter Pidgeon in a tableau from John Ford's How Green Was My Valley, *Philip Dunne's favorite screenplay.*

In what ways is How Green Was My Valley *different because Ford directed it?*

There are a lot of obvious ways. I'm not knocking Jack for this, but he let some of the actors go a mile over. Not the principals, but the bit parts. Here's the strange thing: Ford loves stories of strong ties between men. He got that wonderful feeling between brothers beautifully. But I was worried about the love story. Yet this picture is far and away Ford's best love story. The scenes between Angharad [Maureen O'Hara] and Gruffyd [Walter Pidgeon] are lovely scenes. I say so even though three of those scenes were not in the book. These were mine, and I was very fond of them. In one scene, in the kitchen, she says something to him, and he says, "You're a queen wherever you walk." She says, "What does that mean?" He replies, "I have no right." She says, "If the right is mine to give, you have it."

That was a lovely love scene, and Ford got every ounce out of it. Willy couldn't have done it any better. But I think in general he might have been a little more realistic and less sentimental, that's all. And of course, in all of the angles it would have been much more covered. Ford camera-cut it all the way. Then, Ford did things that Willy might not have done that were very effective. Like when the two boys with their packs were leaving for America, with the choir singing outside the house with the other brothers and the little boy Huw [Roddy McDowall] sitting on the bed suddenly realizing that they've gone out of his life—of course I'd written a close-up of Huw watching. Ford never cut in. He played it in a long shot. I don't know if that was deliberate. I never asked him. But what he *didn't* do was brilliant.

Ford was originally slated to direct Pinky *[1949]. Would it have been a different movie if he had directed it instead of Elia Kazan?*

Totally, in this case. Because Ford didn't really understand about black people. He was having Ethel Waters moaning spirituals. Kazan at least had the modern approach, even though Ethel Waters was playing a deliberately old-fashioned character. At least he knew how to treat blacks as human beings, not as aliens. That is why Ford was replaced. Zanuck saw that. Ford came down with an attack of shingles, which was useful all around, let's say. I think he realized himself that he was in over his head. I felt that, even though we had only two conferences on the picture. He just didn't say much. He seemed a little puzzled by it. Kazan had no preparation time at all. One day, and he was on the set.

Was Pinky *a difficult project to bring to the screen?*

When I was brought in there was already an excellent script by Dudley Nichols. But the problem was, he had followed the book. You could hardly blame him for it, but the book and his screenplay were political impossibilities. You couldn't release a picture like that or you would offend blacks and liberal whites.

Dudley Nichols wrote you a letter criticizing your contribution.

Let's say I thought Dudley was guilty of an injustice to a great many people in thinking as he did on the film.

Did you admire him as a screenwriter?

Yes. He did some wonderful screenplays working with Ford, others too. And *Pinky* was a grand screenplay, except it had this fatal flaw, which was really a political flaw not a writing flaw.

You say it was a political not a dramatic flaw?

It became both. The problem was, the issue Pinky faced was whether to become a black activist (we didn't call it black activist then)—to become a member of the NAACP and work for "her people"—or to use her training as a nurse and go along with the system, in effect. No matter how you came down, you were going to offend a lot of people. That's what made it political. Also, dramatically, it was flawed because it had nothing to do with the main theme of the story, which was the ability of this girl to pass for white. Now, when her dilemma becomes instead, "Do I use this house that's been left to me by my godmother, Ethel Waters, as a clinic and use my training to help my people; or do I run off with this white doctor and pass for white for the rest of my life?"—that was a big moral dilemma, and it also applies directly to the thesis of the story. That's why it was much superior dramatically, and it also solved the political problem; nobody could resent her saying, "No, I'm going to stay here, be what I am." You can't live without pride—everybody has to love that. The solution involved radical changes from the book and Dudley's screenplay, but I was able to use pages of his screenplay that were not affected by the changes. So on the screen today, a good part of it is Dudley's screenplay, wholesale. But the nature of Pinky's dilemma was totally transformed by my script.

You've said the script was king at Fox. Was that very different from Warners or MGM?

Yes, very much so because Warners and Metro were both star studios. The script was king at Twentieth because we had no stars to begin with. I think people started out at Warners by saying, "Let's do a Bogart picture." I know at Metro, Thalberg always worked from the star up. Zanuck never had stars in the early days. For *The Rains Came* we had to borrow Myrna Loy and George Brent. For *Stanley and Livingstone* we borrowed Spencer Tracy. For *How Green Was My Valley,* we borrowed Walter Pidgeon, and otherwise it was a totally starless picture.

Shirley Temple was growing up. Will Rogers was killed in Alaska. They made Ty Power a star. Betty Grable—she was not really a star in the Metro sense but a pin-up. Then Don Ameche, Alice Faye, Dan Dailey—that whole group that worked mostly in musicals. Zanuck didn't have that many big dramatic stars.

Does that translate into, you believe there were better scripts written at Fox than at the other studios?

Well (*laughs*), I'm too biased to answer that question, but I certainly do think so. (*Laughs.*)

Today I think that people feel Warners and MGM were more exciting studios, and whereas there were some standout films made at Fox, in general it was home to more pallid filmmaking.

I'm not saying the great bulk of the product was great. The "B" pictures were a big part of the program. I'm saying, for example, that in the twenty years Zanuck was at Fox I think there were five Academy Awards for best director given to Fox pictures. That's one fourth of the directing awards [during that time span]. That's way above our average when you consider Warners, Metro, Goldwyn, Paramount RKO, Selznick, Columbia, and Universal were all making pictures. Two of the awards were won by Ford, two by Joseph Mankiewicz, and

Philip Dunne with Gary Cooper on the set of Ten North Frederick.

one by Elia Kazan. In a discussion like this I tend to think of the top pictures of each studio, and there I think Fox scripts were the best.

In your book and in our conversations, you make it clear that you admire Zanuck. What were his flaws?

Well, all our friends have faults. He was very cruel and would bully people who tended to be pushovers, including some famous directors. If he ever got the idea you were afraid of him, look out; he'd make your life miserable. I don't think he could have operated without a certain amount of tyranny. He always listened, though. You could state your point of view. But when he made a decision, that was final. So his fault was, in a way, a sidebar of his virtue of decisiveness. As a producer, sometimes what we'd call his nervous system would take hold. He would cut into your motivating sequence so you didn't quite understand what the character did in the last reel because the first reel had been chopped up. In most cases I'd have to say he was probably right, that you didn't need all of that stuff. He was terribly impatient to have the story keep moving, always keep moving. Again, it's a fairly good flaw.

Was he literate?

Yes, he was—surprisingly. I started out with the natural assumption that he was a lot stupider than I was because he was a producer. Not so at all. He was an extremely intelligent man. He was not widely read, but he had plenty of people to read for him, so he knew where to go for sources. I think he was like a president who reads the précis of the day's digest. I don't know if he ever read books, but he absorbed information. Of course he was known as the current events producer, especially at Warner Brothers.

I can't say he was a completely well-read man, but if you put a bit of chi-chi into your script, he would find a way to refute it. I remember in my salad days I once wrote, "They were dancing to a Chopin waltz." The next story conference Zanuck was happy to tell me Chopin's music was never danced to, it was too long. It was played on a piano. Obviously, someone in the music department had told him that after reading the script and sending him their critique. So he loved to score against you. But he would score the other way, too. When his son, Dick, was put with me to learn about the business—Dick was a sophomore at Stanford at the time, it was a summer job—he questioned something I said. Darryl turned on him and said, "You may be a Stanford man, but you are questioning the word of a Harvard man." He was very fond of putting in the needle in all conversations.

Did you write with an idea of the audience in mind?

Always. I always believed you had to do your very best, that you never should write down to an audience, and I wonder now if all that is disproved by the popularity of some things going on today. If *Superman* [1978] and *Star Wars* [1977] are what the audience wants, we've got a pretty juvenile audience. I always wrote for the most intelligent people I could think of. I hoped my audience consisted of Albert Einsteins and Albert Schweitzers. Not the New York film critics—a much higher level. (*Laughs.*)

Did Zanuck think that way too?

He told me that once. He said, "Never write down. Do your best, always." And he meant it. He would say sometimes, as producers will, "I don't understand that," meaning an audience won't understand that. It referred to a lack of clarity. Don't ask too much of an audience in understanding an elliptical thing. If you give them a nice round thing, it can be as complex as you like. But make it clear.

In the 1950s when you did the quasi-religious pictures such as The Robe, David and Bathsheba, Demetrius and the Gladiators, *and* The Egyptian *[1954], did you feel that the subject matter was particularly suited to that neo-conservative Eisenhower era?*

This was all Zanuck. I didn't really like those assignments very much. *David and Bathsheba* I liked because I thought it was a modern play, really, and a wonderful chance to write in the grand manner—a lot of it is in blank verse, you know. *The Robe* was strictly a chore. I was hoodwinked into accepting a credit I didn't want. Later on I read an interview with [the blacklisted screenwriter] Albert Maltz in which he said I *took* the credit on *The Robe*. The whole thing was his own doing because the Guild required you to inform people that you are working on something, and he, of course, worked under the table. The producer never told me, and Zanuck never told me, although he must have known. I hold that against him. *The Robe* was a favor for Zanuck.

As for *Demetrius and the Gladiators,* it was kind of fun to see if we could cook up something out of a lot of sets and costumes and characters—use those left over from *The Robe,* those that hadn't been killed off. On *The Egyptians,* Casey Robinson did the first script. It was a pretty good script, but I had read the book and I was quite impressed by it—Mika Waltari wrote it—because it had a love and a feeling for ancient Egypt. Obviously, the man had done a very scholarly book. He had really been into it. The project fascinated a lot of people, but the casting hurt the script.

Zanuck had his flaws, too, and one of them was that he thought all kings, emperors, and nobility should be played by English actors. That was class, you see. I had unofficial status as producer on the picture. I was in on everything. I was actually sent on the set to keep an eye on Curtiz [the director Michael Curtiz]. Before shooting began, there wandered into my office an actor who was sort of gaunt and a strange-looking color—a very interesting fellow. He had a stage reputation. I said to myself, "My gosh, this is Akhenaten. He's the fellow for the weird epileptic emperor." On the same day an agent brought into my office a lovely dark-eyed, swan-necked beauty—an absolute knockout girl. I said, "My God, she looks like Nefertiti." I sent them up to Zanuck, both of them. They got intercepted by Mike Curtiz. The actor was John Cassavetes, a wonderful Akhenaten. Zanuck, of course, cast Michael Wilding, an English comedian. The actress was Dana Wynter, who does look like Nefertiti. If you had those two . . .

And then [Marlon] Brando was driven off the picture by Curtiz. We had a reading, and Brando read his part [of Sinuhe, eventually played by Edmund Purdon] absolutely beautifully. It was quite poetic. Then Mike said, "How can I, with all my genius, make you play this man who is one moment hero, the next moment villain?" Brando just looked at him. I went down to my office and wrote a long memo to Zanuck, Mike Curtiz, and Brando explaining the character. Zanuck got on the phone right away and asked, "Why did you send that memo?" I replied, "Well, Mike seemed a little confused about the character, and I think Brando was puzzled." He said, "Oh Christ," hung up, and called Brando at his hotel. But Brando was already on a plane back to New York.

Do you think it hurt your career to have done these religious-themed pictures?

Well, we write to please ourselves and our contemporaries. We have certain feelings of prestige within the industry. If you do a *How Green Was My Valley*, a *Pinky*, or even a *The Ghost and Mrs. Muir*, that's wonderful. Those are all good credits. A thing like *The Robe* is to me a bad credit. It's like having a credit on a backstage musical. Lamar Trotti did a lot of those. He didn't really like them; they were his *devoir*.

With the biblical pictures you got off into the DeMille category, which your fellow writers look on with great contempt. Apropos of this, I had a letter from [the novelist and screenwriter] John Fante, who died recently, after I had written a piece for [*The Los Angeles*] *Times* on political speechwriting. In the letter Fante said, "It's hard to believe you did this brilliant piece, you the author of all those biblical epics for Twentieth Century–Fox." A very insulting letter if you think about it. As if to say, "My God, the man can write readable prose." That is the attitude.

You told me you once wrote some short stories. Why didn't you continue writing fiction?

Oh, I never did, really. During the war when I was with the Office of War Information and we were flat broke in New York, I moonlighted a few stories for *The New Yorker*. I showed one to [James] Thurber, who used to come to dinner at our house. Jim took it to *The New Yorker* and they bought it, so I always said Jim was my agent. Then I wrote another one and they surprised me, *The New Yorker* of all places, by putting a happy ending on my tragic story.

Were you drawn to that medium?

Yes, but the movies were already there. I was already sitting at a feast, so why go around to the hotdog stand? I know people who have thrown off movie careers and who have gone off and tried writing elsewhere. Then I know lots who professed to be disappointed and disgusted with Hollywood. They went away seeking higher things, and they turned out some amazingly bad movies when they got away from Zanuck, who was a good editor, and from people who were restraining them. I'm thinking, for instance, of [the writer-director-producer] Joe Mankiewicz, who is a very talented man. He came out of the projection room with Zanuck one day and said to me, "Well, my movie's over, finished. Darryl's ruined it. I never want to hear about it again." Six months later I saw him walk up not once but twice to receive

Academy Awards for writing and directing *Letter to Three Wives* [1948].

Then he left Zanuck and made *The Barefoot Contessa* [1954], which was, in my opinion, unwatchable despite a wonderful cast. Zanuck wouldn't have let him make *The Barefoot Contessa* in the first place, and if he had let him make it, he would have cut it.

I think it was Hemingway who said you need a built-in bullshit detector to be a good writer and that you lose it once you come to Hollywood. Is that true?

I don't think so. I object, for instance, to the notion that F. Scott Fitzgerald was ruined by Hollywood. People forget he wrote a perfectly terrible play—unplayable—before he came to Hollywood [probably referring to *The Vegetable, or from President to Postman*], and nobody says Broadway ruined him. Back in the 1930s there were a lot of us who went around together—Ted Paramore, Nunnally Johnson, John O'Hara, the Hacketts, Arthur Sheekman, Joel Sayre. These were mostly fugitives from New York. And we knew, peripherally, Thomas Mann, Aldous Huxley, Lion Feuchtwanger, Fitzgerald, those people. Nobody was very excited about being at a party with them. Now, people are awestruck when you say you knew Thomas Mann or Fitzgerald. No, we were sorry for Fitzgerald; we were not awestruck by him.

I agree with my old friend Jo Swerling, one of the earliest screenwriters, who said screenwriting is not so much an art as like fine cabinetmaking. I think that's right. Nunnally [Johnson] used to use that analogy, too. He picked it up from the same source I did, I'm sure. We never claimed to be artists, but we thought we were good craftsmen.

When you use that analogy, it's almost as if you're taking a rhetorical position against people who regard film as an art form.

Except in a very few exceptional cases, moviemaking is a collaborative art or craft, whichever you prefer. Of my thirty-six-odd screenplays, only four count as originals, so I was really tailoring other people's work to the screen. Sometimes that involved an enormous rewrite; in other cases, say with *The Late George Apley* [1947], which was a play, I stuck pretty close to the play and the book [by J. P. Marquand]—which differed widely. I tried to marry them. I don't think there's anything wrong with fine cabinetmaking, but I wouldn't pose as an artist.

You said in your book that writing is more important than directing.

Directing is a lot more fun, but, of course, the writing is more important. The architect is more important than the contractor. I'm not saying the writer is more important than the director, I'm saying the writing is more important than the directing. Directing is only interpretation. If the director is also the writer, obviously he can call himself an auteur. He's not one if he isn't both. I don't think he always is even then because I wrote, directed, and produced *The View from Pompey's Head* [1955]—that's three hats. But Hamilton Basso had written the novel. That was the big creative act, the rest was interpretation.

I think all really good movies that are adaptations are fairly faithful to the intent of the author. For instance, *Wuthering Heights* [1939], that was good [Emily] Brontë on the screen. Everybody involved— writer, director, producer—contributed to that. I think [the play-wright-screenwriter] Bob Sherwood did full justice to [the author] MacKinlay Kantor with *The Best Years of Our Lives* [1946], a really good picture. In some cases, as with a novel like *Forever Amber,* which is worthless, it would be foolish to try to recover the intent of the author, which is to please that part of the public that likes to lick its lips while reading. That is all it was.

Someone, I think it was Andrew Sarris, wrote that many writers who became directors did not sufficiently challenge their own material.

That could be true.

How do you rate yourself as a director?

Well, I don't really know. I think I'm very good with actors. I think I got the best possible performances out of actors by letting them do it, not by telling them how to play the scene. But I really don't know because I never got the combination that you need to make a first class picture. *Ten North Frederick* came closest, but it was so skimped on by the studio that it looked like a "B" picture.

How did you work as a writer? Did you get up in the morning and keep regular hours?

I always had spotty hours. I used to get up sometimes at three or four o'clock in the morning and write. And I usually worked at home. At one point, I didn't even have an office at the studio. Zanuck once said, "I'll send that down to your office." I said, "Darryl, I haven't even got an office." He said, "For chrissakes, I keep telling all these people they have to stay in their offices, and you don't even got one. How do you think that looks? You have to *have* an office. You don't have to sit in it."

Being at home encouraged me to work odd hours. If you get an idea in the middle of the night, it's a good idea to get up and write it down, or it's gone. There's a famous story about a writer who always swore he got up and wrote his ideas down. He had a wonderful idea in the middle of the night once, got out his pad and pencil, and wrote it down. He went back to sleep—slept like a baby. He woke up, and he had written: boy meets girl.

Did you ever suffer from writer's block?

All the time. That's endemic. Even doing a little newspaper story like this [Dunne was in the process of writing a newspaper column commenting on the death of Jack Dempsey], to get a lead . . .

Did it ever stop you from writing for long periods?

No. Two or three days. The strangest thing happened. I usually found that resolutely going to a party, having a bit too much to drink, and getting a hangover was an awfully good un-blocker. I don't know why. The other thing is to take a drive. It's probably a bad idea. You should concentrate more on your driving. But if you go out on a long dull highway with no distractions . . .

The block's a terrible thing. I don't know of any writer who doesn't suffer from it occasionally. There's another thing I used to suffer from—the writer's nightmare. I still get it. The dream is: a story you're trying to solve and it just keeps eluding you. There's no solution. The great relief is when you wake up and realize there *is* no story. You don't have to solve it. That sort of roadblock can happen even when you're adapting a published book. A sort of example: when I was doing *Ten North Frederick,* we had a major problem because we weren't allowed to show an abortion on the screen, and an abortion is a major part of the story. So I had to cook up a thing in which Edith Chapin, the wicked mother, so harassed her daughter that she brought on a miscarriage—an emotional trauma. Luckily, I had a great actress in Diana Varsi who could play the trauma and did, beautifully. You can get blocked on something like that because, what are you going to do?

Did you include a lot of description or camera movement in your scripts?

It all depends. I used to, but when I started directing I left it all out. There were two reasons for this: one was laziness, and the other was I could make the script a little longer than they liked by leaving description out. It gave me a little more elbow room. In fact, Rowland Lee taught me that when Eddie Small kept trying to cut us on *The Count of Monte Cristo.* Rowland would tell me to have the secretary put more stuff on the page when she was typing up the script. Then he'd say to Eddie, "See, I cut five pages," when he hadn't cut anything.

As a director, I didn't want too many preconceived notions. Shakespeare rarely used stage directions, you know, and his plays are understood by everybody. You don't *need* a lot of stage directions. Now I have read stage directions that I admire. I remember Ben Hecht for *Viva Villa!* [1934] had wonderful stage directions, undoubtedly thinking of Wallace Beery. One stage direction was, "Villa sweats like a horse." I know just what he means. Or when he was trying to write a letter: "Groans with literary frustration." And Nunnally Johnson wrote beautiful stage directions, although he couldn't photograph them. He would have two teenage girls looking at each other "with the innocent eyes of a couple of Beale Street madams." That's wonderful. Though you couldn't photograph it, it would convey something to a very good actor.

What is the most difficult part of a screenplay to write?

The ending. The beginning is a cinch. The world is full of great openings, not so many great third acts. How many pictures have you seen that fall apart at the end? That can't sustain it?

You worked during what is referred to as Hollywood's golden age. Did you feel then that it was a very special time? Was it as wonderful as it seems in retrospect?

The golden years of anybody's life—you don't realize them at the time. I don't think we were aware of the fact that it was a golden age. You have to remember all the extraneous issues going on: the first part of it was the Depression, then the Guild fight, then World War II, then the House Un-American Activities Committee, then the threat of television. There were always those things going on that diverted your attention from what you were doing. I'm pretty sure that in the time of Augustus, Virgil had no idea that this was the Golden Age of Rome. I think we were just trying to make a living.

Do you miss it?

I don't miss it, although I still resent Century City. I think you really mourn departed years, youth, and glory to some extent. But I'd much rather just stay here [at home in Malibu]. I have a telescope, and I spend all the clear evenings out here watching the stars. The only thing that is really bad about becoming a "senile" citizen is that you lose your friends.

Julius J. Epstein:
A King of Comedy

Interview by Pat McGilligan

What becomes a legend most? In the case of Julius J. Epstein, obscurity. Epstein has made a career out of being the "invisible man" in Hollywood. Initially, he worked as a ghostwriter and dialogue doctor, then as one-half of a writing team with his identical twin brother, and finally as an adaptor faithful to the original ideas of other authors and playwrights. It is only in screenwriters' circles that he is reputed to be one of the crème de la crème. Four Oscar nominations and the Writers Guild Lifetime Achievement Award (awarded in 1955) attest to the esteem of his peers.

In 1933 Epstein, then a lowly press agent, arrived in Los Angeles to bail out two college buddies who had pitched a story to Warner Brothers and could not realize the script. (Although Epstein diplomatically refrains from mentioning their names in this interview, Hollywood lore pinpoints one of the two as the Sammy Glick–prototype Jerry Wald.) After catching fire at Warners, Julius was joined by his look-alike brother Philip G. Epstein, and the twosome clocked in at the Burbank studio for fourteen years, turning out such obligatory four-handkerchief pictures as *Four Daughters* (1938) and *Mr. Skeffington* (1944) and specializing in adaptations of frothy Broadway hits such as *No Time for Comedy* (1940), *The Man Who Came to Dinner* (1942), and *Arsenic and Old Lace* (1944). In this regard the brothers Epstein diverged from the studio's vaunted, hard-boiled, headline-conscious social-statement film-making. They were so adept at champagne comedy that they were extended uncommon liberties as contract writers and eventually promoted to short-lived experiments at producing and directing.

While sequestered at Warners, the Epsteins shared an Oscar with Howard Koch for that celebrated piece of patchwork picturemaking, *Casablanca* (1942), a World War II resistance love story based on a forgotten play called "Everybody Comes to Rick's" and starring the romantic icons Humphrey Bogart and Ingrid Bergman. If legend is to be believed—and there is a lot of legend to be sorted out when one is examining the low-profile career of Julius Epstein—the script was written and rewritten one step ahead of the dailies. Co-writer Howard Koch has volunteered his version of the writing of *Casablanca* in two books, the autobiographical *As Time Goes By* and *Casablanca: Script and Legend.* And the uncredited screenwriter Casey Robinson defends his own contribution elsewhere in this volume. To add to the mix, writer Albert Maltz is said to have sat in on at least one crucial script session.

While Koch and Robinson are adamant about their involvement in the script, Epstein is self-deprecating on the subject, having said at one point, "There wasn't one moment of reality in *Casablanca.*" Yet in this interview, he claims for his brother and himself the primary role in shaping the screenplay of *Casablanca.* This departure from his usual modest pose is spurred, he says, by his children and close friends, who know "the true story" of the script's creation and who are not as willing as he to downplay the Epsteins' role in the making of a classic. The *Casablanca* Oscar is on his mantelpiece, bespeaking the grudging pride Epstein has in a movie that has grown in stature and is now a late-night TV, video, and college circuit staple.

As might be expected of dapper, successful identical twins, the Epsteins cut quite a swath through the film colony of the 1930s and 1940s and were appreciated as much for their oneupmanship (often of each other) and devastating wit as for their disdain for official credits. Both were also earnest Rooseveltian (and later, Stevensonian) liberals, but this aspect rarely crept into their screenplays (with the notable exceptions of *The Male Animal* [1942] and *Casablanca*). Both Julius and his brother were active in the Screen Writers Guild and were prominent in the short-lived Committee for the First Amendment, the delegation of motion picture industry progressives who traveled to Washington, D.C., in 1947 to protest the legality of the House Un-American Activities Committee (HUAC). Jack Warner's contentious relationship with the wise-cracking duo led him to name the Epsteins as probable Communists before the HUAC Committee. This was laughable to people who knew them as staunch anti-Communists, but it was no laughing matter in the panic-stricken film business at the time.

When Philip Epstein died suddenly and tragically of cancer in the early 1950s, Julius continued his writing career as a solo, and he flourished. If anything, his reach broadened: the list of scripts he wrote in

Julius J. Epstein in Beverly Hills, 1984. (Photo: Alison Morley)

the 1950s, 1960s, 1970s, *and* 1980s reflects his range, showing emotional depth, a contemporary savvy surprising for such an oldster, and the maturation of his forte—the risqué, sophisticated urban comedy. Julius Epstein has never been one to sit around and wax nostalgic about the golden age of Hollywood. It took four years of coaxing to persuade him to reminisce for this interview—letters; phone calls; a breakfast in Boston during which I pried details out of him about the Epsteins' uncredited collaboration in the writing of *Yankee Doodle Dandy* (1942). (That territory is covered in my earlier book, the annotated script of *Yankee Doodle Dandy,* published by the University of Wisconsin Press in 1981.)

When, in 1983, I finally interviewed him in the den of his cliff-side home in Beverly Hills, he was nervously awaiting the release of a small, unheralded comedy he had just co-produced and written called *Reuben, Reuben* (1983), from a 1964 Peter De Vries novel. Epstein was certain that *Reuben, Reuben* would be overlooked in the now-age cinema of special effects and souped-up sex and violence. Not to worry—the expertly crafted script, bolstered by a sublime performance by Tom Conti in the title role as a Scottish poet on a sexual rampage through the Connecticut countryside, brought *Reuben, Reuben* mention on many critics' "ten best" lists. And at seventy-four Epstein received his fourth Academy Award nomination. "It is," Epstein said of *Reuben, Reuben*, "the finest piece of screenwriting, the most adult film I've written, and with no concession to any so-called box-office value" (from "Interview with Aljean Harmetz," *The New York Times*, February 5, 1983, Section 2, p. 1).

1934   *Twenty Million Sweethearts* (Ray Enright). Uncredited contribution.

1935   *Big Broadcast of 1936* (Norman Taurog). Uncredited contribution.
        Broadway Gondolier (Lloyd Bacon). Co-script.
        Living on Velvet (Frank Borzage). Co-story, co-script.
        In Caliente (Lloyd Bacon). Co-script.
        Little Big Shot (Michael Curtiz). Co-script.
        I Live for Love (Busby Berkeley). Co-story, co-script.
        Stars Over Broadway (William Keighley). Co-script.

1936   *Sons o' Guns* (Lloyd Bacon). Co-script.

1937   *The King and the Chorus Girl* (Mervyn LeRoy). Uncredited adaptation.
        Confession (Joe May). Co-script.

1938   *There's That Woman Again* (Alexander Hall). Uncredited contribution.*
        Four Daughters (Michael Curtiz). Co-script.
        Secrets of an Actress (William Keighley). Co-script.

1939   *Daughters Courageous* (Michael Curtiz). Co-script.*
        Four Wives (Michael Curtiz). Co-script.*

1940   *Saturday's Children* (Vincent Sherman). Co-script.*
        No Time for Comedy (William Keighley). Co-script.*

1941   *Honeymoon for Three* (Lloyd Bacon). Additional dialogue.*
        The Strawberry Blonde (Raoul Walsh). Co-script.*
        The Bride Came C.O.D. (William Keighley). Co-script.*

---

* In collaboration with Philip G. Epstein.
** In collaboration with Philip G. Epstein and another writer.

1942   *Yankee Doodle Dandy* (Michael Curtiz). Uncredited contribution.*
        The Man Who Came to Dinner (William Keighley). Co-script.*
        The Male Animal (Elliott Nugent). Co-script.**
        Casablanca (Michael Curtiz). Co-script.**

1944   *Mr. Skeffington* (Vincent Sherman). Co-script, co-producer.*
        Arsenic and Old Lace (Frank Capra). Co-script.*

1946   *One More Tomorrow* (Peter Godfrey). Additional dialogue.*
        The Time of Your Life (H. C. Potter). Uncredited contribution.*

1948   *Romance on the High Seas* (Michael Curtiz). Co-script.*

1949   *Chicken Every Sunday* (George Seaton). Co-play basis only.*

1950   *My Foolish Heart* (Mark Robson). Co-script.*
        Born Yesterday (George Cukor). Uncredited contribution.*

1951   *Take Care of My Little Girl* (Jean Negulesco). Co-script.*

1954   *Forever Female* (Irving Rapper). Co-screen story, co-script.*
        The Last Time I Saw Paris (Richard Brooks). Co-script.**

1955   *Young at Heart* (Gordon Douglas). Remake of *Four Daughters*.
        The Tender Trap (Charles Walters). Script.

1957   *Kiss Them for Me* (Stanley Donen). Script.

1958   *The Brothers Karamazov* (Richard Brooks). Co-adaptation.**

1960   *Tall Story* (Joshua Logan). Script.

1961   *Take a Giant Step* (Philip Leacock). Co-script, producer.
        Fanny (Joshua Logan). Script.

1962   *Light in the Piazza* (Guy Green). Script.

1964   *Send Me No Flowers* (Norman Jewison). Script.

1965   *Return from the Ashes* (J. Lee Thompson). Script.

1966   *Any Wednesday* (Robert Ellis Miller). Script, producer.

1972   *Pete 'n' Tillie* (Martin Ritt). Adaptation, script, producer.

1975   *Jacqueline Susann's Once Is Not Enough* (Guy Green). Script.

1977   *Cross of Iron* (Sam Peckinpah). Co-script.

1978   *House Calls* (Howard Zieff). Co-story, co-script.

1983   *Reuben, Reuben* (Robert Ellis Miller). Script, co-producer.

Philip G. Epstein credits also include *Gift of Gab*, co-story (1934); *Love on a Bet*, co-script (1936); *Grand Jury*, co-script (1936); *Mummy's Boys*, co-script (1936); *The Bride Walks Out*, co-script (1936); *New Faces of 1937*, co-script (1937); *There's That Woman Again*, co-script (1938); and *The Mad Miss Manton*, co-script (1938).

Television includes adaptation of *The Pirate*.

Produced plays include *And the Stars Remain, Rufus and His Wife, Chicken Every Sunday, That's the Ticket,* and *But, Seriously.* . . .

Academy Awards include an Oscar nomination in 1938 for co-writing *Four Daughters* with Lenore Coffee; an Oscar in 1943 for writing *Casablanca* with Philip G. Epstein and Howard Koch; a nomination in 1972 for adapting *Pete 'n' Tillie* based on material from another medium; and a nomination in 1983 for adapting *Reuben, Reuben*.

Writers Guild awards include the Laurel Award for Achievement in 1955.

You were born and raised in New York City. What is your family background?
My mother was a housekeeper. My father ran a livery stable. I don't think he finished grammar school.
What side of town did you grow up on?
Well, lower East Side—but I cannot be described as having come from poverty, because my father had a good business. We went to the Catskills every summer. As a matter of fact, during the Depression we went out of town to college—my brother and I. And we didn't work our way through college. We were certainly not rich either. We lived on the one good street—East Broadway—which was brownstones all owned by doctors. They had their offices on the ground floor, they lived on the first floor, and they rented out the second floor. We lived on the second floor. No, not rich, but certainly not poor. Everybody around me was poverty-stricken on the lower East Side.
Where did you go to college?
Penn State—which is isolated in the exact center of Pennsylvania. I went there because they were known for their top boxing teams. They were always producing champions. I was a boxer, so I went there. I was captain of the team in my senior year [and an Intercollegiate Boxing Champion in 1929]—bantam featherweight.

What did you major in?

I became a poli-sci major because, when I went to register, the man said, "What do you want to major in?" I said, "I don't know." He said, "C'mon, what do you want to major in?" I said, "What do you teach?" He said, "History and political science." I said, "Okay, history and political science."

What did you expect to do after graduation?

The main thing was to get a job. I wanted to be a sports writer.

Why?

Because I loved sports, and I was always very active in sports. And, I figured, to see sports and to be paid for it, well, there was nothing better.

Had you done any serious writing in your youth?

In high school? Strictly journalism. I was editor-in-chief of my high school newspaper—Erasmus High. Then in my junior year, I got into the playwrighting course at Penn State—the first one they ever gave at Penn State—and I had to write a play to pass the course. But I can't remember a thing about it. I can't remember a thing about half a dozen screenplays I wrote in the 1930s. They were just hack work. I turned them out—three or four a year.

Why do you think you became a writer?

I couldn't do anything else. (*Laughs.*) It's hard to say. It wasn't ever something I had to do or that I didn't want to do anything else. Of course, I tried to get a job on a newspaper. My father had some connections; there was a Metropolitan News Company that distributed newspapers from the presses to the news dealers by horse and wagon. They stabled at my father's stable. So he had some connections; but everybody said, "We're not taking anybody now." It was the Depression. It was when I got out of school that I found out I was quite slick at writing. I was gifted at being an office boy and a press agent for an orchestra leader.

When you say you were quite slick—you mean, as a press agent?

Well, you took what you could get in those days—1931 and 1932. (*Laughs.*) As a matter of fact, there are quite a few press agents who became screenwriters in Hollywood—Claude Binyon, Paul Yawitz, quite a few others.

How and when did you come to Hollywood?

I came out by accident. I was called to do some ghostwriting by two desperate people who shall remain nameless. They sold an idea to a studio and couldn't write it, so they sent for me and I wrote it as a ghost writer. That's how I started in the business. I arrived in Hollywood on October 14, 1933.

How did they know you could write a script?

They knew me from college, and they knew me as a press agent.
Was this summons from Hollywood a bolt out of the blue?
Absolutely. Thoroughly unexpected. Unexpected in that I got connected with motion pictures, but not unexpected in that I knew these two fellas couldn't write a word. When I was in New York, I thought, "What are they doing out there?" Then I got a telegram saying, "Come out quick."

Did you think you were coming to Hollywood for just a brief stay—for only six months?
No, I thought, "This is the chance." That was not foresight; I just knew it was an opportunity.

Who else did you know in Hollywood besides these two people?
Nobody. Not a soul.

What screenwriters had you heard of or did you admire?
Donald Ogden Stewart, Dudley Nichols, Robert Riskin—Horace Jackson, although he was not in the same class as the others—Ben Hecht, although being a screenwriter was the least of his activities. Not too many; I didn't know of many others. And I didn't admire too many. As a matter of fact, there are very few screenwriters today who are known by the general public. Ask who wrote what, nobody will know. That's why I say, "Who will buy a book about screenwriters?"

Was there anybody who took you by the hand and showed you the ropes?
One of the people I came out for. I came out on a Friday and landed in the railroad station at ten o'clock at night. Twelve o'clock that night I was writing, because they had to take some stuff in on Monday and they had nothing to turn in. Sunday, one of them took me downtown to the Paramount Theatre—I think it was *College Humor* [1933] with Bing Crosby and Mary Carlisle. He said, "That's a fade-out. That's a dissolve. That's an iris-down." That was my education in screenwriting. I think it's all you need.

How did you learn the technical language of the camera?
I learned by looking at other scripts. And I learned very early that directors pay no attention to that. You just write: "master scene," "cut to," or "close shot"—which is very easy, you just mix it up. The master shots and the individual shots were all shot the same way. When I first arrived, I wrote an original story every night. In those days you didn't have to write a screenplay to sell, you could do ten or twenty pages of an idea. In about nine months one sold to Warners. I came in October and sold something in August. After a week Warners put me on a seven-year contract, and I was there under two seven-year contracts.

What was your first impression of Hollywood?

I thought then and I still think that Hollywood Boulevard is the sleaziest street I had ever been on. (*Laughs.*)

Literary Forebears

What writers did you read while growing up?
I read everybody. Mostly playwrights—Philip Barry, S. N. Behrman, Robert E. Sherwood. All the big playwrights of the era.
Sounds like you had a leaning toward light comedy even then.
Yeah—I thought Eugene O'Neill was a big bore, and I still do.
What novelists were you reading?
Everybody. Fitzgerald, Hemingway.
Later on, Faulkner?
Not too much. He was at Warners for years, you know. Never said a word to anybody. Never said a word, just walked right past you.
Why would he do something like that?
We think he was half drunk all the time. He was not a successful screenwriter. Worked on the B-unit, mostly. It was a very friendly, club-like atmosphere, when they had the studio system. It was a real club; that was the fun of it. There were 70 to 75 writers at Warners, 125 at Metro, or something like that—and you were a *club*. You had a writers' table, and only the writers could sit at the writers' table. Faulkner didn't sit at the writers' table. That was his treatment of everybody.
Were you aware of comedic authors?
Ring Lardner, I guess.
Damon Runyon?
Trash, just awful. Not a real writer. He was like Mark Hellinger. The story of Mark Hellinger is that he would take Mondays off; press agents would send him phony material, and he would print it in his column. It was a good thing for press agents. I wrote a phony story about my orchestra leader in which his name was mentioned twenty-four times—and Hellinger printed it! On a Monday! I was making $15 a week, and the orchestra leader raised me to $20; then, he only paid me every other week, so I lost $5 out of the deal. (*Laughs.*)
How about P. G. Wodehouse?
Oh, I loved him! I have all of his works up on the shelf, and I keep rereading him.
Who else in that vein?
The man who has given me a livelihood in the past few years—Peter De Vries. I think he's wonderful. But I didn't start reading him until later.

Did you see many plays on Broadway?

When I was making $15 a week, I saw every play on Broadway. Today you couldn't afford it. It cost me sixty-five cents to see a play; a $1.10 ticket would come to the corner drugstore at the last minute, and they would charge you fifty-five cents plus ten cents; so for sixty-five cents I saw all the plays from the second balcony.

Were you conscious of absorbing influences?

Yeah, yeah. Mostly I liked high comedy. Barry and Behrman, but of course George S. Kaufman and Moss Hart, too.

Did the newspapers of the day affect you?

In those days there were at least ten newspapers in New York—*The Times, The News, The Sun Mail, The World, The Journal,* and so on. You couldn't get away from newspapers. And there were things like the "F.P.A." column in *The World*—Franklin P. Adams. There would be little bits and pieces by contributors like Dorothy Parker and George S. Kaufman—the whole Algonquin crowd—and light verse by Samuel Hoffenstein. The contributors were just the top people. Just a marvelous column. There's been nothing, nothing like it ever since.

Did you read the comic strips?

Never—to this day. The only comic I've ever read is "Doonesbury," and that was only recently. I've never read anything else. I don't think they're funny. They're just not funny.

When did you first become aware of movies?

I used to go to movies all the time when I was a kid. Everybody went to movies. There was no radio until I was about eleven or twelve years old. When I was at Penn State, there was a transition between silents and talkies, and I never missed a picture. There was only one moviehouse there, with a violinist and a pianist when the silent pictures were on.

How did the transition to sound strike you?

Oh, I liked it. I thought most of the silent pictures were silly. You know, Robert E. Sherwood was a movie critic for *Life* magazine when it was a humorous magazine. I'll never forget one line he wrote during the silents days: "You know, 90 percent of all pictures could be titled 'Her Sacrifice.' " Oh, but I always liked going to the movies!

The Contract Writer

In what direction did your strengths as a screenwriter evolve?

Mostly in dialogue. But when you were under contract, you'd do everything—including start from scratch. In those days, each studio had 75 to 100 writers. They did about 50 to 60 pictures a year, and there were about six studios—about 400 pictures a year plus independents. But if you look at the credits, the same names of about 150 to 200 writers kept popping up all the time, and they kept doing 90 percent of all the pictures. The same writers, the same names. You were given the assignments. Today you write something; if you sell it, it's a picture. If you don't sell it . . . The top writers today, if they have one picture every two years, they are doing well. There wasn't a year under Warner Brothers that we [my brother and I] didn't have three pictures. Made! Credits! Not counting the pictures that weren't made. They used to go on the principle of three scripts written for every one that was made.

Would some of the more important stars try to involve themselves in the writing?

Some actors would involve themselves in the writing—to a more or less degree. But it was nothing like it is today, where the actors are ruining more scripts, I think. All the actors today want to be known as improvisers, it seems—which I think is a terrible trend. It's alright for an actor to be a writer; quite a few good writers have come from the ranks of actors—[Harold] Pinter, Clifford Odets. But most of them aren't; they just think they are. A lot of damage is done.

Was that true in the old days as well?

You had some of that. You had it with Bette Davis or with Cary Grant. But not to the degree you have it today.

Did you have it with Cagney?

No. That was a marvelous relationship, an ideal relationship.

If he had an idea, it was on the beam?

Absolutely.

Our first experience with the Cagneys was on *The Strawberry Blonde* [1941], which was based on *One Sunday Afternoon* [1933]—the only Gary Cooper picture that ever lost money. We thought the reason it lost money was it was too bucolic. It took place in a little country town. We said, "Change it to the big city, put it in New York." That's what we did for *The Strawberry Blonde*—which was very financially successful. We did not do the first version of the script. It was done by Stephen Morehouse Avery. When we went on the rewrite, we knew it was for Cagney. That's a help. Plus, we knew we weren't going to give Cagney S. N. Behrman dialogue, you know what I mean? The director, Raoul Walsh, I thought was great. Very businesslike. He never changed a word on *The Strawberry Blonde*. Some writers complained about Walsh. My experience with him was very good.

Was he a better director than Michael Curtiz?

I think he was better, yes. But Curtiz was a good director with the camera—good instincts.

You only worked with Walsh once. Why did you end up with Curtiz so often?

Not by design.

Were you and the other Warners screenwriters chauvinistic about your studio?

No, I don't think so. Each studio had its style. We [my brother and I] did not adhere to the Warner Brothers style—the Warner Brothers style was the punchy, right-out-of-the-headlines pictures like *The Public Enemy* [1931] and *I Am a Fugitive from a Chain Gang* [1932]. We didn't do gangster pictures or headline pictures.

Why not?

Well, first of all, I don't think we were suited for them, and we didn't like them. And they liked the type of thing we did, so they assigned us to them. They had a story department run by a wonderful woman named Irene Lee [the Warners story editor, later associated with Hal Wallis at Paramount] who gave out the assignments, and she knew what we could do best.

Did you and your brother have your choice of Warners assignments?

After a while we had clout. We could turn down things and suggest things. Not at the beginning. We weren't the only ones who could do that; there were quite a few others who could.

Did you ever pursue assignments for one reason or another?

Very frequently; we would go in and look at the shelf of the discarded scripts and take one out and say we would like to do it. That happened in the case of *Mr. Skeffington* [1944]. They had four or five scripts that had never been made, including one by Edmund Goulding and one by John Huston. We took a look at *Mr. Skeffington* and said, "First of all, it shouldn't be English; it should be made with an American family. Secondly, the trick of the book was that its title was *Mr. Skeffington,* and he never appeared in the book. He should be a character in the movie." And it was made.

We also were specialists of turning plays into movies. *The Man Who Came to Dinner* [1942], *Arsenic and Old Lace* [1944], *The Male Animal* [1942]. . . . We didn't say we wanted to do *that.* But in those days they bought a lot of plays, and because plays usually had better dialogue than ordinary pictures, they gave them to us to adapt. So in doing them we'd try to at least maintain some level of the same dialogue the play had.

What problems did you face, typically, with plays?

The usual problem with most of the plays in those days was that they were one-set plays. So you had to open them up. And some plays you had to change completely, like *No Time for Comedy* [1940]. We had to make big changes in that.

It occurs to me that it is a somewhat easier task to write a screenplay if you have the advantage of beginning with a good, solid play.

Sometimes it was very easy. Sometimes it was very difficult. But *No Time for Comedy,* for example, was just talk, talk, talk—no action really, no situations. It was very good talk, but we had to do a lot of changing on that.

I'll tell you a story about *Arsenic and Old Lace.* It had one terrible problem. The whole plot shifted on the Cary Grant character finding out that he's an illegitimate, that is, a bastard. The big laugh of the play was: he turns to the girl, whom he can't marry because he thinks there's insanity in the family, and says, "Darling, I'm a bastard!" The theatre fell down. But you couldn't use the word "bastard" in the movies. You couldn't even say "damn." How were you going to do that in the movies? Everything would fall to pieces if he turned to Gail [the character portrayed by Priscilla Lane in the movie] and said, "I'm *illegitimate!*" Nothing! My brother solved it. He made up a story for the two old women characters to tell Cary Grant that his father was a chef on a tramp steamer. And then Cary turned to her and said, "Darling, I'm the son of a sea-cook!" I don't know why, but it was just as good as bastard. They laughed just as hard.

Why is it that you wrote so few original stories of your own for the movies?

Well, there was a good reason for that. Nowadays you have to do originals. In those days you soon found out that no matter what you wrote, original or adaptation, it never wound up the way you wanted. It was always changed by the producer, the director, or the actor. Someone always had a finger in or a whole hand in it. You felt it was ridiculous to break your neck; it was going to be changed anyhow, and it hurt more when it was an original than when it was an adaptation. So you're getting paid anyhow; what's the difference?

Did you have that experience yourself?

Yeah, I started out writing originals; that is how I broke into the business. I found out you go through the same process on all of them.

You seem to have made that decision for yourself early on.

Right from the first.

Have you done any originals since then?

Only plays—but even there you have problems.

I thought Pete 'n' Tillie *[1972] was partly an original.*

Pete 'n' Tillie was from a novella by Peter De Vries that I combined with a flop play of mine called *But, Seriously.* I took material from the flop play and melded it into the novella because the novella, from the story point of view, was not enough. What I took from my original play made a picture out of it.

And House Calls *[1978]?*

House Calls was originally a play written by Max Shulman, who sent it to me. Then, we sat down and made it from that into an original movie. But there we had a fight with the director, and he brought in a couple of writers and crapped up the ending, terribly so. I have mixed feelings about *House Calls.*

You have to come up with your own ideas today. There is no such thing as a contract writer today. The entire industry puts out eighty pictures a year, and most of them are pick-ups—from Canada, from Australia, from independent filmmakers. Cases in which a studio buys a book or a play and then assigns it to a writer—well, I don't think there are more than ten a year in the whole industry.

Yankee Doodle Dandy (1941)
and Casablanca (1942)

How is it that you and your brother acquired such a reputation in Hollywood as script doctors?

We don't have a big reputation as script doctors. Everybody at the studio was a script doctor—"Who isn't doing anything at the moment? Here, see what you can do with these scripts." Not any more than any other people.

But you scrupulously avoid talking about your uncredited work—I'm thinking of your rewriting on such classic films as Yankee Doodle Dandy.

Everybody in Hollywood knows what we did do and what we didn't do. I don't like to talk about it. It's not important.

It does seem as if you and your brother weren't very aggressive in terms of credits.

The credit situation was different. Now it's very important to have your name on a script because you get residuals. So, *financially* it's important. In those days there was no such thing as residuals. If you got your name on a script or didn't get your name on a script, it didn't matter; you were under contract; the studio knew who did what. See what I mean? The studio knew who did the work on *Yankee Doodle Dandy,* even if your name wasn't on the script. There was a sort of gentleman's rule that anybody who worked on the script would get credit. There was no such thing as credit arbitration. That was only when the residual aspect came in. Even before that, when the studio contract system broke down in the late 1940s after the war—which was before the residual system—then it became important because you had

Members of the Committee for the First Amendment arriving in Washington, D.C., in October 1947. Left to right: Julius J. Epstein, Canada Lee, Oscar Serlin, unidentified, John Garfield, Larry Parks, unidentified, Philip Epstein, Paul Draper. (Photo: Wisconsin Center for Film and Theater Research)

to be hired at other studios. Somebody at Metro may not know who did the work at Warners unless your name is on it.

Even so, William Cagney [producer of Yankee Doodle Dandy *and other films and James Cagney's brother] told me that you and your brother were the most passive and gentlemanly when it came to credits.*

Yeah. Because we thought most of the pictures [we passed on] were terrible anyhow.

Is that true of Yankee Doodle Dandy?

We never liked the subject. It was too sentimental for us. In those days the credits had no financial meaning, so we stepped aside for [Robert] Buckner and [Edmund] Joseph. Besides, we really didn't consider it to be one of our scripts.

*Yet I know from studying the various script drafts that your contribution was crucial to the story. When I wrote about that in my monograph on the script [*Yankee Doodle Dandy, University of Wisconsin Press,*

1982], you were very unhappy that I revealed the circumstances behind the development of the script and your involvement.

Buckner I liked. It [*Dandy*] was given to us, so we worked on it. The Cagneys were very unhappy with the [Buckner] script; wouldn't shoot it. We didn't take credit on it and don't regret not taking credit on it because we got full credit at the studio. In your book, Buckner says, "The boys [meaning the Epsteins] were never shy about taking credit before this," which shows that he was hurt. That saddened me. He was hurt mostly by the Cagneys. The Cagneys were very free in attacking him. Which we didn't do. We just did our job and didn't even take credit on it.

Do you feel the same way about Casablanca? *Don't like it?*

I don't hate it. I just think it was slick shit.

In the case of Casablanca, *I am surprised—because it is one instance where you have publicly defended your credit.*

I was forced into that by my kids, who were outraged. And by my friends, too, who knew the situation. If it wasn't for the pressure from my kids and from my friends, I wouldn't have even been interested.

In Howard Koch's book about the making of Casablanca—

Which I haven't read.

He presents what seems to me to be a very judicious account of the writing and explains that he came in on the back end of what someone else had already written, and consequently embroidered upon the skeleton of the Casablanca *story.*

Exactly the other way around. What actually happened was, war broke out. Frank Capra went to Washington to do a series called "Why We Fight," and he asked my brother and me to go along to work on it. We said we would; the studio said, "No, you've got to do this picture." We said, "We're going anyhow." We never did a line before we went to Washington. And we went. We were there four weeks. And when we came back, they had maybe thirty to forty pages written by Howard Koch. Just between us, they were very unhappy with it. His stuff was not used. If there was an arbitration panel in those days—if such a thing had existed—Howard Koch would not have received a credit. Because you have to have at least 30 percent of a script to get credit. He never would have come close. No way.

Casey Robinson says he wrote a first draft too.

Let me clear that up. Casey Robinson did not write a first draft. He never did a draft of it—never. He wrote some test scenes for the actors, which we rewrote to fit the script. The only line of his that remained that I can remember is, "A franc for your thoughts," which I always thought was a terrible line. We fought to get it cut. Let me just

Famous last words: The airport scene in Casablanca, *with Conrad Veidt, Claude Rains, Paul Henreid, Humphrey Bogart, and Ingrid Bergman. But who wrote what, precisely, is still at issue.*

say this. As I say, the studio knows who did what. They made us producers right after *Casablanca*. We were producers on *Mr. Skeffington* until we gave it up when we found out that Bette Davis had more power than we had. They gave us a new contract. They gave us a whole bungalow with fireplaces.

What about Howard Koch's claims?

I've always liked Howard. I think his memory is just wrong, and he is thinking the wishful thought.

What about Casey Robinson's claims?

I don't know. I never saw a draft of his. We were the first ones on it. That is, we were supposed to be the first ones on it, and then we went to Washington; then we came back and started right from the beginning. As a matter of fact, we wrote our first couple scenes in Washington.

*Have you read Hal Wallis's autobiography [*Starmaker: The Autobiography of Hal Wallis *by Hal Wallis and Charles Higham. New York: Macmillan, 1980]?*

No.

Basically he says all four of you were working on the script.

Listen, he had seventy-five writers trying to come up with an ending. Everybody in the studio was trying to come up with an ending. They were panic-stricken.

There is some debate as to who came up with the ending.

The ending came up on Beverly Glen and Sunset Boulevard. We—my brother and I—were driving to the studio and that's when we thought of the ending.

Philip G. Epstein

Tell me a little about your brother. He died so long ago—

Thirty-two years ago.

Not much is known about him today.

Well, he was just like me.

How did you work in collaboration with him?

As if we were one person. The times I've collaborated with other people—like with Max Shulman—we didn't collaborate the same way. We'd think up a scene and do it separately. Not together. I couldn't do it in the same room with anyone else. I tried it three times with Billy Wilder, and it never worked out. Never got a word on paper. One got made—*Avanti!* [1972]. I started that with him and couldn't do anything with it. Before that, one that never got made. I can't remember the third one—whether or not it was made. Anyhow, it was not a fruitful collaboration.

So you could only collaborate with your brother?

Yeah.

Was it a case of you beginning a sentence and him completing it?

Yeah. Many a time. Or the other way around.

Would you always be writing in the same room together?

Oh yeah, all the time.

Two typewriters?

Never typed. Longhand—one of us.

Did one of you have a better gift for comedy?

No.

For construction?

No.

For character?

No.

Theme?

Same. No to all the questions.

Just completely compatible?

Yes.

If dialogue was your strength and it was the same with Philip, if the two of you were working on the same story, might the dialogue be strong and the story weak?

Sometimes.

I don't mean this question to strike deep, but what was it like to work alone after your brother's death, after working so long and so closely in collaboration with him.

It was more difficult. (*Pause.*) Listen, I did several pictures before we started to collaborate, so it was really going back to the original way.

High Comedy

Is there any genre you couldn't possibly believe in?

Well, I detest science fiction. I thought *Star Wars* [1977] was a big bore, and the others [the sequels] I didn't bother going to see. I just don't believe there is anybody there in outer space. *E.T.* [1982], I thought, was one of the great bores of all time. I was bored from the first frame to the last. E.T. itself was one of the dullest characters ever; he never said anything of consequence, he had no humor, nothing. I think he was just made up to look like Menachem Begin. (*Laughs.*) With as much humor.

How about westerns?

Westerns, too. I'm an Easterner. I think all the stories about the West are probably full of shit. Cowboys were probably uneducated and very dull.

Musicals?

I haven't been asked. I did a musical that was sold three times to Broadway, with a score that was the first ever written by Stephen Sondheim. It was called *Front Porch of Flatbush* until he wrote a song for it called "Saturday Night"; then it was called *Saturday Night*. Metro asked me once every year for ten years to sell it as a movie, and I wouldn't sell it; Paramount offered to back it too—if I would get rid of the score. So it was never produced. Three times it was optioned for Broadway! Something always happened. The last time, in 1959, Bob Fosse was going to direct it. It can still be done, because it's a period thing.

You have a reputation in the Hollywood community as a staunch liberal. Yet Casablanca *is the only one of your pictures I can think of with any politics—any topicality or relation to headlines.*

I've never been considered ultra-left; my politics are much more along liberal lines. I'm a Franklin D. Roosevelt–Adlai Stevenson liberal. But I don't usually go for propaganda pictures. I think they're futile. They're usually dull. I don't like that in plays either. If you're skillful enough that it is entertaining—and it isn't the old agit-prop, as we used to call such plays—well, maybe . . .

I'm surprised your liberal politics hasn't informed your writing.

Hasn't affected it at all. They are two separate things. There is a touch of it in *The Male Animal,* but I can't think of another picture where it figures in.

Besides Casablanca.

That was everybody's attitude then—the Nazis were big heavies.

How do you manage to keep the two strains of thought separate and distinct?

I don't think along political lines. My play, *But, Seriously* had a political angle that was dull as hell—that's what killed the play. There were a lot of laughs in it, which I took and put into *Pete 'n' Tillie.*

One thing I can safely say: over a long period of time you have gained a reputation as one of Hollywood's top comedy screenwriters.

But there are different kinds of comedy. It's not like television comedy. It's not the Mel Brooks kind of comedy.

Have you specialized in comedy by choice?

By natural thinking.

Where do you think you got your sense of humor?

From being Jewish. (*Laughs.*)

Can you elaborate?

How? How can I? Who knows? I have no explanation for it. Steve Allen has a book [*Funny People* and *More Funny People,* New York: Stein and Day, 1981 and 1982] out; have you read it? He says, "If you look at it, 95 percent of all the comedy writers and comedians are Jewish." And *he* has no explanation for it. His only explanation is: it must come in the genes, because the only way the Jews could last all the years is by laughing about it. That explains why the Hittites disappeared. I guess they had no sense of humor. (*Laughs.*)

Does your sense of humor come from the streets at all?

Well, we lived in the streets, which our kids today sadly don't. Maybe the kids today don't have as much humor, I think, as our generation. Maybe that's one of the reasons. You know what Lenny Bruce said? Everybody on the two coasts, by which he meant New York and Los Angeles, is Jewish. Everyone in between is gentile. In other words, he meant if you're in show business or if you *think* alike . . . you're Jewish. Of course, I don't mean literally Jewish. But you have to examine that remark; there's a lot of truth in it.

Would you call your humor cynical?

It tends more toward cynical than to the Will Rogers type.

Literate?

Yeah, I would think so.

Has being a New Yorker influenced your writing?

My characters are usually more sophisticated, urbane. I don't like country-and-western music or country-and-western characters. (*Laughs.*)

So you still consider yourself a New Yorker.

Yeah. That's silly, because I was twenty-four when I came out here and I'm seventy-four next week.

What do you think of the new generation of filmmakers from the film schools—the Lucases, the Spielbergs, the Coppolas?

Look at them. With some exceptions, there's no humor. Spielberg: did you see *1941* [1979]? It's one of the worst pictures I've ever seen. No humor. Coppola is an Easterner; he has touches. But so far, no great humor. Lucas's humor, I think, is childish.

What about American Graffitti *[1973]?*

That was autobiographical. There's one great autobiographical story in all of us.

What's so inherently funny about being from the East Coast?

It's more sophisticated. More street life. There's no street life in California.

How does that lead to humor?

I don't know, but I think there's a relation. Take illiterates— uneducated people with street smarts. They have a kind of humor. The early comics never had any education—the great comics—they were street people. Eddie Cantor, all of them.

Why have you been able to stay so active when so many of your contemporaries have been unable to crack the new Hollywood?

Maybe it's because my type of thing has lasted longer. The old ones who are steeped in the pictures of the thirties and the forties are out of style; maybe they'll come back, I don't know. Maybe I've been lucky. I can't account for it.

Your type of thing being?

It's more of a sophisticated level. I hate to use the word literate.

What is your definition of sophisticated dialogue?

Peter De Vries is a literate writer; Stephen King isn't—because he doesn't write about literate people. You can't give literate dialogue to the sort of characters he writes about.

Robert Riskin gave literate dialogue to ordinary people.

Well, Robert Riskin was a literate writer. And if he hadn't died, I think Robert Riskin would have lasted and lasted and lasted.

Then define it for me further. What is the definition of literate comedy?

It's not the path of least resistance. Have you seen *Risky Business* [1983]? Every other word is "fuck" or "shit." In other pictures I see around, the dialogue is practically nothing but. It's a cheap laugh. Now I'm not above a cheap laugh if I can get it, but it seems to be nothing but, and that's not literate. In *Reuben, Reuben* I think someone mouths the word "shit"—once. That's all. And these are very sophisticated, up-to-date people.

What about comedy has remained constant in movies over the years?

I can't tell you. I've discussed this with a lot of my friends who are very bright and funny. If you can tell me what makes something funny, you'll never be able to do it. It's got to flow. It's got to be natural. You can't write it according to a diagram.

What is funny that was funny fifty years ago?

Basically, the same things are funny. Physical comedy. Slipping on a banana peel is still funny. But I don't do physical comedy. Mostly verbal. I don't laugh much at physical humor. Who knows why? Who knows what the genes are? What the electrical impulses are that enter in the brain?

What has remained a constant in Hollywood over the years?

The constant in Hollywood, which is a terrible thing, is pandering to what they think the public wants. Today they pander to the young kids who go see a movie four or five times—I'm not even talking about teenagers; I'm talking about kids who are nine, ten, eleven, or twelve years old. That's always been true of the studios. But not quite. In the days of the contract system, they all fought to get Ernst Lubitsch. His pictures never made it, they were all losers, but the studios all fought to get him. He could go from studio to studio. They wanted a little class in their program. Today that would be impossible. Today they put up their "classic divisions." They know they won't lose very much money because they can sell it to cable if it's made cheaply enough, and they won't lose any money on it. So a little guilt has crept in there, I think. But the pandering has never been as bad. It was there in those days, too. In those days they wanted to make women's pictures—the four-handkerchief pictures with the Crawfords and the Shearers. So they were pandering to that; today they are pandering to kids. It's the pandering that is constant.

What has changed the most?

There's no more contract system. There's no more machine-belt production. There are no more clubs. There is no studio system, and the way of making pictures is entirely different. And much less fun. Pictures are better. I think pictures are much better today. People who say the golden age of movies was great, that's baloney. But they're not as much fun to make.

Tom Conti as the debauched poet in Reuben, Reuben. *Julius J. Epstein received his fourth Oscar nomination for a hip-cynical screenplay that ranks among his best—and most personal.*

Summing Up

What is the perfect working situation for you as a writer? Time of day?

Well, I usually work when everybody has lunch—about from twelve to two.

Length of time?

Never more than two hours a day.

How do you gear up for the work?

Well, I have a little trick that I don't always follow. If I am writing a scene, I won't finish it; but I know what the last three or four lines of dialogue will be. I won't write it down. I'll start the next morning with those lines that are already written.

Do you think about the writing ahead of you all day before you begin?

You don't consciously, but you can't help it. You'll be shaving or in the shower, and a thought will pop in your mind. More often than when you sit down and say, "What am I going to do?"

How do you wind down afterwards?

Just stop, take a nap, get a little sun, read.
Longhand still?
Longhand.
Do you move ahead to the second scene if the first scene isn't working out?
Never. I never do that. Never in fifty years. I work from one to two to three to four to five.
Ever suffer from writer's block?
I guess I have to knock wood on that. Not seriously. Instead of my usual three pages a day, I might do one or two one day, but I can't remember saying I'm stuck for two or three weeks at a time.
Do you go back and revise after the first draft?
Oh, yes. But not until I've finished the draft. Not daily revising.
Do you listen to music while you're working?
No.
Do you read for inspiration?
No, I just read; but sometimes it'll throw you into something.
Do you brook any interference during those two hours? Is the phone off the hook?
I welcome every bit of interference. I welcome every phone call. It's an excuse.
Do you drink coffee for stimulation?
I haven't had coffee for years.
Drugs? Liquor?
While working? Never! Oy! (*Holding up hands.*) These are the only tools I have.
If you are doing a script, what are the ideal steps of the process? Do you bother with a treatment?
I don't do a treatment. They used to be mandatory in the old studio days, and I hated them. I do a step outline, by which I mean: number one—meets the girl; number two—meets the father; number three—takes a job; number four—they quarrel; number five. . . . One line—that's all.
How many steps?
Depends. Usually twenty to twenty-five steps.
What comes next?
Doing the actual scenes. I don't fitz around with treatments and things like that.
How long will a script take?
The whole script? It has varied. About two to three months.
What's the fastest script you've ever knocked out?
I think we did *The Male Animal* in about four weeks.
Have you ever tried to write a novel?

No, I don't like prose. I don't like to write it; I don't even like to read it. (*Laughs.*)

Why haven't you attempted a novel?

I'm not very good at it, I guess. I remember once speaking to Philip Barry's widow and asking her if he ever wrote a novel. She said, "No. It all came out dialogue." The same with me. I'm too impatient to get the people talking rather than describing what they look like.

Does that mean there is no extended description in your scripts?

The smallest amount possible.

You've had so many credits. Are you a workaholic as a writer?

The absolute opposite.

Lazy? I find that hard to believe.

All through my career. Max Shulman says he can't go more than a week or so without writing. I know Norman Panama goes crazy if he isn't writing something every day. If I don't work for two or three months, it's fine with me. And I've had periods where I said I'm not going to do anything, and I just sat around without doing anything. Even if I'm not a workaholic, I'd accumulate a few credits after fifty years.

You have described so many of the movies you helped write in derogatory terms. Which do you take particular pride in?

I did a picture called *Take a Giant Step* [1961], which was a black picture before its time. *Light in the Piazza* [1962] was an underrated picture—neither film is a comedy, by the way. I'm very fond of *Pete 'n' Tillie.* I like *Fanny* [1961]. I like *The Tender Trap* [1955].

Not Four Daughters *[1938],* The Strawberry Blonde, Mr. Skeffington?

Yeah, but not so much. Listen, those pictures were made in the days when the language was not real because of censorship problems. Situations were not real. Like *My Foolish Heart* [1950]—she had to suffer because of her divorce. It was ridiculous! That was another picture of mine that was not a comedy, by the way.

Aren't there any pictures that you worked on from that era, where the language may not have been real but where you did work that you are still proud of? The Male Animal, *perhaps?*

I liked *The Male Animal.* I thought it was a good job. There are some pictures that don't require naturalistic dialogue.

What about Arsenic and Old Lace?

Too much like the play. So you can't really take much credit for that.

At a certain point in your career, you must have had considerable prestige within the industry. Were you in a position to direct and therefore to better protect your own writing?

I tried directing once—on a test for *Forever Female* [1954], with Bill

Holden. I was supposed to direct that picture, but the test was so terrible that that was the end of my direction. I'm not tough enough. I knew what the actor was doing wrong, but I couldn't convey to him how to do it right. That's why actors make good directors. I knew exactly what was wrong and exactly how it should be done, but . . .

I didn't know how to communicate with an actor. But I'll tell you something else: when I have a *good* relationship with a director, I can stand behind him. I can go over to him on the sly, and I can say, "No, that's wrong, it should be *this* way." But I can't do that to the actor. I don't know why. I would say today that no writer should start out without first learning direction. It's a way of protecting your work.

Do you ever regret having expended your tremendous creative energy in movies and in Hollywood?

No. I don't know what else I could have done. And I think, especially today, once censorship was done away with, pictures are far superior to the theatre or the stage—a much more important medium.

But you look down your nose at so much of your own work.

Yeah. But take the top playwrights. How many Tennessee Williams plays were really good? Maybe three or four out of a whole forty years' work. So if you've done sixty or whatever pictures I've done—a lot of them on the machine-belt at Warners . . .

Then you feel it is enough to be proud of at least a handful.

Yeah, a handful. But that's enough.

Frances Goodrich and Albert Hackett: Perfectionists

Interview by Mark Rowland

In his memoir, *Heyday,* the screenwriter, producer, and former MGM studio head Dore Schary claims that *Father of the Bride* (1950), which eventually netted an Academy Award nomination for Best Screenplay by Frances Goodrich and Albert Hackett, was nearly derailed at its outset by the reluctance of its would-be authors to write it. "The book was darling but we don't know what to do with it," was, according to Schary, Goodrich and Hackett's initial reaction. But they decided to give it a shot after a series of pep talks from understanding Uncle Dore, and lo and behold, their screenplay turned out to be "wonderful."

"The Hackett-Goodrich syndrome appeared each time they went to a new screenplay," Schary concludes. "All I needed for a cure was patience and a variety of soothing reassurances" (pp. 217–18). What Schary in his self-congratulatory spiel neatly overlooks is that over the course of three decades at MGM, with or without Schary's "variety of soothing reassurances," Frances Goodrich and Albert Hackett wrote films of consistently high quality and remarkable range. Indeed, today their credits read like a revival theatre's dream bill—cosmopolitan whodunits (*The Thin Man* and two clever sequels); Nelson Eddy and Jeanette MacDonald favorites (*Rose Marie, Naughty Marietta*); rousing musicals (*Seven Brides for Seven Brothers, Easter Parade*); westerns (*The Virginian*); social drama (*The Diary of Anne Frank*); and even a bonafide Christmas classic (*It's a Wonderful Life*). Through it all they remained "simple people with simple tastes," as Frances once put it—perfectionists who always took their craft far more seriously than themselves or their surroundings. "There isn't anything glamorous about us," Frances liked to observe. "We just have the capacity for hard work, and it has paid off."

Both Goodrich and Hackett began their careers as actors and later as playwrights. Albert, who was born in New York City and educated there at the Professional Children's School, made his stage debut at the age of six. Frances, nine years his senior, grew up in Bellevue, New Jersey, graduated from Vassar, and made her theatrical debut in 1916 with Ruth Chatterton in *Come Out of the Kitchen*. Her first two marriages, to the actor Robert Ames and to the writer and historian Hendrik Willem Van Loon, ended in divorce; by the time she met Albert, both were aspiring playwrights. Not too surprisingly, their first collaboration, *Up Pops the Devil* in 1930, was a comic sketch about a group of artistes living in Greenwich Village whose lives bore more than a passing resemblance to the authors and their social circle. Spiked by the sort of snappy dialogue and sly turns of wit that would eventually become their trademark, the play was an instant hit, with rave notices and an extended Broadway run.

Albert was first lured to Hollywood as dialogue director of *Devil's* film adaptation; but, rather than relegate Frances to the role of "writer's wife" (they had married by then), he elected to return to New York with her, where they penned a second successful comedy (*The Bridal Wise*). Now MGM offered them both writer's contracts, and their film careers began in earnest.

Success came quickly; after a few forgettable efforts, they scripted Dashiell Hammett's *The Thin Man* (1934). Myrna Loy, who played Nora Charles in the film, lauded her character's "gorgeous sense of humor. She appreciated the distinctive grace of her husband's wit, and laughed at him and with him when he was funny"—comments that apply with equal felicity to the Hacketts themselves. Through the thirties Frances and Albert were actively involved in the Screen Writers Guild, socialized with other "expatriate" New York writers at MGM like Dorothy Parker, Alan Campbell, Lillian Hellman, and S. J. Perelman, and still adhered to a grinding work schedule that often kept them at their desks for such lengths that, as Albert once joked, "We had to bring a flashlight into our garden to see how the vegetables were doing."

By 1939 the Hacketts were burned out, and they returned to New York for a breather. Within weeks Albert's friend and the playwright-director Owen Davis had persuaded him to co-star in a new comedy, *Mr. and Mrs. North*. Albert, who had come to appreciate acting again because "actors don't have to think—all they do is remember," took to his part with relish. ("A good actor having an uncommonly good

Frances Goodrich and Albert Hackett at work on The Diary of Anne Frank.

time," wrote one drama critic.) The Hacketts did pen a Broadway play
of their own (*The Great Big Doorstep*) before returning to Hollywood,
where they served on the Writers' War Board for the war's duration.
One of their tasks included trimming Lillian Hellman's *Watch on the
Rhine* (1943) by twenty minutes for an Armed Forces presentation.
The Hacketts were understandably worried about the playwright's reaction; but Hellman found their edit quite satisfactory (she later

lopped off three more minutes herself), and several years later she recommended the Hacketts to producer Kermit Bloomgarden when the latter was casting about for a possible theatrical adaption of *The Diary of Anne Frank.*

In the interim the Hacketts had reached the apex of their screen-writing careers, producing a series of first-rate scripts that were in turn filmed by some of Hollywood's leading directors. Nearly all of these projects were musicals, comedies, or both. *The Diary of Anne Frank* posed a completely separate set of challenges and absorbed the Hack-etts' energies for two years. In preparation they spent considerable time with Anne's father, Otto Frank, toured the attic where the family had sequestered itself (so narrow "you could put out your hands and touch the walls on each side," Frances recalled), studied war records, and even immersed themselves in other teenage diaries to better plumb Anne's psychology. "No one working on *Diary* thought about money," said Frances. "We all felt we were working for a cause." The play opened in 1955 and won that season's Critic's Circle and Pulitzer prizes. In 1959 the Hacketts adapted it for the screen, with George Stevens directing. Ironically, it turned out to be one of their last cred-ited pictures.

I interviewed Frances Goodrich and Albert Hackett in December of 1983 in their spacious and comfortably appointed duplex on New York's upper West Side. Albert met me at the door and escorted me to a table at the far end of the living room by a window overlooking Central Park, where Frances, physically infirm but still possessed of her natural elegance of bearing, exceedingly alert, and good-humored, was seated. (Her first remark, as I brought out a bottle of wine as a present, was a mock accusation of bribery.)

The Hacketts insisted that their careers were of no interest but that they would do their best to answer whatever questions I might pose about their work. In fact, they used my queries as a springboard into the rich memories of their past, and they proved effortlessly amusing and insightful in the process. Every fifteen minutes or so, Frances would interrupt the reverie with her assurance that I had done my duty and the interview was over. At this point I would look for help to Albert, who would persuade his wife to put up with the interloper for a few more minutes. After living and working together for over fifty years, their clear enjoyment of and affection for each other was noth-ing short of inspirational. Both were far too gracious to refuse my request for another talk after the Christmas holidays but warned that I wouldn't get away twice without being forced to drink my own wine. A few weeks later, Frances Goodrich died. She was ninety-three years old.

1930   *Up Pops the Devil* (Edward Sutherland). Based on their play. Dialogue director.*

1933   *The Secret of Madame Blanche* (Charles Brabin). Adaptation.
Penthouse (W. S. Van Dyke). Adaptation.

1934   *Chained* (Clarence Brown). Uncredited contribution.
Fugitive Lovers (Richard Boleslawsky). Co-script.
The Thin Man (W. S. Van Dyke). Script.
Hide-Out (W. S. Van Dyke). Script.

1935   *Naughty Marietta* (W. S. Van Dyke). Co-script.
Ah, Wilderness! (Clarence Brown). Script.

1936   *Rose Marie* (W. S. Van Dyke). Co-script.
After the Thin Man (W. S. Van Dyke). Script.

1937   *The Firefly* (Robert Z. Leonard). Co-script.

1938   *Thanks for the Memory* (George Archainbaud). Remake of *Up Pops the Devil.*

1939   *Society Lawyer* (Edwin L. Marin). Co-script.
Another Thin Man (W. S. Van Dyke). Script.

1944   *Lady in the Dark* (Mitchell Leisen). Script.
The Hitler Gang (John Farrow). Script.

1946   *The Virginian* (Stuart Gilmore). Script.
It's a Wonderful Life (Frank Capra). Co-script.

1948   *The Pirate* (Vincente Minnelli). Script.
Summer Holiday (Rouben Mamoulian). Remake of *Ah, Wilderness!* Script.
Easter Parade (Charles Walters). Story, co-script.

1949   *In the Good Old Summertime* (Robert Z. Leonard). Co-script.

1950   *Father of the Bride* (Michael Curtiz). Script.

1951   *Father's Little Dividend* (Vincente Minnelli). Script.
Too Young to Kiss (Robert Z. Leonard). Script.

1953   *Give a Girl a Break* (Stanley Donen). Script.

1954   *The Long, Long Trailer* (Vincente Minnelli). Script.
Seven Brides for Seven Brothers (Stanley Donen). Co-script.

---

* Albert Hackett only.

1956   *Gaby* (Curtis Bernhardt). Co-script.

1958   *A Certain Smile* (Jean Negulesco). Script.

1959   *The Diary of Anne Frank* (George Stevens). Based on their
play. Script.

1962   *Five Finger Exercise* (Daniel Mann). Script.

Produced plays include *Up Pops the Devil, Bridal Wise, The Great Big Doorstep,* and *The Diary of Anne Frank.*

Academy Awards include an Oscar nomination for adapting *The Thin Man* in 1934; that same year the original story for *Hide-Out* by Mauri Grashin earned a nomination (the script was by Goodrich-Hackett); a nomination in 1936 for the screenplay of *After the Thin Man;* a nomination in 1950 for the screenplay of *Father of the Bride;* and a nomination in 1954 for the co-screenplay (with Dorothy Kingsley) of *Seven Brides for Seven Brothers.*

Writers Guild awards include the Best Comedy of 1948, *Easter Parade,* co-written with Sidney Sheldon; the Best Comedy of 1951, *Father's Little Dividend;* the Best Musical of 1954, *Seven Brides for Seven Brothers,* co-written with Dorothy Kingsley; and the Best Drama of 1959, *The Diary of Anne Frank,* based on their own play. In 1955 they received the Laurel Award for Achievement.

When did you first meet and decide to collaborate as writers?
Hackett: We were on the stage, that's how we first met.
Goodrich: He was in one company, and I was in another in Chicago at the same time.
Hackett: Right. I'd just come there for one day. I'd gone up from Cincinnati where I was playing stock to see Paul Kelly, who was doing *Up the Ladder.*
Goodrich: I remember Albert visiting Paul in the dressingroom, and his voice. I thought, *"That fresh kid!"* Well . . .
So you became involved romantically at that time?
Hackett: We began to write together. We were both trying to make some money writing; then we exchanged views on things; and then we started to rewrite each other's stuff. That was how we got involved, exchanging those dreadful comments. Wasn't that it?
Goodrich: I had a very nice woman in a play [probably an unproduced script]. And Albert rewrote her character and made her bitchy. Very curious, don't you think? Well, anyway, it was a long time before we got the first play done.

Hackett: Meanwhile, we were still *in* plays. Then we had a play that was going to go on up in Skowhegan, wasn't it? Then we had another play that was being tried out in Long Island or someplace. That is the one that eventually became *Up Pops the Devil.* Well, we rewrote it, and it became something of a hit [in 1930].

Goodrich: It ran over a year [146 performances at the Masque Theatre].

Hackett: It was sold to Paramount. Then, we decided to get married because we had enough money. I left the cast and was off as dialogue director at Paramount.

Goodrich: Then [David] Selznick offered you a seven-year contract. And Albert was out there on his own as dialogue director. Well, anyway, he was sweet and gave it up and said, "I'll wait until we both get a contract." So he came back to New York and put on a play [*The Bridal Wise*], and we *did* get a contract together—at MGM.

What made you decide to leave New York and go to Hollywood together?

Hackett: Well, that was where the money was.

Goodrich: No it wasn't, Albert! My God, it wasn't! Those were the years when Mr. Mayer would call in everybody and you would think it's going to be something lovely [and he would say], "Cut 50 percent!"

Hackett: Well, at that time we were both out there working for much less than we'd got in the theatre acting, and with a 50 percent cut we were practically sending home for money.

Goodrich: But it was a new field and interesting for that reason. And you could always go back to the theatre. You thought! (*Laughs.*)

What were the differences you found in writing for the screen?

Hackett: It was a lot easier. Because there was movement in the thing. Sometimes in a play you got stuck in the middle of a big scene, and you couldn't get the goddamned curtain down. But here you just kept moving.

Goodrich: We started to write movies as we would a play. Because we had a director, Charles Brabin, a beautiful director, who told us, "Don't write stage comedy. Don't write anything but the words. I'll do the rest."

Hackett: We worked for one man who committed suicide after we finished a script. He was a producer at MGM, and he committed suicide right after his marriage to the blonde bombshell [Jean Harlow]. What was his name? Paul Bern.

Goodrich: We had written a simple scene, and he called us in for a conference: "My secretary could do it better!" Then Albert read it for him, and he said, "Well, why didn't you *write* it like that?" We said we did. That is when we learned that when you write, "Yes, I would like to go . . ." (you add), "Her face lights up. Then she turns to him . . ." All this awful *dreck*. But that's what he wanted.

Hackett: This was supposed to be for a picture with Joan Crawford and that little boy actor [Jackie Cooper], who was going to play her son. Well, we knew Joan Crawford wasn't going to play mother to that little boy. But that problem wasn't the only reason the script wasn't very good. It was about a woman who was a prostitute, and we were not very good on writing about prostitutes. We went down to talk to some woman in the government in Los Angeles, and she talked to us about women prostitutes. She said they make the best mothers, you know. She said there was one who used to put her boy out there on the fire escape when the men came in—pull the shades down, let him play out there, and have a fine time: it kept him healthy. So that the disadvantage of having a regular mother . . . Well, anyway, the picture never got made. (*Laughs.*) But we did finish the script. And that night we went to a party—

Goodrich: At the Freddie Marches'. And Paul Bern was supposed to come with his bride.

Hackett: I remember Bern said, "Well, I'll see you there." So we looked for him but never found him that night. And the following day a paper was out—an extra—that Paul Bern had committed suicide that night.

That must have given you some pause.

Hackett: Well, naturally we wanted to find out if we were to blame. And whether he'd done it because of that script of ours was a question.

Goodrich: Because one day while we were still working on the script we had met Freddie March on the lot. And he said, "How's it coming?" And we said, "We hate that man, Paul Bern. It's just outrageous the way he tears down what we do. So we're thinking about moving back to New York." And Freddie said, "Don't do that. He has in his family a history of suicide, and we're all scared he'll commit suicide." That's exactly what he did. So we weren't entirely responsible.

Hackett: We were only responsible for *his* death—not the other members of his family.

Goodrich: I think we helped.

Did you criticize each other's work?

Goodrich: Oh God, yes!

Hackett: Show the scars! Show the scars!

Goodrich: (*Laughs.*) I'd *scream* at Albert. Once I screamed, "Over my dead body does that line go in!" I screamed so hard I lost my voice for three days. And Albert once said to me, which was a much *crueler* thing, "If you think that's good, you should be *scared.*" You know, you couldn't say anything worse than that, could you? Quietly, he said it. Didn't lose his voice at all.

Would you write the same scenes?

Hackett: Always. We each wrote a scene and then handed it to the other. Then said, "Oh, boy!" But that was wonderful about the two of us; we could say how scandalous we thought it was. Whereas, if we were working with someone we didn't know, you know, we had to be more delicate. With each other we could say right off, "That's it, that's right," or "You can write it better," or "Do you think that's better?" So eventually the scene came out so that neither of us had any objections to it.

Goodrich: Also, it was a great benefit having been in the theatre. Because we could play the scene and see if it worked, you know?

Hackett: That was what we were always doing—getting up and playing the scene. So then we knew how long a scene was and how tight and what part held and when it didn't begin to hold.

Goodrich: Those were wonderful days out there, those early days, because you really had authority, which I don't think you have now. At least we hadn't any when we left—no authority at all. And we really had quite a backlog of successes. But no authority. It always had to be Mr. So-and-So, some other producer. At first we had a really wonderful producer, Hunt Stromberg. He was good, he encouraged us, he was darling to us. And when we were working with him we never had any trouble, did we?

I'm curious about your relationship with MGM, which wasn't really known as a great studio for writers.

Hackett: Well, they had 155 writers under contract while we were there.

Goodrich: One hundred and fifty five. Now they don't have any people under contract, I think. A director comes in with his writer and his script and his star. And that's that.

Hackett: And his own couch. (*Laughs.*)

Was there much camaraderie among the writers there?

Goodrich: We had a wonderful table there in the commissary. Just think of the people who were there! Dashiell Hammett, Ogden Nash, Sid Perelman, Laura Perelman, Dorothy Parker, and Alan Campbell. You know, it was a wonderful group of people. Stromberg used to call us "his stable." (*Laughs.*)

Hackett: But then in the center of the room there were the big writers that had the die in the cage and would toss it to see who paid the bill. Those were the big boys.

Goodrich: Those were the ones who tried to break the Guild.

You're talking now about Patterson McNutt, James Kevin McGuinness—

Goodrich: Yes, McGuinness, and John Lee Mahin, and—

Hackett: The one [Howard Emmett Rogers] who was saving two bullets—one for himself and one for his wife.

Goodrich: Those were very interesting times—when the Guild was being formed and all that excitement. Albert and I would go around at luncheon time, taking our lunch time to talk to young people—

Hackett: I think one of the junior writers was Art Buchwald. (*Laughs.*) But I don't remember putting the sleeve on him.

Goodrich: I never knew that, until you tell me now.

Hackett: I'm sorry I kept it from you. Well, you see, our lives will be different from now on.

Goodrich: So we'd go 'round at lunch time. Then we'd be up in the Alps and look down at the walls of the studio, and we'd see the "Four Horsemen" that took studio time to break the Guild.

Hackett: They could go anywhere. They didn't have to have office hours.

Was there a difference in hanging out with the writers in Hollywood versus, say, the Algonquin Circle in New York?

Hackett: Oh, we'd never be allowed near the Algonquin people. (*Laughs.*) They were mostly critics and writers and newspapermen and lots of lady stars. Some witty people.

Goodrich: In Hollywood we were just working people having lunch together. That's really all it was.

Was that at all indicative of a difference between Hollywood and New York?

Hackett: No. When we were in New York back then, there were a lot of actors and people in the theatre that we knew. When we got to California, if you were a writer the only people you ever knew were writers. The actors, the big ones, all were friendly with producers. The only exceptions were Freddie March and a couple of stars we had known in the theatre; a couple of times we'd go to dinner with them. But most of the time . . .

Goodrich: There was such a caste system out in Hollywood. There was never anything like it. There were layers and other layers, you know. And the lowest layer was the writers.

Hackett: Less than dust.

But still you enjoyed each other's company.

Hackett: Fortunately.

Goodrich: It wasn't really nine to five, but half past nine to half past four over at the office every day, even Saturday. We worked hard—very hard—to get the stuff out.

Did you work in the same office together?

Hackett: Yes. We had two offices but we always ended up getting together in the same office. Neither of us had a secretary, you know. You finished something, you'd send it over to the script department, and they'd copy it for you quickly and well. We never thought a secretary was necessary.

Would you trade ideas as you worked?

Hackett: Well, before we would write a scene we would talk about the scene and say something about it; and then we would go and write a few things and then make our changes.

Goodrich: It was curious out there. They did not want you to write an original. They preferred to buy something, look at it, know they had it, and then adapt it. We only did about two originals, even when doing sequels. Not any originals; didn't want it. Either buy a play from New York or a book or something, and you work on that.

Hackett: Actually, the ideal thing was, if they could have a picture out for every week of the year—fifty-two pictures. They had the theatres to play them, and anytime they were not able to put their own picture in there they had to put in somebody else's. In *their* theatre. So they were always trying. Once the word went out that everybody was to write a "B" picture *fast.* That was the time when we looked through stories and finally found part of an idea that we could use, [and it kind of went with] part of a play we'd started to work on in New York, so we just threw our idea in along with it. Then they said, "Take your time, take your time." It was called *Hide-Out* [1934], with Robert Montgomery and Maureen O'Sullivan, a real rush job.

Van Dyke, who directed it, was a wonderful director, and he had done many other westerns. In this picture there was this Irish actor from New York, Whitford Kane, who MGM got to come out and play a part opposite Elizabeth Patterson. These were *stage* people. In one scene where Montgomery is wounded and in bed, Kane was told, "Now you start right here at that doorway. When she answers the door, you take the cup and saucer, come down around the bed, and carry it right off." That was the rehearsal as far as Van Dyke was concerned. Kane says to someone, "What happens now?" "They're going to shoot it." "Shoot it?!" They had to cut the sound out, he was shaking the cup and saucer so much. He got back to New York so fast. (*Laughs.*) Couldn't understand how anyone could stand it. No rehearsal or anything. Whitford Kane from the Abbey Theatre . . . *The Thin Man* [1934] was supposed to be some sort of record, Van Dyke was so quick. He shot the film in about twelve days or something like that.

Goodrich: We did the script in three weeks. My God, when I think of what we used to do.

Hackett: Anyway, by 1939 we were exhausted so we just quit and came back to New York. Back where it was quiet.

It's been said that your screenplays for The Thin Man *series were based as much on yourselves as on Nick and Nora Charles, the characters created by Dashiell Hammett. Is that true?*

Hackett: No, not any more than usual. You do put a lot of yourself in scenes. But those were the sort of scenes you'd have written in the theatre.

How faithfully would your pictures adhere to the script?

Hackett: Well, it depends. With Stromberg, the scene we wrote was what they played. We had another director—Richard Boleslawsky—who, if someone was supposed to do this, he'd do just the opposite. Just a dreadful man—arbitrarily changed everything. But it [*Fugitive Lovers* in 1934] was one of those things where it was done fast and wasn't very good.

Goodrich: As writers we were never on the set, never asked to be on the set. The script finished—okay—shot and that's it. And only for a rewrite were we called in.

Did you get as much satisfaction writing adaptations as originals?

Goodrich: Adaptations were all we did. Except for *Father of the Bride* [1950], where they wanted a sequel. When we saw Spencer Tracy on the lot, he said, "I've got a wonderful idea for the sequel." This is the third one, by the way; we'd already done the baby one [*Father's Little Dividend* in 1951]. Tracy said, "Elizabeth is very tired after having the baby; I have to go to Europe on a conference, so I take her with me."

Hackett: That was his idea.

Goodrich: Which just meant that [Joan] Bennett would be on the wharf to say goodbye and then hello when they got back. Bennett—out!

Hackett: And Tracy and Elizabeth Taylor would have all the scenes together.

Goodrich: Then I went to dinner at so-and-so's house and sat next to [the producer] Walter Wanger, who was Bennett's husband at the time. He said, "I've got a wonderful idea for the third *Father of the Bride* series. Elizabeth Taylor says to Joan, 'Mummy, tell me, when did you fall in love with Daddy? When did you first meet him?'" Well, of course, that eliminates Spencer Tracy entirely!—because Joan Bennett could play an eighteen-year-old and look lovely, but *he* couldn't. Then he [Wanger] shot the agent [Jennings Lang] in the scrotum in the parking lot, remember? That was the end of that series.

Hackett: Yes, that saved us.

The original version of Hammett's The Thin Man, *which was modeled after Hammett and Lillian Hellman, but also applicable to screenwriters Frances Goodrich and Albert Hackett. Myrna Loy and William Powell (with Asta) played Nick and Nora Charles.*

Did you enjoy working on adaptations?

Hackett: Sometimes, you see, you got a hold of something where there wasn't anything there, and you had to tear your hair out to find an idea; those were the tough ones. But if there was a story there, your job then was to fill it in and pad and get something going in it.

In *Easter Parade* [1948] we had seventeen songs by Irving Berlin, but one little song that he composed—"she loves him and he loves her and she loves him"—was supposed to be the idea of what this story was about. That was the deal when MGM bought the songs from Berlin. We looked at that song and looked at the other songs, and we couldn't make anything out of it. But we could make a story out of "Easter Parade," which was one of the numbers in the thing. So Berlin—

Goodrich: He was just the dearest man who ever lived. He said, "Forget it; it doesn't matter. I'll use the other song again, don't worry about it."

Hackett: The story wasn't too good, but it served. Got those [musical] numbers in there.

Beginning with the Nelson Eddy–Jeanette MacDonald films, you worked on a number of important musicals. How did you adapt yourselves to the limits of that form?

Hackett: With *Naughty Marietta* [1935] and *Rose Marie* [1936] you had certain scenes in there and certain songs that were all part of that business—my God, those were famous songs. They had to be there and come out in pretty much the same form as they did in the show. The only thing we tried to do was make it seem a little bit more real than the stage version. The thing is to try to make it work for everybody. If you can satisfy the music department with what you're doing . . .

Did you find that each of you had certain complementary strengths as writers—for comedy versus drama, say, or dialogue versus structure?

Hackett: No, no.

Goodrich: Just a long battle. For every line and every word. And a *violent* battle. At least Albert was more polite than I—except when he said, "You should be *scared.*" That one is emblazoned on me.

Would you work through several drafts?

Hackett: You'd do a lot of writing and cutting and trimming. But the point is, once you've got the thing moving, it's a lot easier then.

What about male and female characters? Was one of you better at that?

Hackett: We thought of everyone as being homosexual so we never had to worry about that.

Were there scripts you felt were particularly successful?

Hackett: The script we did for *Ah, Wilderness!* [1935]. At first, when it was talked about, W. C. Fields was going to be in the thing, and it was very exciting. W. C. was going to play the part of the uncle, so we tailored the part and gave him a couple of special scenes. The guy [Wallace Beery] from *The Champ* [1931] ended up playing the part—and he wouldn't say the lines. He wouldn't say O'Neill's lines! Anything that came into his head he'd say but not O'Neill.

Goodrich: That picture was entirely O'Neill. That's when doing an adaptation is really wonderful, you know, when you've got a lovely thing like that to do.

Tell me about It's a Wonderful Life *[1946]. You came in rather late on that picture, and four different writers [director Frank Capra, Jo Swerling, and Goodrich-Hackett] are given credit.*

Hackett: Well, none of the early writers had even written the story that that picture was about.

What was the origin of the story?

Hackett: It came from a Christmas card. I don't know if we actually ever saw the card, did we? Anyway, the idea was, "I wish I'd never been born." There wasn't any story to it. But Marc Connelly wrote a script, [Clifford] Odets wrote—I don't know if he wrote a full script . . .

Goodrich: And [Dalton] Trumbo wrote any number of scripts. But they just didn't pay any attention to the story.

Hackett: So when we saw the script and were asked, "What do you think of it?" we said, "Nobody's told the story that's on the card." And Capra said, "Well, that's the way I feel about the thing."

Goodrich: So, fortunately, we didn't have to rewrite. We did our script.

That was the script of the movie?

Hackett: I don't know; it's hard for us to remember that, because we never stayed on the thing all the way, not for a rundown.

Goodrich: Not for that horrid man.

Hackett: I remember he [Capra] said to one of our agents, "When are the Hacketts going to be finished?" And the agent said, "Tell him they're finished right now." Well, that's the way we felt about it. We quickly wrote out the last scene, and we never saw him again after that. He's a very arrogant son-of-a-bitch.

Goodrich: He couldn't wait to get writing on it himself. Beulah Bondie was in it—you know, actors *never* know who wrote the script. And we saw her at a party, and she said, "Oh, what a wonderful man that Capra is. We were given a scene that was impossible to speak. These long speeches—impossible! So Capra said, 'Dismissed for the day.' And the next morning, a simple lovely scene." So there it is.

Hackett: She didn't know we'd had anything to do with it.

Goodrich: We had rewritten and rewritten.

Hackett: We've never seen the thing.

Goodrich: It's the only unpleasant experience we've ever had.

That's pretty ironic. It's a very touching movie, a classic.

Goodrich: (*Laughs.*) Oh, when I read in *The New Yorker* that they run it every year, that they have an organization . . . I remember what we went through.

You can't bring yourselves to watch the film?

Hackett: No, we've never seen it.

After a series of upbeat musicals your careers took quite a turn with The Diary of Anne Frank *[1959].*

Goodrich: Well, it just got to be that you had no authority. There was no one like Stromberg who would say, "We'll take the Hacketts' script!" Nobody who had enough knowledge or faith in their own judgment.

Hackett: We worked with somebody we will not mention—he's passed beyond—and he didn't know what the hell you were writing about. We handed him a scene, and he'd pick up his blue pencil and say "let me see!" without ever reading the scene.

So what inspired you to write The Diary?

Goodrich: It was submitted to us as a picture, but the studio [MGM] would not buy it. Then word came from [the Broadway producer] Kermit Bloomgarden that he'd like us to do it as a play. Then, a long battle. And Albert said to me at one point, "You turned it down as a picture, what are you doing?" I said, "It's a perfect play—one set." So we came back to New York to do it as a play.

Hackett: You see, someone had started to write that play before, and there was a lot of breast-beating in it; and we could never write that sort of thing. When the producer came to talk to us and to ask us what we thought of it, we said we don't see it as a picture. And he said, "I don't think if it's a breast-beating thing, it'll ever get over. But that child, if we can only hold on to that child . . ."

Goodrich: The young girl. That [her character] was another thing that we just put on paper. Completely altered that diary. Completely. That was a tremendously moving and interesting thing. I cried for two solid years while we did it. And then we never had another offer for a comedy or musical ever again. (*Laughs.*) But someone wanted us to write about—

Hackett: A gang rape or something like that.

Goodrich: That's the kind of offer we'd be getting. That was one of the things that made us say, "Let's forget pictures for a while."

Do you still write now?

Hackett: Oh, no. We just do what we have to do. What we have to buy in the store, you know. Grapefruit, that's what we like. Milk, butter, eggs.

Goodrich: Albert still has writing very much on his mind. He had pneumonia about two years ago—three years ago?—and he was up in the hospital. He had it bad; they were feeding him penicillin and God knows what else. At one point I said to the nurse, "Have your lunch; I'll watch him. It's alright, take your time, have a little rest." So I sit there reading. I'd only looked away for a moment; I look over and he's taken the penicillin needle out and he's writing. With *penicillin.*

Hackett: You see, it's in my blood.

Norman Krasna:
The Woolworth's Touch

Interview by Pat McGilligan

In the fullest sense of the word, Norman Krasna represents the screenwriter as *auteur.* For the most part, Krasna wrote original plays and screenplays without the benefit (or hindrance) of a collaborator, and his stories and the peculiar themes that have preoccupied him derive from his own rags-to-riches experiences.

As a poor youth without means or prospects, Krasna worked at Macy's department store while plugging away at night-school law courses. Inspired by the journalism wars and the colorful newspaper personalities of New York City in the 1920s, he borrowed a quarter and went downtown to the offices of *The New York World,* where he talked his way into a temporary job as a copy boy for the Sunday feature department. There, on the periphery of the Algonquin Circle and surrounded by his idols—people like the columnists Heywood Broun and Franklin P. Adams, the editorialist Walter Lippmann, the drama critic Alexander Woolcott, and the famed reporter Louis Weitzenkorn, who wrote *Five Star Final*—Krasna fell in love with the written word, quit law school, and much to the chagrin of his parents, pronounced himself a writer. He was an errand boy for the big names of *The World,* but a notorious up-and-comer in his own right, who is remembered for his demonic energy and impetuous blunders. He was awarded a byline reviewing second-tier acts at the Palace. He was not yet twenty.

With the imminent collapse of *The World,* Krasna went to work for the editor Martin Quigley at the movie trade journal *The Motion Picture Exhibitor's Herald World.* When, as fate would have it, he was offered a job with Hubert Voight in the publicity department of Warner Brothers, he moved to Hollywood, where he further enhanced his eccentric reputation by contriving wacky publicity stunts of questionable taste and ethics. At night Krasna drafted a satire about his adventures as a Warners tub-thumper, and the result was his first play, *Louder, Please!*, which he described as "nothing but screaming, like *The Front Page*—the best play I ever saw in my life." After *Louder, Please!*, which starred Lee Tracy, opened to good notices on Broadway, Krasna returned to Hollywood—no longer as a press agent but as a junior writer at Columbia. Shortly, he was up for the first of his three career Oscar nominations for the story and screenplay of *The Richest Girl in the World*, a period trifle starring Joel McCrea, Miriam Hopkins, and Fay Wray, and directed by William A. Seiter. The 1934 comedy was the first manifestation of the mistaken identity motif that was to become his trademark.

Among his subsequent accomplishments were two hard-hitting, slice-of-life melodramas directed by Fritz Lang; Alfred Hitchcock's only screwball comedy; a play and screenplay in partnership with Groucho Marx; the vintage thirties and forties romantic comedies *Hands Across the Table* (1935), *Bachelor Mother* (1939), *The Devil and Miss Jones* (1941) (inspired by his Macy's memories), *The Flame of New Orleans* (1941) (directed by friend René Clair), and *It Started with Eve* (1941); an Academy Award for writing the screenplay of *Princess O'Rourke* (1943), which he also directed; numerous film adaptations of his plays, including *Indiscreet* (1958), which was directed by Stanley Donen and ranks among the best of his films; and *Let's Make Love* (1960), one of the last pictures to star Marilyn Monroe.

His career as a writer is unusual in several respects. With impunity, he shuttled between Broadway and Hollywood, producing successful plays as well as acclaimed screenplays; he dabbled in directing and producing; he often wrote without a studio contract and almost always without a co-writer. Krasna has been given short-shrift as a screenwriter by some latter-day film critics and pigeonholed as a comedy writer obsessed with plot contrivances. When I interviewed him, he was aware of this stigma and embittered about it. How wrong these critics are. This interview shows how close the themes of impersonation and mistaken identity were to the heart of Krasna and how infinitely adroit he was at exploring them within the framework of a movie story.

In the late 1950s, Krasna left Hollywood and emigrated to Europe for a period of time that stretched over twenty years. When he returned he found himself a screenwriter without a "recent credit." Our interview was conducted in his Swiss villa–style apartment across the avenue from Twentieth Century–Fox and around the corner from the

Norman Krasna working with Olivia de Havilland between scenes of Princess O'Rourke. *(Photo: Academy of Motion Picture Arts and Sciences)*

Hillcrest Country Club, where Krasna liked nothing better than to spend the afternoons on the greens.

At seventy-four, he was humiliated by the mighty effort necessary to revive his dormant screenwriting career. He died on November 1, 1984. According to *Variety,* "He had not been in ill health and had played golf the day before."

1932   *Hollywood Speaks* (Edward Buzzell). Story, co-dialogue.
    That's My Boy (Roy William Neill). Script.

1933   *Meet the Baron* (Walter Lang). Co-story.
    Love, Honor, and Oh Baby! (Edward Buzzell). Uncredited adaptation.
    Parole Girl (Edward Cline). Uncredited story contribution.
    So This Is Africa! (Edward Cline). Story.

1934   *The Richest Girl in the World* (William A. Seiter). Story, script.

1935   *Romance in Manhattan* (Stephen Roberts). Co-story.
    Hands Across the Table (Mitchell Leisen). Co-script.
    Four Hours to Kill (Mitchell Leisen). Adaptation of his play *Small Miracle*. Script.

1936   *Fury* (Fritz Lang). Screen story.
    Wife Versus Secretary (Clarence Brown). Co-script.

1937   *As Good as Married* (Edward Buzzell). Story.
    The King and the Chorus Girl (Mervyn LeRoy). Co-story, co-script.
    Big City (Frank Borzage). Story, producer.

1938   *Three Loves Has Nancy* (Richard Thorpe). Producer.
    The First Hundred Years (Richard Thorpe). Story, producer.
    You and Me (Fritz Lang). Story, co-adaptation.

1939   *Bachelor Mother* (Garson Kanin). Script.

1940   *It's a Date* (William A. Seiter). Script.

1941   *Mr. and Mrs. Smith* (Alfred Hitchcock). Story, script.
    The Devil and Miss Jones (Sam Wood). Story, script, co-producer.
    The Flame of New Orleans (René Clair). Story, script.
    It Started with Eve (Henry Koster). Co-script.

1943   *Princess O'Rourke* (Norman Krasna). Story, script, director.

1945   *Bride by Mistake* (Richard Wallace). Story.
    Practically Yours (Mitchell Leisen). Story, script.

1946   *Dear Ruth* (William D. Russell). From his play.

1949   *John Loves Mary* (David Butler). From his play.

1950   *The Big Hangover* (Norman Krasna). Story, script, director, producer.

1951   *Dear Brat* (William A. Seiter). Based on the characters from *Dear Ruth.*
        Blue Veil (Curtis Bernhardt). Co-producer.
        Behave Yourself (George Beck). Co-producer.

1952   *Clash by Night* (Fritz Lang). Co-producer.

1954   *White Christmas* (Michael Curtiz). Co-story, co-script.

1956   *The Ambassador's Daughter* (Norman Krasna). Story, script, director, producer.
        Bundle of Joy (Norman Taurog). Remake of *Bachelor Mother.*

1958   *Indiscreet* (Stanley Donen). From his play *Kind Sir.* Script.

1960   *Who Was That Lady?* (George Sidney). From his play. Script, producer.
        Let's Make Love (George Cukor). Story, script.
        The Richest Girl in the World (Lau Lauritzen). Danish remake of 1934 film.

1962   *My Geisha* (Jack Cardiff). Story, script.

1964   *Sunday in New York* (Peter Tewksbury). From his play. Script.
        I'd Rather Be Rich (Jack Smight). Co-story, co-script.

Produced plays include *Louder, Please!, Small Miracle, The Man with Blonde Hair* (also directed), *Dear Ruth, John Loves Mary, Time for Elizabeth* (also directed), *Kind Sir, Who Was That Lady I Saw You With?, Sunday in New York, Watch the Birdie, Love in E Flat, Kein Problem* (Berlin), *Bunny* (London), *We Interrupt This Program . . . ,* and *Off Broadway* (a.k.a. *Full Moon*).

Academy Awards include an Oscar nomination in 1934 for the original story of *The Richest Girl in the World;* a nomination in 1936 for the original story of *Fury;* in 1939 Felix Jackson earned an original story nomination for *Bachelor Mother* (Krasna wrote the screenplay); a nomination in 1941 for the original screenplay of *The Devil and Miss Jones;* and an Oscar in 1943 for the original screenplay of *Princess O'Rourke.*

Writers Guild awards include the Laurel Award for Achievement in 1959.

Throughout your career you made a point of working alone, without a collaborator—and often, which is more unusual, "writing on spec," without a studio contract. Why?

I don't know where I got this blown-up confidence in myself. First I was a press agent at Warners, and I wrote a play by myself—that means at night. When it was on Broadway, I came back as a junior writer at Columbia. While I was at Columbia, I wrote my second play, *Small Miracle,* at night and put it in the vault—you bet at night, because I worked damned hard there. It wasn't an eight-hour day, it was a fourteen-hour day.

Also, while I was at Columbia I wrote *The Richest Girl in the World* [1934] and got an Academy nomination. I was twenty-two years old then and socially way out of my depth. Groucho [Marx] and his first wife Ruth took me downtown to the Ambassador for the awards, and we had a table together, the three of us. I had a white tie on—rented; my socks were showing through my pants. There were only three writers nominated—everybody told me I was going to win an Academy Award.

It's Prohibition. Groucho has a flask, he gives me a drink—one sip and I'm drunk. I had a whole speech prepared. Now comes the category: original story and screenplay. Three nominees. I don't win. Now I think everybody's looking at me. I'm embarrassed. In reality they don't know who the hell I am. Groucho gives me another drink. He's dancing with his wife, and I'm alone, drunk. I get up on the table. "Everybody!" The whole affair stops. Do you know what that means to be at the Oscars and the whole affair stops? "Everybody! Come to my house." A thousand people there! The whole industry! And all I had was a can of anchovies and a bottle of crème de menthe in case I could inveigle a girl up there. Groucho pulls me down, and they carry me out to the car. And that's Krasna's Academy Award. I was a little baby. I didn't know any better. Not that anybody knew who I was; when everybody stopped, they probably thought it was a fire or something. I threw up half the night.

But you ask me why I wrote by myself? I got to be pretty vain. *The Richest Girl in the World,* Academy Award nominations for story *and* screenplay—that was unheard of. And I was only twenty-two years old.

Was working alone partly a question of ego?

Temperament. I'm crazy about being alone. I'm an only child. I didn't get married for the first time until I was thirty. I'm used to it.

Did working alone have anything to do with fear that your point of view might become distilled?

No, I've worked with some good people—and sometimes for free, frankly. I keep saying I'm an only child because if you're an only child, you speculate by yourself. That's the Walter Mitty syndrome. When I'm by myself, I'm my own boss, whether I'm in the bathroom scratching or whether I think of something and write it down. Even when I'm not writing, I am thinking out a story from beginning to end. In the old days when I would tell a story, it would take thirty, forty minutes. I would tell you every scene, so when you bought it you would always say, "Well, you sure wrote it the way you told it." Because it was all done already. I didn't need anybody to get in my fucking way. When I'm working with or helping somebody, that's a separate thing; it has nothing to do with my writing. It's kind of showing off or proving something. For me, to write is to be by myself—strange hours, get up in the middle of the night if I have an idea, write the notes or three or four pages of a scene, then go back to bed. It's a continuous process if you're writing. If I'm my own boss.

You did collaborate with Groucho Marx. That's a distinction.

Groucho is the only person I wrote with—twice. *The King and the Chorus Girl* [1937], a movie, and a play called *Time for Elizabeth.* When I say we wrote *Time for Elizabeth* together, it took ten, fifteen years to write it—through his marriages, my marriages, his career, my career.

Was it difficult, writing as a collaborator with Groucho?

Groucho was a very dour man. He wasn't funny, funny, funny. He didn't always do madcap stuff—rarely. He was a very serious man. When I say we collaborated—he let me do the construction. I wrote at the typewriter, and he'd be great unless he started being Groucho *at* me. If he would comment funny on what we were doing, then we'd be in trouble. But he wouldn't most of the time; he was a real collaborator. *Somebody* has to sit at the typewriter. Groucho was a very, very dear friend. My play, *Dear Ruth,* is about his whole family. He liked me very much, and when the Marx Brothers were at their height, that was some endorsement. They said, "If Groucho likes him, the kid must be pretty good to keep Groucho's interest."

I worked with [Billy] Wilder a little bit, but with Wilder, *I'm* the secretary. You've got to let somebody carry the ball. Mostly, I'd rather work by myself. I always did. I used to invest in an original screenplay, write it, and try to sell it when that was unheard of. Nobody did that but me. Nobody! I had very few contracts. I was unique in that respect.

Did you always aim for an idea that you knew would sell? Or did you ever write a story that you cared so much about that you weren't going to lose any sleep over whether or not it would sell?

It's too easy to put myself on the side of the angels. But I have really taken some liberties. Best notices I ever got were for *Small Miracle,* a religious play in contemporary terms set underneath a lounge in a theatre. Later, after reading *The Nation,* I got the idea for *Fury* [1936]. I got so worked up after reading about a lynching, I thought, what could I do? I told my idea to [the MGM story editor] Sam Marx and Joe Mankiewicz. They were crazy about it. They went and told it to Mayer. I never even wrote it. Joe dictated the whole thing for me to get the check. For the record, I told him the whole story, and I never even saw what he wrote. But you're talking social significance? Remember *Fury* with Spencer Tracy? You know what Mayer said? He said (he was going to drive me out of the business), "What, Krasna! Anybody else I wouldn't pay a penny more than $10,000! Don't you give him a cent more than $15,000!" I never followed the logic of that.

I wrote what I liked, and I'm not this tremendous intellectual figure; I wrote what interested me, if it lent itself. For instance, I'll go by *Mr. and Mrs. Smith* [1941]. I was crazy about that idea of two happily married people, [Carole] Lombard and [Robert] Montgomery, who find out they're not married. That inspiration of having that little gimmick was enough of a drive, do you understand? Did I have in mind that it was commercial? I don't know. I told it to Lombard, she liked it; she had me tell it to [the RKO producer and executive] George Schaefer. He said, "How much do you want for it?" and I sold it. Hitchcock came into it later.

It's only when we sit here in later years that we say, "Oh, no, I wouldn't have done a *cheap* comedy." Yet I did a Wheeler and Woolsey [*So This Is Africa!* in 1933] when I was a kid. Cohn said, "Can you do a Wheeler and Woolsey so we can start in six weeks?" I did it in *three* weeks. Wheeler and Woolsey! You can't tell me I had any aspirations toward great art there.

Did you ever tailor your stories, generally speaking, for a particular star?—apart from writing Mr. and Mrs. Smith *for Carole Lombard.*

No. I always said, "I have a bagful of things to sell. Who do you want a story for? You tell me." Because I had so many plot ideas; I was very fertile, I thought. When I heard [Paramount] needed a story for George Raft, it interested me. The head of the studio [the production executive William LeBaron] said to me, "Gee, Raft. Can't you think of something for him?" I said, "Will you let me direct it?" He said, "Certainly. But I haven't heard the story yet." I came back in a few days, and I told him a George Raft story. They said, "Great." I wrote the script. That was *You and Me* [1938]. I don't think I ever saw it, how about that? I was very mad. I'll tell you why.

What happened is, they said I could direct it. I even did tests of an actress; everything was going fine. But they sent the script to Lombard first. She said, "Gee, that's great." They said, "But gee, Krasna—we can't let him direct a Lombard picture. It's one thing to let him do a Raft . . ." Now they called me down to the office to tell me—politely, because I was a real hotshot writer—that they're sorry I can't direct the picture. They'll give me another one. I said, "Oh, that's terrible." (Of course, I knew when I came down what it was for.) I said, "What are we going to do about the script?" They said, "Oh, the script—the script belongs to us; you wrote it under salary." I said, "Oh, I meant the story. You own the script because I wrote it under salary, but my contract says all original material belongs to me and that was a story I had before I came here." They said, "What good is the story without the script?" I said, "No, you've got it wrong. Now, I'll tell you the story again." And I told them the whole story with a circus background instead of a prison background. I said, "What you mean is, what good is the script without the story?" A long silence.

Mr. Zukor [Adolph Zukor, president of Paramount] was there, along with William LeBaron. They said, "What do you think this story is worth, Norman?" I said, "Well, it's certainly worth equal to the script; as witness I can use the story without the script, but you can't use the script without my story." They said, "What do you want for it?" I said, "I'll tell you what we'll do. You give me a figure, and whatever the figure is, it'll be a do-or-don't. I'll either take it, or I'll write you out a check for that amount and I'll own the property. That seems fair to me—no haggling."

That's when they called in the story editor [Richard Schayer] and told him, "You make this deal." I went out with him. He said, "Do you want to give me a hint as to the neighborhood?" I said no. "But I'm warning you," I said, "it'll be only one crack. Whatever number you say, I'll either say 'yes,' or I'll write out a check for that amount." Now I was mad. I was really a fresh kid in those days; I've got plenty of money, and they're not going to get the property. I walked up and down the outer office, and I watched this fella—Richard Schayer—from across the corridor. Inside another office, three steps away, were Zukor and LeBaron, waiting to hear the results. They were in a helluva spot. I walked out the door; I saw the story editor; I said hello; I saw he hadn't made up his mind yet. Two or three times.

Finally I wandered in with the others, crossed my legs, and said, "Whenever he gives me the number, I'll give you my decision." And Zukor said, "What do you think is fair?" I was still seething; I was going to direct; what a dirty trick! In sarcasm I said, "Do you think $10,000 is fair?" I was needling him; I had no notion of $10,000. And Zukor got up, put his arms around me, and said, "You're the finest young man I've ever met in my life." He wasn't acting. Someone once said to me, "Aaah, he was smarter than you!" It isn't true. He knew what a terrible thing they had done. I didn't know what to say.

After such fanfare for Fury *and* You and Me, *why did you empha-*

size comedy in your work as your career developed? Do you prefer comedy?

I can't be persuaded away from comedy; I like comedy. It gives me more chances to do the kinds of statements I want to make. I claim there was a tremendous social statement in *The Devil and Miss Jones* [1941]. King Vidor in *The Crowd* [1928] would do it to the employee; I do it to the richest man in the world, so you'll smile at him. "Are you chewing gum?" "No, I'm not." "Open your mouth." He swallows his gum. I can break your heart with the story of a girl who is four months pregnant and needs a job badly—only I prefer to do it in *Bachelor Mother* [1939] by making you laugh. I do it on the lighter level, but I don't think less of me because of it.

I'm a big believer in comedy. I watch a Bette Davis picture, I admire it; but for five reels I can't sit in the theatre; for the sixth I cry because the kid's in an oxygen tent. You can't do that in a comedy. Thirty seconds are dull?—get it out, skip that. That's why I stayed in comedy. It was a bigger challenge, a bigger technique.

In his TV Movies *[New York: Signet, 1982], critic Leonard Maltin makes a point of referring to your work as "social comedy."*

Well, you can't give me a better compliment than that. I like to think about myself that I wrote social comedies, as witnessed by my point of view. I'm a big fella for the underdog. You can't say that I'm not. I can point out what my attitude is, whether it is in *The Devil and Miss Jones* or even *Bachelor Mother,* which are as much of a protest as I can make against the existing system, and it's all in the framework of a comedy. A big political thinker would say, "That doesn't help us one millionth of an inch." He couldn't see it. Not that I mean it that way, except that's my point of view.

I always get in my social comment—but limited according to what the subject needs. I certainly don't go on the wrong side. I will not write that if you have a lot of money you're a better person. I try and show you my idea of *pure*—for instance, *The Richest Girl in the World.* I'm talking about 1931—fifty years ago, my God. If I use as a plot that the richest girl in the world [Miriam Hopkins] poses as her own secretary in order to get some privacy, how clever! The only thing is, eventually she ought to fall in love and get married. I like that idea. So what I do is—the fella falls in love with the richest girl in the world, only he thinks *she*'s the secretary. There you are—he's pure in heart. To his credit. That's everybody's daydream. I give you a reward. I make you laugh. But I always show you what the right side is: your emotions go along with the underdog.

Did you ever encounter resistance from stars, directors, or producers because of this avowed sympathy for the underdog?

No—but as a matter of fact I heard that [the director] Sam Wood saw *The Devil and Miss Jones* and was horrified because he was an extreme rightist. I do it at such an angle—not to fool people—but because I believe it's the best way to do something of social significance. I feel that *Pygmalion* is one of the great social dramatic comments, you understand? Ibsen would shout it. I think Shaw's point is stronger and more effective than Ibsen's. Unless you write on the nose for political reasons you are not labelled a writer for social betterment. But we're just talking, and I'm telling you what I think of myself.

Was the censorship of the 1930s and 1940s inhibiting at all when it came to dealing with sex?

I think the restrictions made for more cleverness than open-ended camerawork. I know it's kind of silly to keep one foot on the floor when you're talking to a girl in bed. But I'm not going to give credit to the picture business for that. Films only reflect what we live through. If you would have told me thirty or forty years ago that I would have a grown daughter who's living with a fellow—and they're not married!—I wouldn't have believed you; I wouldn't have allowed such a thing; I would have handcuffed everybody and got myself a gun. You know what I'm trying to say? The picture business just followed; the world has changed. I'm not going to say that the little colony of us out here changed the world. The world changed; we tried to follow it.

I remember when [the director] Leo McCarey did *The Awful Truth* [1937], which started with them [the Cary Grant and Irene Dunne characters] getting a divorce. That meant they had slept together! Unbelievable! It was a breakthrough. What happened was: we would see those pictures, like *The Awful Truth* or Capra's *It Happened One Night* [1934], which won all the awards, and we would jump on the bandwagon. Which is not to say we were copying it. But we would say to ourselves, "Are we allowed to do that? To have lovers quarrel instead of just being ingenues?" So we'd do it, and we'd go on from there. Five years later you might run it in a projection room and say, "Good God, is *that* what they liked back then? Was *that* the big hit?" It's not fair. Capra had to be the first one to do something like *The Taming of the Shrew*. Then we did so many variations on it that he got discredited, and people began to say, "Look how elemental it is." Out of context, there's no way to judge this.

For instance, *Guess Who's Coming to Dinner?* [1967]—a big breakthrough. A black fellow is a Nobel Prize winner; the white girl isn't good enough for him! They had to weigh it for that much shock value and then for having Spencer Tracy and Katharine Hepburn—who were beyond what their roles represented—accept the Nobel Prize–winning black fellow. It's ridiculous if you look at it now. If there was a discussion about that picture today, someone would say, "I saw that. You really think it is such a marvelous picture?"! Not fair, not fair. Where were you when we needed you?

What happened in the case of The Flame of New Orleans *[1941]? I understand you had some censorship problems on that picture.*

The Flame of New Orleans was a collaboration between [the director] René Clair and me. We finished the picture, and the Hays Office said, "Keep it, it's dirty." We couldn't get away with the sex stuff. A small studio like Universal *can't* keep a picture. Things were changed in the storyline. They found that by dropping the middle two reels, it could still be released. The picture is missing two reels. But Marlene Dietrich wasn't right for the picture. René Clair and I worked together on the script; I turned it in and it was ideal. I went on to something else. I explained something to René Clair, who was absolutely brilliant. I said to him, "Look here, you've got Dietrich—one of the great, famous still faces in the world. She knows all about lighting for herself, and everything else turns out just great. Who we need to play the leading man is someone like Cary Grant—but you can't get him. It's got to be a great comedian to make her look funny. A talker." I'm a big believer in this. In *Indiscreet* [1958], Ingrid Bergman turned out to be a wonderful comedienne, but Cary Grant was opposite her. Everybody thought Olivia de Havilland was a great comedienne in *Princess O'Rourke* [1943]; it's not true. She's just darling, an ingenue. And everybody else is in on the joke—Jane Wyman, Bob Cummings, Charles Coburn; they were great comedians all around. So it comes out as a comedy, and they go and put her in *Government Girl* [1943] for Dudley Nichols, and she falls on her ass. Don't let *her* be the comedy!

Lubitsch once explained Dietrich to me: "Miriam Hopkins talks all the time," he says to me, "and everything is witty. But when you come to Dietrich, watch; the big trick with her is you think she is going to say 'no,' and by God, she says 'yes.' It's what has to be built up for her." So I said to Clair, "Since you've got one frozen face, try and get someone like Cary Grant for the other part. Otherwise it won't even be talking heads; it'll be *looking* heads." They got Bruce Cabot—as far away from Cary Grant as you can get in the world. He stands still; she stands still. But there's only one person in the world who stands still more than both of them. For the third part I said, "Get Menjou." And they went and got Roland Young. You couldn't tell if his lips were moving. Between him, Cabot, and Dietrich—three people who didn't move!

Your career was also unusual in that, during the 1930s, 1940s, and 1950s, you shuttled back and forth between New York and California, writing stage plays as well as screenplays with equal success. There were playwrights who worked in Hollywood only with the intention of making enough money so they could afford to work in the legitimate theatre. Did you feel that way about the film industry?

Well, that's kind of fashionable to say. I'd like to give you that attitude too: I'm really a *theatre* fella, see. Aaagh! I like the writer—I forget who it was, someone very big, Shaw or Voltaire or somebody—who said nothing good was ever written except for money. There were theatre fellows, I'm sure, who came out, did pictures here, and then went back and immersed themselves in the theatre. No. If I had an absolutely fabulous idea for a movie, frankly, I would do nothing but devote my life to it as a movie—a television series, anything. I'd work hard on any idea that merits it.

Like, in the 1950s, I tried hard to sell a funny idea for a picture in Russia about the Moiseyev Ballet, which we had seen in Paris, with the Red Army chorus behind the titles. It was going to be a two-a-day picture. Oh God, how we were mixed up with the Russian government and our State Department! I tried to involve the biggest people— RKO, Disney—and I was dealing with the Russians myself. That was a *giant-sized* idea. And we finally had things arranged. I got René Clair to direct—he's a favorite in Russia—and wrote a whole script too, called *Hello, Russky!* I'll never forget. We all had our reservations; we were ready to embark from Paris, and the U-2 was shot down.

Would you say that the theatre is a purer medium for writers?

I would like to tell this anecdote. When I was active in all spheres, we'd have two contracts in Europe or New York—on the desk—for stage play and picture work. I could use either one for my purposes at the moment—writing at home. The first picture contract was then $175,000, or 25 percent of the profit. In the old days (I know what it's like now), we'd have two first-class tickets for my wife and myself. We were met at the airport by a limousine. We stayed in a hotel suite (which we might have paid for out of our own money, although sometimes they even picked that up) and had all kinds of goodies and side things that were really very flattering. Let alone the influence! The theatre tickets supplied, a press party at "21," and the press agent is with you to pick up the check. God, what they'd do for you! You're a very, very big man. That's the picture contract.

Now comes the stage money: this contract is a $500 advance. Thirty-five dollars a day, sometimes $25. Economy ticket for one. Ain't nobody meeting ya. No interviews at "21" with the press agent picking up the check. Now you come to the theatre to rehearse. The best they could get is either a small ballroom or upstairs of the Winter Garden on 42nd Street. You can't believe it; you're afraid to sit down—dirty, peeling paint. Big shows in the theatre are *lucky* if they can get that room upstairs. How is it that everybody is so crazy about trying to get into the theatre?—writers especially? Because when you write this wonderful script that you wrote for the film, the director, the star, or the producer, they can put on another writer or they can throw the script away; they can change it on the set—or before, if that's their theory.

Now we come to the theatre. The star comes onto the stage and says, "Well, good morning." And a little, thin script girl says, "Excuse me, sir, there's no 'well.' " He says, "I'm sorry." He comes on stage again and says, "Good morning." The reason for that is as follows: it doesn't matter that I claim I wrote "Well, good morning" and then "Good morning" fifty times before I decided on "Good morning." You see, I haven't been paid for the stage play—$500 was just a Dramatists Guild option. You decided to do the play; I want to see *my* play on—whether I fail or not.

In the picture business they paid me $175,000; they paid for two first-class tickets; they paid for lunch at "21." I won't say that's being a whore like some extremists do when they are talking about Hollywood. But I tip my hat, and that's why I don't complain when they want to change something. I try to arrange it so it doesn't happen to me. And I don't think any writer has had more original screenplays filmed without one word changed. Because I look for that set-up. If they paid you, it's theirs. Bow your head a little; you took the money quick enough. But in the theatre not even one word will be changed.

Now there is a realistic side, too. You don't know where you'll get good suggestions from. It may be that "Well, good morning" is the most marvelous line you've ever heard. You're the one who decides. And you can imagine how much money it has cost us for me to have my last three or four plays on? Because we live great—we can afford it—in the best hotels, and travel! Fifteen thousand dollars minimum— that's just for doing rehearsals. Curtain goes up, curtain goes down. The fact that I've had road companies out, other plays on, and tremendous smashes means that I'll take my chances. I tip my hat to the theatre because it's the big gamble. It's the one my peers think most of. But I don't write a picture like that. I write a picture, you give me my money; and later on I hear what the grosses are, *if* I believe it.

Would your motives be any different when you were writing a play? Would your impulses be less commercial?

As a matter of fact, the one who gave me the lesson in that regard was a great man, a friend of mine, Moss Hart. I had written a play before the war that I really wrote to win the Nobel Peace prize. It was about some Nazis who had been interned in Canada while England was in the war, their escape, and the search for them by Canadian authorities. I thought it made a timely statement.

The night before the play opened in New York at the Belasco Theatre, we had invited a full audience from Mount Sinai—the staff, interns, nurses, and so on. The shouting that went on in that theatre! My God, how it was received! They thought like I did. It was just sensational. I went to sleep thinking there was a medal coming to me and wondering where to put it. The next day the curtain came up, and the first time the audience heard the word Jew—we're talking about 1938, now—they were uncomfortable. Winchell [the columnist Walter Winchell], whom I knew well because I was a kid around the Algonquin group, was looking to *hit* me, he was so offended.

When I think of the scars that I have and why I went into *Mr. and Mrs. Smith* rather than . . . but that's what I felt at the time. And if you're young, when are you going to be full of juice and do things that you like? Between *Fury,* between maybe *Small Miracles* and *The Man with Blonde Hair* (that was the name of the play), I took my shot at knockin' 'em dead.

But you say the experience left scars.

I don't know, I'm just talking now. I was smart enough to know what to leave behind. I really wasn't bewildered then. Anyway, Moss said to me, "You know your trouble, Norman. You think what you write in pictures is a matter of style—commercial. You're an expert in that, I see. But when you go to the stage you're trying to kill 'em, as witness *The Man with Blonde Hair.* You're trying to be Shaw. Norman, you've got it all wrong." Next door under the same roof was another writer, Jerry Chodorov, who had sold *Junior Miss* for, I think, $400,000. Moss continued, "You belittle it, but you're envious. You say, 'Why *Junior Miss?* That's nothing but Andy Hardy.' Why don't you do one of those for the stage?"

Then I wrote *Dear Ruth,* which is the biggest commercial hit I've ever had. Moss Hart produced and directed it. And *Dear Ruth* could never have sold as a movie. It's about a twelve-year-old girl who writes a letter to a judge, not about grown-ups mixed up on romance. It's interesting even as I think about it now. Think of that—it's what I had belittled. Moss knew better. He said, "Write what you do best." He once said on radio or television—and he apologized to me, but I understand exactly what he meant—he said, "Norman Krasna has the best Woolworth's touch I know." He said he didn't mean it derogatorily; he meant he would trust me with a general audience.

How did you decide what would make a good play versus a good movie?

It [a good play] lends itself; it will never look as good on film. You smell out which ones will be practical, easy to write. I can *do* them as stage plays, do you follow me? That's what governs the most. In my time the big trick was to be able to write a romantic comedy in one set. The sheer manipulative skill was in keeping the thing going with the entrances and exits in a realistic comedy—meaning that you can believe it. The theme, the *appeal,* I think of—that's obviously primary. But the technical side of sitting down—act one, scene one—I just know that it better not cover four years.

In 1943 you directed your first motion picture, Princess O'Rourke *and won an Academy Award for writing the screenplay as well. At that point you were one of the handful of first-rank writers—like John Huston, Preston Sturges, and Billy Wilder—who were being given an opportunity to prove themselves as directors. Yet you only directed two other movies.* The Big Hangover *in 1950 and* The Ambassador's Daughter *in 1956. Why?*

I'm not a good director, not at all. I know how to direct what I write; but then I write knowing that I'm able to direct it.

What reservations do you have about your own directing?

I guess it was alright. If I hadn't gone into the Army, I probably would have kept on writing and directing. But in my opinion, you develop different interests in life. I worked twenty-four hours a day when I was a kid. The plays I wrote I wrote when I had a full-time job; I just sensed time was running out. I had the energy then. Later on there weren't enough hours in the day to work that hard.

So it was partly that directing is too all-consuming a job?

Oh, yeah. Nunnally Johnson said that to Groucho. He said, "Groucho, you're on your feet all day!" And if it doesn't go good . . . aaagh! Willy Wyler—his blood doesn't circulate. George Stevens—nothing frightens him. Gee, I'm conscious of spending $40,000 a day when I'm shooting. And they never let you alone. I really like a lot of privacy. "What do you think of this hat? What do you think of her hair? Do you want three hundred extras for tomorrow? If you can get through today, can you use one shot less? Where do you want the camera?" There's no end. You turn around and they're lined up, waiting to get your attention. Also, I'm not a great technician. I used to watch the big ones, and they'd ask for a two-inch lens. What do you mean a two-inch lens? I don't know what a two-inch lens looks like. Then, the cutting. I'm great in spurts, but you can't spurt as a director. It's a long, long process.

Tell me about your short-lived production company with Jerry Wald at RKO in the 1950s.

At the time I really didn't feel like being alone in writing. Wald was head of the studio, practically—according to the publicity. I always was reasonably prominent socially, but now I was at the head of the pecking order. So it was a wonderful adventure—going to New York, giving interviews. For three or four months we were busy. After about six months more, I saw it was hopeless, and I was back playing golf. Hughes [the RKO owner Howard Hughes] had hired Jerry. Jerry said he wanted Norman, and Hughes didn't even know who I was in the beginning. Jerry was absolutely fabulous; he did all the public relations. We were going to do the Greeks! We were sincere in the beginning; I wasn't cynical in the beginning. We had meetings at the [William] Morris office and at Allenberg's [the talent agent Bert Allenberg, whose partner was Phil Berg] house. We took our contracts and showed them to them. We said, "Here's our trick. We're not entitled to *anything*. We've got a distribution company. We've got Howard Hughes. You know what we want to do? We want the best in the world—Huston, Kazan. Give us something! We'll do everything we can to give them full autonomy. They'll never have it so easy. We don't think we're smarter than these fellas. It'll be the goddamnedest studio; it'll be what United Artists was supposed to be."

Everybody was taken with this. We were sincere about it. That's what we meant to do. So, let me see *you* try and get Hughes on the phone. We started to holler. Colonel Wilkerson [the publisher of *The Hollywood Reporter*] used to call Hughes up for us and so did [the columnist] Louella Parsons. It didn't interest him. He thought he was doing well enough. A very busy fellow, doing one thing at a time, a genius. We just couldn't get any decisions from him. How long do you think it took for the Morris office and everybody else to catch on? "The poor kids mean well but they can't deliver." So we lose one deal after another, you know what I mean? And about this time I catch on this is all bullshit.

If you want to know what I think of the whole thing, Hughes was using RKO as a whorehouse. If he made a lot of money out of some magic pictures, fine. Otherwise, as someone explained it to me, it was set up so if he lost money, he made money. But he hired us at a time when he had a lot of pictures that had to be cut or have things inserted. He would do such things as the whole picture was done and scored, and he would want better cleavage. So he would build up the sets again and put vaseline between the girl's tits and shoot the scene over. Do you know how much that costs? And holding up the release?

Did he do that to your pictures?

We lived through and did that for him as favors. Mostly Wald, who came in at five in the morning. I wouldn't do that.

*What did you do on the three pictures [*Clash by Night *in 1952, and* Blue Veil *and* Behave Yourself *in 1951] that you are credited with co-producing with Wald?*

What I did most was *Blue Veil*. I worked with Curtis Bernhardt, the director, and Norman Corwin, who did all the writing and who was just great. That was enough to take up my time. Meanwhile, Jerry was getting into all kinds of jams. It was a turmoil. It wasn't worth it. Then I met Earle, Al Jolson's widow, and she said to me, "You're a writer. You're going to put up with this kind of nonsense?" We got married; we went to Europe together, and I kissed that money goodbye. I didn't need money then, and I don't need it now.

Tell me about the genesis of Let's Make Love *[1960]. It's a very clever idea, one that is quintessentially a Norman Krasna idea, yet it doesn't quite come off. Why?*

Ideas come from funny places. I'll tell you what happened. This is how you get killed in the business. This will encapsulate for you how it happens from beginning to end.

I'm always looking for themes. I go to the Writers Guild awards and [George] Burns and [Gracie] Allen bring on Burt Lancaster, or some-one like that, and they do a dance. Everybody applauds. Lancaster can't dance; I think to myself, why did Lancaster get such a big hand? Fred Astaire and Gene Kelly wouldn't have gotten such a big hand for such a lousy dance. It's a *dog walking*. That's my slant. If they're going to laugh at someone inept, how am I going to dramatize someone inept? And I work backwards from that premise.

So I decide to do it in a framework in which I'm familiar—an impersonation. I've got a story to tell. The entertainment will be: I'll put someone in a position where he has to do things in show business that you'll have to applaud, even though it'll be lousy, because look who's doing it. How will I justify it? I do it as follows: I get one of the very, very rich fellows, whose press agent comes to him and says, "Down in the Village they're doing imitations of all kinds of people, and they're doing something about you and girls." Pretend it's Howard Hughes in your mind; I actually had in mind Jock Whitney [a financier who, at one point, was chairman of the board of Selznick International]. "You have to come down and look at it and ask them to soften it; that's the only way to deal with these people."

He gets into his Rolls, goes downtown, and sees impersonations of all kinds of people—Eisenhower, the Whitneys, Howard Hughes. And he's fascinated. He's a man who's been spoiled all his life; he always gets what he wants. There's a girl who is very attractive who is dancing in the show. When they come around to picking someone from the audience to participate in a joke, they pick him. He's embarrassed; he doesn't look too good at it, but he's fascinated by the girl for the moment. And everybody's *laughing* at him. That's the whole story.

The big trick is, look at the span I take: you want to be loved for yourself alone. That's my big theme. He doesn't know what to do; he's only been introduced to people who fall back over his diamond bracelets. So he'd like to win her by himself on her own territory. So if you're the majority stockholder in the American Tobacco Company, Lucky Strike, you get Jack Benny to teach you how to do a routine; you get the real Gene Kelly to teach you how to dance. (He can't turn left, he can only turn to the right.) Now I have an excuse to show a guy doing all that stuff. And finally, at the end, she finds out who he *really* is, of course.

Now I explain this to Jerry Wald, who is producing the picture. I write the picture. I say, "Now we should limit the casting to these people—Gary Cooper, Jimmy Stewart, Gregory Peck." See, we need people who are shit-kickers. Remember, I need the dog who walks on his feet. Well, we get Peck. Peck comes to the house every day for five days or something like that, and we go over every line of the script. Real gentleman. He changed twenty words, and he kept apologizing. At the very end we shook hands, and he said, "Norman, maybe I was being picky, but I felt I was comfortable here. This I promise you—we won't change one more word." That's it. I kiss him goodbye, and my wife went ahead to Europe. I stay behind because I'm producing *Who Was That Lady?* [1960] for Columbia.

Wald calls up. He says, "What a break! You know what I found out. We can get Marilyn Monroe." Monroe is tremendous, but she's not what I had in mind. I was thinking of a musical comedy star like Cyd Charisse—who's kind of a lady, great legs. You would believe those two together, Gregory Peck and Cyd Charisse. There's a class to it. But Monroe's so darling, who can say she isn't an asset? Not what I had in mind, but it's alright. Okay. I tell the whole story to Marilyn in her hotel suite. She loves it, kisses goodbye, and I go to Europe. In Europe I get the phone calls because I own part of the picture. The phone calls are from Jerry Wald: "Peck, when I told him, said 'okay, but no changes in the script.' But Arthur Miller thinks it needs some changes." Now Peck's out. Marilyn Monroe's in, but we've lost Peck. This is what happens when you get too close.

Finally we're getting closer and closer to production, and Wald calls and says, "By God, would you believe it? We've got Yves Montand." I said, "Hold it. You remember the whole scheme was the dog walking. Montand gives concerts; he sings and dances." Wald says, "The motion picture audience doesn't know that." I say, "Jerry, it's not important that they don't know it. I need a whole generation of people who have *seen* him shit-kicking. Stewart, Cooper, and Peck—you *know* they can't sing and dance, you understand. Not Montand." Wald says, "If not Montand, we haven't got a chance. I called you to tell you we've got him for the picture, but the truth is she wants him badly. She's stuck on him."

So . . . the picture didn't get such great notices, although it'll be better ten years from now than it is now; it's a very well-mounted picture of its kind. *But,* the gimmick that started it (*genius* is the word I mean when I say gimmick—gimmick is not a word to be sneered at) is Lancaster trying to sing, Lancaster getting all those laughs by dancing so lousy. The casting ruined it. The central idea was fucked, there's no doubt about it. No use my telling people how good *Let's Make Love* might have been.

Looking back, of all the screenplays you wrote expressly for the screen, which do you feel best about?

The Devil and Miss Jones and *Princess O'Rourke*, obviously. I like *My Geisha* [1962], which I produced, *Bachelor Mother,* and *Mr. and Mrs. Smith*—although it will never be considered the best of Hitchcock because it's way outside his vein. He liked it very much, by the way. He was very disappointed—he wanted me to do the next one, *Rebecca* [1940], I think. I told him I only write comedy, and it didn't interest me.

Were these scripts filmed the way you wrote them for the most part?

Word for word. Just the way I wrote them. But I fell into that too; I'm looking for bows. I went over everything with Hitchcock *before* shooting, alright? I had one sequence where we went to New York and used the World's Fair. I had a better opening than he had. Everything else was the same. And if it was Sam Wood and *The Devil and Miss Jones,* I was co-producer, don't forget. Sam Wood was a fabulous technician who knew nothing about the word, so that script stayed the same too. You've got to remember that part of my job is to satisfy the man who is going to make the picture from beginning to end; so I say nothing has been changed . . . (*Shrugs.*) On the other hand, there have been scripts that have been taken away.

In Film Comment, *the Hollywood screenwriter issue [Winter, 1970–71], you make a point of saying that the only scripts filmed to your satisfaction were the ones you directed.*

That's me being a smart aleck.

Have you read the film critics who say that you have had a career-long obsession, in your stories and in your movies but especially in your romantic comedies, with themes revolving around impersonations or a mistaken identity?

Oh, sure. I'll tell you how they know. I will point out to them how many variations I've done on this theme I like. Then I'll quote Gilbert and Sullivan (who wrote a dozen fabulous operettas, always on the same kind of note), and I'll talk about the influence of George S.

"A champion of the underdog": Norman Krasna's The Devil and Miss Jones *with (front row) Jean Arthur, Charles Coburn, Spring Byington, and (standing) Robert Cummings.*

Kaufman and the third act of *The Front Page*—it's a very learned routine I've got. And what do you think I'll finally see in an interview? "My observation: he only writes on this one note." What I have told them comes back to haunt me.

When you ask me about my obsession with mistaken identity, I must tell you that strikes a chord. There is this kind of a cloud hanging over me. Are you going to tell me that's all I can write? You want to see what I have bound in leather—all my plays? How come? It came from me, big-mouth, explaining, impressing some interviewer. It gets written in the morgue, and I get stuck with it. Well, to me, it's a compliment.

I do it often, I like it. I like the theme. If you think I invented *Prince and the Pauper,* you're crazy. But the big trick, which people don't understand, is that even though I do this one theme, does anyone say I have ever repeated on it? You stay on one theme? You betcha! I couldn't be prouder if I had written thirty, forty properties—whatever I've done, more!—and every one of them was on one theme.

Think how hard that is. So I don't care about that criticism. It's a valid enough theme. I use the mistaken identity—but to tell a *theme* that I like. A theme that I like.

Take *The Devil and Miss Jones.* If that wasn't done on what I consider the right terms—being that witty, I say witty and touching—to show you how tough life is. Gee, that's the best picture I ever wrote, in my opinion. I worked in Macy's when I was going to law school, and I know what working in a department store was like. *The Los Angeles Times,* which was an arch-conservative newspaper at that time, knew enough to write an editorial against the picture. But the guy who came from some labor magazine—I think called *Labor*—got up at the press preview in the studio and said, "You copped out." He should have turned toward the audience and said, "That's what it's like, exploiting the lower classes." I looked at this amateur. He hadn't the vaguest idea of how propaganda works and what social statement I wanted to make. The editorial writer for *The Los Angeles Times* knew this was a dangerous picture.

When did you first begin to get interested in the theme of mistaken identity? How did that evolve in your writing?

The Richest Girl in the World was the first one. I may have done that one because I liked its Cinderella story. After that I did *Fury,* but even *Fury,* come to think of it, had a mistaken identity. The fact that it's *me* that's writing it has more to do with it than anything else. Pick out a picture you like and watch how I'll reduce it to mistaken identity. I know that works as a spine for everything. I don't sit down and say I am going to do a mistaken identity story. I'll do the whole story, and it'll turn out that way. You will say to me, "Look, you've done a mistaken identity story again." And I'll say, "Is that so?"

When I mention the film critics who have harped on your preoccupation with mistaken identity, I don't mean to sound pejorative. The mistaken identity theme works on several levels; that's what's so fascinating about it. You can skip one level and still enjoy the entertainment value. And while the story makes a social point, it is also basically Freudian.

The last one is the important one. I'll explain to you the highlights of myself. When I was twenty-five or twenty-seven I already had all the antique furniture you see here. I had built a home, and I had a second-hand Rolls Royce. The impression you got from reading the Sunday pieces was that I made more money than the president of the United States.

One evening I decided to see my idea of the best play I ever saw in my life—after *Front Page—Green Pastures.* I go in my Rolls Royce, park it, and walk to the Warner Theatre in a sweatshirt, moccasins, and a three-day growth of beard. I stop and look in the window of a one-arm joint on the corner called the Busy Bee; I'm looking through the window, hands in my pockets, with some time to kill. Maybe my nose pressed against the window. And I'm meeting the eye of a girl who's sitting there—my kind of girl, a thin, dark girl—and I see she's embarrassed and looks away. I say to myself, "Holy mackerel, she thinks I need a meal. I'll be a son-of-a-bitch. She's going to come out and maybe offer me a meal. If she does, I'm going to buy her a diamond bracelet. If this girl will only get up and come out and offer me ten or fifteen cents, she will remember it for the rest of her life." I stayed at the window, trying to attract her, and I guess she couldn't afford it. I could see she felt terrible, because she never came out.

When you say Freudian, how would I remember a story like that? Forty years or more ago. The idea of mistaken identity, it must have always been on my mind. When I was a shoe salesman at Macy's, I remember how tough the buyer was, insulting everybody. God, to have a job during the Depression, what it meant! I said to myself, "Some day, I'll get so rich that I'll go apply for a job—like at Macy's— and I'll be sitting there and somebody's going to do something like this and I'm going to stand up and say, 'Go fuck yourself.' " This is about as far as I went in my thinking. I would imagine that it was such a strong emotion with me that it carries over. I feel the drive in all that of mistaken identity.

So there is a psychological basis. Was there anything Marxist about your perspective? Because in your stories, there is always a distinction being drawn between boss and employee, upper and lower class.

No. Don't forget that I'm governed by all the most elemental stories we were all raised on—Cinderella stories. Mostly it was a Walter Mitty syndrome—*if I was in power.* Whether my character is a rich man or a general—whatever his authority is—I put him in a position where he is a small fella, poor and helpless, and it points up inequities and how you correct inequities. I was a big believer in that, and you'd better be if you're poor and young. To me, it was a great formula, to always put it in those terms—that's all.

Even so, that's class politics, right?

Oh, there's no doubt about it. But listen, when I look at *Fury* and see all those kudos—whether I typed out a two-page outline or what— I almost resent that I was considered such a big thinker when it was no more of an invention than my comedies but set in a world of obvious social significance. See, I give myself all kinds of gold stars for *The Devil and Miss Jones* because the truth is, there is as much of a social statement in a farcical comedy like *The Devil and Miss Jones* or *Bachelor Mother* as in *Fury.* Only *Fury* was done as a melodrama straight-on—the lynching of this fellow. The gimmick, the hook, the invention, the *inspiration* is that he is still alive. I use the word gimmick;

although it's derogatory, I don't consider it derogatory. That's the *genius*—same word as gimmick. My great *genius*—not gimmick—was that he was still alive. Then comes the moral of the story in that he is doing the same thing by killing them. But *Fury* is not any more impressive to me—or the brain cells that I am using are not any different creatively—than my lowest comedy effort.

You have said that your great theme is that someone love you for yourself. Is that rooted psychologically in your own background? Do you have any idea why that theme should emerge so powerfully from your writing?

That's so discerning that you frighten me when you say it. I wonder, I wonder. I sure would like your observations on it. I'll put it this way. I picture myself now as I came out here [to Hollywood], and I'm working with these people, all of whom are my idols. In New York I had a photograph of Sylvia Sidney above the typewriter. Usually you grow up and you meet these people and they're little old ladies and you say, "When I was young . . ." But do you know, I grew up quick enough to live next door to Sylvia Sidney, and when I met her and took her to dinner, I said to myself, "You know if I drop dead right now, it's a whole cycle that's been completed."

Except this—she had been living with [B. P.] Schulberg. She was my age but 120 years old. First of all, any woman compared to any man at the same age! But remember, when she was a hit in *Bad Girl* in New York [in 1930], she was only seventeen years old—this little, round Jewish face, and I was fascinated. Five years later she's twenty-two or twenty-three and so am I. I just couldn't get over it. We were great confidantes. She was crazy about me. Only she was like an aunt. She showed me manners, what fork to use, and so on. That's not your girl. That's the girl you're crazy about who's patting your head. This was an aunt of mine who happened to be the same age.

Even then I was losing my hair. I had glasses, no sense of fitness. I'd go into a room, and it would be full of young stars and starlets. I'd be much younger than all of them. I was very attracted to some of them. I'd talk to this girl, trying to be charming and witty, eh? Nothing. She thinks my name is "Mr. Ganzer." I looked so-o-o young.

Then more people come into the room. And, let's say, Lubitsch or somebody comes over and puts his arm around me; and this little girl I'm aware of, the only one that I'm interested in in the whole room, pretty soon she catches on that I must be *somebody*. Then she knows my *name*. Because of Wilkerson (whom I saw so much of), I had publicity much beyond what my career entitled me to. Slowly, politely, because it's kind of human nature, she realizes I'm a *somebody* in the picture business. I'm sure a somebody in this group. But I can't look at her anymore because: "You didn't like me before you knew I could suggest you ought to play the other sister." I liked to be liked for myself.

When I would see such an attractive girl (and I'm really that successful that I'm entitled to this girl), my vanity was such that I'd like her to like me, *not knowing* that Hecht and I were the highest-salaried writers in Hollywood. What *she* likes is my scrapbook. That's all I am is that scrapbook. I wanted to be liked for my scrapbook, but if she sees my scrapbook and Mr. Lubitsch's arms around me and decides *that's* who I am, what kind of values has she got? This is something that must be elemental for all of us. I'm only trying to say that I would not have any interest in a girl who was only interested in me after she found out who I was.

A real-life anxiety over mistaken identity. Is it possible that, on the surface, when you were a young and successful screenwriter in Hollywood, you had an overweening self-confidence but that beneath the surface you had a tremendous emotional insecurity that was born of a real incongruity in your situation. Because you were not particularly well-educated or brought up in an upper-class milieu—you were clever and you were lucky. So that, in fact, what was always going on, partly, and what would play itself out in your stories on the screen, would be Norman Krasna's fantasies of being discovered for who he really is?

I suspect that you are right. I protest, but I'm afraid you're right. That interests me very much, what you're saying. Usually I have to pay for this on the couch. Why a boy my age will buy a lot during the Depression in Beverly Hills, build a home, and buy all this English furniture—which was a big obsession of mine—that came from a kind of insecurity. My wife says I'm a nester. And I *wanted* a home—dating back from having to make my bed every day in the kitchen when I was growing up. That was obviously a drive to accumulate material things.

Now, I didn't walk into this room with this mythical girl and with Lubitsch's arm around me. I made that up. I don't remember any specific times. I didn't come into rooms nervous. Anything but, in my life, God knows; I sometimes even wonder about it. I've been in important situations with people like Lindbergh, Chaplin, or Noel Coward, who were my real close friends. I'm the biggest fan in the world of those people. Yet I'm not panicky about it. I'm entitled to it. I'll kowtow to them if I have to, but those people don't command any intimidation like that. Yet I wonder if the mainspring, the machinery, the motivation inside me to go that strong wasn't what you say.

After this conversation I can't help but see your films as very personal films. I see Norman Krasna in each and every one of them. Not only because they are original stories of yours, but because they are stories with such a private resonance for you.

Norman Krasna in a "story conference" (for publicity purposes) with (left to right) Jerry Wald, Clare Boothe Luce, and René Clair.

I like to hear that. There are some people who are professional writers because they wear steel-rimmed glasses and look like writers and have a whole list of credits. You can live a whole life as a writer in Hollywood without ever having *written* a movie, and you can still be considered one of the great ones. Such writers will do either an original story or write the screenplay of someone else's story. The story can be so full that fleshing it out is not my idea of sensational; or they'll write the story, and somebody else can make something absolutely fabulous out of it. I don't consider that you're a real, real screenwriter unless you sit down and do a movie from beginning to end. Or if the idea is frail enough and the contribution is just marvelous.

You're saying that there is a distinction to be drawn between originating and adapting.

You betcha there is. You betcha there is. I claim that if you've been in the business thirty or forty years and you look back, I would think that one of the things that ought to stick out is what pictures you did that reflect what *you are,* your experiences. You may only have had a few, two or three or four, but you're a writer. You write motion pictures. To make a living at adapting is a big trick; but out of thirty or forty years, goddammit, didn't you write anything that is *yours?* I use that word subjectively. I belittle the writers who took a great book and adapted it; that's all? I think I wrote what showed me off—romantic comedies. In the end they were never the big, big pictures; but they were mine. At the end of the whole picture, I'm the hero's witness.

Screenwriting in Hollywood has been called hack work—both as a compliment and as an insult, I think. But it seems that screenwriters rarely think of themselves in terms of being aspiring artists. How do you regard yourself?

I'm more vain than that. I think I'm great. But remember, I write on the head of the pin. I go back to that. I call what I'm writing very, very difficult to do. If you're reading "The Lord's Prayer" on the head of a pin, you've got to admire me. I didn't write "The Lord's Prayer," but how about writing it on the head of a pin? That kind of comedy can be very hard. I like to believe I belong—way below—with P. G. Wodehouse, W. S. Gilbert, or Molière. Although that's overdoing it.

It may be that you have been luckier than most screenwriters in being able to preserve your integrity in Hollywood.

Don't forget, I wrote a lot of screenplays *before* I sold them. That's a big edge. I don't say you've got to stick to the script, but you bought it, why not? What I've often done, to my great credit, is I will be with a director, if he's a fancy director, and he'll want a change that makes absolutely no difference, but he needs it for his ego. The changes don't make any fucking difference to me—just some extra work. I'll throw him three, four, five pages and even encourage him and say the changes are right. He needs it in order to feel creative. Where the hell were you when the pages were empty?

Has storytelling in motion pictures changed greatly since the old days?

When we did a story, it had a beginning, a middle, and an end. It had a *theme.* Usually it was the same one; they didn't sleep together until the end. A happy ending couldn't be Gable going to jail for thirty years and Harlow saying, "I'll wait for you," and we're left with a lump in our throats. A happy ending—we were excited! They were going to *sleep* together!

When you are committed to the skeleton of a beginning, a middle, and an end, the cleverness was in concealing the skeleton. This is a cliche, but you had to surprise them with what they expected. It has to be an odd way of telling it, but they want to know which way it is going. You have to anticipate what they want, and the trick is in how you lead them to it. Now that means you would have truly rather dull patches, if you want to say that, if you weren't clever enough to pep everything up; but the story had to have an inevitability about it.

Here's the big change in storytelling: they've given up the theme. Never mind the end. You see the most wonderful pictures today; scenes are just great, great, great. Then, suddenly the crawl comes. I don't expect the crawl to come for another ten minutes—they haven't *resolved* anything. But you know, they haven't got any dull periods. They give you these great scenes, you've had a good time for two hours, and you've only had an unsatisfactory thirty seconds. People are accustomed to it. You go out and see this picture, which doesn't add up and is about nothing, and people say, "I didn't like the ending, but . . ." Now movies can be enjoyed by people who haven't got the only time-consuming experience, which is learning. Instruction. I've got thousands of books of dramatic literature. Do you see all the thousands of books I've got here on the shelf? Since Aeschylus. In my generation they gave up plots with character formation. I had to be born now!

TV has taken up the notion of a beginning, a middle, and an end. I'm fascinated. It's child's play now. I'll look at "M*A*S*H," "Alice," or "The Jeffersons" every time I can put my feet up. I know what the rules are, and I couldn't do it as well. They're witty in what they do and how inventive they get. But when you are talking about a whole movie, I would think that by now TV has used up all the plot twists, and you need something stark and wild. Maybe the art form has advanced. But if I was Vermeer, I would be sick to my stomach that Jackson Pollack is making all this money. I would say, let me see you do a thumb!

My masters were Lubitsch and Wilder. They, maybe, sometimes, made mistakes but their standards! Every frame, every shot had to mean something. Unless you work with someone like René Clair, you don't understand about the technique of these old-timers. When René Clair came to Hollywood, he was considered one of the world's greatest directors; they gave him a dinner and introduced him as that. If I had a scene at a table and then wanted to cut underneath to show a couple playing footsy, he wouldn't allow that. "Why did the camera go under the table?" he would ask. "The camera went there . . ." I'd say, "What do you mean?" "No," he'd say, "something has to fall off the table before the camera can go under the table. And I have to have a tick or something, a thread that has to be established earlier." Jesus, the standards of these people! All the finger-points; the wonderful chess game; that's what I like.

It doesn't work that way now. Even Billy Wilder says, "It's a puzzle how pictures are shot. When you had to shoot on a bridge in the old days, what trouble! What expense! One hundred people, the trucks, all-night-long permissions, and expenses." He says, "You know what they do now? Two guys go with a hand-held camera. They stop traffic quick, and they run before the police come. I wouldn't know how to do that. They'd put me in jail."

In the early 1960s you moved abroad and stayed there for twenty-one years; and although you continued to write plays, your career as a screenwriter in Hollywood was effectively curtailed. You're back now. Are you tempted to begin anew as a screenwriter? Do you still have that drive?

It's just that I slowed up a little bit. I *should* be more ambitious. I should be trying to cast my new play now. I'd like to have it on. But to tell you the truth, I can't wait for the sun to come out and to play golf. I've worked hard all my life. I'm older than you think.

John Lee Mahin:
Team Player

Interview by Todd McCarthy
and Joseph McBride

*Hardly a man here is in the big money who has
not a bestseller or some striking stories or a successful play to his credit. (A few exceptions to
this are John Lee Mahin and Robert Riskin, who
are among the half dozen best picture writers in
the business.) But the rule still stands.*

F. Scott Fitzgerald,
The Letters of F. Scott Fitzgerald

John Lee Mahin, who died in 1984, belonged to that rarest of
species: the happy Hollywood screenwriter. When we interviewed him
in 1979, the seventy-nine-year-old Mahin, with a long and successful
career behind him, spoke with satisfaction of what happened to virtually all of his work once it left his typewriter. He had only a few horror
stories to tell, and he seemed to accept those as a necessary price for
the comforts of having worked within the studio system. Mahin spent
most of his career at MGM, where he was known as the favorite writer
of both Clark Gable and the director Victor Fleming, and worked on
such classic studio entertainments as *Red Dust* (1931), *Bombshell*
(1933), *China Seas* (1935), *Naughty Marietta* (1935), *Captains Courageous* (1937), *Test Pilot* (1938), and *Boom Town* (1940).

Although he was more of a team player than an individualist, Mahin
did have a distinctive personal touch in his screenwriting. He shared
with Gable and Fleming a flair for rousing adventure material, and at
the same time he wrote some of the raciest and most sophisticated
sexual comedies of that period. The same qualities are evident in his
two best films away from MGM, Howard Hawks's *Scarface* (1932) and
John Huston's *Heaven Knows, Mr. Allison* (1957).

Mahin's last produced work was on "The Jimmy Stewart Show" for
television in the early 1970s, although in 1979 he returned to his type-

writer to adapt an A. B. Guthrie, Jr., novel into a screenplay that remained unfilmed. Despite his admirable list of credits and his industry trophies (the Laurel Award for Lifetime Achievement from the Writers Guild of America, Oscar nominations for *Captains Courageous* and *Heaven Knows, Mr. Allison*), he was little known outside Hollywood, and he resisted suggestions to write his memoirs.

As might be expected from his easy acceptance of the MGM way of working, Mahin was a deeply conservative man. A veteran of the political wars waged by Hollywood writers over the formation of the Screen Writers Guild (predecessor of the Writers Guild of America) in the 1930s and a paladin of the subsequent McCarthy-era blacklist, Mahin unapologetically described himself as "an old rightist" and stood by his convictions to the end of his life even though he was well aware that history has passed a contrary judgment.

History is written by the victors, and the history of Mahin's era is being written by those blacklisted writers whose survival and moral triumph have given them a heroic stature today. We felt it was instructive, however, to reach behind Mahin's wall of silence, since so few people on his side of the struggle have been subjected to questioning by today's generation. Mahin's forthright, if somewhat uncomfortable, responses shed light on the reasons why the Hollywood establishment acquiesced to political repression.

1931   *Unholy Garden* (George Fitzmaurice). Uncredited contribution.

1932   *Beast of the City* (Charles Brabin). Script, dialogue.
        Scarface (Howard Hawks). Actor, co-script, co-dialogue.
        The Wet Parade (Victor Fleming). Script, dialogue.
        Red Dust (Victor Fleming). Script, dialogue.
        Tiger Shark (Howard Hawks). Uncredited contribution.

1933   *Eskimo* (W. S. Van Dyke). Adaptation.
        Bombshell (Victor Fleming). Co-adaptation.
        The Prizefighter and the Lady (W. S. Van Dyke). Co-adaptation, co-story.
        Hell Below (Jack Conway). Actor, co-dialogue.

1934   *Laughing Boy* (W. S. Van Dyke). Co-script.
        Treasure Island (Victor Fleming). Script.
        Chained (Clarence Brown). Script.

1935   *Naughty Marietta* (W. S. Van Dyke). Co-script.
        China Seas (Tay Garnett). Uncredited contribution.
        Riffraff (J. Walter Rubin). Uncredited contribution.

John Lee Mahin (right), with the director Clarence Brown, Clark Gable, and Joan Crawford on the set of Wife Versus Secretary. *(Photo: Academy of Motion Picture Arts and Sciences)*

1936   *Small Town Girl* (William A. Wellman). Co-script.
        Wife Versus Secretary (Clarence Brown). Co-script.
        The Devil Is a Sissy (W. S. Van Dyke). Co-script.
        Love on the Run (W. S. Van Dyke). Co-script.

1937   *A Star Is Born* (William W. Wellman). Uncredited contribution.

Captains Courageous (Victor Fleming). Co-script.
The Last Gangster (Edward Ludwig). Script.

1938   *Too Hot to Handle* (Jack Conway). Co-script.
Test Pilot (Victor Fleming). Uncredited contribution.

1939   *Gone with the Wind* (Victor Fleming). Uncredited contribution.
The Wizard of Oz (Victor Fleming). Uncredited contribution.

1940   *Boom Town* (Jack Conway). Script.
Foreign Correspondent (Alfred Hitchcock). Uncredited contribution.

1941   *Dr. Jekyll and Mr. Hyde* (Victor Fleming). Script.
Johnny Eager (Mervyn LeRoy). Co-script.

1942   *Tortilla Flat* (Victor Fleming). Co-script.
Woman of the Year (George Stevens). Uncredited contribution.

1943   *Adventures of Tartu* (Harold S. Bucquet). Co-script.

1945   *Adventure* (Victor Fleming). Uncredited contribution.

1946   *The Yearling* (Clarence Brown). Uncredited contribution.

1949   *Down to the Sea in Ships* (Henry Hathaway). Co-script.

1950   *Love That Brute* (Alexander Hall). Co-story, co-script.

1951   *Show Boat* (George Sidney). Script.
Quo Vadis (Mervyn LeRoy). Co-script.

1952   *My Son John* (Leo McCarey). Adaptation.

1953   *Mogambo* (John Ford). Script.

1954   *Elephant Walk* (William Dieterle). Script.

1955   *Lucy Gallant* (Robert Parrish). Co-script.

1956   *The Bad Seed* (Mervyn LeRoy). Script.

1957   *Heaven Knows, Mr. Allison* (John Huston). Co-script.

1958   *No Time for Sergeants* (Mervyn LeRoy). Script.

1959   *The Horse Soldiers* (John Ford). Co-script, co-producer.

1960   *North to Alaska* (Henry Hathaway). Co-script, co-producer.

1962   *The Spiral Road* (Robert Mulligan). Co-script.

1966   *Moment to Moment* (Mervyn LeRoy). Script.

Academy Awards include an Oscar nomination in 1937 for co-screenplay (with Marc Connelly and Dale Van Every) of *Captains Courageous;* a nomination in 1957 for co-writing with John Huston *Heaven Knows, Mr. Allison.*

Writers Guild awards include the Laurel Award for Achievement in 1957.

What did you do before you became a screenwriter?

I wanted to be a playwright, but I got sidetracked. First, I was in the newspaper business for two years, I was a reporter. Then, I got to be an actor for a couple of years, and then I went into copywriting. My father was an advertising man, really a big pioneer in the advertising business. He was born in Muscatine, Iowa, and my grandfather owned a paper there, the Muscatine *Journal.*

Were you interested in movies as a young man?

I reviewed movies on the side when I went to Harvard. I worked for the Boston *American,* a Hearst paper, as movie editor. The drama editor loved girl shows, and he'd give me all the good plays, like the Russian theatre, so I got to review those, too. Which was nice. He didn't like them. He didn't understand them. He'd say, "Fuck 'em, all this highbrow shit!" And I reviewed all the movies, and I got thirty bucks a week for it.

It's unusual that you'd write for a professional paper rather than for the Crimson.

Yeah, I didn't want to. I didn't seem to fall in with the club life at college. I made one boo-boo on the *American.* Luckily it didn't get in the paper, or we would all have been fired. I panned the hell out of Marion Davies. I said she was "a silly, no-talent blonde."

Just like Joseph Cotten in Citizen Kane*!*

Yeah. I'd never seen her before. I knew nothing about the Hearst connection. I panned her, and this guy said, "Jesus Christ! What is this? Don't you know your ass from a hole in the ground?" Later, I got to know Marion and she was a very dear, nice person. Then, I was a reporter for the New York *Sun,* the *Post,* and the *City News.* My father thought I was crazy to quit college, because he was a self-made man. He said, "Well, who's the girl? Come on, who's the girl?" And when I went into the theatre, he thought I was absolutely mad. He wouldn't speak to me.

Was your newspaper work a good learning experience?

Oh, it was great. I think it's the best thing in the world, because you've got to write something every day. Whether you like it or not, you've just got to write. Getting your stuff edited, you learn terseness. You realize how important editing is.

Did you quit acting because you thought you weren't good?

I *knew* I wasn't good. I quit because other people didn't think I was good. But, boy, did it get me around the theatre! I learned a lot. I started as a chorus boy in Gilbert and Sullivan's *Patience* at the Provincetown Playhouse, which was run by Robert Edmond Jones and Kenneth MacGowan. John Huston was there too.

Did you act in any movies?

I had a bit in *Scarface*. I play a reporter named Charles MacArthur from the *Journal*. And I was in a thing called *Hell Below* [1933], another script I wrote. We were over in the Pacific, and they needed an actor. I wrote all the best jokes for myself, and Bob Montgomery would say, "You son-of-a-bitch!"

Besides journalism and advertising copy, what had you written before you came to Hollywood?

Just short stories and some skits.

Which playwrights did you emulate at the time?

Ben [Hecht] and Charlie [MacArthur]. My wife and I lived in kind of an artists' colony. We had an old Dutch colonial farm house in Haverstraw, New York. I commuted two hours each way. I used to meet Ben on the ferry. Ben lived in Nyack and so did Charlie. We used to have parties, and I saw them. I was a copy chief at Kenyon and Eckhart; me and a girl and another guy were the copy department. One day Ben said, "I hear you're in advertising, but you're writing on the side." So I showed him some stuff, and he liked it. He said, "Nutsy and I"—that's Charlie—"are going to Hollywood in two or three weeks. You wanna come along?" I said, "What do you mean?" He said, "Well, work with us, give us something to sneer at. We want to do our plays, and we've got to do this thing we have to do for Sam Goldwyn."

It was *Unholy Garden* [1931]. They'd thought of an idea in an elevator going up to see Goldwyn and had sold it to him. They were stuck with it, so they had to come out here. George Fitzmaurice directed it. Ronald Colman was in it. Ben said, "Maybe you could work on that, and give us a chance to work on our plays. We'll give you $200 a week and guarantee you a job when we leave." So I went. I didn't do a helluva lot of work, because to try to do Ben's work for him is silly. I don't know why he brought me out. I'd try to work, and he'd say, "No, no," and then he'd sit down and rattle off something.

Then Hecht brought you along on Scarface *[1932]?*

Yeah. Hughes was in trouble with the script on *Scarface,* and Howard Hawks came to Ben and asked him to do a new treatment on the whole thing. Ben said, "If you give me $1,000 in cash—I want it in cash, no checks—every day." He did sixty pages in two weeks. He could have gotten $60,000 if he wanted, if he'd stalled, but he wanted to get back to New York. He took $14,000, and he said, "Now you've got to fix it up." I was a Merton of the Movies, and I said, "This is wonderful." It reads like a beauty. He said, "It's so full of holes, this thing, John. There's hardly any dialogue. This isn't a script, this is a full treatment. You're going to have trouble, but this is your job that we promised you." Seton Miller was working on that too. He had worked with Hawks on some of the silent pictures. Seton put all the numbers down, and I just redid the dialogue. We did the final script with Hawks. We started from page one, redoing the dialogue.

Were the three of you together in the same room when you were working on the final script with Hawks?

Yeah, but then we'd go away and write the scene and we'd bring it to Howard. And then I worked on the set the whole time, just me and Hawks.

Was W. R. Burnett on it when you were?

No, he had worked before on the thing, I guess. And another guy [Fred Pasley] was on the credits too.

Who thought of putting the incestuous undertones into the relationship between Paul Muni and Ann Dvorak?

That was Ben.

Hawks claimed he went to Hecht and said he wanted to do Al Capone's story as if it were the Borgias, and that "Scarface" [Muni] and Cesca [Dvorak] had the same kind of incestuous relationship as Cesare and Lucretia Borgia.

Ben said that to *Hawks.* I heard him say that. The Borgias have always been Ben's favorite characters. Howard, bless his heart, probably knew who they were, but I think he looked them up in the encyclopedia. Howard was such a liar! That's a typical example. Like he said he invented the nickel thing. He didn't at all. It was all in the script. Ben put it in the script. Raft flips a nickel constantly, nervously. I can remember the way Ben said, "He flips a nickel nervously."

Even George Raft claims that Hawks thought that up.

I don't think he'd read the script. You mustn't feel that I'm trying to be derogatory, because this was all discussed with us openly. Vic Fleming and I would kid Howard about his lying. He just pretended we never said it; he'd just change the subject. I loved the guy; I think he was a lot of fun. But you know Howard. Now, the script's been OK'd in every department, and the actors have had it. He had a sheet of paper; he'd take the scene they were going to shoot and spend all the time writing it out in longhand—*from the script!* He might change "yes" to "yes, sir" or cut out a "yes" with a nod of the head. He'd hand it to the girl and say, "Make copies and give it to the cast." We'd all joke about it, everybody would. But it looked as though he was kind of rewriting it on the set.

Did Hawks collaborate more than most directors in the writing before the shooting started?

Yes, sure, he did. I think he always wanted to be a writer.

Was he a good writer?

No. He appreciated good writing, I'll say that.

*Hawks used to claim that he had made some contribution to the scripts of three films you wrote for Victor Fleming—*Red Dust *[1932],* Captains Courageous *[1937], and* Test Pilot *[1938].*

Did Howard say *that?* Jesus! He's a complete liar! A complete liar, bless his heart!

Did you work with him on anything else besides Scarface*?*

After I went to Metro, he did a picture with Eddie Robinson called *Tiger Shark* [1932] at Warners. He called me up, and he said, "John, I'm in trouble. The story's pretty good, but the dialogue's lousy. Would you do it?" I was just getting $200 a week at Metro, like I was getting on *Scarface.* Irving Thalberg said, "We're not millionaires here like Hughes, but we'll give you a job and try you out." *Scarface* hadn't come out, but he said, "You have very good references from Hawks and Charlie MacArthur." Since I'd written a gangster movie, they decided to put me on a gangster movie, *Beast of the City* [1932]. Did the script in three weeks, and that got me my contract. So Howard said, "Can you do some work at night, bootleg it, and I'll pay you another $200 a week as long as it takes you?" So I did. I rewrote the script to *Tiger Shark,* working at night. Well, I'm sure that Howard told Warner Brothers that he had rewritten it, you know. But that's alright, I don't mind, it's just one of Howard's charms.

You couldn't get credit on Tiger Shark*?*

No, I was bootlegging. I shouldn't have done it. That's the only time I did it.

The film holds up very well.

Really? The dialogue was very pedestrian, so we rewrote all the dialogue. We tried to lighten it up.

Didn't Hawks shoot some of another script of yours, The Prize-fighter and the Lady *[1933], at MGM?*

Yeah. He was two days on that, and he was six days behind schedule. He probably thought he could get away with it at Metro. But Mayer just put his foot down and said, "This has got to stop." Woody Van Dyke took over.

Hawks just didn't fit in at MGM, did he?

No, I don't think so. He wouldn't take the regimen. He wasn't used to it. You know, he wouldn't allow Hughes on the set. From there on, even at Warners, I think he got away with it. And that's pretty tough to do when you're talking about Jack Warner. But he couldn't get away with it at MGM.

George Stevens said he left MGM after only one film, Woman of the Year *[1942], because there was too much interference. He said, "Good directors didn't stay long at Metro." What enabled directors like Clarence Brown, Victor Fleming, and Woody Van Dyke to thrive at Metro while others were unhappy?*

I think they were clever enough to get their way. I really do.

But isn't it true that MGM was not a studio where the more independent-minded directors like Hawks or Stevens felt comfortable?

Yes, that's true; but again, I found those directors were respected and people listened to them. I worked with George on the ending of *Woman of the Year.* They needed a new ending, so I wrote it. Mayer was away, and [the MGM executive] Sam Katz was in charge of the studio. Hepburn came into Sam's office; *wham,* she threw what I'd written on the desk and said, "That's the biggest bunch of crap I've ever read!" Sam was bewildered; he was looking at Stevens. Tracy was stuck on her, but he knew this ending was for him and not for her, so he was sitting there and he wasn't saying a word. Finally, Sam said, "George, what do you think?" George didn't even answer. "Sam," he just said, "why don't you put that apartment up on stage three, we'll shoot it in the morning." And Sam said, "Oh, that's fine, that's fine."

A lot of directors at MGM objected to the policy of scenes being reshot by other people.

You'd feel that way if you'd written a nice short story, and some guy came in and wrote the three last paragraphs. You wouldn't feel it was yours. I used to go down and direct quite a lot. I did stuff when I was working with [the producer] Hunt Stromberg, because the directors were off on other pictures.

What pictures did you shoot scenes for? Only the ones you wrote?

Yes, and only with Stromberg, because Stromberg believed in me. He wanted to make an actor out of me, and I wouldn't. I shot some stuff on *Beast of the City.* On *Eskimo* [1933] Van Dyke was off doing something, and they needed some new scenes. I shot a couple of things with some Eskimo girls. I directed some of *The Prizefighter and the Lady.* Van Dyke was off doing something else. He was working all the time. He'd miss a lot of close-ups.

That experience didn't inspire you to want to direct your own scripts?

No, you had to get up too early. I think it's much more satisfying to be a writer. If I directed my own things, I would have a feeling of being so subjective that I'm afraid I wouldn't do so good. I think the guys are very brave to do their own things and very sure of themselves. I welcome another opinion, if I respect it.

You're listed for five movies in 1932. In addition to Scarface, *which was made in 1930 but released in 1932, you had* Beast of the City, Tiger Shark, The Wet Parade, *and* Red Dust *all in the same year.*

We worked hard.

How did you get along with Thalberg?

Fine. He said, "If it isn't for the writing, we've got nothing." Mayer went to him once and said, "Oh, these writers! Some of these writers are getting drunk, and they have three-hour lunches in the Derby. We ought to put our foot down. Jack Warner over there runs a tight ship!" Irving said, "No, Louis, they're signed for fifty-two weeks. If I get forty-two weeks a year out of them, that's fine with me. It's worth it. Let them alone, they're doing fine." He had no kicks about the product.

You were considered one of the top writers at MGM in the 1930s, weren't you?

Well, yeah. They had 110 writers under contract at one time. But there were about twelve of us who really turned out the work. I did four in one year, and then I'd do three; maybe I did five in one year, I think.

Did you have any other ambitions while you were writing screenplays—to be writing books or plays?

No. I was very happy.

Maybe that's one reason that you were happy. You weren't complaining that you didn't have time to write your novel.

Probably. I paid more attention and took it seriously and believed that I was a little proud, maybe, of what I'd done. I wasn't ashamed of it. And maybe that comes out. I think it's a craft more than it is an art. In the first place, I was paid while I was doing it. I was very satisfied. If I'd wanted to be a novelist and I'd had it in me, I'd have gone out and been one, I guess. But I was just meant to be good at my craft, that's all. Successful.

There's a lot of debate today about whether the old studio system, with people under long-term contracts, was better or worse than the current system, with almost everyone freelancing. How do you feel about it?

I think for a lucky young writer, it was very nice to have the old system. But if you are an established writer, freelancing gives you a wider range. I was a very lucky young writer. I worked with the best company, the best stars, and more or less the best directors and producers.

Some of the studio writers, like the directors, complained that it was too much of an assembly line, that they were rewritten too often.

It didn't happen to me. Maybe if I wasn't available, sometimes. Don [Donald Ogden] Stewart wrote the very end of *Red Dust*. But I always worked singly.

What about cases where you shared credit with other people?

That was because they'd done enough work on it to gain credit. They had done a lot of ditch digging, and I was just putting in the lace and the jokes.

Did you work on films at MGM you didn't get credit for?

Lots of 'em. When you were working at Metro you were a factory boy, and you'd help out. You could turn things down; but if they were in a jam it was only fair to do the best you could, because you weren't going to get credit; it didn't make any difference. You could only fix good ones, not bad ones.

Why wouldn't the original writer do it?

Because he had written himself out, or he'd left or something, or they couldn't get on with him.

What were some of the films you worked on without credit?

Well, that thing that Gable did when he came back from the war— *Adventure* [1945]. "Gable's Back and Garson's Got Him." Pretty bad. Very mystical thing. Made a lot of money because it was his first picture since the war. It was originally for Freddie Bartholomew, but it ended up with Gable and Garson!

I worked on *China Seas* [1935]. Tay Garnett directed it. They tried to do another *Red Dust*. Thalberg called Jim [James Kevin] McGuinness and me and said, "You fellas look this script over. And Jim, you help John. Let John do the dialogue and some scenes here. I think something's wrong." What we found was embarrassing. Jules Furthman, who did the script, had stolen so much—practically word for word out of famous pieces. Things by Mark Twain and Somerset Maugham—and there was a well-known English novel of the time that he had taken a whole speech from. We discovered these, and we had to do quite a lot of rewriting. Granted, nothing's new, but Jesus, you don't just take whole lines of dialogue!

Did Furthman often do that?

Evidently. Vic Fleming used to give an imitation of Jules Furthman writing. He drives up to the studio in his big car, parks it. He's got a writer's portfolio with all his scripts in it; he's got some books under his arm; he's got his beret on and a scarf. He comes to his big office in the Thalberg Building, says "hello" to the secretary, sits down, and puts his books on the desk. He writes with a pen—doesn't use a typewriter; like Maugham, he writes with a pen—he sits down, takes out his pad, and then he starts to write. That is, he opens the book, reads it, and starts to write.

Hawks was also known to borrow things from other sources.

He did an aviation picture in South America [*Only Angels Have Wings* in 1939, written by Furthman] that was stolen directly out of *Test Pilot.* He asked me to get the script for him for that. I wouldn't do it. I said, "Howard, I can do just so much. It's Vic's script, ask Vic."

Was this before Test Pilot *came out?*

No, it had come out. I guess he wanted the script so he wouldn't have to go to the movie.

Victor Fleming is a director who doesn't get as much attention today as some of the others.

I know he doesn't. There's a book out about sixty great directors, and he isn't even mentioned in it. Here's a guy who did *Gone with the Wind* [1939] and the *Wizard of Oz* [1939]!

Maybe that's because a guy like Hawks obviously had a very well-defined personality in his films, while Fleming's personality isn't as defined.

That's true.

What do you think Fleming did best?

I think he was a good all-round director. Vic and I did seven pictures. On *Captains Courageous* I said, "Geez, this is a beautiful kid [Freddie Bartholomew], Vic. It seems to me you're not getting the close-ups of this kid." He said, "Wait till we need 'em. Wait till they'll have some effect." I said, "Well, when will that be?" He said, "When he starts crying and breaking. That's when we'll go in to see him." And this tough bastard starts to move in on him. He was right.

Hawks and Fleming were close friends, weren't they?

Very close. I'm sure that Vic might have gotten something from Howard. Vic might have gotten a lot of taste from Howard. Howard had class, you see. Vic had innate class, but he wasn't born to the purple like Howard was. He didn't have the advantages of his young life, the rearing. He came from a very poor family. He was part Indian and very proud of it, as he should be. Howard was always very jealous of Victor. He went to the preview of *Red Dust* with us. I rode home with him to Vic's house, and Vic drove somebody else. It had gone over very well. Howard was silent for a long while; then he said, "I wonder where Vic got that story." I said, "What do you mean, where did Vic get that story?" Howard said, "Where'd he steal it?" I said, "It came in a fifteen-page treatment of a story to MGM called 'Red Dust,' and it was a very purple melodrama about a poor little slaving whore—she got whipped by the heavy, fell in love with Gable from afar, and that's all that happened. So, we decided to turn it into a comedy-drama." He said, "Well, I don't know. I think I've heard that story somewhere." He just couldn't face the fact.

Did Fleming work on the scripts with you too?

John Lee Mahin (right), with the director Victor Fleming, during the filming of Captains Courageous.

Yeah. The first one I did for him was *The Wet Parade*. Then *Red Dust*. There was another director on *Red Dust* at first, Jacques Feyder. It was supposed to be John Gilbert and Jean Harlow, and Jean was supposed to help Gilbert's waning popularity—make a bull out of him. I saw Gable in a picture, and I went to Hunt and said, "Oh God, Hunt, this is a perfect team!" He was a promotion man, and I knew it would tickle his fancy. He had never seen him. He ran a picture of Gable's that night. He went to Irving and sold Irving. They took Feyder off, rebuilt the sets, and upped the budget; and that was the team.

You had some of the raunchiest lines of all time in Red Dust. *There are tremendously sexy double entendres.*

It holds up pretty well. You do it with inferences. Let people use their minds; let 'em work. You can say almost anything you want to. I think cleavage is the most exciting thing about a woman. But when they get so explicit, you might as well go to an X picture or go to a whorehouse.

One of the sexiest scenes in movies is the scene where she's taking a bath in the rain barrel. Gable's standing there looking at her, but you don't see her body.

Sure. But you know what he's looking at.

He's looking at her, and she doesn't care.

No. And I think that's the way to do it. We didn't have any trouble with that. The Legion of Decency didn't mind the bathtub scene, because we didn't show anything; now isn't that funny? But the priest picked up on a line Harlow said. I thought of a line, I rushed down, and I told it to Stromberg. I said, "It's a great fade-out line for this scene with her and the Chinaman. She's crying, she's cleaning the parrot cage, and she says to the parrot, 'What have you been eating, cement?' " I thought, if she isn't crying it won't be very funny; it'll just be unpleasant if she says it angrily to the parrot. But if she's crying at the same time, if she's broken-hearted, then it's funny and it's sweet. You can see the difference.

You were often described as Gable's favorite screenwriter, and you played a large part in shaping his image. How would you characterize him?

Quiet, determined—no, not determined, just quiet. I said to Hunt once, "This guy's got eyes like a child and a build like a bull."

He was renowned at the time for having such a frankly lustful way of looking at women, unlike any other actor.

Yeah, but it wasn't a leer. It was a pleasant look. His eyes were open and frank like a child's are, you see what I mean? There wasn't any filth in them. Gable was frankly admiring. A woman never feels bad when she's told that she's got a lovely body, and that's what his eyes said. Gable was a very gentle guy, as a matter of fact. Until he became irritated with a dame who was making a fool of herself, he was a very gentle man.

When MGM remade Red Dust *as* Mogambo *[1953] and you rewrote the script for John Ford to direct, what did you try to do to make it different or improve it?*

You were in a much classier atmosphere—with safaris being what they were then, with trucks and traveling toilets. It just raised the whole thing in class. We thought of a maharajah, and she's coming out there to be with him.

By raising it in class you lost some of the earthiness of it.

Probably. I didn't realize I was doing it.

The remake is more glamorized. For one thing, it's shot in color on African locations, and the original was done in the studio.

Yeah, it was all in the studio. The river was on the back lot. Nothing was in Saigon at all.

Yet somehow the first one is better.

Somehow it is. I don't know why.

Wasn't there a fair amount of second-unit work in Mogambo *that Ford didn't do?*

Ford wouldn't shoot the gorilla stuff, and he wouldn't shoot the stuff in the canoe. I don't know why. The scene in the canoe was when she said that the elephant reminded her of somebody.

That was quite a funny bit of phallic symbolism.

I didn't mean it as a phallic symbol, but everybody took it as that because that son-of-a-bitch bull elephant raised his trunk! The ears were flapping! Maybe the guy who shot it thought it was a good idea. It always got a laugh.

After Red Dust, *you did* Bombshell *[1933] with Harlow and Fleming. That's a very funny, racy film.*

Yeah, in spots.

Was that based on Harlow's own life?

No, that was based on Clara Bow's life. That came in, again, as a very purple movie, a treatment about this poor girl who worked all her life and in the end committed suicide. Nobody understood her, and she had all these people on her, her father and her brother. It was a tragic thing. I said, "Let's turn this into a comedy. It's funny. You must have known people, Vic, in the early days . . ." He said, "I know one right now, Clara Bow. She was my girl. You'd come into the room—there's a beautiful Oriental rug with coffee stains and dog shit all over the floor, and her father'd come in drunk . . ." And I looked at Hunt, and he said, "That's enough. We got it." That was Clara Bow's life. It was based on her. Her secretary was stealing from her. There was later a lawsuit about it.

Did you work on Gone with the Wind *[1939]?*

Yeah. Fleming and I were put on it.

After Selznick had fired George Cukor and halted production and they were panicking?

Right. We were working nights because I was working on something else, and I was going to be relieved to work on the script in about a week. I said, "For God's sake, let's get back to Margaret Mitchell's book and Sidney Howard's wonderful script." Sidney did the first script and then they'd brought in some people and they fooled around with it. Vic and I worked for about a week and then I had a fight with David, a misunderstanding, and I was off it.

Hawks claimed that Fleming told him, "I haven't time to read this damned book. I'm going to people I like, and I'm saying: 'What stuff did you like in the book?' And then I'm doing those." Hawks said he mentioned Tara, and Fleming said, "What's that?"

Oh, God! Oh, Howard! That's terrible! Vic read the novel. Every night Vic would say, "Now look on page so-and-so." He knew the novel by heart. Vic always went back to sources.

They replaced you with Ben Hecht. In his memoirs Hecht said he spent a week rewriting it while they were on hiatus.

Yeah, but there wasn't much to do.

Hecht claimed he never read the novel. Is that true?

It's possible. It's more believable than Victor. Because Hecht could sense a story, and if he was in a hurry, he'd talk to anybody he respected who had read it and say, "Did this happen?" Being a writer, he'd sense how Mitchell would have gone ahead.

How did Fleming feel about the work George Cukor had done on the film?

Vic was a great admirer of Cukor. Vic has gotten so much bad publicity on *Gone with the Wind*. I remember him saying to somebody, "George would have done just as good a job as I. He'd probably have done a lot better on the intimate scenes. I think I did pretty well on some of the bigger stuff. George came from the stage and taught us what directing a dialogue scene was about. He knew. And nobody could direct a dialogue scene like George Cukor. It's bullshit that he's just a woman's director. He's not. He can direct anybody." Vic was very fair. I heard him say that many times. And he's never been given that credit.

I think Gable thought Cukor was paying too much attention to the girls, but I never asked him. I was there when Vic told Vivien Leigh to stick it up her ass. David and I had made up, and I was visiting the set. Vic was feeling very ill, and he was nervous and tired. He had terrible pain in his kidneys; he had stones, and you could just see he was drawn. She was getting more and more bitchy, because she was approaching the scene where she was an awful bitch, and she was getting scared of it. They were doing that scene, which later resulted in him leaving her. She said, "Victor, I don't like this line. I think it should be rewritten." And Vic said, "Well, wait a moment, we all said we're going to do the book. This is right out of the book. Now, come on, this is the character. We're doing Scarlett. She *was* a bitch." She said, "Well, I just won't do it." And Clark said, "By the way, Vic—" Oh, Jesus, then I knew it was coming! Clark said, "That scene we're shooting tomorrow, where I walk out and say, 'Frankly, my dear, I don't give a damn'—I think that's a little strong." Vic just looked at Clark with contempt, rolled up his script, and said, "Miss Leigh, you can stick this script up your royal British ass!" And walked out. Oh, she screamed! Two nights later, the three of them, David, Clark, and Vivien, went to Vic with two lovebirds in a cage, and they said, "Come back, Vic, we'll do the scene."

Did the writers at MGM have an opportunity to recommend literary material to the studio?

Yes. The only picture I wasn't happy about was the one that I really got them to buy. *Laughing Boy* [1934]. God, that was awful!

It doesn't play anymore.

It didn't play at all! They would laugh it off the screen. Ramon Novarro as Laughing Boy! The poor guy was a fag; and he was an old fag then, so it was coming out. And he looked like an old whore, with his hair hanging down and a blanket on. Oh, Jesus Christ! They should have had some virile young guy, Tyrone Power or somebody. Lupe Velez played Slim Girl. She was great. If you'd had somebody comparable to her and if you'd played the sad ending, you would have had a movie. It's very hard dialogue too. I don't know whether anybody could have played it. Their speeches were so up in the clouds. Oh, it was awful!

After the movie came out, you met the author, Oliver La Farge.

I met him in the Harvard Club in New York a couple of years later. He was a classmate of mine in college, but I hadn't know him. He said, "Oh, you went out into pictures, didn't you? God, they ruined something of mine!" I was sitting there with a drink, and I didn't know whether to tell him or not. I said, "Oliver, I did that script." He took his drink, and he threw it right in my face. He could have cut me; it [the glass] broke when it hit the floor. He came back and said, "Oh, God, I'm sorry. What happened?" And I told him. He said, "Oh, those vicious people, why do you work for them?"

We should have done it like *Eskimo* and had that lovely language. The vernacular, the idiom, was beautiful, and we should have let them speak in Navajo. They took it down in Navajo country. But Van Dyke had English-speaking Indians reading their parts. We never thought of it, but we should have, because Van Dyke had done *Eskimo* with Hunt and the same people. I also got MGM to buy *The Yearling* [1946]. I started out with it, and I was taken off because I "didn't realize the sensitivity of it."

Who took you off?

The guy who was going to produce it, Sidney Franklin. I got them to buy it because I loved it so. Vic started out to direct it with Spencer Tracy. They shot in Florida, and Tracy looked so big and so capable that it just didn't work. Well, then they did it with Gregory Peck, and they had Clarence Brown directing it. When they had me on it with Vic, Sidney Franklin said, "Oh, of course, we can't kill the deer." I said, "*What?* You can't kill the deer? That's the *story!* This is the story of a boy growing up. He grows up because he's got to kill the deer!" He said, "You just can't do it. The audience wouldn't go for it." I said, "Sidney, what the hell did we buy this thing for?" He said, "We buy lots of things that we change." And I thought this guy Sidney Franklin was a very sensitive, fine man. He was smart. I couldn't understand this. I said, "You're a fucking idiot, and you're gonna fuck up this picture." He said, "Well, I don't want to talk anymore today." So they took me off because he said I wasn't sensitive enough, that I used bad language.

Years later we became very friendly. He said, "Johnny, I know you hold it against me, but I was so wrong." Which is tough for a guy to say. I love people who are able to say it and say it gracefully and well. He said, "I was so wrong. And the end still wasn't right." I said, "I know it. You finally killed the deer, yeah, that's because Clarence insisted on it. But you had him dreaming of the deer at the end instead of dreaming of digging the well, of killing the bear, of being a man."

In the early fifties you left MGM.

I left with Mayer, and I was with him for four years before he died. We had an office on Canon Drive.

And he lent you to MGM to work on Show Boat *[1951],* Quo Vadis *[1951],* Mogambo *[1953], and others?*

Yeah, he was the best agent I ever had. Whatever pictures I did after he left, he guaranteed me so much, and he'd lend me out at a big profit. He'd take 20 percent, and he'd still make more than I'd make. People would send me things, I'd knock wood, and they'd send me more things.

Were you involved with the Screen Writers Guild at the very begin-ning, in the thirties?

Yes, at the very beginning. I put money up, a lot of us put money up, and then we found out who was really running the thing, with Lawson and his minions. We used to call him George Washington Lawson, who was going to lead us into a great rebellion, but we found out they had other interests; the [Communist] Party was in there heavy. Then we split, and we formed the Screen Playwrights Incorporated. They called us a company union. Yes, we were a company union, formed by the workers themselves. We went cloak-and-dagger, and we found out that all the heavy, leading, hard-working guys in the Guild were members of the Party. We sent guys to meetings. Frankly, we spied on them. A couple of them admitted it. But then we couldn't convince a lot of the people that they were, and some said, "Yeah, we agree with you, but you ought to stay within the Guild." We said, "To hell with it; we don't want to have to watch them all the time. Let's form a guild where we will welcome them in, but we don't want to be run by them." We simply felt we could deal better with Uncle Louis than with Uncle Joe.

We started to form the Playwrights—156 people—and then it got around to Thalberg, and he said, "Now what the hell is this?" We said, "You're going to have to recognize writers sooner or later, Irving, because the Federal Labor Relations Act is coming in and they've got a right. And you'd better recognize us, because you'll be in trouble with that other bunch until they clean house." So Irving signed, and we ran writers' problems for four years, until the Labor Relations Board finally came into real being, as did the Guild, who greatly outnumbered us, because two weeks' work in a studio gave you a voting membership in the Guild, and we required three screenplays or two years' work.

There was a lot of bitterness over that power struggle between the Guild and the Playwrights.

Oh yeah, a lot of people called us fascists, anti-Negro, anti-Jewish, anti-labor—the same old tired jokes they make today. The only thing we were never called, strangely enough, was anti-Communist. Why? Now they got a thing called "McCarthyism," which they use because McCarthy made an ass of himself. Anytime there's a blacklist or a hint of people not being able to work, it's called McCarthyism. McCarthy was a fool. I remember talking to him on the phone, several of us did. I got Mayer to speak to him, because I thought he might get some money from Mayer for his next campaign. McCarthy was making an ass of the whole thing.

How do you feel about the events of the blacklist era now?

We didn't want the blacklist, but those things happen. It's not our fault that they joined the Communist Party, and I didn't give a damn if they worked or not. I could care less. I used to kid Dalton [Trumbo] and Jack Lawson. I'd say, "You're gonna get in trouble because the American Legion and the Catholic Church are gonna have you black-listed. You're gonna scare these guys to death, and you're gonna get blacklisted." And, by God, they were. We didn't blacklist them. Some of them were very good writers.

Couldn't you have done something about it?

We couldn't do anything about it. They weren't members of our guild, our Screen Playwrights. If they had been and if they could prove they were blacklisted, we'd have tried to do something about it.

But this was in the late forties and early fifties, and there was only one Guild then, wasn't there?

Yeah. In 1938 we quit, and the real Guild took over by law.

It's hard to understand that when writers and other people were being blacklisted, the Guild didn't stand up for them.

I don't know. I didn't rejoin the Guild until around '45. I went in because they had found out that what we had always claimed was true, and they'd gotten rid of a helluva lot of the big, major influences of the Party.

Do you really think the Party had that much influence on screenplays?

Sure it did, sure it did.

But so much of it was exaggerated, wasn't it, like the famous case where Ginger Rogers's mother attacked Dalton Trumbo for being "communistic" because he wrote the line "share and share alike" in one of her daughter's films [Tender Comrade in 1943]?

Ginger Rogers's mother was an eyesore. There was a lot of damage done by stupid people. Hedda Hopper, for instance. *The Reader's Digest* ran a debate between their gang and our gang, and Hedda was one of the four people on our side. The night before, we saw what she was going to talk about. She had a whole list of movies that were Communist-controlled, with Communist philosophy in them. One or two were ones where they had a banker who held a mortgage. He was the heavy because he was a money man holding the mortgage over a poor family. We said, "Jesus, Hedda, a banker holding a mortgage on a family has been a heavy for five thousand years! This is not Communist!"

Frank Capra would have been deported if it had been.

Frank Capra had a picture of Mussolini on his bedroom wall—a big oil painting—he adored him. And he was against us. So it's very strange bedfellows you got. I spent as much time telling people that so-and-so was *not* a Communist as I did saying that I believed or had proof that somebody was. I never said a thing about anybody unless I had proof.

But what do you think the threat to pictures was? All the pictures that were accused of being Communist-inspired are so innocuous.

They never got made. Or they were so innocuous that they didn't mean anything. The threat was to us, as writers, as members of an organization, to our way of operating; we had to watch every step, and we didn't want to. There was no threat to pictures.

Or to the American way of life?

No, not at all. If they were a threat to the American way of life, the American way of life isn't worth a shit, you know?

People like Louis B. Mayer and Harry Cohn wouldn't have made Communist pictures.

Of course they wouldn't.

But in Hollywood, money rules; and if Communism sold, they'd make a Communist picture.

They would. Listen, they hired them all [during the blacklist], all the good ones; they all worked under different names.

If fascism sold, they'd make a fascist film. I've always thought Hollywood has really no morality.

Sure. I agree with you. Look at the crap—the horny, almost pornographic crap that's being put on now. Why? Because it makes money. I think L. B. and Thalberg and Sam Goldwyn would never have done it. Mayer was a pirate, and he had some questionable ethics; but he was smart enough to have good taste, and I don't think he would have done that.

You worked on one of the most anti-Communist films of that period, My Son John *[1952].*

Leo McCarey was a brilliant man who let the Communists drive him absolutely crazy. He actually went crazy. I said, "I'll do the film if you just make Robert Walker—alright, he's a Communist; but he could just as well be in the government employ and be discovered to be an embezzler, as far as I'm concerned. Let's not preach against the Communists. We've done enough of it. People know it's bad; that's all we have to say. He's a spy, he's a member of the Party, and his mother is Helen Hayes. That's her favorite son. And you have a movie."

But then he wanted to carry it a lot farther?

Oh, he carried on and he preached and everything. I did the original script. Then he called in Myles Connolly, and they rewrote it. I went down to see Helen on the set. I hadn't seen her in a long time. I didn't know what they'd done. I knew Myles was going to be there, but Leo said something about my sort of letting him down on the script. I said we'd agreed we wouldn't get on the soapbox, because it's boring. I went up to Helen (Leo was in his office), and she said, "What happened to the script?" The script that I wrote they'd sent to Helen to get her to play it, because she hadn't done a picture in years. I said, "What's wrong?" She said, "What happened to the script that I accepted, that you wrote, John? When I got out here I was handed a different script. Now a lot more of this crap is going in it about how bad communism is." He'd gone crazy. He lost his sense of humor. I was aghast when I saw the picture; so was Helen. She called me and said, "Oh, God! I really came back to Hollywood fine, didn't I? This is my last time."

In Film Comment, *the Hollywood screenwriter issue, you said* Heaven Knows, Mr. Allison *[1957] was the film you are most satisfied with.*

I think so, yeah. It was a tour de force, and I really felt it was kind of a little gem. John Huston, on the other hand, never mentions it when he is interviewed. I thought it was a nice film.

It was very risqué but charmingly so; it was never salacious.

"A little gem": Heaven Knows, Mr. Allison *with Deborah Kerr and Robert Mitchum, co-written by John Lee Mahin and the director John Huston.*

We handled that with a great deal of care. It was a very dirty book by Charles Shaw. Gene Frenke bought the book, and he had to be a producer on it [with Buddy Adler]. So I turned the script in to him and gave a copy to Buddy Adler, and Frenke kept saying, "It's not sexy enough, it's not sexy enough." I said, "What do you mean, not sexy enough?" He said, "She's gotta have an itchy cunt!" I said, "Oh, for God's sake, will you stop this?" I went to Buddy, and he said, "Just hand the stuff in, and don't pay any attention to him." When John [Huston] took it over, he said, "I'm going to have a conference now," and Frenke said, "Well, I've got to be in on this." And Buddy said, "You can be in on it if you don't open your goddamned mouth."

I like Huston. He said to me, "You've done a hell of a job, John; I love it. I'd like to go away with you to Ensenada for about three weeks"—you see, he couldn't work in this country because his citizenship was in Ireland—"and there are a couple of things I'd like to put in; I've got some ideas." I said, "Fine, I love it," because I respect him. And Gene Frenke is sitting there, and he says, "Tell you what it needs, Mr. Huston. She's gotta have an itchy cunt." And John says,

"What? What? What?" And Buddy Adler said to Frenke, "Get out! Go! Get out of this office! Go!" Isn't that awful?

Did you consult with any religious authorities before making the film?

I talked to a nun who ran a hospital here. A hell of a woman, lovely-looking, about forty-two. I interviewed her for about two hours. She later saw the film, and she was very pleased with it. I said to the nun, "Now I'm going to ask you the $64 question, sister. You can ask me to leave, but I've got to ask it. Now that you have taken your vows, don't you as a woman miss the desire that comes to a woman? Don't you miss the fulfillment of that desire? You know what I'm talking about." She said, "I know exactly what you're talking about. Of course we do. Our lives are built on sacrifice. If you're not conscious of the sacrifice, what's it worth?" We had that in the picture, that line; Huston took it out. I said, "John, why did you take it out?" He said, "She was too glib; she was too quick with it. She should have searched for it."

When you knew Huston in the early days, did he want to make his career as an actor?

He didn't know what he wanted to be. I knew he was writing. I wasn't writing much in those days. I had just started to write, and I knew he was trying to write. I'd had a couple of short stories published, I think. He was a strange boy. He's a strange *man*. In the hotel we were staying at down there in Tobago, there was a night club, and he got drunk and showed up in the night club quite naked. God, it was awful. And he didn't know where he was. He's a bad drinker. He wants to fight. He gets mean. He wanted to fight, and people surrounded him. They rushed the publicity department down from the studio, and they covered it up. They said it wasn't Huston, it was a tourist named John Hamilton; and he was kicked out of the hotel. Three days later it was his birthday, and we had a little cookout with some friends on a ranch they had. He got a big sombrero, and my wife knitted in blue lettering across it, "Heaven Only Knows, Mr. Hamilton." He had to laugh.

How did it come about that you produced The Horse Soldiers *[1959], with Martin Rackin, for John Ford?*

At Warner Brothers I had done a script of Pearl Buck's novel *Letter from Peking* with Rackin before *The Horse Soldiers*. Jack Warner decided against doing it. But that's how I got together with Marty. We decided to go into business together. We took out an option on this book [by Harold Sinclair], and we said the perfect guy, a Civil War buff, is Ford. He fell for it like a ton of bricks when we took it to him. We wanted Gable to play Duke's part first, and we almost had him. Ford was wonderful, but that was an unfortunate picture. Bad movie.

Ford lost interest at the end, didn't he, when the stuntman, Fred Kennedy, was killed?

Yeah. There was supposed to be a big, bloody battle at the end, and then the guy died.

Ford just wrapped it up and came back from location?

Yes, he did. I said, "Marty, we've got to shoot it." I pleaded with the Mirisch brothers [the producers Harold, Marvin, and Walter Mirisch of the Mirisch Company, Inc.]. They said, "No, we've got Ford, Holden, and Wayne; we'll make a million." I said, "This picture goes right out the window. It's a little shaky up to there anyway, so let's at least have a finish." They said, "No, we won't spend the money."

What about the ending that's in the picture now?

Ford ad-libbed it. If you'll notice, in the charge across the bridge, one man fell off a horse, and the bridge wasn't even splintered. He just dove off his horse. That's all that was. It was awful.

Did Ford have much influence on the script while you were writing it?

No, we more or less had the script, but he edited a lot of the scenes.

Did he suggest the scene of the boy soldiers?

He did that, you bet. That was one of the best scenes in the piece. He ad-libbed it. Bending the tracks, I think he put that in. He put Grant in. He understood Grant, the drinking and all.

Ford always said he hated producers; did that cause any problem for you?

No, no. Marty drove him crazy because Marty was always cracking jokes. He'd say, "Get that son-of-a-bitch off my neck; he's driving me crazy."

So he was the scapegoat for Ford's hatred of producers.

Maybe. He said, "See, you have humor, he has jokes." I think he was trying to flatter me. But he was kind of wily. I wondered if he was trying to split me and Marty to get his way. But he wasn't. It was just that Marty irritated him. We both walked on the set one day, and they were doing the banquet scene, where she served them food in her house. Ford was using a pretty well-known bit actor, Walter Reed; he had him in a Union outfit. He had already played a Confederate soldier. Well, he's a guy whose face you remembered, but here he was in two uniforms. We didn't know how to tell Ford. I said, "I'll tell him," and Marty said, "Don't, Jesus, he'll go crazy." So we went to Duke and said, "We want some advice, how do you tell this guy?" Duke says, "Well, you just go tell him. I agree with you. Jesus, we've already cranked two hours on the guy." Finally we went down on the set and told him. Ford said, "Alright, alright, that's it! You take over, you take over!" Wouldn't accept the fact. We just cut around him.

I understand you recently came out of retirement to do another script.

Yeah, a thing that Eddie Grainger finally got me to do. We call it "The Town." It's from a little book by A. B. Guthrie, Jr., called *Arfive* [Boston: Houghton Mifflin, 1971]. "R-5" is a brand, and he called the town "Arfive." It's the story of his father, who went to Montana around 1900. He became a high school principal in a town like Missoula, just off the Bitterroot range there on the plains. The town was just about ready to graduate a high school class—it had grown up that much. It was still a rough town; it had a whorehouse and a sheriff and all that. It's just his experiences. It's a bawdy book, but there's nothing dirty about it, nothing offensive. The characters were so good, I said, "I've got to try it again, see what I can do." I took about ten months, and I just finished it a couple of days ago. At least I have a Movie of the Week, I know that. It's a very simple little story. It may be too bland. It's a déjà vu thing, in a way. But it plays beautifully and it's entertaining. I was so glad to see the possibility of doing an old-fashioned kind of movie and also of having the freedom that exists today.

Richard Maibaum:
A Pretense of Seriousness

Interview by Pat McGilligan

Of all the screenwriters featured in this anthology, Richard Maibaum is the only one who asked to approve the transcript of his interview, to edit out offensive material, and to revise inadvertent phraseology. This is the mark of a perfectionist as well as the survival instincts of a canny old pro who has remained *au courant* in Hollywood for half a century by rolling with the punches. One of the few early sound-era screenwriters still active, he is, in his mid-seventies, at the top of his profession and is embarking, as this is being written, on his twelfth James Bond title.

His evolution as a writer seems extraordinary even by Hollywood standards. As a playwright in New York City in the 1930s, he was noted for experimental drama, plays influenced by the German Expressionists, and impassioned social consciousness works. (As a sideline he acted in Shakespearean repertory.) Brought to Hollywood by MGM in 1936, he labored at MGM and Columbia to turn out star vehicles and genre potboilers that were (and are today) a notch above the average. At MGM he was introduced to Cyril Hume, the novelist and the Tarzan screenwriter, who became his mentor and his collaborator on nine films.

A young Turk who nonetheless broke with the left wing in theatre and film circles, Maibaum was active in the fight to establish the Screen Writers Guild and remained a staunch liberal. During World War II he headed up the Combat Films Division in Washington, D.C., and channeled and supervised military documentaries. Acquiring producer credentials as a result, he returned to Paramount and wrote or produced a number of films starring Alan Ladd—including a faithful version of *The Great Gatsby* (1949)—and suffered through a prolonged if misbegotten association with the director Mitchell Leisen.

The 1950s found Maibaum scrambling—and thriving—on several fronts. Not one to look down his nose at the new game in town, Maibaum wrote with distinction for television—including co-authoring the teleplay for "Ransom!"—and later served as executive producer of MGM-TV from 1958 to 1960. With Hume he wrote the now-cult classic *Bigger Than Life* (1956) for the actor James Mason and the director Nicholas Ray. Recommended by Alan Ladd to the Warwick producers Cubby Broccoli and Irving Allen, he shuttled between Great Britain and the United States and wrote or co-wrote a series of profitable adventure pictures that the company specialized in at the time.

Then came the smash success of the first James Bond picture, *Dr. No* in 1963, and with it twenty-plus years of steady employment, accolades, and lucrative work. One of the longest running serials in cinema history, the Bond movies are distinguished not only by their inflated budgets and bosomy starlets but by their sophisticated storytelling; the in-jokes, one-liners, double-entendres, and witty repartee; the relationships in the continuing storyline and the complicated capers.

In the Bond films Maibaum, a frustrated playwright, has sought to achieve a synthesis of his literary good taste with the box-office demands of mainstream entertainment. The Bonds are not so much a betrayal of his once "serious" aspirations as they are a throwback to the romantic imagination of his boyhood—to the tales of Alexandre Dumas. In this respect, Maibaum is an example of a writer who sacrificed dearly for status in Hollywood but remained true to himself in the process of accommodation.

1936	*We Went to College* (Joseph Santley). Co-script.
	The Gold Diggers of 1937 (Lloyd Bacon). Co-play basis only.
1937	*They Gave Him a Gun* (W. S. Van Dyke). Co-script.*
	Live, Love, and Learn (George Fitzmaurice). Co-script.*
1938	*Stable Mates* (Sam Wood). Co-script.
	The Bad Man of Brimstone (J. Walter Ruben). Co-script.*
1939	*Coast Guard* (Edward Ludwig). Co-story, co-script.
	The Lady and the Mob (Ben Stoloff). Co-script.
1940	*Foreign Correspondent* (Alfred Hitchcock). Uncredited contribution.
	The Amazing Mr. Williams (Alexander Hall). Co-script.

* In collaboration with Cyril Hume.

Richard Maibaum in Pacific Palisades, 1984. (Photo: Alison Morley)

Twenty-Mule Team (Richard Thorpe). Co-script.*
The Ghost Comes Home (William Thiele). Co-script.

1941   *Hold Back the Dawn* (Mitchell Leisen). Uncredited contribution.
I Wanted Wings (Mitchell Leisen). Co-script.

1942   *Pride of the Yankees* (Sam Wood). Uncredited contribution.
Ten Gentlemen from West Point (Henry Hathaway). Script.

1945   *See My Lawyer* (Edward Cline). Co-play basis only.

1946   *O.S.S.* (Irving Pichel). Story, script, producer.

1947   *The Big Clock* (John Farrow). Producer.

1948   *The Sainted Sisters* (William Russell). Producer.

1949   *The Great Gatsby* (Elliott Nugent). Co-script, producer.*
Song of Surrender (Mitchell Leisen). Script, producer.
Bride of Vengeance (Mitchell Leisen). Co-producer.*

1950   *Dear Wife* (Richard Haydn). Producer.
Captain Carey U.S.A. (Mitchell Leisen). Producer.
No Man of Her Own (Mitchell Leisen). Producer.

1953   *Hell Below Zero* (Mark Robson). Adaptation.

1954   *Paratrooper* (a.k.a. *The Red Beret*) (Terence Young). Co-script.

1956   *Cockleshell Heroes* (a.k.a. *The Survivors*) (Jose Ferrer). Co-script.
Ransom! (Alex Segal). Based on his co-teleplay, co-script.*
Bigger Than Life (Nicholas Ray). Co-screen story, co-script.*
Zarak (Terence Young). Script.

1958   *Tank Force!* (a.k.a. *No Time to Die*) (Terence Young). Co-screen story, co-script.

1959   *The Bandit of Zhobe* (John Gilling). Screen story.

1960   *The Day They Robbed the Bank of England* (John Guillermin). Co-adaptation.
Killers of Kilimanjaro (a.k.a. *Adamson of Africa*) (Richard Thorpe). Co-screen story.*

1961   *The Battle at Bloody Beach* (Herbert Coleman). Story, co-script, producer.

1963   *Dr. No* (Terence Young). Co-script.

1964   *From Russia with Love* (Terence Young). Script.
         Goldfinger (Guy Hamilton). Co-script.

1965   *Thunderball* (Terence Young). Co-script.

1968   *Chitty Chitty Bang Bang* (Ken Hughes). Additional dialogue.

1969   *On Her Majesty's Secret Service* (Peter Hunt). Script.

1971   *Diamonds Are Forever* (Guy Hamilton). Co-script.

1974   *The Man with the Golden Gun* (Guy Hamilton). Co-script.

1976   *Logan's Run* (Michael Anderson). Uncredited contribution.

1977   *The Spy Who Loved Me* (Lewis Gilbert). Co-script.

1981   *For Your Eyes Only* (John Glen). Co-script.

1983   *Octopussy* (John Glen). Co-script.

1985   *A View to a Kill* (John Glen). Co-script.

Television credits include executive producer of MGM–TV, 1958–60, and author of numerous teleplays, including "Fearful Decision,"* "S*H*E," and "Jarrett" (also producer).

Produced plays include *The Tree, Middletown Mural, A Moral Entertainment, Tirade, Birthright, Sweet Mystery of Life, See My Lawyer,* and *The Paradise Question.*

As a kid, I used to sneak into theatres—risking my life to climb up fire escapes and through men's rooms, then emerging into the balconies—because I liked the early serials and thrillers.

At the same time I must admit I was kind of scornful of movies because, from a literary standpoint, they left much to be desired. From when I was about eight, I was a compulsive reader. For instance, that series of books up there on the shelf—the green ones, the [Alexandre] Dumas books—they had a great influence on me. I read them three, four, five times—*The Three Musketeers* and others. My father loved Dumas too. They're marvelous adventure stories. When I was about nine, I wrote a novel. I have a copy of it somewhere. It's laughable now—about Indians and stuff like that. But to persevere for 150 typed pages—a kid of nine—indicates I had a precocious facility with words.

The University of Iowa

When I went to the University of Iowa, my theatrical life really began. Going there was the best thing I ever did, because people from New York can get insular, too—provincial in reverse. It was an amazing place, Iowa. Full of inspiration and enthusiasm and experimentation. The University was two hundred miles from Chicago, so culturally it was a matter of do-it-yourself. There was so much going on—poetry, music, drama, art.

I met the man there who was to prove a great influence on me— E. C. Mabie, of whom you have undoubtedly heard. Mabie was head of the drama department and responsible for Iowa's thrust in fine arts. He was a powerhouse—a broad, chunky, big-voiced eccentric who didn't suffer fools, shirkers, or phonies gladly. A very, very difficult man, but unique. He believed profoundly in regional theatre.

Anyway, I went to Iowa City two weeks early in January of 1930, and there was a try-out for Eugene O'Neill's *The Hairy Ape*. I got the part of the ape. That was really an experience. Mabie had a friend— Kenneth MacGowan, the critic—who came out to Iowa to see *The Hairy Ape;* and it's immodest of me to say this, but I still get a kick out of reading a review for *The Daily Iowan* in which he said there were moments during my characterization of the ape that surpassed that of Louis Wolheim on the Broadway stage.

After *The Hairy Ape* was over, I sat down, and in four days and nights of working practically nonstop, I wrote a play about a lynching, called *The Tree,* which became my first Broadway play. I gave it to the "boss," as we called Mabie, to read, and he was enthusiastic about it. When I was an upper soph we put the play on in a tiny experimental theatre in Iowa City; and I played the lead and directed it. Paul Green, the Pulitzer Prize–winning playwright [for *In Abraham's Bosom* in 1927] from North Carolina, came to see it and encouraged me.

The next time I was home in New York, I met a woman called Agnes Mapes, a literary agent—a prim, little old lady who would sit in an office about as big as this room, filled with scripts. She read *The Tree* and said she'd handle me. Then I went back to school, and, sure enough, she found a producer for it—Ira Marion—who got a talented young man named Robert Rossen to direct it. This was in '32. The play was produced at the Park Lane Theatre with Barton MacLane, Truman Quevli, Laura Bowman, and Marc Lawrence, who made his debut in it. Bob Rossen got good reviews for his direction; they launched his career. But it was a terrible time for the theatre during the Depression, and *The Tree* only ran a few days. However, Brooks Atkinson wrote that I was a writer who "has more than a common awareness of the strange things that pound in the blood of human beings." The critics didn't know I was only twenty-three years old. They thought I was a professor at the University. And I didn't disabuse them.

By the time I had graduated and taken my master's I was pouring out plays. I wrote eleven three-act plays in one year. I was particularly influenced by the German expressionists, and I wrote all kinds of experimental plays. I thought that, after *The Tree* and the reviews I received, I'd be able to sell them, but I couldn't. They weren't buying experimental plays at that time. Don't forget the Depression was in full blast.

After I went back to New York to write and look for a job as an actor, I heard of a company in town called the New York Shakespearean Repertory Theatre. I tried out for Percy Vivian, the director, who had been a protégé of Sir Ben Greet. Vivian had put together quite a good company with Ian Maclaren, Curtis Cooksey, Irving Morrow, Martin Gabel, and so on. I did a Bolingbroke speech from *Richard II,* and he was impressed. My first part was as Charles the Wrestler in *As You Like It.* We had the longest run of any Shakespearean repertory company in the history of New York theatre; it lasted into the spring of the following year. In all, I played in seventeen Shakespearean plays.

I continued writing; I went back to the University of Iowa from time to time to try out new plays, even though I was headquartered in New York. I was an ardent liberal and wrote a four-hour play about corruption in politics, a play about an explosion in a coal mine, a play about euthanasia, and *Birthright,* which was the first anti-Nazi play on Broadway written by an American. It was about a German-Jewish family in Berlin and what happened to them the night Hitler became chancellor. Again it received a few excellent reviews but didn't run.

One of the plays I wrote was *Tirade,* which was the story of a schoolteacher who was thrown out of his job for being a "radical" and inveighs against the world and the things he thinks are wrong with it. It was fashionable then to write plays like *Awake and Sing!*—not any sort of criticism of the radical movement. Some people thought *Tirade* was a reactionary play, but it was just a character study of a failure who blamed the world for his own shortcomings.

Finally I began to ask myself, "Are my plays no good, or is the subject matter too grim?" Around that time I met a demon insurance man, Mike Wallach, who told me a funny story about the insurance business. He gave me $25 a week to write a play with him; I did the writing, he supplied the background. It was called *Sweet Mystery of Life,* a story about a corrupt board of directors, who loot the treasury of their company, insure their president for $5 million, and then try to worry him to death. It took about a year to get produced. Herman Shumlin brought in George Haight, who had written *Goodbye Again* and who was supposed to be the fair-haired boy, as a collaborator to help rewrite. The play grew to sixty scenes and twenty sets and three revolving stages. We opened at the Schubert Theatre in 1935.

Two hours before the play opened, Warner Brothers, who was backing it, caught up with us in George Haight's office in the Sardi Building, and we signed a contract to sell the motion picture rights for $100,000. Everybody was so sure it was going to be a smash hit. Well, it opened and the stages didn't work. You'd have a funny scene and then hear a rumble like a battleship coming into dry dock as the stages turned. Benchley said in *The New Yorker* that it was "the triumph of lumber over a good idea." It became one of my first movie credits, when *Sweet Mystery of Life* was later converted into *The Golddiggers of 1937* (1936) at Warners, although I had nothing to do with the screenplay.

At that point, enter the movies. MGM was sending a group of playwrights to Hollywood, and I was one of the bunch interviewed by Sam Marx, MGM's story editor. The others were Gladys Hurlbut, Jack Murray, Allen Boretz, Emmett Lavery, and Everett Freeman. I was very ambivalent because I had two other plays on option. So I thought I'd go out to Hollywood and see what it was like; if I didn't like it I'd come back.

A week before I was supposed to leave I got married to my high school sweetheart, Sylvia. Our trip west was our honeymoon. We were met at Pasadena—at that time the V.I.P.s got off there. A limousine was waiting, so you didn't have to go through the crowd at the station in Los Angeles. An assistant of Sam Marx met us. He sat in front while Sylvia and I were in the back holding hands. As we passed the observatory, this guy says, "The Griffith Observatory—see it before you go back." Sylvia and I looked at each other. We went to the Hollywood Roosevelt Hotel. That night we strolled along Hollywood Boulevard, still holding hands. We got to Musso and Frank's and walked in. There was a place in the back where the writers gathered, and somebody was eating a salad with a lot of garlic at the next table. It smelled great, so we ordered it. A chiffonade salad. We still call it "our salad."

The Screenplay Form

Quickly I learned the difference between a play and a screenplay. Structurally, a play has to be much tighter. It is more difficult to do a play in that you must compress the material because you have, at most, one, two, or three sets. With the flexibility of the screenplay form, you need less exposition. You can open the story up; you can go anywhere; you can do anything. This is a lure too, because you mustn't go so far that it becomes diffused. You must find that proper balance.

People who have written plays know that there are certain basics that apply to all dramatic literature. One of the troubles with a lot of young writers today is their disregard for those basics. It's all arbitrary, capricious; there's no necessity to go inevitably from point to point, to surge right straight through to a satisfying resolution. Things don't end anymore; they just stop. All of a sudden you get a freeze frame, and everything is left up in the air. Like life itself, I suppose, but not always art.

One thing about screenwriting at that time; MGM had a stable of writers as well as a stable of actors; they knew, for instance, they were going to make three Wallace Beery pictures a year, so they always had six in the works. As you wrote, you tailored to the star you were writing for, whether it was Gable, Beery, or Tracy. I did three pictures for Beery. I found out my acting was helpful because I would sort of impersonate the star as I wrote for him.

The first picture I worked on for Beery was *The Bad Man of Brimstone* [1938]. I believe it was the first funny western *intended* to be picaresque and exaggerated. It was the story of a bandit called Trigger Bill [played by Beery] and a young man, an ex–prize fighter, who comes to town to collect taxes from Trigger Bill, something nobody has ever been able to do. Trigger Bill's henchmen ask him why he doesn't knock off the newcomer. Then Bill discovers the boy is his long-lost son.

So Trigger Bill arranges a phony legacy to get his boy out of town, presumably to Chicago to study law. However, Bill wants to give him some advice before he goes. They had done nothing but clash up to that point. So as the boy is about to ride away, Trigger Bill waits to say "goodbye" to him and says, "Jeff, I want to give you some advice before you go." And he gives him a reverse version of Polonius's speech from *Hamlet:* "To thine own self be true," and all that. Only Bill's version is: "Never stand up to a man in a fair fight. Always sneak around and shoot him in the back. Never drink water; it has all kinds of germs in it. Whiskey is the only drink for a man. And never have anything to do with any decent woman. She'll hog-tie you something terrible." Jeff replies, "Get out of here, you old so-and-so." He doesn't know Bill's his father, you see, and has arranged all this.

None of this was in the picture, because when Beery looked at the length of the speech, he said, "Who wants to say all that junk? I just want to say 'goodbye.' " So he cut it all out. Beery used to come to the studio in the morning, and as he got made up, he'd say to his stand-in—a fright of a hulk with a face that would stop Big Ben— "Read me the titles." He never called it dialogue; he always called it titles. The stand-in couldn't read very well either, so you can imagine what kind of version he read Wally. Then Wally'd go on stage and wing it.

The perfect tag-line for Beery was written by [Ben] Hecht and [Charles] MacArthur for *Viva Villa!* [1934]. When the reporter who's supposed to be John Reed [played by Stuart Erwin] comes up to Villa after he's been shot, Villa says, as he always used to say, "What you say about me now, Johnny? What you put about me in the papers?" And Reed, with tears in his eyes, says, "I'll say he did many things that were wrong, but he loved his country very much." Beery looks up at him and asks, "Johnny, what I do wrong?" Then he dies. That is one of the best tag-lines of all time. "What I do wrong?" Villa had murdered, pillaged, and raped—and "What I do wrong?" Hah! Now that's *writing,* because in terms of character, it makes the greatest possible statement about Villa and about all men like him. And about Beery—the perfect title for a Wallace Beery picture would have been *The Son-of-a-Bitch*—because he was such a lovable ignoramus.

Cyril Hume

When I was at MGM, I was called into [the producer] Harry Rapf's office and introduced to Cyril Hume. He was very tall, very blonde— almost an albino. Harry Rapf said, "Dick, you two are going to collaborate." And despite everything, despite never having known one another before, we collaborated. We worked on nine films together. Cyril was a very important factor in my development as a screenwriter. Such a brilliant man. There couldn't be two more different people in the world than Cyril and myself. He was a novelist from the twenties and a very successful one—*The Wife of the Centaur, My Sister, My Bride, Cruel Fellowship,* and so forth. He was descended from Hume, the philosopher, and had gone to the same prep school as F. Scott Fitzgerald, and then to Yale. Next to Fitzgerald, I personally believe his novels of the twenties were the most revealing.

When Cyril first came to Hollywood, he did *Flying Down to Rio* [1933]. Then he was brought to MGM, and they assigned him to, of all things, *Tarzan, the Ape Man* [1933]. Later, after he had done about three or four of the *Tarzans,* I said to him, "How can you do those things?" He said, "What do you mean? Kipling did *Jungle Tales,* didn't he?" A perfect response. He took them seriously, not tongue-in-cheek; and that's why they are good, good to this day. Cyril got in trouble at MGM; he fought with everybody eventually. But they kept bringing him back because he was the only one who could do a successful *Tarzan.*

We clashed immediately because we were absolutely different people, but gradually we began to see that our basic interests were the same. I respected him tremendously because he was one of the most deeply intellectual men I have ever known—also one of the most stubborn and opinionated. Socially, he was very formal, very stiff. In any situation, writing or speaking, he had an overpowering desire for the proper word, *le mot juste;* and he had a superb command of the language—greater than anyone I've ever known.

You see, I was a playwright and he was a novelist, and I think that is why we worked well together; I helped him with the form because he was inclined to novelize or overwrite. He overcame that somewhat with his economy of dialogue, but still, he would have little tricks that we would argue about. For example, he hated anything trite to such an extent that he'd avoid the trite expression even if it was the correct one to use. I always had a sense of structure because, after all, I had come from writing plays, and he was writing novels, which is a looser medium, where you can be interior and employ stream-of-consciousness techniques that you can't utilize in a screenplay.

Uncredited Contributions

Without receiving credit I had some interesting writing experiences. Charlie Brackett and Billy Wilder hadn't quite finished the script of *Hold Back the Dawn* [1941]; they had to write *Ball of Fire* [1941] for Goldwyn, so somebody had to hold the fort. I was brought in to work ahead of them on the script. Then, each weekend I would work with them. It was a pleasure. Charlie would curl up on the sofa with a pencil and paper, taking notes, while Billy would stride up and down swinging a cane or a tennis racket. I would be listening or making suggestions. I knew I was not going to get any credit. We were all friends.

I was writer about number thirty on *Foreign Correspondent* [1940], and primarily I rewrote the Albert Basserman part of the old statesman who was kidnapped. I worked for about four weeks on *Foreign Correspondent.* With Joan Harrison—Hitch had great confidence in her. He said to me, "Did you read what we've got?" Which was half a screenplay. I said, "Yes." He said, "What do you think about it?" I replied, "It's not very logical." He grimaced and said, "Oh, dear boy, don't be dull. I'm not interested in logic, I'm interested in effect. If the audience ever thinks about logic, it's on their way home after the show, and by that time, you see, they've paid for their tickets."

Herman Mankiewicz and I were put together by Sam Goldwyn to write *Pride of the Yankees* [1942]. There are many versions of this story, and the one by Richard Merryman in his book about Mankiewicz [*Mank: The Wit, World, and Life of Herman Mankiewicz*] isn't factual. I had run into Mankiewicz before on *Live, Love, and Learn* [1937]. Charlie Brackett had written about fifty pages of script and had to go on to another assignment. And they had already started to shoot the picture. So all the MGM writers were called in, shown the four and a half reels, and asked, "How can we end this?" There were about fifty or sixty writers present who tried to come up with the answers, and it all came down to what Cyril and I wanted to do versus what Herman Mankiewicz wanted to do versus what Dore Schary, who was a writer at MGM at that time, wanted to do.

So we met in Mannix's office with George Fitzmaurice, the director; Bob Montgomery, the star (a very articulate, bright guy); Cyril; myself; Harry Rapf; and God know who else. The first one to tell what he wanted to do was Herman, and it was quite good. Then I told what Cyril and I wanted to do. I always did the talking for Cyril and myself, for some reason. I don't know, I guess I was glibber, or maybe Cyril realized that he would be too assertive, too caustic, so he always let me tell the stories. Then it was Dore Schary's turn. Dore says, "I think what Dick and Cy want to do is wonderful, and I don't think my way is as good." And Eddie Mannix grabbed him by the hand and said, "Dore, that's one of the finest things I've ever heard a man say." Dore was marvelous; whether he won or lost, he came out as the memorable one. In order to pacify Mankiewicz, Mannix said, "You go ahead, Dick and Cy, finish the script, and then we'll let Herman polish." In any event, Herman left the studio; and Cy and I did it and it turned out to be a good show—one of the nicest comedies I had anything to do with.

That was the only previous association I had with Mankiewicz. Then Goldwyn invited us to dinner at his house and said to me, "I've seen the things you've written, and your writing has kind of an emotional content to it; and Herman is very experienced, so work together." So we did; that's the way things were done. Herman was drinking heavily and didn't show up. The war was on. I had to be in Washington in six weeks; I'd been commissioned as a captain. Also, my wife was pregnant and lost the baby—all this during a very rough time. And here I was trying to write *Pride of the Yankees* and my collaborator didn't show up. So I sat down to write it by myself. We had discussed what we wanted to do the one time we had met, and I was pounding away, wondering when Mankiewicz was going to come in and talk again. Lefty O'Doul, the great batter, was technical adviser. When Sam Goldwyn introduced Lefty to me, he said, "One of the greatest football players who ever lived." Such a marvelous guy, Goldwyn—football, baseball, ping pong, what the hell.

Anyway, Sam began to get impatient. Where were the pages? He called a meeting. Collier Young was his story editor at the time, and in the meeting Sam said, "It's going so terribly slow, why don't we get Dorothy Parker to write the love scenes?" I was desperate. I said, "I think that's a good idea, Sam." When we got back to the office, Herman, who we had managed to get to that meeting, said, "What the hell is the matter with you? Why do you want Dorothy Parker to come in on this?" I said, "You're no help, you're never here. I had to call your brother [Joseph Mankiewicz] to find you." He says, "You have no complaint. What you're doing, we talked about; and they're all my ideas. You shouldn't be left alone with a typewriter." That was one of his stock lines, which he had forgotten he told me once about Budd Schulberg. I said, "That does it, Herman. I feel I've got no responsibility to you anymore." I called up Collier Young and said, "The reason the script is going so slowly is because Herman is drinking and he hasn't been here and I've got to get this finished because I'm going into the Army in two or three weeks."

Next thing we knew, there was a big meeting in Sam Goldwyn's office. Sam said to Herman, "You ought to be ashamed of yourself. I only hired you this time because I like your wife very much. That you should do this to me, especially after the break I gave you to work on this, and then not be available—I'll never forgive you, and you'll never work for me again." Then he turns to me and he picks up the script and says, "You did this all by yourself?" I said, "Yes, sir!" He said, "I don't like it. I think we should get new people on this story." I said, "Well, Mr. Goldwyn, if you want to do that, it's alright with me." He said, "I wouldn't want to hurt you, but I think it would be best." I get home and Collier calls up and says, "You'll hear from us in a couple of days, because we want to put another writer on you." So I wait and I wait and time's a-wasting. About a week later I called up Collier, and I said, "What is going on there?" He says, "Well, Dick, this is kind of hard to tell you, but we've got Jo Swerling in to work on the script, and he's going to work with Herman." That's what *really* happened. I've never seen the finished film to know if any of my writing survived into the final version. I have a block about seeing it.

World War II

The Academy of Motion Picture Arts and Sciences had a group; Darryl Zanuck was head of it. Well, they knew what was coming and that the military effort was inevitable, so they began to ask people to sign up. Now, I was a college graduate, I had taken ROTC, I had a Phi Beta Kappa key, I was fairly successful in my job, and at that time I was thirty-two. Also I was Jewish and I didn't like Hitler. They commissioned me as a captain. Then I went into the Army and worked harder than I ever had in my life. I started out as a captain; I soon made major and I ended up as a lieutenant colonel. For the Industrial Services Division I wrote and produced nine films, which were screened in factories to show war workers their importance in our military effort. Eventually, I became the director of the Combat Films Division, where all the combat film taken by cameramen was funneled into Washington for various propaganda or morale purposes. I had a great many writers, directors, producers, and editors I could call on.

I was a member of the Inter-Services Film Committee. The Army, the Navy, the Marines, the Coast Guard—everybody had a film unit. There was a lot of duplication; everybody would photograph the same thing. So you'd have to know in advance that an operation was coming up against, let's say Okinawa, and we'd all get together and say, "The Army will cover the landings, the Navy will do the bombardment, the Air Force will do so forth and so on." I did some interesting documentaries in the service: *Appointment in Tokyo, The Liberation of Rome, Twenty-Seven Soldiers.* One of my branches made a five-hundred reel history of the war. Capra and Wyler did the *Why We Fight* and *Know Your Enemy* series, which were magnificent. Wonderful work was done, and I think the American documentary came of age during the war.

Producing at Paramount

While I was in the Army, a friend of mine, Harry Tugend, got to be the executive producer at Paramount. When the war ended, I was still in the Army because I was the youngest officer in grade in my outfit; they wanted me to stay on and be Eisenhower's photographic officer in Europe. That was kind of tempting. But I had already given four years to Uncle Sam, from age thirty-two to thirty-six, and these are usually the most creative of a man's life. I didn't mind it; it was little enough to do. But I had picked up producing experience while in the service, and now Harry said to me, "I'd like to have you with me," so I was signed up to come back to Hollywood as a producer-writer.

I remained at Paramount for the next four years. Paramount was like a delightful country club at that time. It was the days of Brackett and Wilder and *Sunset Boulevard* [1950] and all the other wonderful pictures and good writers. The atmosphere around the place was so good, and of course, the motion picture business was so easy. There was no such thing then as that terrible phenomenon called television. Which really didn't have any impact until 1949 when it hit us like a ton of bricks.

Every studio in Hollywood was racing to come out with the first O.S.S. film. When I was in Washington, I knew some of the O.S.S. people, so I had a head start on the subject. When I came back, my first assignment was to make a film called *O.S.S.* [1946]. I wrote the script and produced it. I liked producing initially because I had more control—especially over casting. I thought *O.S.S.* was well-cast; and that's where I met Alan Ladd for the first time. It was just the most wonderful relationship—my wife and myself, with Alan and Sue and their children. I never saw another actor who moved as gracefully as Alan, who had that kind of coordination. A beautiful, deep voice. Everybody said he was a nonactor, but they were wrong. He knew what he was doing. He was overly modest, shy, an introvert. But once you won his confidence, you could do no wrong.

Paramount had Alan Ladd pegged as a dubious actor, but I didn't believe them. I was at his house, and he took me up to the second floor, where he had a wardrobe about as long as this room. He opened it up, and there must have been hundreds of suits, sport jackets, slacks, and shoes. He looked at me and said, "Not bad for an Okie kid, eh?" I got goose pimples, because I remembered when Gatsby took Daisy to show her his mansion, he also showed her his wardrobe and said, "I have a man who sends me clothes from England every spring and fall." I said to myself, "My God, the Great Gatsby!" And he was, in a way, the Great Gatsby. Success had settled on him as it had on Gatsby. Being a movie star, he had the same kind of aura of success, but he didn't quite know how to handle it. He had the same precise, careful speech, the controlled manner, the carefully modulated voice. So I said to Sue and Alan, "How about we do *The Great Gatsby* [1949] because Paramount owns it?" Sue read it and he read it and they liked it; they were a little dubious, but I talked them into it.

When I went to the studio, the powers-that-be said, "Oh, come on, for God's sakes, *he* can't do it." Additionally, there was a real objection to Fitzgerald at that time, more than to any other writer. Because Fitzgerald represented everything that the Johnston office was against. They said *The Great Gatsby* had an unpunished murder, illicit sex, extramarital affairs, a low moral tone, and so on. So the studio said, "Nothing doing." But Alan said, "I'll take a suspension if you don't let me do this." They said, "Alright, do this other picture first, then you can do *Gatsby*."

Richard Maibaum conferring with Alan Ladd on the set of The Great Gatsby *(1949). (Courtesy: Richard Maibaum)*

Naturally, I got Cyril Hume to collaborate with me on *Gatsby*. Cyril and I had discussed the novel many, many times. But the studio didn't like our script, and we had difficulties with the Johnston Office—[the Production Code official] Joe Breen. I argued myself blue in the face. Finally I said to Breen, "How can you object to this book? All of Fitzgerald's works are really versions of the Faust story. A man makes some kind of pact with the devil or devotes his life to some dubious goal, and then discovers after achieving what he wants that it's all dust and ashes. *Gatsby* is really a morality play." Breen said, "Nonsense. If it's a morality play, where is the voice of morality?" He was always holding forth about the voice of morality. I said, "Well, if I can find it will you OK the script?" He said, "Yes, but you won't find it."

So I looked in the Bible for weeks, and finally one day I came across it. It's in Proverbs, where it says, "There is a way which seemeth right unto a man, but the end thereof are the ways of death." I said, "There it is," and Breen said, "OK, where are you going to say it?" So we had to put it right in the opening where Nick and Jordan, now married, stop at Gatsby's grave and quote the chapter and verse from Gatsby's tombstone. I had to do it, which I now think was all wrong and very un-Fitzgerald-like. To moralize like that was something he never did; he was always indirect. It was the price I paid to get the film done. Even so, of the three *Gatsby* films that have been made, I think ours was a more faithful rendition than the other two—especially the [Robert] Redford one [in 1974] in which they didn't seem to know what the story was about.

Mitchell Leisen

Then my Mitch Leisen ordeal began. I had worked with him before—on *I Wanted Wings* [1941] and on *Hold Back the Dawn*. But I didn't respect him, and he didn't respect me. I thought he was a talented man—facile, but shallow. He saw things differently than I did. He lived a different kind of life. He would never really listen to dialogue when he was directing. He always had a dialogue director around to do that for him. When the scene was over, he would look at the dialogue director and get a nod before they'd print. I don't know; he made some good women's pictures, but not with me. I had a terrible time with him.

The studio teamed us because Mitch was difficult to handle, and Henry Ginsberg thought that since I get along with most people, I'd be able to work with him. But I couldn't. Consequently, the pictures he made with me—except *Song of Surrender* [1949], which was an unusual little picture with Claude Rains and Wanda Hendrix—were not happy experiences. I think he thought I was the studio's watchdog to keep him from spending too much money on the picture for clothes and things like that. He was always fussing around with the clothes and the props.

After my fourth stab at producing with Mitch—*No Man of Her Own* [1950]—I was told Paramount was not picking up my option because the house had fallen in on the business, the house called television. In 1948 they were making $48 million a year at Paramount. In 1949 they practically went broke. So I left. Mitch left shortly thereafter. I was glad to go. The films I'd made with other directors had some quality and did quite well. But outside of *Song of Surrender,* the ones I made with Leisen I just didn't like. That is sometimes one of the hazards of producing motion pictures. You have an illusory control.

Enter, Cubby Broccoli

After I left Paramount I sat around for a year and a half without being able to get a job. Sometimes, when you're to the point where I was—making three big pictures a year for a studio—you're important, and people are hesitant to hire you. They wonder why you left and stuff like that. Things were very bad.

I was kicking around here, playing golf, when a gentleman named Albert ["Cubby"] Broccoli showed up in my living room and said he had a script called *The Red Beret* [a.k.a. *Paratrooper,* 1954], which several people had already worked on. He had just made a deal with Alan Ladd to make three pictures with him for a company called Warwick in England. Cubby's partner was Irving Allen, and the Ladds had told them they'd like me to script the first one. So Cubby signed me up, and that was the beginning of our relationship. I went to England with them and did *The Red Beret* and others.

Meanwhile, Cyril and I had written a one-hour show for U.S. Steel called "Fearful Decision," which was nominated for Best Teleplay by the television academy in 1955. "Fearful Decision" was probably the best thing Cyril and I ever did. It was about a father who refuses on principle to pay the ransom for his kidnapped son. Then we wrote a play about it, which the Theatre Guild wanted to do; but they had such dismal notions about changes that we wouldn't let them do it. While I was writing *Cockle-shell Heroes* [1956] for Warwick, Metro bought "Fearful Decision" for $85,000—a lot of money in those days. At that time, Dore Schary was head of the studio. It's funny how the Hollywood wheel turns.

So I came back from England, and Cyril and I did the screenplay, now called *Ransom!* [1956] for Glenn Ford, who was not as effective as Ralph Bellamy had been on television. Alex Segal, who had directed it as a television show, repeated it as a picture. But, interesting thing, I told Alex that if he directed the two-hour picture with the intensity with which he had directed the hour show, it would never hold up. He wouldn't listen. As a result, just when the story should have gripped you the most, the audience was emotionally depleted. Although I thought it was a good film, I wasn't as fond of it as of the TV show.

Bigger Than Life (1956)

After *Ransom!* Cyril and I were asked to come over to Twentieth Century–Fox to do *Bigger Than Life,* with James Mason as the producer and star. It was a story that dealt with the overuse of cortisone, which at that time had side effects that people weren't warned about. I thought our screenplay was well-written. But then Nicholas Ray came in to direct it. I don't know; Nick was a fine director, but I thought he muddied things up somewhat.

Clifford Odets, a pal of Ray's, was brought in to rewrite one or two scenes, and those were the scenes that I disliked—one at the end and one somewhere in the middle. Ray exaggerated some scenes and diluted others. Some directors don't realize that there are scenes that are like music: if you knock out a few notes, it becomes discordant. That happened again and again throughout the picture. It was still an interesting picture, because of James Mason's performance, and it has become kind of a cult picture.

The James Bond Films

In 1956 or 1957, when I was in England writing for Cubby and Irving Allen, Cubby gave me two of the James Bond books to read. I read them and liked them enormously. Cubby was very excited, too, but Irving Allen didn't share his enthusiasm. So Cubby put them aside. It's my personal opinion now that that was a wise thing to do, because with the censorship of pictures that existed then, you couldn't even have the minimal sex and violence that we eventually put into the pictures. They just wouldn't have been the same.

Later, when Irving Allen and Cubby broke up, Cubby got together with Harry Saltzman, who had an option from Ian Fleming, and he and Cubby joined forces. Cubby went to New York and convinced the United Artists board of directors to give him and Saltzman what eventually amounted to $1 million to make the first picture. I didn't know Saltzman at the time, but Cubby told him about me, and I was asked to go over there and write the first James Bond script.

Thunderball [1965] was actually the first; we decided it was the one to start with. I finished a first draft, and then Kevin McClory jumped up with a lawsuit against Ian Fleming, claiming he wrote the novel after they'd done a screen treatment together. So we put *Thunderball* aside until that was settled and decided to do *Dr. No* [1963]. I was then in London, after having finished the first draft of *Thunderball,* so I began to write *Dr. No* with Wolf Mankewitz. Cubby and Harry didn't like our first treatment, so Wolf bowed out; and I went on to do the first draft of the screenplay. Later, after I left, a novelist named Aubrey Mather (Jasper Davis is his real name) did some work on it with a girl playwright, Joanna Harwood.

On *From Russia with Love* [1964] they had Len Deighton start, and he did about thirty-five pages; but it wasn't going anywhere, so they brought me in. I did the screenplay and got a solo credit on it. Joanna got an adaptation credit, because she worked some with the director, Terence Young, and made several good suggestions. I was a little put out that she was given an adaptation credit because I didn't think she deserved it, but there are always politics in these things.

Richard Maibaum (right), with Ian Fleming and the Duchess of Bedford. Harry Saltzman, co-producer of the James Bond films, is visible behind Fleming's shoulder. (Courtesy: Richard Maibaum)

On *Goldfinger* [1963] I did a first draft. Harry Saltzman didn't like it, and he brought in Paul Dehn, a good writer, to revise. Then Sean Connery didn't like the revisions, and I came back to do the final screenplay. That was the first time that happened: where I was followed by someone and then called back to finish up.

I worked on *Thunderball* again and got a solo on *On Her Majesty's Secret Service* [1969], which is one of the best of the *Bonds* despite [George] Lazenby [who played Bond]. After I did the first script on *Diamonds Are Forever* [1971], I left and Tom Mankiewicz came on. They liked his work, so Tom stayed on to do *Live and Let Die* [1973]. Then they used Tom again on *Man with the Golden Gun* [1974]. He had a disagreement with [the director] Guy Hamilton, and I was asked to come back and rewrite that. Then, on *The Spy Who Loved Me* [1977] I did the first draft, followed by Christopher Wood, who also wrote *Moonraker* [1979]. Gilbert [Lewis Gilbert], the director, liked his work; I didn't. Then, after *Moonraker* I began to work with Michael G. Wilson, an unusually versatile, talented young man, and we did *For Your Eyes Only* [1981], *Octopussy* [1983], and *A View to a Kill* [1985].

I'll tell you something about a James Bond script. How many scenes would you think are in the *Octopussy* screenplay, for instance? Over one thousand! Whereas it's rare that scripts have more than two hundred or three hundred scenes. Sometimes directors don't want the writers to break it up to such an extent, but I always do. I figure, you're fooling yourself and everybody else if you don't do that. It's pretty well worked out in advance—especially with men like John Glen and Peter Hunt, who were great editors. You can't take short cuts. (I remember once, when I was doing the script for one of my favorite early pictures, *Ten Gentlemen from West Point* in 1942, I wrote, "Then follows the Battle of Tippecanoe." And Darryl Zanuck noted in the margin: "Who are you kidding, kid?")

Basically, in a way, the pattern of the story is the same in all of the Bonds, and I think that is one of the attractions of the pictures. You have that engine working, the James Bond syndrome—with all the conspicuous consumption, the luxurious locales, the beautiful women, the larger-than-life villains. We've carried it much further than Fleming. Bond is absolutely dedicated and devoted to serving Queen and country; he never questions what he does or the morality of it. In an article he wrote, Charles Champlin says that Bond is the man who rides into town to set things right, and he calls him the Musketeer. Well, I told you: the Dumas books had a helluva influence on me.

Ian Fleming

I met Ian Fleming several times while he was still alive, but I did not speak to him about screenwriting. He didn't seem very interested. He didn't have script approval, but as a matter of courtesy we gave him the scripts to read. He would make minimal notes in the margin, in very tiny handwriting, that usually dealt with questions of protocol— what Bond called M in the office as opposed to what he called him at their club, things like that.

He did say to me once, "The pictures are so much funnier than my books." He was a little bemused and a little obtuse about it, I thought, because he really didn't understand that we were *trying* to make them funnier. That was the thing we changed most about his books as far as the pictures were concerned. We made Bond more humorous, throwing away those one-liners that are now obligatory in Bond films.

Fleming was strange about the books. I think he got bored with the Bond stories after a while, especially after *On Her Majesty's Secret Service,* on which he really did a superb job. As a novel I think it's the best of them and the one we had to do the least with to make a good motion picture script. It was a solid novel, more of a serious effort than most of his books, which are really one hundred pages of brilliant exposition and then some good, swift action.

I told this to Fleming once, "There is an untransferable quality in your writing." It's all very well; Fleming writes two and a half pages describing the fish underwater, the beautiful waving weeds, the colors—but, what the hell, it's just a pretty piece of celluloid when you see it on the screen. In other words, we had to popularize to a great extent. I won't use the word vulgarize, because we've tried very hard, and Cubby has tried very hard, to keep the pictures from being vulgar. If someone suggests something that is really vulgar, he'll wince. Partly the difference is in going from a kind of cult audience to a mass audience. It was only a cult audience of readers that kept Fleming alive for a long time before the pictures really discovered him. As books, they were not caviar to the general.

A Pretense of Seriousness

Penelope Gilliatt once said that Bond films were "modern mythology." In my opinion, they started this whole larger-than-life approach to action-adventure pictures. There have been others, of course; and Burt Lancaster always ribs me about imitating the style of *The Crimson Pirate* [1952]. But I do think the Bond pictures started this whole cycle, and then everybody else climbed on the bandwagon. That's not generally accepted. I think *Raiders of the Lost Ark* [1981] was, except for having a wonderful gimmick (the ark itself), a kind of Bond picture. The action, the villains, the unexpected!

You know, Hitchcock once told me, "If I have thirteen bumps in a picture, I think I've got a picture." A bump is something like someone says, "I'm looking for a man who has a short index finger," and a totally unexpected guy says, "You mean like this?" That's in *The 39 Steps*. After *Dr. No* Cubby, Harry, and myself decided that we weren't going to be satisfied with thirteen bumps in a Bond story, we wanted thirty-nine.

As a writer I think one of my contributions to the Bonds is that I maintained a pretense of seriousness. I took them seriously, the way Cyril took the *Tarzans*, as if they were really happening, although of course such things don't. There are no secret agents like Bond; secret-agenting is really a pretty dull business most of the time, despite all the legends and the myths. But I took it seriously, and I learned something quickly: the audience is willing to be lenient about what is real and what is not real. They will allow you to be humorous, and then they will allow you to strike the humor and be serious for a moment as long as they are being entertained. Any time you are not serious about it, the picture suffers.

Then, I think, my work on the first four films set the pattern and had something to do with the character of Bond—his humor, his savoir faire. I know I insisted on the elegance of the villains—especially after I saw how great Joseph Wiseman was in *Dr. No.* "You disappoint me, Mr. Bond; you are nothing but a stupid policeman." I tried to add a touch of elegance to the dialogue, and some of the directors didn't approve. Terence Young would say, "Oh, for chrissakes, stop writing Chinese, Dick." I wanted Bond to have some of that elegance, too, and not to be the monosyllabic hero that, for example, Harrison Ford is in *Raiders of the Lost Ark.* He has not a flicker of class or humor, even though he is supposed to be an educated anthropologist.

I feel, about dialogue, Chinese or not, that I try to use words that are proper from a semantic standpoint. And, of course, I object when what I consider to be a good line is omitted. In *Octopussy,* for example, when Bond goes clandestinely into East Germany, M says, "Take care, 007." My line for Bond's reply was, "I promise to look both ways before I cross the street, sir." It put a father-son relationship between him and M. All gone! The line was cut, I suppose, because Roger [Moore] didn't like it. But a star can say any goddamned thing he wants really. You know what William Goldman says in *Adventures in the Screen Trade,* that a star is a person no one ever contradicts. He has to be pampered even when it hurts the scene.

Of course, directors also change dialogue. Terence Young is a writer too, but I groaned each time he threw in his favorite cliche, "Easy come, easy go." But there are always some added lines that are funny, lines I ruefully wish I had thought of. That is one of my strong points as a collaborator: I have a tolerance of other people's ideas and am able to select the good ones and fight like hell against those I think are bad. I am able to take an idea someone else has thought of and go beyond it.

In retrospect, I've had a great deal of fun doing the Bonds, although the fun was mixed up with many problems that had to be solved, problems that look so simple once they are solved. Once I become involved in a Bond film, I get fascinated all over again with the difficulties and the possibilities. In between, I keep saying, "Well, I'd *like* to do another Bond, but to try and think up a new caper, something we haven't done . . ." But something new always comes up. And, of course, I'm well paid.

Writer's Block

I never lost my first love: the theatre. In 1939 I wrote a play, *See My Lawyer,* which was produced by George Abbott and ran for 227 performances. But not all of my theatrical experiences have been that enjoyable. In 1954 I wrote another play with Walter Hart, a fine director, who had written *The Primrose Path.* We had been good friends when I was a young actor, and he directed me in *Men Grow Taller.* Our play was called *The Paradise Question.* It was a comedy about the United Nations and concerned a professor of geopolitics from Iowa University who was on a committee to determine the fate of the Paradise Islands, which nobody wanted—very timely and very amusing. Leon Ames played the professor.

It opened in Skowhegan, and we thought we had a hit. In New Haven it was not as good. In Philadelphia, worse. It seemed to retrogress. Leon was obviously losing interest, and we didn't know why. Then we discovered the reason: [Howard] Lindsay and [Russel] Crouse had written a play, *The Prescott Proposals,* which was also a comedy about the United Nations. We were going to beat it into Broadway, but at the last moment just before we were to open in New York, Leon "lost his voice," so we had to replace him. Later, we decided not to bring the play in. Still later, Lindsay and Crouse announced they had signed Leon to star in their TV series, "Life with Father." Coincidence or deep-dyed plot?

I was walking on the eleventh floor of a hotel in Philadelphia after being told we were closing. The window was wide open, and I stood there, so wrought up and distressed I almost jumped. That's when I said to myself, "This is too much goddamned trouble." You spend a year during which you don't get paid—it's all speculation—and it just isn't worth the heartache and the headache. Of course, even as I am telling you this, I know if I got an idea I think would make a great play, I would sit down and write it.

But I haven't written a stage play in thirty years. Every now and then I get a possible glimmer, but I haven't been able to overcome my block. Did you happen to see the letter I sent *Time* magazine about writer's block? They had an article about it that suggested a cure: "Don't try to write, just go for a long walk, have a drink, and then see a James Bond picture." So I wrote to *Time* and said, "I was pleased by the suggestion to see a James Bond movie to cure writer's block. Any thoughts about how to cure mine?"

Casey Robinson:
Master Adaptor

Interview by Joel Greenberg

> *Casey Robinson was Warner Brothers's master of
> the art—or craft—of adaptation. Whether the prop-
> erty was a five-hundred-page novel in need of dras-
> tic scenario surgery (*Now, Voyager*) or a sophisti-
> cated transatlantic comedy hit requiring the gentlest
> of nudges past the censors and into the mass-
> audience heart (*Tovarich*), Robinson brought to
> the task a chameleonic ability to "adapt" himself to
> the inner rhythms of the author's prose, as well as a
> remarkable sense for editing plots and dialogue
> into entertaining screenplays.*
>
> Richard Corliss, *Talking Pictures*

Casey Robinson belongs to that fortunate generation that was born
at precisely the right time—around the turn of the century—to enter
the cinema when it too was young and to grow up with it. Known
chiefly as one of the most accomplished and professional Hollywood
screenwriters of the thirties and forties, he has in fact worked in films
since the twenties, not only as a writer but in other capacities as well.

His virtues of craftsmanship, discipline, and a precise understanding of
the mass audience's needs have suffered an eclipse in recent years. Certainly the audience for which he unerringly tailored the great vehicles that
starred Errol Flynn, Humphrey Bogart, and Bette Davis has significantly
changed. While the tastes of that period were perhaps broad, simple, and
predictable, Robinson did not simply pander to them. Whatever we may
think today of *Dark Victory* (1939), the movie broke new ground in the
popular cinema by introducing a terminally ill heroine. *Kings Row* (1941)
dealt, however discreetly, with matters that might have been more appropriate to the dark worlds of Luis Buñuel, Henri-Georges Clouzot, or
Ingmar Bergman. And *The Macomber Affair* (1947) belongs with Ranald
Macdougall's version of *To Have and Have Not* (*The Breaking Point* in
1950) as one of the most uncompromising and faithful transferences of
the Hemingway mystique to the screen.

Robinson wrote no less effectively for women than for men; and he
could write comedies, melodramas, soap operas, historical romances,

or westerns. Yet he was never just facile. Each genre made its own demands and operated according to its own laws. While his scripts may not have been especially distinguished as pure literature (although no less an authority than Somerset Maugham praised one of Robinson's scripts highly), they nonetheless formed the basis for films that, while not consciously striving to be artistic, nevertheless occupy a valued and honorable place in the history of American cinema.

The interview that follows represents a condensation of parts of a lengthy oral history conducted with Casey Robinson in Sydney, Australia, between July and September 1974. Naturally, in a career embracing half a century and some seventy film titles, much has had to be omitted here. I have chosen to concentrate mainly on Robinson's nine years at Warner Brothers—years in which he wrote some of that studio's most enduring cinematic successes. The discussions of key titles here reveal something of their gestation and the technical problems involved in achieving viable screenplays; and Robinson's remarks on the status of writers at Warner Brothers, their working conditions, and their relations with management tell us much about the glories and vicissitudes of that put-upon profession in Hollywood's heyday.

1927   *The Private Life of Helen of Troy* (Alexander Korda). Co-titles.
The Patent Leather Kid (Alfred Santell). Uncredited contribution.

1928   *Bare Knees* (Great Britain: *Short Skirts*) (Erle C. Kenton). Titles.
Mad Hour (Joseph C. Boyle). Co-titles.
Turn Back the Hours (Great Britain: *The Badge of Courage*) (Howard Bretherton). Titles.
The Chorus Kid (Great Britain: *Her Great Ambition*) (Howard Bretherton). Titles.
The Hawk's Nest (Benjamin Christensen). Titles.
United States Smith (Great Britain: *The Fighting Marine*) (Joseph Henaberry). Titles.
Out of the Ruins (John Francis Dillon). Titles.
Waterfront (William A. Seiter). Co-titles.
Do Your Duty (William Beaudine). Co-titles.
The Companionate Marriage (Great Britain: *The Jazz Bride*) (Erle C. Kenton). Titles.
The Head of the Family (Joseph C. Boyle). Titles, supervision.

1929   *Times Square* (Great Britain: *The Street of Jazz*) (Joseph C. Boyle). Titles.

1930   *The Squealer* (Harry Joe Brown). Continuity.

1931   *The Last Parade* (Erle C. Kenton). Story.
    Masquerade (Casey Robinson). Script, director. (Short subject.)
    The Girl from Hong Kong (Casey Robinson). Director. (Short subject.)

1932   *Is My Face Red?* (William A. Seiter). Co-script.

1933   *Strictly Personal* (Ralph Murphy). Additional dialogue.
    Lucky Devils (Ralph Ince). Co-story.
    Song of the Eagle (Great Britain: *The Beer Baron*) (Ralph Murphy). Co-script.
    I Love That Man (Harry Joe Brown). Co-script.

1934   *Eight Girls in a Boat* (Richard Wallace). Script.
    She Made Her Bed (Ralph Murphy). Co-script.
    Here Comes the Groom (Edward Sedgwick). Co-script.

1935   *Golden Harvest* (Ralph Murphy). Script.
    McFadden's Flats (Ralph Murphy). Adaptation.
    I Found Stella Parish (Mervyn LeRoy). Script.
    Captain Blood (Michael Curtiz). Script.

1936   *I Married a Doctor* (Archie Mayo). Script.
    Hearts Divided (Frank Borzage). Co-script.
    Give Me Your Heart (Archie Mayo). Script.
    Stolen Holiday (Michael Curtiz). Script.

1937   *Call It a Day* (Archie Mayo). Script.
    It's Love I'm After (Archie Mayo). Script.
    Tovarich (Anatole Litvak). Script.

1938   *Four's a Crowd* (Michael Curtiz). Script.

1939   *Dark Victory* (Edmund Goulding). Script.
    Yes, My Darling Daughter (William Keighley). Script.
    The Old Maid (Edmund Goulding). Script.

1940   *All This and Heaven, Too* (Anatole Litvak). Script.

1941   *Million Dollar Baby* (Curtis Bernhardt). Co-script.
    Kings Row (Sam Wood). Script.
    One Foot in Heaven (Irving Rapper). Script.

1942   *The Pride of the Yankees* (Sam Wood). Uncredited contribution.
    Now, Voyager (Irving Rapper). Script.

1943	*This Is the Army* (Michael Curtiz). Co-script.
	Casablanca (Michael Curtiz). Uncredited contribution.
1944	*Passage to Marseille* (Michael Curtiz). Uncredited contribution.
	The Racket Man (D. Ross Lederman). Story.
	Days of Glory (Jacques Tourneur). Script, producer.
1945	*The Corn Is Green* (Irving Rapper). Co-script.
1946	*Adventure* (Victor Fleming). Uncredited contribution.
	Saratoga Trunk (Sam Wood). Script.
1947	*The Macomber Affair* (Zoltan Korda). Co-script, co-producer.
	Desire Me (No director credit). Adaptation.
1948	*The Mating of Millie* (Henry Levin). Uncredited contribution, producer.
1949	*Father Was a Fullback* (John M. Stahl). Co-script.
1950	*Under My Skin* (Jean Negulesco). Script, producer.
	Two Flags West (Robert Wise). Script, producer.
1952	*Diplomatic Courier* (Henry Hathaway). Co-script, producer.
1953	*The Snows of Kilimanjaro* (Henry King). Script, uncredited producer.
1954	*A Bullet Is Waiting* (John Farrow). Co-script.
	The Egyptian (Michael Curtiz). Co-script.
1956	*While the City Sleeps* (Fritz Lang). Script.
1959	*This Earth Is Mine* (Henry King). Script, co-producer.
1962	*Il Figlio del Capitano Blood* (Great Britain: *The Son of Captain Blood*) (Tullio Demichelli). Story.
	Il Segno di Zorro (Great Britain: *Duel at the Rio Grande*) (Maria Caiano). Co-script.
1975	*Scobie Malone* (Terry Ohlsson). Co-script, producer.

Academy Awards associated with Robinson's career include the nomination for Best Original Story for Rupert Hughes's *The Patent Leather Kid* in 1927–28 (Robinson's titles were uncredited); and the *Casablanca* screenplay Oscar in 1943 (again, his contribution is uncredited).

Writers Guild awards include the Laurel Award for Achievement in 1967.

I was born in a small college town, Logan, in Northern Utah. I was one of seven children of W. O. Robinson, who was a professor of music and dramatics at Brigham Young College. I graduated from Cornell University at nineteen. There was a professor at Cornell by the name of Joseph Q. Adams, the greatest authority on Shakespeare in America, possibly in the world. We studied three Shakespeare plays during the year: *Hamlet, King Lear,* and *Othello.* Whether consciously or unconsciously, Professor Adams was conducting the greatest course in writing that could be given. Most of what I know about writing I learned there.

The next year, I taught English in a high school in Brigham City, Utah. At the end of that year, I came to California for a vacation. I was walking down Hollywood Boulevard one day, and I heard my name called out sharply. I stopped; and stopping nearby me was an open Packard car, and in the car sat Gerry Duffy, a reporter I knew from New York. Gerry Duffy was now the head subtitle writer for First National Pictures, which later became, and still is, Warner Brothers.

Gerry received a call one day from the head of First National, [the production supervisor prior to Hal Wallis's ascendancy] Al Rockett. They had an emergency, Gerry was told. They had just completed a picture called *The Patent Leather Kid* (1927), starring Richard Barthelmess and written by a very popular novelist, Rupert Hughes. They liked the picture very much, but they didn't like the subtitles.

How Gerry Duffy convinced Al Rockett that a young man named Robinson was a great new literary talent, I don't know; but I guess he did, because we went to work. We started about ten o'clock on July 4—this was 1927. We worked that day, that night, the next day, the next night, and until early afternoon of the third day without touching head to pillow. That was my introduction to the motion picture business.

Writing subtitles was as good a way for a new writer to begin as any. It took you right into the editorial rooms—handling the film yourself; spotting the places for the titles that carried the thread of the story and dialogue, the sense of the scenes, and what the people were presumably saying on the screen. In those days, unlike today, they believed that a writer, as well as anybody else, could serve an apprenticeship. We didn't have the instant geniuses that abound today.

One could ask, "Were screenplays written for these things?" Of course they were. But they were not the voluminous documents that we have today. They would be fairly thin. All of the action was described and usually in great detail. The sense of dialogue scenes was there in what they called "temp" or temporary titles. After the picture was finished came the work of polishing, editing, and framing the whole thing.

With the coming of sound I was out of a job, and lean times de-

A publicity shot for This Is the Army: *Casey Robinson, Michael Curtiz, and Hal B. Wallis. (Photo: Warner Brothers Collection)*

scended. For one thing, no subtitles were needed. For another, the executives were terrified of a new word, "dialogue." And if you hadn't written a play, you couldn't possibly write dialogue. And I had never written a play. On the last possible day that I could exist—it wasn't that tragic but pretty close to it—I sold a story called *The Last Parade* [1931]. I also received a four-week contract; this was at Columbia.

The first seven or eight pictures that I wrote, Harry Joe Brown produced. It was a very close friendship. He was a wonderful man. He liked two things: people and comedy. The common touch. And you can see all through my early work—what today is a little bit corny sometimes—that man's heart beating through me into the script.

Now, Harry Joe goes to Warner Brothers, and we continue right where we left off. I went with him. Warner Brothers was a great place for a writer. This was not because Jack Warner loved writers. Jack Warner despised writers. He thought they were the least needed thing in the world. I remember him saying during the negotiations for me, "Why should I pay a writer $1,000 a week when I can buy four for that price?" Pay attention to the word "buy." But it was the greatest studio in town for a writer owing to some of Jack's characteristics that are not particularly admirable. He wouldn't pay for rewrites or for reshooting, so your stuff got shot as you wrote it. If it was good, you went up; if it was bad, you were out. It was as simple as that.

It was very much a one-man studio in the sense that Jack Warner never read scripts. In all my nine years at Warner Brothers, I think he read only one of my scripts. His attention was to the contracts, to the fights with actors—he was always having fights with actors—and to publicity. He watched that like a hawk, and you were fired if you had a publicity agent of your own. He ran budgets, how much you could spend—purely administrative.

This is the greatest studio set-up you could have. I've seen it only twice in my life: at Warners, once Hal Wallis became the strong arm, the administrator responsible for making the pictures; and at Metro-Goldwyn-Mayer, when Thalberg was alive. There, the division of work was absolute. Mayer took care of the actors and finding new talent. He was a genius at it, so the scenes in Mayer's office would win Academy Awards. He'd cry, he'd weep, he'd beg, he'd kiss, he'd love, he'd hate, he'd scream—he'd do anything! And Thalberg made the pictures. At Warners there were no producers, there were associate producers. Jack Warner was the executive in charge of production, and whoever sat in that office next to Jack Warner was the producer.

But Hal Wallis came to conduct that studio the same way that Thalberg conducted Metro. Now you must understand that it is a tremendous load to produce thirty pictures a year. And so you've got to put your trust somewhere, you've got to delegate. With Thalberg—and it became so with Wallis—it didn't matter whether your title was associate producer, director, or writer—if he trusted you, he'd throw you the load. This is the only way that a great studio can be run successfully, and these were the two greatest organizations that ever were in Hollywood.

Writers at Warner Brothers during the thirties and into the forties were at once the most despised of all creative people and the luckiest. They were the luckiest for two reasons: because the boys' work got shot since Jack Warner would not pay for rewrites or reshooting, and because of the attitude of Hal Wallis. Hal had been brought up from the publicity department. Having to make thirty pictures a year, he needed any help he could get—the type of writers who could prove their worth on the screen, who got it done on the screen. And so out of this peculiar circumstance of Jack Warner's pecuniary stinginess and Hal Wallis's need for and recognition of talent, there grew up the greatest staff of writers that ever existed in any studio in the history of motion pictures.

But let me go back once more to Jack Warner and the regulations. A writer was expected to appear at the studio at nine o'clock in the morning and leave at five o'clock. He was expected to restrict his outside calls to the minimum; they were monitored. Let's face it; you didn't say anything you didn't want heard. A writer was not permitted on the set without written permission from Jack Warner. This was a regulation. A writer was never invited to see his rushes. He was never invited to a preview. If he wanted to see his own pictures on the screen, he paid his money and went in and saw them. That was the regulation. In the beginning, that was Jack Warner's attitude toward writers.

The boys in general met these regulations with a mixture of great anger and amusement. It became a game to circumvent them. For example, the boys would check in through the gate at nine o'clock; immediately pass out again through the gate (past the friendly gate-keeper, who didn't notice or would choose *not* to notice that they had left); go across to the drugstore to have breakfast, have their talks, and so on; and then come back to work.

I participated about 1938 or 1939 in the first writer's strike, not on my own behalf but on behalf of Seton ("Hap") Miller, who was having a preview that night and wasn't invited. We all used to go to the Lakeside Country Club and have lunch when we didn't want to go to the commissary. And that day we decided not to go back to the studio. We each called our secretaries and said that if anyone was looking for us, we were at the Lakeside Country Club having lunch. Well, along about four o'clock all hell broke loose, and we were all called in to Hal Wallis's office. Poor Hal! He was about to leave on a vacation that night, and he was almost in tears. He said, "You are spoiling my vacation!" "We're sorry, Hal," we said, "but that's it. No more work from *any* of us unless Hap can go to his preview and all writers can attend their previews." And that broke it, that settled it!

I was luckier in that I had come to the studio with Harry Joe Brown. They wanted Harry Joe, and they couldn't have him unless I came along; so for the first year or two years, I had that protection. And then, I had a peculiar psychological advantage over Jack Warner. When I was writing and directing short subjects in New York, the very first one I did was at the Warner Brothers Brooklyn studio. It was a two-reel dramatic picture called *Masquerade* [1931]. It got to the Coast, and I was called in to the office of Sam Cox, the head of the thing, who said that Jack Warner wanted me to come to California and sign a contract as a writer-director. At the same time, Walter Wanger of Paramount [based at Paramount's New York studios at Astoria, Long Island] offered me a contract. The next week Walter was fired, and so I never got the feature. On my first day as I walked into Wanger's office at Paramount with Leland Hayward, my agent, Wanger held the telephone out to me and said, "It's Jack Warner." I had never met Jack Warner, so I got on the phone and said, "Hello, Mr. Warner." And his words—I'll never forget them—were: "I just want you to know, smart ass, that you will walk into a Warner Brothers studio again only over my dead body!" And he hung up.

So when Harry Joe and I were brought up to Jack Warner's office for him to say "hello" and "welcome to the studio," I had the good sense or good luck to recall to Jack Warner his conversation with me. He looked at me and grinned and said, "Well, I must be dead! How's *your* health? Welcome to Warner Brothers!" I knew I had the advantage, so I adopted the system of simply pretending he wasn't there and doing exactly as I pleased. This worked because I was doing my job. He was getting three pictures a year out of me and for less money than I could have gotten elsewhere.

After a preview of *It's Love I'm After* [1937], which was a screaming success, Hal Wallis and Jack Warner cornered me in the lobby, and Warner said, "You are now going to sign a new contract with the studio." Imagine Jack Warner coming to you and asking if you'd sign! But weeks, months went by, and there was no new contract. He delayed and delayed. Jack was a very peculiar fellow. Once you got to him, Jack was a patsy. You got what you wanted. But getting to him was murder: he was barricaded behind that office, behind his secretary.

So finally I went on strike. I chose a beautiful time to go on strike. I was about two thirds of the way through the screenplay of *Tovarich* [1937]. I used to play tennis in those days, so I went over to the West Side Tennis Club, called my agent, and said, "If the studio asks where I am, tell them I'm at the West Side Tennis Club playing tennis, and there I expect to remain until I see Jack Warner and get my new contract." "You can't do this," he said. "You already have a contract, and you are breaking it." "I want to break it," I said. "I'm mad about Jack breaking his promise." Well, that afternoon I saw Jack, and a new contract was negotiated. It was not only for more money but had several provisions I'd put in: one, that I would choose my own material from this point on; two, that I would under no circumstances be asked to rewrite anything; three, that I had to talk to a director only twice, once before I started a screenplay and once after I had finished a screenplay, and more only if I chose. When I struck that blow, I felt as though I was striking it not just for myself but for everybody—especially for the boys at Warner Brothers who, up to that time, were pretty much the abused, misused, low men on the totem pole.

Captain Blood (1935)

The first picture I wrote for Warner Brothers was *Captain Blood*. It wasn't the first picture shot because there was some trouble with the casting. It's a good script even today and a remarkable script for that time, I believe. I say this because after perhaps eight scripts I felt for the first time that I could call myself a professional writer.

Today, I'm afraid, if somebody writes one script then he's a pro. But I felt that I had gone through the mill. I knew both sides of the camera. I knew something about acting, about directing, about producing; and I regarded myself as a professional. But I was still very young; I was always very much younger than my years, and I hope I still am. Now that I'm getting on, it's a blessing; then, maybe, it was a curse.

Rafael Sabatini wrote marvelous historical adventures. And *Captain Blood* was based upon a historical character, Henry Morgan, a pirate. Piracy in those days, of course, was a legitimate activity. It was a patriotic activity—part of the war between England and Spain. And Henry Morgan, who did all sorts of things—he sacked Maracaibo, he took Panama—that were not included in the picture, was rewarded as a patriot by being made governor of Jamaica. This is history.

We kept the historical basis, that I know. There was also another antecedent; *Captain Blood,* which we made in 1935, was a remake, actually. Very few people know that. It had been made at least once before [in 1924] and starred Milton Sills. So, I would say, the principal thing that was done in the production with Flynn was to humanize the movie. To say we took a more modern approach is partially true; but we got inside the character of a young man who was a doctor in England, who was unjustly accused of conspiring against the throne, and who went into virtual slavery with a great feeling of the injustice done to him. This led immediately to the theme of man's injustice to man, because Morgan was not alone; he was with a lot of others who were transported to the Indies. And that theme, which was completely absent from the Sabatini novel, contributed greatly, I would say, to the success of the film. We humanized all the characters. Sabatini drew historical characters that, if they had been translated directly to the screen, would have been merely wooden figures, puppets moving in costume. This is the great danger in making costume pictures; this is the thing that has to be avoided.

And so, we humanized the love story between Flynn and young Olivia de Havilland. She was a girl with whom the audiences of that day, and of today, could readily identify. We humanized her father and made him rather funny. I remember I introduced two quack doctors, which was certainly not part of it, and got a lot of amusement out of them. In other words, we were getting entertainment into the story.

What did we keep? We kept the historical basis of the story. It was certainly not a literal translation of the book; it was not even a faithful translation. I remember that several years after that I re-read *Captain Blood,* and I didn't recognize it from any memory I had of the picture.

It was altogether a delightful experience, because we combined the freshness of the approach with the freshness of two beautiful young people. It was Flynn's first [American] picture; it was de Havilland's second picture. And actually, you could count it as her first, because all she had done before, if my memory serves me correctly, was to appear in that spectacle, *A Midsummer Night's Dream* [1935]. So, as an actress this was actually her debut along with Flynn's debut, and this added to the total excitement of the whole project and, I am sure, contributed greatly to the reception—the instant reception—that it got from the audience.

Dark Victory (1939)

Warners had never made women's pictures. It was a man's studio. Metro-Goldwyn-Mayer was the great women's studio, where they had Crawford, Shearer, Garbo, and later, Greer Garson. There were two women on the Warner lot, and they were both lost. Bette Davis was one; Kay Francis was the other. During the early part of the thirties, Miss Davis was abused and misused at Warner Brothers. They didn't know what to do with her. Either she was treated as an ingenue (which Bette never was), and a silly ingenue at that, or she was treated as one would treat a male actor—never as a full-bodied, complete woman. We just happened to cast Bette in *It's Love I'm After.* It wasn't written for her. It was the first time I ever met her. I realized that here was a great, great untapped talent, and this led directly, although after quite some time, into *Dark Victory.*

In 1935 I had gone to New York and looked around for material. My agent, Leland Hayward, told me of a play called *Dark Victory,* which he had sponsored and which starred Tallulah Bankhead. And the play was a failure, a complete dud. "There must be something wrong with the third act," he said, because they had tried out three or four third acts on the road and nothing worked, nothing saved it. He asked me if I'd like to read it. I took it back to the hotel, and a miracle occurred. I remember it was a bitterly cold day in New York, and to warm up I took a hot bath. As I was bathing I started to read the play, and the whole concept of the picture, the whole structure, descended on me.

I went back to the studio and, as always, reported to Hal Wallis. I said I had found something terribly interesting, a play that had flopped called *Dark Victory.* His first question was, "What's it about?" I said, "It's about a woman who dies of cancer of the brain." Well, the man turned white, of course. He stuttered. One must remember that this is the mid-thirties and that cancer was a dirty word. If someone died, they died of heart failure or some obscure cause. Now, measure Hal's great depth of vision, his confidence in those he had confidence in: his next question was, "Do you really like it, Casey?" I said, "I love it." His next statement was, "We'll buy it."

I was on cloud nine for two days, and then came the news that the thing had been sold to David O. Selznick. So for three years I had a prayer every night: "Please don't let David's writers get the right ideas." Well, he had, I believe, four scripts prepared. He had very good writers. But nothing was happening. Finally, I heard that Ben Hecht had said to him, "The only way to save this is to make it a comedy." And I guess they tried that. At any rate—and now we are into 1938—word comes that Selznick is willing to sell *Dark Victory*. At the same time the situation in the studio was such that they needed something for Bette Davis to go into.

From the moment I had seen her work in *It's Love I'm After,* there was only one person in my mind to play it, of course. I'd even talked to her about it. I told her the story and said, "It's too bad it can't happen." "Maybe I can get loaned out," she said. I suggested to associate producer David Lewis that we buy *Dark Victory* for Bette Davis. Hal Wallis said, "How do we sell it to Jack? Jack won't like it." I said, "Well, how would it be if you told him that you are not only buying the property to get rid of a Davis commitment, but you are buying a David O. Selznick script that Casey can fix up?" That worked. The deal was made. Four scripts were delivered to the studio, and I dropped the four scripts into the scrap basket. That sounds very conceited; but I'm very impressionable, actually, and I didn't want to be tainted by influence.

The play was about a rich, spoiled girl who gets carcinoma of the brain and is going to die. In the second act she learns she is going to die and accepts it gallantly. Oh, there was a little sadness about it; she was in love with her doctor and that part is still in the picture. But what had happened is that they had played the third act in the second act. Where were we going to go? If she accepts death, this is the end. Are you going to play the third act in heaven or wherever she was going to?

It was dissipated. It was all gone. And they just had a lot of gabble in the third act that meant nothing. There had to be, in the middle of the piece, a period of great rebellion against fate—of anger, which, of course, was mixed up with her love for the doctor. Also, the anger that she hadn't been told, and so on. That was an entirely new development in the screenplay and a very important one.

Now, *Dark Victory* is about two things: love and death. And I decided that these two elements should be kept apart as long as possible—that when there was a scene about love, it wasn't about death; when there was a scene about death, it wasn't about love. That is, on the surface. So when there was a scene about love, death was underneath it; when there was a scene about death, love was underneath it—all the time until the very end, when they would reunite into a sort of requiem. Now, in order to do that, I needed a character, and that was the birth of Ann [Geraldine Fitzgerald], the secretary-companion of the heroine Judith Traherne. She was not in the play at all.

Eddie Goulding's fault was that a new idea always appealed to him as better than the old idea—simply because it was new. This is something I don't believe in at all. We had a conference at his house, and I must say he contributed greatly to the screenplay. His analysis of it was: "Let's see, Casey, if every bit of this script consists of strips of film, not words on paper." While I may have been writing in strips of film, I never quite had that approach in mind. It's something actually rather indefinable, something a screenwriter eventually, if he progresses, uses naturally—to think in strips of film.

The Old Maid (1939)

Dark Victory made Bette Davis into a box-office star, and so there was an immediate and urgent need for another vehicle for her. *The Old Maid* had been a successful play on Broadway. It had been purchased by Paramount, and Virginia Van Upp, a very competent woman writer, had written a screenplay. Hal Wallis called me into the office one day and said that Paramount, being unable to cast the vehicle or being dissatisfied with it, was willing to sell it. What did I think of it as an idea for Bette, and would I be willing to do it? I had not seen the play nor had I read it, so I said, "Let me read the play first, and I'll get back to you." I did not ask to read the script; that would have been uncharacteristic of me at that time. I read the play, came back to Wallis, and said that I found it to be a super-saccharine story in its treatment. And I said that I couldn't accept it as it was, but if we injected a new element into it, it would make a suitable vehicle.

That element was hatred. I believed that putting salt into the sweet would make it a more rounded vehicle altogether and certainly more suitable for Miss Davis. We purchased the vehicle, and I went to work. Now, hate is like love; you don't portray hate by having a scene in which you say "I hate you" unless all other devices fail. And a scene in which you say "I love you" is a very bad love scene. It has to be in the whole atmosphere of the piece. It must underline everything. It must be between the lines. Later in the piece I was able to express it when I had Miss Davis say, "All this time we've been pretending with each other that we actually have hated each other." The development of that was largely a matter of casting, and we decided on Miriam Hopkins as ideal for the other woman.

Everything seemed ideal, but in the playing it didn't come off quite as intended. There were plenty of fireworks on the set. There was the antagonism of actress to actress. I remember Bette saying to me one day, "Casey, throwing a cue at this woman is like throwing a tennis ball in a blanket"—meaning, of course, that nothing came back. Actually, what Miriam was doing was underplaying, so that Bette was forced to do all the work. She was upstaging her at every opportunity. She was being super sweet but without the strength of sweetness, always just sort of retiring and prissing around. I am as astonished at this today as I was at that time. I'm amazed that Eddie Goulding didn't pick it up and correct it. It *is* a flaw in the picture, as far as I'm concerned. However, by then Bette was popular and carried everything along. It became a very successful picture.

Now, Voyager (1942)

Writing the screenplay [for *Now, Voyager*] was without the challenge that really excites a writer when he undertakes the adaptation of a book. It was a cakewalk to write—no enormous problem. It was, in fact, a Hal Wallis individual production. He had changed his contract at Warner Brothers, and I guess I wrote all his individual productions. We had our offices together in a bungalow, and our association, which had always been in existence behind the scenes, was now out in the open. We were collaborators in every sense of the word.

There was a small annoyance in the beginning in that Hal Wallis kept sending the material back to the author, and we used to get a few letters from Prouty [the author Olive Higgins Prouty], picking on this little point or that. Now, I don't want to be misunderstood: I try, when I'm writing a screenplay from somebody's original work, to be as faithful to it as I can be (within the limitations of a screenplay and remembering that the novel medium and the screen are entirely different). As I say, this was an annoyance; but it was no more than a mosquito bite, and the work progressed without any difficulty whatever. I've never read Bette Davis's book [*The Lonely Life*. New York: Putnam, 1962—in which Davis claims that she "used Miss Prouty's book and redid the screenplay in her own words as we went along"], but there was never,

"A cakewalk": Bette Davis and Claude Rains in Now, Voyager, *from Casey Robinson's screenplay.*

never one word changed in any of the scripts that I wrote for her—by Miss Davis, by a director, by anybody—and that is a flat statement, a true statement, and final.

Kings Row (1941)

I was leaving with my wife of that time for a vacation to the Philippines and the Orient. This was 1940. Hal sent me a bon voyage present—an advance copy of the book *Kings Row*. That is how it first came to my attention. Well, I encountered nothing that could be used and everything that could not be used, or so it seemed at the time. There was one case after another of insanity and of subjects that were forbidden: two love affairs between young people, miscegenation, and incest, of all things—Dr. Tower's [Claude Rains] sexual affair with his daughter.

I was pretty horrified and understood why I had heard that this was a book that could not be translated to the screen. I remember well the time I finished the book. We were sailing on a little boat from the Philippines down to Bali, through the Sulu Sea. It was one of the most beautiful evenings you could imagine. I took the book and threw it overboard, saying, "Nobody else is going to see this bunch of trash!" And as it hit the water I got the idea that solved the major censorship problem of the book—to change the subject from incest to an inherited tendency towards insanity. I cabled Wallis immediately: "Buy it."

While I was out there, I also got the idea of the theme for the picture: the idea that some people just grow old while other people grow up, the struggle of young people to grow into manhood and womanhood. As a matter of fact, I wrote the first scene, the death of the grandmother, in which that theme is stated, on a piece of Manila hotel stationery. Well, I got home and found a quite irritated Hal Wallis. He thought I had lost my mind. So I told him my solution to the main problem, the censorship problem, and I let him read the speech that the grandmother made before she died. He was, of course, delighted and said, "Go ahead."

Sam Wood never saw the script until it was completed. "I hear that all one has to do with one of your scripts, Casey," Sam said to me, "is set up the camera." You would think that a writer would jump up and down with glee at that, but I was horrified! "Here comes trouble," I thought to myself, "a man who has not made his mark in the studio." Sam's first suggestion was that the picture start in the middle, with the love affair between Parris [Robert Cummings] and Cassandra [Betty Field]. It is true it would have been an interesting opening, a startling opening, but where do you go from there? Two people meet. They haven't seen each other for years, and pretty soon they climb into bed together. We don't know anything about them. "It was a lousy idea, wasn't it, Casey?" Sam says, "Now let's start at the beginning." That began one of the most pleasant associations of my life. We sat in Sam Wood's office with a great art director and designer, William Cameron Menzies, and we went over the script scene by scene, putting it into a shooting script. While we discussed the script and the content (and agreed on it so we weren't two people thinking of a picture but one person thinking of a picture), Bill Menzies sketched every scene, every camera angle, every set-up. He numbered them so that, when Sam finally went on to the set, all he would have to say to [the cinematographer] James Wong Howe was, "Jimmy, this is scene number ten," and Jimmy would go to work lighting the set while Sam worked with the people. And that is how the picture was made. This is my idea of a perfectly ideal relationship between a writer and his director, and I've always quoted it as such.

I wrote the love affairs between Cassandra and Parris and between

Drake [Ronald Reagan] and Randy [Ann Sheridan] with as great care as one could write them. I intimated rather than showed. I did everything I could to protect those scenes from the censors, by which I mean that I used good taste. Now we are at the point where the script is finished. Hal called me up and said, "The censors have totally refused to let us make the picture, and [the Production Code official] Geoff Shurlock is coming over at ten o'clock to talk about it." They said that we had not eliminated the sexual angles or the incest. True, it didn't happen with the father now; it happened with the young man. And as for our camouflage of saying it was instead a tendency toward insanity—they had decided that the girl's insanity was nymphomania, believe it or not. That was a day long to be remembered. As Hal and I stuck at it, I acted every scene in the piece. At the end of the day—it went right through lunch—Shurlock said, "Well, the boy gets off scot free, and he shouldn't." The girl died—she was killed—and so I had to put in a speech that he was sorry, that he felt responsible. As for the other love affair, we said, "Look, the sin is punished. Drake loses his legs." And that took care of that.

Kings Row was almost entirely a studio project. Such things as the freight yard and the passenger train were studio. And because of this kind of intense close shooting—more effective than if you'd gone to a freight yard or shown the passenger train coming in—Sam was right on top of the story all the time. He could control it; he wasn't showing scenery. When Parris arrived home, you just saw a little scene between two cars and you saw a boy's face, worried. That's what the story was about. It wasn't about a train coming into a station. And the beginning—there was never a long shot of that town. The town was shown in bits and pieces. First there was a sign, "Welcome to Kings Row." That was to tell people it was not a costume picture. Then the next things we saw were a schoolhouse, a bank, the exterior of Parris's office—in other words, you accumulated the town as you went along, which was real picture language, a magnificent, brilliant idea of Sam's.

Casablanca (1943)

It used to be the custom that, when Hal would go to New York, I would go with him. Hal wouldn't fly. I can't sleep on trains, and he would come to me with a pile of stuff from his desk and say, "You're not going to sleep anyway, so go through this stuff and see if there's anything worth my notice." So I read all night and encountered an unpublished play called, I believe, "Everybody Comes to Rick's." It was set in Casablanca, Africa, and there the relationship with the picture almost ends. There was one gimmick or "weenie," as we some-times call it in writer's terms, in it: namely, there is one exit visa and two who want to use it. This was a story about two Americans and was totally unrelated to World War II. I got the idea to use not two Americans but a European girl and an American and to tie the story into World War II and refugees.

Something very specific gave me this idea: I was falling in love with a Russian ballerina named Tamara Toumanova; writers sometimes have such personal reasons. She had movie ambitions. Also, I had already determined to leave the studio at the end of my contract, which was coming up not too long from then, and I wanted this for my first independent production. But I was under contract to Warner Brothers; I couldn't buy anything for myself. So, the next morning when I met Hal at breakfast I said, "I found an unproduced play, and it's pretty lousy. But it has one idea, and I want you to promise me that you will read the whole thing, because you'll get a big bang out of it when you get to the last page."

So he took it and came back in about an hour. I've never seen him so angry; on the last page was a telegram to Walter McEwen, story editor at Warner Brothers, saying, "Get me the asking price on 'Everybody Comes to Rick's.' Am very interested. Signed Wallis." I had sent a telegram in his name; we were always kidding each other. He was angry; but he started to laugh and called me a few names and I said, "Look, Hal, if you don't want it, I do, because I'd like to use this as my first independent production." "You're welcome to it!" he said. But it bothered him while we were in New York. He couldn't figure out why I would be so interested in this thing. And so he'd keep egging me, and gradually he got a little information out of me about the World War II situation, the refugees, the foreign girl, and so on—but not the story, not yet. On the way home we met the producer Pan Berman, and Pan astonished him by saying that he thought the man they had at Warner Brothers who had the most appeal to women was Humphrey Bogart. And Hal warmed up to it, and told me that he had bought the play.

So it's gone, and I go about my business. Pretty soon I hear that he has put the Epstein brothers to work on it, and I'm furious! Here's my pal! Something I've found! And he's given it away! "Well," he says, "you've got *This Is the Army* [1943] going and you've got *Saratoga Trunk* [1946]; you are too busy." After a few weeks he came to me and said, "What was that story you told me?" And furiously I said, "For how much?" Well, we settled that. The next thing I hear is that the Epsteins have finished, and they have a man named Howard Koch on it. I don't know him, but he's a pretty fair writer, I believe.

So they started shooting, and Hal comes to me and says, "We

need some help. There's a little trouble." I found out shortly that the little trouble was big trouble because Bogart had said, "I won't shoot this ————"; and he had used a very nasty word and gone home. The production had broken down. He didn't like the relationship between him and Bergman. "This is no love story," he said. "It ought to be a great love story." And the reason Hal had come to me is that they had promised Bogart that I would write it. Hal said, "If Casey will write the love story, will you come back and go to work?" Well, Bogart loved me because I had gotten him out of gangster roles with that romantic trainer in *Dark Victory,* and on that basis he came back. They started shooting, and I wrote ahead of the camera from that point on.

Frankly, I never read the script, because I had already written this script in my mind. I do know that the [Epstein] boys wrote the police stuff and the comedy, and they wrote it very well. And the breaking into and closing down of the club—they wrote that. So what it came to was I wrote the love story. I wrote the scene where she came to him ("I hope you enjoyed it, it's over . . ." and so on), the scene where the husband comes to Rick, and the finish of the thing.

I heard Bergman on the [David] Frost show saying that the nerve-racking thing about this picture was that they didn't know how it was going to end. Well, they didn't know how it was going to end because I was home writing it—of course, always in consultation with Hal. There was, incidentally, never any question about the way the story would end—whether Bogart or the husband would go with her. The ending was clear as far as I was concerned and as far as Hal was concerned, once I was on the picture. We never even discussed it.

But I want to give credit where credit is due. The last line in the picture—"Louis, I think this is the beginning of a beautiful friend-ship"—that's Hal Wallis. He wrote that line, and it was marvelous. It was inspired. One more thing about the finish: Roosevelt and Chur-chill had just met in Casablanca, and the order came down from Jack Warner that *Casablanca* would finish with the conference between Roosevelt and Churchill! How we got out of that I don't know.

Now about that credit. I am angry still. I was pretty smart-assed in those days, too. I wouldn't put my name on the screen with another writer. I was very proud of the fact of my solo screenplays. Except in those cases when somebody came on after me—as in *This Is the Army* or *The Corn Is Green* [1945], where Jack Warner ordered it rewritten or where I rewrote somebody else—then that's fine. But to go on the screen with three other writers with my piece—because I regarded it as *my piece!* And I wouldn't put my name on the screen. It was a very bad mistake, because the boys proceeded to earn an Academy Award.

Metro-Goldwyn-Mayer

After I had left Warner Brothers, I fell into the trap of going to Metro, because they offered me $5,000 a week. Metro was a place where, if they wanted somebody, money was not an object. They paid more than any other studio for their stars, their directors, even for their writers. I shouldn't have done it. I knew better, because I have always said that Metro is the graveyard of writers. And so it proved to be. I remember my first conversation with Louis B. Mayer. He paid me the honor of asking me to come up and talk with him personally. At that time there was great rivalry between MGM and Warner Brothers. They were, by far, the two most successful studios in town. And Mayer said to me, "Tell me, Mr. Robinson, to what do you attribute the present success of Warner Brothers?" And I said, "Well, Mr. Mayer . . ." And that's as far as I ever got because Mr. Mayer then proceeded to spend a half hour telling me that the Metro system was the only system, what a great organization MGM was, and how, at last, it was being run as only a great organization could be run. Right then I knew that I had made a mistake; and six months later I paid $80,000 to get out of my contract.

Actually, the truth about Metro—I don't want to tear down a great studio—was that it had marvelous directors, great stars, and some bright people. But when Thalberg died, Mayer made the same decision that Jack Warner tried to make when he brought in Hal Wallis: that he would never have a strong man again. And it developed into a system where they had committees for everything. That's why I thought it was the graveyard of writers. Their solution to fixing a script that had something wrong with it was to bring in another writer. You'd see four, five, six names—it was just crazy! Because they were run by committee, there wasn't someone who could say "Yes" or "No," who could make decisions. They had a committee to select stories; they had a committee to select casts. They were top heavy with executives who all had to have their say. Now the thing wrong with a committee is that it can only make a compromise. Bravery is gone, courage is gone, and it's wasteful. But it's worse than that, because all you can develop with that kind of a system are formula stories.

Twentieth Century–Fox

Zanuck ran a one-man studio. He was a mixture. There's a phrase in the Bible that describes him absolutely: "The Lord giveth and the Lord taketh away. Blessed be the name of the Lord." You never asked

Darryl for a thing. He liked to give. He also, necessarily, took. He was a remarkable executive in that his desk was never jammed up with anything left over from the previous day. Write Zanuck a note in the morning, you had an answer in the afternoon.

He was a fantastic worker. He worked every night. Work and play were his life. To produce for Zanuck meant, in a way, that you were an associate producer, that you got your way if it agreed with Zanuck's way. However, if it came to a difference of opinion, his way always prevailed. He was a great listener. He loved to listen. He would listen to anybody. He had a very open mind. He was not a hog for credit. I'm not speaking of credit on the screen, I'm speaking of giving credit to people. I never heard him claim the credit for a successful picture. I never heard him lay the blame for a bad picture on anybody but himself. Now, this is remarkable. I mean, if someone makes a picture that comes out badly, Zanuck would say, "Well, I let you do it, didn't I? It's my fault. I should have stopped you, shouldn't I?"

He was a great dramatist. He had this enormous office, and he would walk up and down during a conference while his personal secretary, Molly Mandeville, took notes of everything that was said and got them out to you immediately. He might just expound about the picture in general, or he might begin to write scenes. Of course, Zanuck, as you know, started as a writer; in fact, he made Warner Brothers by writing for *Rin Tin Tin*. Their whole success was based on his writing; and so, as I say, he might start to write scenes, and she'd take them down and send them to you. But woe betide the man who sent him back that same scene in his script.

You couldn't be a sycophant with Zanuck. Contrary to legend, you could not be a yes-man. That legend sprung from the fact that Zanuck always liked to have a couple of clowns around, people he could pick on. These were not the people who were making pictures. These were court jesters. He loved gags—that was a fact of many years' standing—but he respected contributions, he respected talent tremendously. He gave you your head, provided you delivered the goods and provided he didn't get some quirk about something.

Allan Scott: A Nice Life

Interview by Pat McGilligan

If Allan Scott had stopped writing movies in 1938, his place in screenwriting annals would be secure as the co-writer of six of the ten Fred Astaire–Ginger Rogers musicals. As it is, his résumé also includes numerous vehicles for the leading ladies of RKO and Paramount; an Oscar-nominated screenplay for a World War II topical melodrama (*So Proudly We Hail*); other musical fare for Astaire, Jack Benny, and Bing Crosby; a co-writing credit with Dr. Seuss (*The Five Thousand Fingers of Dr. T.*); and his involvement in the lavish remake of *Imitation of Life* for the director Douglas Sirk. As a writer-producer he worked behind the scenes for David O. Selznick, Stanley Kramer, and Kirk Douglas, among others.

Born in Arlington, New Jersey, Scott matriculated at Amherst and earned a Rhodes Scholarship to Oxford (Jesus College). Affiliated with the Theatre Guild, he wrote his first produced Broadway play in 1932. His erudite education, cosmopolitan travel, and flair for light satire served him well in his work as the final writer and touch-up man on the Astaire-Rogers classics. But it might be said that his recruitment for *Top Hat* was a quirk of fate, and it is interesting to note that his list of favorite scripts does not include any of the better-known musical titles.

Like other Hollywood writers whose talents were diverted into comedy, Scott had political concerns that animated his life. He was an early advocate of the Screen Writers Guild and a board member. His younger brother was the producer Adrian Scott, one of the jailed Hollywood Ten. A subscriber to various anti-fascist and progressive causes, Scott wrote position papers for the Democratic Party and was a figure in the wings of the Richard Nixon–Helen Gahagan Douglas campaign.

Alone among the subjects in this book, Scott's interview was conducted by mail and pieced together through correspondence and passages from his unpublished autobiography.

1933   *Goodbye Again* (Michael Curtiz). Co-play basis.

1934   *Let's Try Again* (Worthington Miner). Uncredited contribution.
The Gay Divorcée (Mark Sandrich). Uncredited contribution.
By Your Leave (Lloyd Corrigan). Adaptation.

1935   *Village Tale* (John Cromwell). Script.
In Person (William A. Seiter). Script.
Roberta (William A. Seiter). Additional dialogue.
Top Hat (Mark Sandrich). Co-script.

1936   *A Woman Rebels* (Mark Sandrich). Uncredited contribution.
Follow the Fleet (Mark Sandrich). Co-script.
Swing Time (George Stevens). Co-script.

1937   *Wise Girl* (Leigh Jason). Co-story, script.
Quality Street (George Stevens). Co-script.
Shall We Dance (Mark Sandrich). Co-script.
Damsel in Distress (George Stevens). Uncredited contribution.

1938   *Joy of Living* (Tay Garnett). Co-script.
Carefree (Mark Sandrich). Co-script.

1939   *Fifth Avenue Girl* (Gregory LaCava). Story, script.
In Name Only (John Cromwell). Uncredited contribution.
Primrose Path (Gregory LaCava). Co-script.
Man About Town (Mark Sandrich). Co-screen story.
Lucky Partners (Lewis Milestone). Co-script.

1941   *Honeymoon for Three* (Lloyd Bacon). Co-play basis.
Skylark (Mark Sandrich). Script.
Remember the Day (Henry King). Co-script.

1942   *Holiday Inn* (Mark Sandrich). Uncredited contribution.

1943   *So Proudly We Hail* (Mark Sandrich). Screen story, script.

1944   *I Love a Soldier* (Mark Sandrich). Story, script.
Since You Went Away (John Cromwell). Uncredited contribution.

Allan Scott in Los Angeles, 1985. (Photo: Alison Morley)

1945   *Here Come the Waves* (Mark Sandrich). Co-screen story, co-script.
        Blue Skies (Stuart Heisler). Adaptation.

1946   *Notorious* (Alfred Hitchcock). Uncredited contribution.

1947   *The Paradine Case* (Alfred Hitchcock). Uncredited contribution.

1948   *Portrait of Jennie* (William Dieterle). Uncredited contribution.

1949   *Tell It to the Judge* (Norman Foster). Uncredited contribution.
        Let's Dance (Norman Z. McLeod). Script.

1951   *The Guy Who Came Back* (Joseph M. Newman). Script.

1952   *Wait Till the Sun Shines, Nellie* (Henry King). Co-adaptation, script.

1953   *The Five Thousand Fingers of Dr. T* (Roy Rowland). Co-script.
        The Four Poster (Irving Reis). Script, producer.

1954   *The Caine Mutiny* (Edward Dmytryk). Uncredited contribution.

1957   *Top Secret Affair* (H. C. Potter). Co-screen story, co-script.

1958   *The Defiant Ones* (Stanley Kramer). Uncredited contribution.

1959   *Imitation of Life* (Douglas Sirk). Co-script.
         Beloved Infidel (Henry King). Uncredited contribution.

1960   *Inherit the Wind* (Stanley Kramer). Uncredited contribution.

1962   *Tender Is the Night* (Henry King). Uncredited contribution.

1966   *The Confession* (William Dieterle). Uncredited contribution.

1973   *Don't Look Now* (Nicolas Roeg). Co-script.

Produced plays include *Goodbye Again, Joy to the World, The Last Act, Dubloon, In Clover, Third Side of the Coin, Ballad for Beginners, The Piper's Son,* and *Memo.*

Academy Awards include a nomination for the Best Original Screenplay of 1943 for *So Proudly We Hail.*

How and why did you first come to Hollywood?

What actually happened was that [the director] Mark Sandrich had seen one of my plays in New York and liked the dialogue. At the time, I was working with [the producer] Jed Harris, revising some of his things, and he was busy then negotiating *Gay Divorce* [play basis for *The Gay Divorcée,* 1934]. Dwight Wiman, who produced *Gay Divorce,* mentioned to him that I had revised *Gay Divorce* for opening in London, although I had not revised it an awful lot. Mainly, I was recommended because I had recently gotten back from a long time of living abroad, and he thought I might be useful. I had a chat with Mark, and he wanted me to come out and work on *The Gay Divorcée,* but I wasn't available at the time. But I told him that I was negotiating with RKO and was to report the following year or so, if we came to terms. I had had many offers from Hollywood, but when my wife [the actress Laura Straub] became pregnant and there was no immediate production or play in sight, I left for Hollywood to make some money.

Tell me a little bit about RKO in the early 1930s.

At that time, although RKO was a major studio with a host of stars, compared to MGM it was a minor-major studio. The big stars at RKO, like Ann Harding, Diana Wynyard, Constance Bennett, and so on, were fading, and a new group, headed by Irene Dunne, Katharine Hepburn, Ginger Rogers, Cary Grant, and Joel McCrea, were on the upsurge.

RKO did not make huge, plush pictures like MGM or gangster melodramas like Warner Brothers, but it was known for its "classy pictures." More, as I look back, because of the taste and showmanship of [the producer] Pandro Berman, who worked on comparatively limited budgets. Pandro was a shrewd enthusiast who let the younger directors and writers have their head.

My first office was in the newly erected building called "The New Writers' Building"—very pleasant, large paneled woodwork offices with a room for one's secretary. Actually, I wrote mostly at home, which you were able to do after they realized you were really working. Between assignments you'd come in, gossip, have lunch, wander around the lot, talk with the other writers—a nice life. To my left was Dalton Trumbo—not political yet—and to my right were Julius and Philip Epstein, who became one of the best screenwriting teams of the next quarter century. Further along was Irwin Shaw, working valiantly on a football picture, doubtless because he had played football in college. It wasn't until after the war that he became a short story writer and novelist.

On the second floor was our father confessor, Dudley Nichols, a master craftsman, and in another more luxurious suite was Donald Ogden Stewart, always ready with wry advice and quietly cynical suggestions—quite a witty gent and useful to a writer. Dudley was the one who impressed me most, because even though he was now directing pictures, he was interested in the plight of the Hollywood writer. A gentle, affable guy, he had been a newspaperman at the "old *World*" [*The New York World*], as they used to call it, and he was very busy now trying to form some kind of writers' guild. Because he knew I was a member of the Dramatists Guild in New York, we had many conversations about the possibilities. In the end he was one of the founders, along with me, of the Screen Writers Guild and our first president.

The first floor, with really luxurious offices, was inhabited by the directors, Leo McCarey and Gregory LaCava.

We were a collection of talents previously successful in other fields, never in competition with each other (how can writers compete?); but we laughed together, lunched together, and met together at night, when our real intellectual life took place, to debate politics, contemporary literature, or whatever. For some of us, political expression afforded a means of personal expression. Dalton was a chief exponent of this. He was a genius at public relations and probably the best pamphleteer of the period. Others of us still engaged in writing plays— myself, for example. I had that in my contract. Others had other kinds of work in progress, and later, when the refugees from Europe arrived, there were all sorts of salons where one met the likes of [Bertolt] Brecht and [Lion] Feuchtwanger (whose brother I had known well in Munich as an editor-in-chief of one of its papers). We lived a dual life, writing fantasies by day, and in the evening becoming social idealists, who agonized over Spain, fascism, anti-Semitism, or defended democracy by aiding the allies (as Roosevelt said)—a democratic island in a world gradually becoming totalitarian.

How did RKO's treatment of writers compare with the other studios?

We were treated generously. There was none of the committee writing so prevalent at other studios. Pandro permitted us to do what no other studio permitted at the time—for example, I was on the set constantly during shooting, something new for writers in those days. At other studios, those writers who were low on the totem pole were treated as a necessary evil but not for long once films began to talk. Hollywood was at its height, powerful, alone, dispensing its pictures all over the world, seemingly impregnable, and under no direct assault from outside sources. A small, almost inbred community. They kept referring to it as the "industry," and the heads of the studios kept thinking of themselves as the captains of industry. There was no question they had the buildings, the equipment, the actors, the directors, and all the machinery to make pictures. Except that without writers, they were alone with blank pieces of paper, and all the machinery stopped.

How did you, a freshman writer, wind up being assigned to the Astaire-Rogers vehicles?

Pandro, in the first weeks, told me to wander around the studio. He introduced me to various people, others I met at luncheons. In particular he introduced me to Billy Hamilton, an old-timer who was the best cutter (nowadays known as film editor), who explained to me all the technical terms (dissolves, lap dissolves, jump shots, opticals) and what they meant—all on his movieola.

By chance one day I wandered onto the set of *Gay Divorce*, which was now changed by the censor's office to *Gay Divorcée?* (with a question mark). According to the Code, there was nothing gay about a divorced woman. Now as I say, it happened, unknown to RKO and even to Astaire at that time, that Dwight Wiman, the original producer of *Gay Divorce* in New York, had asked me to rewrite some of the play for London. In New York, *Gay Divorce* hadn't been a major hit, despite its score, and it was the first time that Fred had danced without his sister. Her place had been taken by Claire Luce—not the writer, but a good dancer and a fine actress who later played straight plays unto Shakespeare.

When the shooting stopped, I greeted Mark Sandrich, who was behind getting me to come to RKO. I asked Mark if he had seen the London production and the London script of *Gay Divorce*, and he hadn't. I mentioned that at the point they were shooting, the following things happened. He wondered if I had a copy of the script, and I didn't but indicated that I could remember the revisions. So, taking his secretary outside and with him looking over my shoulder, I dictated maybe a scene of two pages. "That's it," he said, grabbed the pages, and ran back.

Without knowing it, this turned out to be a lucky break. Mark and I ended up making some twelve pictures together both at RKO and later at Paramount—light comedy, musicals, serious dramas. But I am getting ahead of myself.

When Pandro asked me if I thought I was ready to write a picture, I told him I thought I would like to try. Suddenly I was deluged with scripts from the head of the "B" department—"The Keeper of the 'Bs'," we used to call him. T. S. Eliot, I remember, said, "Movies supplanted the stage in melodrama. Melodrama is perennial and the craving for it is perennial and must be satisfied." With rare exceptions, say of John Ford, melodrama on the RKO lot consisted mostly of imitation "B" pictures of Warner Brothers—G-man pictures or chase pictures, and so forth. After seriously reading the deluge, I wrote to the Keeper of the "Bs": "There's nothing I can possibly add to any of these to make them worse." He immediately protested to Pandro, and a day or so later, Pandro Berman, smiling, came to me and just said, "For chrissake, be a little more polite; he's my uncle. Just say 'it's not my cup of tea,' but remember, I didn't hire you to write what other people want to write. I just want you to write what you really feel like writing." At that, he handed me a script saying, "Here's one by somebody you admire." It was a screenplay by Marc Connelly based on the Philip Stong novel [*A Village Tale* (New York: Harcourt Brace, 1934)].

It began in the observation car of the Super Chief, with two men looking at the countryside as it whirled by a Midwest village. One man said, "Look at that town." The other man took a drink, grunted, and said, "Yup. Yeah, nothing every happens in a town like that." And the camera stays on the town. I read the screenplay and the Phil Stong book. It was second-rate but popular. I told Pandro that I knew nothing about the Midwest, but that I did know, at least I thought I knew, about a small town. I could write about Arlington, New Jersey. He said, "Write about what you know."

So I transplanted the people I knew from Arlington into the screenplay. Pandro liked it, and suddenly out of nowhere, John Cromwell, who was one of our star directors, liked it. Cromwell persuaded Kay Johnson (his wife at the time) and Randolph Scott (a rising movie star who was probably the last of the period Arrow-shirt-type heroes) to be in it. I had seen Kay many times in New York. Also, I always felt during this picture that Randolph was at a big loss without his horse. The picture was pretty well received by the New York critics, but the local wags—the dailies—landed on it heavily because I had dramatized the petty viciousness (also the fun) and near tragedy of a chivaree played on an innocent person. The local critics deemed it sordid and "not the kind of picture we need at this time." I got one fan letter. It read: "This is the stuff to feed the troops." And it was signed by Eugene O'Neill.

Although I remained filled with serious intent, I couldn't interest anyone in subjects I wanted to do. Whereupon Mark Sandrich reappeared with the first draft of the script of *Top Hat*. It was written by Dwight Taylor, who was the son of Laurette Taylor and the stepson of Hartley Manners, a prolific playwright in the early part of this century. Dwight had also written *Gay Divorce,* which was a revised version of one of Hartley Manners's plays. Mark said, "Read it [*Top Hat*], and let's have some fun." I read it, liked it, rewrote it completely, and then Mark and I polished it together. He knew exactly what he wanted; and gradually I learned construction and wrote the scenes.

Did you put much camera movement into your scripts in those early days?

Most of the camera movements were the kind I might have made in the theatre—to emphasize points. I always wrote in medium-long with occasional close-ups for emphasis. There was little reason for writing camera movement, because most of the time, although you described the sets in your script, you never knew how large or small they'd be— unlike the theatre—so you left it up to the directors. In general, the scripts of that period were shorter, maybe 130 to 140 pages. On the other hand, Gregory LaCava, who was so adept at comedic pictures, didn't care how long the scenes were, because the final version wasn't prepared until the day of shooting. My first picture with LaCava was 270 pages long. It was mimeographed after the picture had been shot. Otherwise, there would have been a series of heart attacks in the front office.

How involved in, how crucial to, the success of RKO was Pandro Berman?

Pandro was an affable, intelligent, quick-witted gent who was sure of himself and wide open to suggestion. Once he made this decision about a director and a writer, he would stick to it. He was the most accessible of studio heads. I often wondered what made him tick, and I found out. It was his "smeller." Once, when a new play of mine was waiting my arrival in New York, he let me go even though I still had some scenes to do on *Roberta* [1935]. But he kept me on salary; he said he had to go to New York too. So, as I would write the scenes for *Roberta,* he would get off the Super Chief, say in Kansas City, and wire several scenes back to the set. We finished up the script and sent it by telegram from the Waldorf-Astoria Hotel.

Then I asked him, "Now can I go to my meetings? My director is waiting for me." He said, "I have one more favor to ask you. Please come see a play with me tonight. It's called *Stage Door.*" I told him I'd already seen it, but he insisted. At the end of the first act I said, "Now can I go? I don't like this one, Mr. Berman." At the end of the second act I said, "Now can I go, please? I've got a date." At the end of the third I said, "Now are you convinced? It isn't any good at all. May I go now?" He said, "Let's have a drink first."

So we walked to Sardi's, and over a brandy we talked about the play. I wanted nothing to do with it. I mostly wanted to get on to see my director. But Pandro suddenly said, "I'm going to buy *Stage Door* because I see Katharine Hepburn in it." "There's no part in it for her," I said. "And I see Ginger Rogers in it." "Doing what?" I asked. "Directed by Gregory LaCava," said he. And in a sense we were both right.

LaCava made a stunning picture out of it with Katharine Hepburn and Ginger Rogers. He used practically nothing of the play except its name, and actually he used not the plot or the characterizations but one line of dialogue. [Screenplay by Morrie Ryskind and Anthony Veiller based on the Edna Ferber and George S. Kaufman play.] It was Berman's "smeller" that night as we sat over brandy that made him perceive the the hit that *Stage Door* [1937] finally became.

What about Mark Sandrich? He seems to have escaped lionization by film buffs. Although he directed five Astaire-Rogers pictures, his reputation seems to be mainly that of an effective technician under Astaire's thumb.

He is the man most neglected in practically all the writings about the Astaire-Rogers films. The lynchpin, the prime mover, and the creator of the idea of the pictures, although he didn't direct all of them, was Mark Sandrich. Mark was a man I loved and admired for his talent. Long before *The Gay Divorcée* hit the screen (as opposed to big musicals like *42nd Street,* "43rd Street," "44th Street," and "Lexington Avenue Street" with all the big Busby Berkeley mob scenes), Mark was experimenting with small musicals, like *So This Is Harris* [1932] and *Melody Cruise* [1933], which was actually done in a kind of rhymed doggerel.

As I found out later, he was instrumental in signing Astaire, although with no foreknowledge, say, of *Gay Divorce,* and it was later at his insistence that Ginger was partnered with Fred even though Fred strenuously objected to it, saying in effect she was not enough of a lady to play the refined Englishwoman of the script. Fred was a snob, and even after their first hits together, he still objected to being a team. He had been a team with Adele, his sister; but his objections carried no weight with Pandro Berman, who knew what he had in the pair.

Being a physicist and engineer by education, Mark helped perfect the playback system of recording. That is the system that enables the number to be prerecorded for the cutters. Up to that time the cutters had enormous troubles getting the music tracks to fit the dance steps. Up until then most musical numbers, particularly songs, were filmed and recorded on the set with the full orchestra; later the dancers were recorded with just the pianist, Hal Bourne, playing the music as it would be played by a full orchestra.

Mark was also the one who insisted that the numbers be shot in one take—no cuts to other people watching or to an audience responding, only shots of the feet dancing. This was done with the concurrence of Fred. I'll admit he was a far better showman and producer than director. But he was an enthusiast and was under no one's thumb. He was a sweet, gentle, and inspired man who created confidence in others— very warm and enthusiastic. For films, he practically invented the musical form.

I'm curious about the writing credits for the Astaire-Rogers vehicles. So many names . . . In her book, The Fred Astaire and Ginger Rogers Book *[New York: Outerbridge and Lazard, 1972], Arlene Croce refers to you as a rewrite man for Dwight Taylor. What was the nature of your collaboration with him?*

I was not a rewrite man for Dwight as Arlene Croce dubbed me. By the time I got to Hollywood, Dwight was already considered a veteran writer, and on the basis of *Gay Divorce,* he was given first shot at the script. But actually, after the first picture, which I also contributed to without seeking credit, what usually happened was Mark, Dwight, and I would sit down and hammer out a kind of storyline; and because usually I was busy working on the shooting script or some other project, Dwight would work on a first draft. Then, I would read his draft, confer with Mark and the composers, and rewrite completely according to our needs.

For example, on *Top Hat* [1935] he did the first script—breaking the story down, suggesting possible dance spots—while I was writing for other actresses on the lot—Hepburn or Lombard or Irene Dunne. About three months before the piece was slated to go, I got it and made the second draft based on Dwight's storyline. I never had a conference with Dwight—we never really *collaborated*—except I knew him, of course. After I had finished my draft, Mark and I would sit down and go over it page by page—improving it, making better suggestions for the lyrics—and finally I would give it a final polish. Then—something new in Hollywood, which Pandro Berman permitted, although it is commonplace enough today—I would stay on the set in a mobile dressing room that Mark and I inhabited, watch the rehearsal, fix anything that we thought needed fixing, go back to the dressing room, and start work possibly on an entirely different picture. This was the way Mark and I always worked, even later when it became a partnership, until his premature death at the height of his talent when he was about forty-five.

The only official collaboration I ever did at RKO was as a special favor to Pandro. Pan had bought a story [probably the story basis for the 1937 *Damsel in Distress*] by P. G. Wodehouse, who insisted on doing the screenplay, too. Since that prodigious worker wasn't supposed to know much about the screen, I told Pan I would try it. When Wodehouse would show up occasionally for a conference, he would listen to what I proposed and would say, "Amazing, my boy, keep it up!" Then he'd head off for lunch somewhere. He used to drive Berman crazy. Wodehouse was getting $6,000 a week. He would come in and sit in the first quadrangle on the bench and peruse a two-week-old copy of *The Times* of London. Pan, exasperated, would watch him from his window. This went on for approximately ten weeks. When I had finished the script, he said once again, doubtless with his quiet irony, "Amazing, old boy, simply amazing—what you did with my little story!" He said he would like to make changes, so I gave him the script and he took it home and came back. I searched through the script, and found one change he had made in red ink. I had written for someone to say, "Well, I'm off." He had rewritten it to say, "Pip, pip, I'm off, chaps." So, he took the $60,000 bucks and walked out of Pandro's existence. He was too busy to *run* with the money with any dignity.

What about Ernest Pagano? His credit crops up on a few Astaire-Rogers movies as co-writer.

Ernie Pagano was a veteran who had been a gag-man in the silents, and he helped me enormously. The gag-writers of the silent age, as I understand it, were always trying for visual effects, and the few remaining, like Ernie (who was a humorous gent although he didn't write very well), were fun to be around. For example, in one of the pictures [*Carefree*, 1938] where Freddy was supposed to be a psychiatrist who had hypnotized Ginger, we were looking for something for her to smash. Ordinarily, in fact as I remember it, I wrote that she just smashed a plate glass window and got into trouble as a result. But Ernie had a real gag idea. He said, "Why not a truck carrying plate glass mirrors and plate glass itself? In this way, she can begin to follow it, keep it under surveillance, and finally pick up her rock and heave it through the vehicle." So, as a consequence, Ginger kept the truck on surveillance and followed it a couple of blocks and the gag developed; the audience found it quite funny.

I remember Vincent Lawrence used to dramatize his theory about comedy. Vinnie was a New York playwright, and at Lucy's (which had formerly been a speakeasy) across the street from Paramount, after he had downed twelve martinis in a row, he would show you his idea of comedy. He was like a nervous pitcher on the mound. He would wind up carefully and carefully slam the ball theoretically at the catcher. "Strike one!" he'd say. He'd wind up again, look nervously around, and fling the ball to home plate. "Strike two!" and then "Strike three!" It was his way of demonstrating the "one and the two and the three." Take a single incident good enough to make you laugh; explode it into another; and before they have recovered from the first, set off the third—like a series of firecrackers. It was not new, but what was new was the way we treated it. It was a development, particularly American in my opinion, that combined all that anyone knew of stage, burlesque, black comedy routines—all refurbished for legitimate actors and actresses. Things that were only just funny or that bombed in burlesque were hysterical with Cary Grant. Then we made the dialogue, in addition to the action, ripple instead of just relying on the visuals of the gag-men who were still haunting the sets.

Did you work closely with the Astaire-Rogers composers, and how did they adapt to Hollywood methods?

The differences between stage and the kind of musicals I got involved with were simple. We had people like Fred, Bing, and so on to key on, whereas the stage musicals (like Rodgers and Hammerstein's *Oklahoma!*) had huge casts with twenty or so songs or dances. Most of our composers, in fact all that I remember, had been Broadway composers who were used to writing fifteen to twenty-five different songs for each show. In our musicals we never had more than four or five, so the numbers and the songs had to thrust the story forward. All of them had to be intimate except for the last one, which was usually done with a chorus of girls and boys, and so on. A song like "Cheek to Cheek" was supposed to have been a love scene in the script, for example. As a musical number it was so much more lyrical.

For example, with the Gershwins I worked very closely with Ira. Ira would call me, and then George, who kept a notebook—a big notebook of melodies—would go to work. Once, I had come back on the *Isle de France* and gone down to the boiler room to see the different mechanical pieces working up and down. It occurred to me that maybe this would be a marvelous place for Freddy to do a single ["Slap That Bass" from *Shall We Dance,* 1937]. We were always looking for ideas for Freddy to embellish in his one single in each show, and George wrote the music for this one eventually.

Sometimes, as in "Isn't It a Lovely Day to Be Caught in the Rain?" the ideas were lifted right out of the scenes by Irving Berlin. Irving had been brought in as composer [for *Top Hat*]. At this point, he had suddenly developed a big lull, in songs *and* shows, in his career. He knew virtually nothing about picture making, and Mark, who was really the innovator of this particular kind of musical, had him write thirty-one songs. Irving was used to this for shows in New York, but remember, we could only use five. And although Irving always had a bundle of songs, he had to write, for the first time in his career, directly for the needs of the picture. I recall, for example, one of the thirty-one, which we knew was a good song, was "White Christmas," which we ended up using some years later. Actually, if you look at the old sheet music you'll find out it has nothing to do with war or soldiers but rather with Irving being alone in Beverly Hills wishing for a white Christmas from the East.

Swing Time [1936] was really the first book musical, and I wrote it with Dorothy Fields and Jerome Kern all the way. Kern only lived a few blocks from me, so instead of going to the studio, I would go up to Jerry's house. This way the songs were integrated in the script from the beginning, except for "Waltz in Springtime," which was just a marvelous piece of musical lyricism—a white vision, impossible to describe. Kern at his musical best, Fred and Ginger so full of passion—almost unbelievable in its sheer delight. No wonder someone called Fred the Mozart of the Dance.

The melodies just used to pour out of Kern. I remember sometime later, after Paris fell, we were about to break for lunch when a telegram arrived for Jerry. He read it and said, "Go in and lunch alone, will you? I suddenly got something to think about." About half an hour later, when I came back, he said, "Listen to this," and he played a tune—a rather sad tune with funny little squeaks occasionally. "Remind you of anything?" he asked me. I said, "Kind of like the taxi horns of Paris." He had received from Oscar Hammerstein the lyrics of "The Last Time I Saw Paris" and the tune was completed in that short time.

Were there any tricks to writing for Astaire?

Freddy was very professional—a good light actor—the only thing to keep in mind was his "image" and not write anything that was contrary to it. All he wanted to know, even before we did something, was what we thought would be needed. He took no immediate interest in the scripts and worried only about what he called "taste." So I would put in several lines that might be a bit raw so that he could ask that they be deliberately cut out; this then made him happy. As I say, Freddy was a terrible snob—I imagine he still is. I remember, for example, that I wrote (to be deleted later) an American millionairess's mother saying, "Considering the riff-raff we're getting from English nobility these days, a dancer isn't so bad." This pained Freddy to no end because his

Fred Astaire and Allan Scott during the filming of Follow the Fleet. *(Photo: Academy of Motion Picture Arts and Sciences)*

sister had married nobility. So I deleted it and again had my way on the script. I was never, except professionally, involved with Freddy. He was a very private person, and so was I; and outside of the pictures we were doing, we rarely saw each other except at the barbers' or something like that.

In your other RKO pictures, and later at Paramount, you seemed to specialize in vehicles for leading ladies—Ginger Rogers, Claudette Colbert, Irene Dunne, and Katharine Hepburn. Why did you write so well for women characters?

I think it was because at RKO in those days the really big stars were women. Other than that, I've been interested in women as long as I can remember—pre-virginity. Curiously enough, I was criticized for my plays because most of the major parts were for men. But at RKO the female stars outnumbered the males enormously. And can you imagine writing anything (except possibly for his horse) for Randolph Scott? In fact the end of his horse had more warmth and geniality than poor old Randy himself.

The reason I think that actresses liked my scenes was that I verbalized the inner feelings of the characters. In other words, instead of just a kiss and then a shot of a mussed-up bed (or something to indicate that the people had fallen in love and into bed at the same time), I remember a script conference once with Zanuck and Henry King . . . I've forgotten which picture [probably *Remember the Day,* 1941, before casting was finalized], but we were examining the final script and cutting here and there and we came to a love scene of some kind and Zanuck said, "Now, we come to one of those goddamned, fucking, sensitive, lyric scenes of Allan's between Colbert and Milland." Zanuck said, "Henry, can we cut this?" and Henry said, "Not unless you want to cut Colbert out entirely," and Zanuck said, "Okay, shoot the damned thing."

Zanuck would have loved the way they kiss today on the soap operas, where the protagonists lunge at each other, open-mouthed, with their tongues unleashed, performing tonsilectomies upon one another.

Can you comment, briefly, on the major RKO actresses and their involvement with the scriptwriting process? Irene Dunne?

Irene was the easiest of all to please. A deeply religious woman—very involved with church affairs. Irene had been a star on Broadway in musicals, so she became an actress (a straight actress, that is) really when she came to Hollywood. Being from the theatre, she always came to the set thoroughly prepared. If she had any problems with a scene, she would always select out the author, sit down with him, and talk it out—never making any suggestions but just saying she was having a bit of trouble and asking what she was doing wrong.

Claudette Colbert?

She also had come to films from the theatre and so was very conscientious about characterizations. Sometimes I'd get a phone call late at night, and she'd say she was having trouble. Then, because she was such a thorough professional, I'd know something was wrong, and I'd correct it. She usually was right.

Katharine Hepburn?

Kate never uttered a word until the script came out; then we would make a date to meet somewhere and go over the script scene by scene. She made notes—very sharp, intuitively right for her. She is a great spirit and great fun to argue with.

Ginger Rogers?

Ginger never involved herself in the writing. The scripts I wrote for her solo vehicles weren't tailored for her exactly but were done in collusion with her on several occasions. I'd show her a story I liked for her, and a couple of times we got the studio to buy the original mate-

Ginger Rogers, Lucille Ball, and Harriett Hilliard with Allan Scott on the set of Follow the Fleet. *(Photo: Homer Dickens Collection)*

rial—short story or novel. She was a very gay (in the decent sense of that word) person and led an elaborate social life. I remember one particular joke about Ginger that developed over the years. If Ginger was having trouble with a scene, she always said, "There's something radically wrong with this scene." It took us a couple of pictures to realize that when Ginger said this, it meant that she was not prepared and doubtless had been on the town the night before. So, when we burst into laughter at her saying it (because we were counting on her saying it), she was embarrassed. But she worked very, very hard.

Can we talk about the other directors you worked with, apart from Mark Sandrich? Specifically, how they applied themselves to the script. Gregory LaCava?

It's extraordinary. He was one of the most talented of them all—a skillful technician, who was heavily influenced by the Depression, which affected most of his work. The Depression was going on at the time he had already made pictures, and he talked about it all the time. He had been a political cartoonist before coming to Hollywood, and he had a satiric nature. On the other hand, he was a reactionary Republican and hated Roosevelt.

Greg was an artist, but his chief weakness was booze. There was a legend that he never had a script when he began shooting a picture. This was, of course, untrue. We had many conferences, and I would write sometimes as many as four and five different versions of each scene. But because of his mistrust of the front office and his theory of acting, there was never a script shown to anyone but only an outline given to the various departments. His idea was that if the actors had a script, they'd get stale. Literally, on the day of the shooting we'd stay in our trailer with his secretary of many years, with all the versions I had written, and with the notes he had made strewn around, and he would dictate what he liked of my scenes, annotating them as he liked. Then the secretary would type up the necessary copies, the actors would get the script, and within the hour we were shooting. This way, he believed, and actually he got, a kind of spontaneity that was sometimes lacking—because we didn't rehearse enough in those days. He was right, in a way, because in the theatre there is a certain staleness after the first two weeks of rehearsal, and it isn't until the end of the third week, with the apprehension of opening night on the horizon, that a play, particularly a comedy, begins to regain its life.

For example, when I was working with Lewis Milestone, "Milly" insisted on getting the scenes as I turned them out. When I was finished with act one, he had read the scenes so often that they were stale to him; so I had to redo act one just to amuse him. He never got over this, and he was a pain in the ass to work with because of that, as much as I loved him. He was almost afraid to begin a picture—very insecure, particularly about comedy.

George Stevens?

George had come up through the studio ranks and had realized as he achieved director-producer status that he'd neglected his education. I was pompous enough to give him reading lists. Actually, he educated himself. He was slow, thoughtful; he'd drive you crazy in conferences, because of the long silences—presumably he was thinking. A great man and a marvelous drinking companion, but sometimes you never knew what the hell he was shooting. Still, it all added up. One lesson I'll never forget I learned from George Stevens. I had a tendency to overwrite. George said, "Stalk a scene. And always remember in your mind, the film is rolling and rolling, constantly."

Henry King?

Henry King was the reverse of George. He'd come up through the theatre as an actor and director. The written word was most important to him. The first draft I would do myself—except that I could see him whenever, at any time. He insisted that I write on the lot in case he needed me for casting or something. After the first draft came the most painful draft. We waded through the script together, shot for shot. How should he introduce this scene? Should the camera come in on a pole and wander over to someone who was looking at something else? It used to drive me crazy. It was a longer nine-to-five day with Henry. And if we got stuck, he'd say, "Let's clear our heads." That meant driving to the Burbank airfield and getting in his plane. Because he was an elderly gent, I would be terrified. But we always managed to land in Texas or Missouri with our heads entirely clear of everything except fear.

It appears from your list of official credits that you wrote less or stopped writing altogether after World War II.

I became a writer-producer. My name is not on several screenplays because of the rules we were going by in those days, which have since been changed. Even though I may have initiated a project, I would hire a fellow writer to do the first draft sometimes, and sometimes I would completely rewrite it. But the rules stated that I could not take credit for the screenplay. Apart from which, I was sympathetic with writers who differed with producers, having been in that position myself.

From the earliest days I remember being called a rebel, simply because I was against anybody who tried to tell me exactly what to write. That's why I was considered, in their terms, a tough son-of-a-bitch to work with. I happened to stumble on a ploy that worked for me early, and I used it constantly thereafter. For example, when I attended a full-dress story conference with the heads of the studio, the yes-men, and the other producers along with their ass-lickers (particularly those who hadn't even read the script except possibly for a synopsis prepared by their secretaries), someone would open the session by beginning with, "Well, Alan . . ."

There would be a silence, and I was supposed to start defending what I had written. Thereupon, I would say, "Look, fellas, I am here to listen to the improvements you have in mind and your suggestions. I'm interested really in your second thoughts." Their second thoughts were mostly about other studios' pictures they had seen the night before or pictures they had previously made themselves. Someone would say, "It's too long." Somebody else would say, "It's too short." All of them would address the boss rather than me.

They couldn't have caught my eye anyway, because I would be furiously writing down the chaos I was hearing. When finally they had exhausted themselves, there would be a silence, and I would continue scribbling. Then I'd get up and say, "Thanks. When anybody gets a better idea, I'll do my goddamnedest to write it." This was again followed by a silence, stunned looks were exchanged, and I would leave. As the door closed behind me I could hear the usual pandemonium break loose. I must say this ploy worked for me most of the time. It was the reason I became what is now called a "hyphenate"—a writer-producer—so that I could work directly with directors and not have to trip over a lot of live corpses.

Over the years were there projects you worked on, or wanted to write, but for some reason were frustrated?

After several experiences in the beginning when I found I could not write something I believed in, I took refuge in writing comedies. The cry one kept hearing was, "Please don't uplift me when I go to the movies." I remember one producer telling me, "You can get all the social significance you need at home. Leave it out of my pictures." That's why this particular producer scrapped [Sinclair Lewis's] *It Can't Happen Here*—out of deference to Hitler and Mussolini.

There are a number of specific projects I worked on for which I did do a screenplay, although they never were made. For example, at Selznick's I think the best screenplay I ever wrote was for *Tess of the D'Urbervilles*. It had been long a favorite of mine, and I had even gone to England and shot with the second company. David loved the script, and his wife [Jennifer Jones] was going to play the lead; we had the rest of the cast on the lot.

I never quite knew what happened, because I left the lot to do a play in New York and London; and when I got back, Jennifer, in tears, came to my office and said that David was abandoning the project and trying to sell it to Metro. I was a bit outraged, and when I met up with David I asked him why. He said Metro could do it because he had other things he wanted to do, but since Jennifer liked it so much he was trying to sell it, her, and the script to Metro. The deal fell through because, as a friend of mine—Arthur Hornblow, who was the interested Metro producer—told me, David was asking a million dollars for the script alone. That was horrific sum in those days. Actually it had cost David $15,000 for the novel and about twenty weeks of my services. I was getting, at that time, $5,000 a week. But I was not only writing it but producing other pictures. So it never got made.

Did you lose your passion for the theatre by concentrating on movies—even though you continued to write plays on occasion?

I never did. But the reason I stayed in movies was to learn my craft. In the theatre in those days (even worse now) you had to wait a year or more to see your work in front of an audience. In pictures, when you wrote three or four scripts a year, you'd see your work—see mostly your mistakes—because in both media, nothing is complete without an audience. The thirties was a great learning period for me, and what the studio (or Pandro Berman, perhaps) was pleased to call my gift for first-class dialogue got me over the early days.

It's ironic that you, with your social conscience and outside political activity, became known primarily for high-toned musical comedies. Did you ever regret your immersion in the Astaire-Rogers movies?

Not at all. They were great fun to write. Actually, I'm very proud of having written some of those screenplays and of breaking new ground for the Hollywood musical as a consequence. And they were so successful that I could always say I was working on one or another to avoid writing some piece of claptrap. They were terribly difficult to write because of their artificiality. But the big thing was to keep them bubbling humorously and entertainingly, and we worked very hard at this so that the numbers always flowed out of the situation.

Which of your screenplays, as filmed, remains your favorite and why?

So Proudly We Hail [1943]. Originally, we were asked to make a two-reel film for the Red Cross, because at that time they were in charge of getting nurses for the Army. I happened to be in Washington (I was one of a group of speech writers) when I heard that the nurses rescued from Corregidor were at Walter Reed Hospital. They were being kept from the press; but through Harry Hopkins I had met Eleanor Roosevelt, and she arranged a meeting with five or six nurses who could reasonably be questioned—the remainder were still in terrible shock. I heard the story from these girls—the atrocities and rapes that were committed on their comrades in the Bataan peninsula. To this day the Army has not revealed that particular catastrophe. The "long march" left no survivors among the girls other than . . . well, no point in going into it. I wrote a first script. It was censored by the Army only because it told the truth. However, I did get an excellent script eventually, and it was one of the most distinguished pictures of the war.

Skylark [1941]—It was a Samson Raphaelson play that had been a success in New York. It was very like the kind of plays I wrote myself but without a third act, so I rewrote it—barely managing, for the first time, to take an anti-Nazi stand in a comedy, just because it was a comedy.

Primrose Path [1939]—This had been a novel by a very gentle woman I'd met, but it was to be directed by LaCava. He left me alone until shooting time, and I devised an entirely new story.

The Four Poster [1953]—I saw this in London when it was a play and wired Stanley Kramer that I thought it had the makings of the kind of picture we were buying for Columbia (we had to make pictures for $150,000 on our deal) with Harry Cohn. Stanley wired back,

Veronica Lake, Paulette Goddard, and Claudette Colbert (left to right) in So Proudly We Hail; *the screenplay earned Allan Scott an Oscar nomination.*

"Buy it." I did, for $15,000, even though the play closed. I persuaded Rex Harrison to play it with his wife Lili Palmer. It was the first two-character play made in Hollywood, taking them from the time of their first night together, throughout their life, and until her death. In addition, for what I called inter-scenes, I had John Hubley—a beautiful cartoonist—animate scenes so I could avoid double exposition. I also produced it. A big success.

Looking back over the length and breadth of your career, did you feel at all compromised by impersonal studio assignments? How would you summarize the accomplishments of your career in terms of how you managed to express your personality or your ideas or even the full range of your talent in your screenplays? Do you feel you accomplished as much as you would have liked to accomplish, or did the studio system take away as much as it gave?

In films I never had a coherent theme because, with some exceptions, the stories were in a sense chosen for me, or I'd choose stories I thought they'd make. The Astaire-Rogers pictures were full of optimism and happy turns of events, slightly tongue-in-cheek and unrelated to the world around us—escape into fun, jokes, dancing. As a matter of fact, my approach was even more satirical, but Mark deleted some of the things I had written. In the theatre, on the other hand, my plays that have been produced are marked by satire and irony—with essentially serious undertones—about the irrational comic side of man (and woman).

Looking back, for someone who was working in the phenomenon of film, I never fooled myself as to quality, and I was never patronizing. I was aware how the stars, quite unconsciously, became prisoners of their own images, believing the things we wrote for them to say, and how their images became part of their public lives. So big were they on the screen that the stars saw themselves, in actuality, as "big head close-ups."

Unlike the freedom in the theatre, I sometimes found out what I had really written—at least according to the critics—after a production had been done. Although I was fully conscious of what I was doing, many times it was blurred by directors into something vague. I once wrote a scene in which a director somehow (I'll never know how he did it) put on the screen the exact words written in the scene but got the opposite meaning of what was intended. He was not a tyro but an egocentric intellectually. One was always running into these lapses in comprehensibility. Naturally, we had to reshoot the scene.

The literature of a scene is just as vulnerable as any other kind of writing; this I found out looking back on some of the scholarly essays that I once wrote on Emerson, Milton, or secondary sources of the more preaching critics. Even in the works of my favorite novelists (Fielding and Jane Austen) one can find faults and contradictions and flaws—but who the hell cares? The same goes for the best of the movies. Movies are as vulnerable as human beings are vulnerable.

I was always aware that the future would soon be the present, so I took a great joy in the passing moment; I think I made many mistakes in plays and pictures and sometimes believed more in the characters I invented than in "real life" (what happened to be the truth rather than my fancy). And from time to time, I paid too much attention to the criticism of others. (In the early days, particularly, and most particularly in the first draft, when there is not a writer alive who doesn't need, at that point, approbation.) Like St. Ignatius when he went to Monserrat and confessed, I have never received absolution.

For myself, I have never thought that pictures were a doorway to romance, and all the other cliches. All I ever asked and ever knew was whether I had an aptitude for it or not. It was the pursuit of writing—not an adventure; sometimes, just hard labor to achieve a kind of proficiency. Boundless patience, fraught with dry potholes of disappointment along the road. Nor did I ever put on the prophet's cloak.

So I never had to buy a bigger hat because of successes, and with the failures I made do with a new haircut.

I think writing is the only way to live that I have been interested in. Not to liberate my soul or correct any imperfection in an imperfect world. Just for the incredible pleasure of working and the discipline now of daily being surprised at what is happening as I live; so that when the end comes, I shall doubtless be found with my head mashed on the keys of the typewriter.

All I'm trying to say here is that I think the craft of fiction, whether on stage or bookshelves, is just a jigsaw puzzle; and half the fun is doing it, and it's impossible to tell how it will all turn sour. Characters go through one's mind from childhood to what you make them—who dominates and how the story turns out and how it sometimes twists almost away from you. At least, I hope audiences found it interesting.

Donald Ogden Stewart:
Politically Conscious

Interview by Allen Eyles and John Gillett

The son of a judge, Donald Ogden Stewart was born with a silver spoon in his mouth, and he never lost it. He went to Yale and became one of the "in" people as a celebrated humorist in print and lecture appearances; then, entranced by the Hollywood high life, was easily persuaded into a writer's cubicle at the studios, supplying an uncredited polishing job here, a badly needed exit line there, an episode for this, an adaptation of that, and even an occasional original contribution.

Yet his name is enduringly linked with his studies of American high society and his adaptations of Philip Barry plays. And justly so, for it is in these vehicles that he gently pokes fun at the pretensions and attitudes of the rich (a heroine in *Laughter* who is aghast to find herself nearly dancing with the butler). In this way Stewart found a way of expressing his affection for the oddballs, the rebels, and the people who overcame conventional standards in order to achieve liberation and happiness. Working with suitably gentle directors like George Cukor and Harry d'Abbadie D'Arrast, Stewart made his funny characters unusually touching and sensitive.

Beneath the professionally humorous exterior, Stewart was himself keenly sensitive to social concerns, and was among the first in Hollywood to publicly denounce fascism. He subsequently wrote a forthright exposé of fascism's evils, *Keeper of the Flame* (1942), which remains his proudest achievement, and became an unhumbled victim of Hollywood's blacklist. But even in as serious a framework as that of *Keeper of the Flame,* the old joker pops up momentarily as a motorist, finding his car damaged by another driver, says, "Thanks. How much do I owe you for the improvement?"

At seventy-five Stewart wrote his autobiography (*By a Stroke of Luck!*), which he confessed was not very commercial because he liked all of the people in it too much. In this interview he talked about his Hollywood career and about his involvement in politics, which put him on Hollywood's blacklist.

1926   *Brown of Harvard* (Jack Conway). Adaptation.

1930   *Not So Dumb* (King Vidor). Actor.
        Laughter (Harry d'Abbadie D'Arrast). Dialogue.

1931   *Finn and Hattie* (Norman Taurog). Based on his book *Mr. and Mrs. Haddock Abroad.*
        Tarnished Lady (George Cukor). Story, script.
        Rebound (Edward H. Griffith). Play basis, dialogue.

1932   *Smilin' Through* (Sidney Franklin). Co-dialogue.
        Red Dust (Victor Fleming). Uncredited contribution.

1933   *The White Sister* (Victor Fleming). Script.
        Another Language (Edward H. Griffith). Additional dialogue.
        Going Hollywood (Raoul Walsh). Script.

1934   *Dinner at Eight* (George Cukor). Additional dialogue.
        The Barretts of Wimpole Street (Sidney Franklin). Co-script.

1935   *No More Ladies* (Edward H. Griffith). Co-script.

1937   *The Prisoner of Zenda* (John Cromwell). Additional dialogue.

1938   *Holiday* (George Cukor). Co-script.
        Marie Antoinette (W. S. Van Dyke II). Co-script.

1939   *The Women* (George Cukor). Uncredited contribution.
        Love Affair (Leo McCarey). Co-script.
        The Night of Nights (Lewis Milestone). Story, script.

1940   *Kitty Foyle* (Sam Wood). Co-script.
        The Philadelphia Story (George Cukor). Script.
        That Uncertain Feeling (Ernst Lubitsch). Script.
        A Woman's Face (George Cukor). Co-script.
        Smilin' Through (Frank Borzage). Co-script.

1942   *Tales of Manhattan* (Julien Duvivier). Co-script of remake.
        Keeper of the Flame (George Cukor). Script.

Donald Ogden Stewart, in London, England, 1970. (Photo: Allen Eyles)

1945   *Without Love* (Harold S. Bucquet). Script.

1947   *Life with Father* (Michael Curtiz). Script.
        Cass Timberlane (George Sidney). Script.

1949   *Edward, My Son* (George Cukor). Script.

1952   *The Prisoner of Zenda* (Richard Thorpe). Uncredited contri-
        bution to remake.
        Europa 51 (United States: *The Greatest Love*) (Roberto
        Rossellini). English dialogue.

1953   *Melba* (Lewis Milestone). Uncredited contribution.

1955   *Summertime* (David Lean). Uncredited contribution.
        Escapade (Philip Leacock). Script under pseudonym.

1960   *Moment of Danger* (United States: *Malaga*) (Laslo Bene-
        dek). Co-script.

Produced plays include *Los Angeles, Rebound, Fine and Dandy, How
I Wonder, The Kidders,* and *Honor Bright.*

Books include *A Parody Outline of History, Perfect Behavior, Aunt Polly's Story of Mankind, Mr. and Mrs. Haddock Abroad, The Crazy Fool, Fighting Words* (editor), *Mr. and Mrs. Haddock in Paris, France, Father William: A Comedy of Father and Son, Rebound, Exeter Remembered* (contributor), and *By a Stroke of Luck! An Autobiography.*

Academy Awards include an Oscar nomination in 1930–31 for collaborating on the original story of *Laughter* with Harry d'Abbadie D'Arrast and Douglas Doty; a nomination in 1940 for co-writing *Kitty Foyle* with Dalton Trumbo; and an Oscar that same year for writing the screenplay for *The Philadelphia Story.*

I was on a lecture tour in the twenties, and one of my stops was Los Angeles where I had four different lectures at different places. There was a little embarrassment there because it was the same lecture but it had four different titles—I was afraid that people might come to one lecture, then go to one with another title.

One of the titles of the lecture was "Life, Liberty, and the Pursuit of Happiness." It was a horrifying experience at first because I would be introduced (usually it was to women's clubs and in the afternoon) as the funniest man in America or something like that, and I would notice the women in the front two rows suddenly set their jaws determinedly not to laugh. I would fix my attention on them and try to get a laugh and toward the end of the lecture I usually had them loosened up. I'd started in New York and played Chicago and San Francisco on the way out. By the time I got to Los Angeles and Hollywood, it was going pretty well, and I got some of the film people to come to the lecture. That was the way I ran into Mrs. William DeMille, whose husband, of course, was the brother of Cecil and was himself a very fine director; and through her I met Agnes DeMille and got into the film colony. A classmate of mine at Yale named Harry Crocker was working with Charlie Chaplin at that time, and Harry took me out to see King Vidor and Eleanor Boardman. Of course, I fell in love with a star that I had been very fond of on the screen named Patsy Ruth Miller—she was great fun. I'd been going to pictures for a long time, and I met Mabel Normand, Lew Cody, Jack Gilbert, Charlie Ray. It was a wonderful experience, and I was so eager to get back.

I had just published a book called *The Crazy Fool,* and I got King Vidor, and [the director] Jim Cruze, and two or three other people to read it. The next year—I was in Paris, of course (in those days you always went to Paris for the summer!)—I got this marvelous cable saying that MGM was very anxious to do *The Crazy Fool,* and would I come out and do the script? I very eagerly trotted out to Hollywood, and there it was that I found out that King Vidor had taken the wrong book to MGM. He'd taken another book of mine, which had been published a couple of years before, called *Perfect Behavior*. One Sunday at Irving Thalberg's house, he read extracts from this, thinking it was *The Crazy Fool* (or at least Irving thought it was); so they bought it, and I had to go to work on *The Crazy Fool*. That was my first introduction, and actually it was rather typical, because the first picture they asked me to do after that was *Brown of Harvard* [1926] (I happen to be a Yale man). That was the only silent film I ever did. MGM still owns *The Crazy Fool* and they still think it's *Perfect Behavior*. I think they got two or three other writers to work on it and try to make something out of it, but it never became a film.

After I'd done *Brown of Harvard* and I'd met a lot more of my boyhood heroes and heroines, I went back to New York. I'd never written a play, I'd never acted, but a friend of mine who had been at Yale with me, named Philip Barry, had written a play called *Holiday,* which was put on, I think, in the fall of '28. And he'd written a part into it that was a little like me in terms of the "life of the party" part, and he asked me if I'd like to play it. I did and suddenly found myself in a Broadway hit. Katharine Hepburn was just out of Bryn Mawr and was the understudy to Hope Williams, the star, in *Holiday*. The producer Arthur Hopkins had seen her in something else and taken a liking to her. At first, we all rather disapproved of her. She was so fresh and perky, and we made up our minds that, goddammit, she'd never get a chance to play the part if we could help it. So, Hope Williams would be dying of a cold or something, but we'd brace her up and get her onto the stage; so Katie never got to play the part until we went on the road with it, and Hope couldn't make it.

The actual fact was that Phil Barry had written this one part about me, so I could play it alright. And that was also true of the girl who played my wife; she was very wealthy society girl. And Katie was a really good actress, and she must have known instinctively that we were amateurs. Anyway, we disliked her, and then when she went on in *Holiday,* she did it so well. The next year I was by chance in the elevator with Katie; she'd just come up from Washington and had been given a very good part in a play that was trying out, and they'd fired her. Well, she was so damned spunky about it that I sort of fell in love with her then and have been every since. She, I would say, is the best friend I have in the profession.

I wrote my own first play, *Rebound,* which went on, I think, in '29, and I acted in that, too. Then Walter Wanger of Paramount, which then had studios out on Long Island, asked me to do a picture, and I went out there and worked with Harry D'Arrast on *Laughter* [1930].

When I saw it the other day, I found myself, to my surprise, enjoying it, although I hadn't seen it for forty years.

Walter Wanger also wanted me to do a picture for Tallulah Bankhead. I think Tallulah was in his mind as a possible star. I made up a story and did the script. *Tarnished Lady* [1931] was her first picture, and it laid an awful egg. I'm not ashamed of it at all; but it just didn't do Tallulah any good, and it wasn't successful at all. But I'd gotten to know George Cukor through that and liked him and respected him. Later on when he went out to Hollywood, I was out there too. George and I understood each other and respected each other. I've always gotten along very well with directors, and George was one of the best.

Marion Davies and W. R.

I was asked to act in a picture called *Not So Dumb* [1930], directed by King Vidor with Marion Davies as the star. It was my first and only experience as an actor in films. I liked Marion very much indeed. I used to go to what they called the "ranch," which was Mr. Hearst's place, with Jack Gilbert quite a bit; and that was rather a terrifying experience, because if W. R. was not in the right mood everybody would be afraid to say anything. As you probably know, he'd bought a castle in Wales, I think, and had taken it over stone by stone and reconstructed it in California. You were given a room that was full of priceless art treasures, and you also found it very difficult to find the bathroom. I mean, he hadn't brought a bathroom over from Wales; at least he didn't on my first trip there.

It all depended on W. R.'s mood as to whether you had a good meal or not. As a matter of fact, at my first meal there I couldn't quite take just sitting there at a long table silently, wishing that somebody would laugh, so I thought I'd try to make people enjoy it more. I got up and began making a speech about the various art treasures, taking them one by one and showing Mr. Hearst that they weren't really what he thought they were, that they were fakes. And there was a terrible moment of silence. I was dying. Suddenly W. R. laughed very loud and very long, and that encouraged everybody. I never felt so relieved in my life.

I wouldn't say that Marion Davies was a great actress, but she was an awfully good comedienne, and in the picture I wrote for her, *Going Hollywood* [1933], with Bing Crosby, the two of them did a very good job together. She had a real hoydenish, don't-give-a-damn feeling about her, and it came across on the screen. She was a good mimic, and she loved to make fun of people; but mainly she loved to *have* fun.

There was great spirit in her along the fun line, and it was enjoyable to be with her.

Filming the Haddocks

Paramount bought my book, *Mr. and Mrs. Haddock Abroad,* and Joe Mankiewicz did the script. The first thing I knew about it was Joe coming to me to apologize for it because it wasn't *Mr. and Mrs. Haddock Abroad* as I had written it or as I saw it, but largely a vehicle for Leon Errol to do the many very funny things he used to do with his legs and with dialogue. They had just ruined the whole spirit of the Haddocks, and when I saw it I quietly tiptoed out of the theatre.

A Hollywood Contract

My very good agent Leland Hayward got me this job with Metro, and I went out [to Hollywood]. The first thing I did, having acquired a reputation as a humorist because of my books, was *Smilin' Through* [1932], which wasn't exactly a laugh riot. Irving Thalberg needed some help with the dialogue there; they had shot half of it, I think, and I rewrote some of the scenes. That was my first real introduction to Hollywood.

Thalberg and Selznick

Thalberg was younger than any of us, but he became sort of a father figure to us. There was an Irving Thalberg stable, and I was very fortunate to become one of its members. I learned a great deal not only about screenwriting but about play writing from Irving. He would never praise you. You would take a scene into him and he'd read it and then the best he would ever say to you was: "Hmmm . . . not bad." He could remember every scene he'd ever seen in pictures, and with that memory he would make suggestions for your own scenes or he would be able to judge them. He was the only producer that I worked for that I could say was also a creative person.

I don't think David Selznick was in a class with Irving Thalberg. He was the kind of producer who would shoot everything and then really begin making the picture in the cutting-room—quite an expensive process, but with David it seemed to work. He was alright to work with. He gave me credit on *Dinner at Eight* [1934], when all I did was about a week's work of dialogue or scenes—just polishing—and it was very nice of him to give me that credit. But he was a terribly overbearing person. He was *right,* and you weren't supposed to argue with him. I can remember one scene in, I think it was *The Prisoner of Zenda* [1937], when I suddenly became aware that David was telling *me* about the characters, and by that time I'd had quite a lot of experience. Irving Thalberg never did that. Irving would help you, encourage you: "No, this isn't it, try it again." But David was a much more overriding sort of personality. I know I ended up without much respect for him compared to what I felt for Irving Thalberg.

F. Scott Fitzgerald

When Scott Fitzgerald and I worked together a year or so before Scott died—he was writing *The Last Tycoon*—I remember we talked about Thalberg a great deal, because Scott had worked with Irving too. We were writing the screenplay for *The Women* [1939]; we didn't get the credit. They gave it to someone else after Scott and I had worked on the picture. I had known Scott two or three years before I became a writer. I was working up in Minneapolis with the American Telephone and Telegraph Company—this was right after I graduated from Yale. We both lived in St. Paul, and we got to know each other quite well; and the next year or so he exploded into greatness with *This Side of Paradise.* By that time I was—as most Yale men were—in the bond business, and I got fired because I wasn't very good at it. I went to New York to try to get some kind of a job, and Scott sent me round to *Vanity Fair.* I was going to get a job in the advertising department. Edmund Wilson was the editor, and he asked me to write something just to see if he could send me to the advertising department; and I wrote a parody of Scott. To my amazement they bought it; and it was as casually as that that I became a writer.

Career Technique

In those days the first thing you had to learn as a writer, if you wanted to get screen credit, was to hold off until you knew when they were going to have to start shooting. Then, your agent would suggest you might be able to help. The producers had the theory that the more writers they had to work on the scripts, the better the scripts would be. It was the third or fourth writer that always got the screen credit. It wasn't beyond you to try to possibly screw up another writer's script so that your script would come through at the end. It became a game to be the last one before they started shooting so that you would not be eased out of the screen credit. They thought that if you did a script too quickly, it couldn't be very good. The plot was not to be too quick. They were paying you a marvelous salary; if you took three or four months over it, that would impress them. There was a general feeling that the more money spent, the better the script must be.

Pride in the Work

You became quite proud of being a good screenwriter in the same way that—I think it was Lewis Milestone who said it—a machine-gunner, who, for instance, didn't like being a soldier in the army killing people but was interested in his craft. I got terribly interested in becoming a good screenwriter and worked terribly hard at it. The competition was very great. You couldn't make mistakes because there were other writers waiting to step in and fix your script up the way you were fixing somebody else's. One of the first things you had to learn was to not let them break your heart, because if you really put yourself into a script and began creating and caring terribly about it, then the producer, the director, and the star would go to work on it; and they would break your heart with what they would do to something you were very proud of. Cukor would always ask me if I liked this or that. We had a good partnership. Every once in a while George would ask me to come down on the set to see how it was sounding, but most directors wouldn't do that.

On *A Woman's Face* [1941] they got Albert Bassermann, who was one of the big German stars, and it was an important part yet a small one, so I took care to get just the right words. I didn't know he didn't speak any English at all. So I went down on the set to see how it was coming. They pointed over in the corner, and he had another German with him and he was learning my lines by heart. He didn't have the least idea what they meant, he just learned them. When he played the part, he almost stole the picture—somehow it worked to have him sing these speeches, although I thought they should have had John Barrymore to bring the right emphasis to the verb and the noun. Otherwise, I didn't really go on the set. Generally, you were working on another script by that time. They weren't crazy about having writers come around, especially with any suggestions.

I worked with [the writers] Ernest Vajda and Claudine West; I think we did three pictures together. They were great favorites of Sidney Franklin. We did *The Barretts of Wimpole Street* [1934]; and we worked especially hard on *Marie Antoinette* [1938], and then they turned it over to Woody Van Dyke. I think we worked two or three years on that. I got screen credit. I don't know what Van Dyke did to it, but I think there was only one line of mine in the whole picture. It certainly didn't have the Cukor touch.

It hurt terribly to have done what you thought was a very good scene and then to find that Lana Turner didn't like it very much, so they'd have you rewrite it the way Lana Turner wanted it to be. The one trouble, at first, with *Cass Timberlane* [1947] was Lana. Spencer Tracy was a terribly professional actor who worked on the script and knew it by heart, and Lana'd come onto the set not having the foggiest idea what the thing was about, not knowing the lines or anything. Spencer was very angry during the first couple of weeks. Then it got better, and at the end he said: "That is a good actress." She got his respect eventually, and I think *Cass* was quite a good picture. She had quite a lot of influence with the producer, in terms of her not liking a certain scene or something like that, which is always irritating to a writer.

The Hays Office

You had, of course, to write with an eye on the Hays Office. There was one scene in *Love Affair* [1939] in which Irene Dunne met Charles Boyer on a boat, but before she met Boyer she had lived with another man. The Hays Office had the ethical or moral code of the Catholic Church as one of its guidelines, and in that code, if you sinned, you had to pay for it; and that payment had to be on the screen. If you'd sinned before the picture even started and the audience knew about it, then you had to pay. So Irene and Boyer were going to meet on top of the Empire State Building, and it came back from the censors that she had to atone for this previous affair before she achieved the bliss of marriage to Boyer. So they suggested that I have her run over by a truck on her way to the Empire State Building; and that's what happened, she never got to the top. You dissolved to her in a hospital with her realizing that God hadn't wanted her to meet Boyer until she was sorry for what she had done before. So finally she married Boyer, and all came out well.

In *The Philadelphia Story* [1940] Katie Hepburn had a swimming pool in her place, and it came back from the Hays Office that they were worried about the nude statues around the swimming pool—they must not be unusually exciting; the angles on the statues had to be such that they didn't show certain parts. In *The Prisoner of Zenda*

A scene from Donald Ogden Stewart's Oscar-winning adaptation of Philip Barry's The Philadelphia Story, *with Cary Grant, Katharine Hepburn, and James Stewart.*

Ronald Colman looked exactly like the Englishman *and* the king—of Ruritania, I think it was—and the reason he did look like that king was that three hundred years ago his great, great grandmother had been rather naughty with a king of Ruritania. Well, the censors said that would never do, and so I put it in the script that she had died in childbirth—that took care of the sin that had been committed. You would learn to put in four or five incidents or bits of dialogue that they could take out so that they would let you leave in other things. You didn't make a deal with them, but they wouldn't want to take out too much; so you'd give the Hays Office five things to take out to satisfy them and you'd get away with murder with what they left in.

An Oscar

Getting an Oscar for *The Philadelphia Story* was the easiest Oscar that you could imagine. All I had to do was get out of the way (which was one of the things to learn in screenwriting). A lot of writers worked to improve a very good novel or play, and it was quite a thing to learn to appreciate what the original author had done and let that come through. *The Philadelphia Story* was such a good vehicle, and Katharine had played it in New York. They had made a recording of it in the theatre with all the laughs, you see, and they'd play this for me; and if I hadn't included a laugh that was in the play I'd have to go back and do it again. I was really writing against a tape recorder.

A Political Awakening

From about 1930 on (when sound came in), I was out in Hollywood at least half of each year, and I hadn't the foggiest idea about politics. At Yale I had taken a course in economics in which it was proven to me that socialism wouldn't work. That seemed to me to be the answer; at least I never disputed that. And then came 1929 and the Depression began. It didn't affect Hollywood at all as far as income was concerned. That is, more and more people wanted to go to the movies and forget, and Hollywood manufactured dreams to help the box office. There wasn't any connection between the Hollywood I was living in and the world itself, politically there wasn't any reality.

I remember Upton Sinclair ran for governor of California, and Louis B. Mayer, the head of MGM, was a staunch Republican and friend of Herbert Hoover, and a lot of us were asked to donate a certain portion of our salary to defeat Upton Sinclair. Of course, we didn't like to refuse. I know that, later, on account of the Depression, we were asked up to L. B. Mayer's office one by one. When I was summoned to the throne, I came into the room and L. B. began to cry behind his desk. "It's this Depression; it's just terrible, isn't it?" he said. And I said, "Why, yes I suppose it is." He said, "Don, I'm gonna have to ask a terrific favor of you. To help us out, I'm gonna have to ask you to take a cut in your salary." And he began to cry again. I said, "Well, L. B., for heaven's sake . . . I'm very glad to be able to help," and so forth. And politically that was about as far as I was knowledgeable. That was the cause, incidentally, of the big fight later between Thalberg and Mayer, because the only person they found out who didn't take a cut was L. B. Mayer. When Thalberg called him on that, there was a big fight; and I think Irving went to the South of France—walked completely out of the studio.

Little by little, some of us began to feel . . . partly guilt, I suppose; but we wanted to do something. We became, as they said, "politically conscious." And by the next time I went out to Hollywood, they were organizing the Hollywood Anti-Nazi League. This was in '35 and Hitler had come to power. I worked with the people at the head of the

League—there was Dorothy Parker, Oscar Hammerstein, Freddie March and his wife, Herbert Biberman, and other people. And we really got Hollywood politically connected with the world for almost the first time. We would have very good speakers come out—senators and so on—and [André] Malraux came out and spoke.

The Anti-Nazi League got up a meeting, and we read Irwin Shaw's *Bury the Dead,* which had just come out. It was very anti-war. Irving Thalberg sent the story editor round. He said, "Close the door" and "Irving won't like it if you take a part in this." And Irving in high school in Brooklyn had been a boy socialist, gone out on the corner, and made speeches. But this was something else—he didn't want his dear writer to get involved. But I did. I was in awfully good company. Freddie March and Florence Eldridge read the play and I was emcee. It was a marvelous evening; everybody was beautifully worked up and collections were big. Most of the big stars ducked any commitment; Freddie and Florence were very brave.

Most of the writers were with us, and the producers at first were very anxious to help us—especially the Warner brothers. We got going quite well; we had five or six thousand members. The Warner brothers did one or two quite good anti-fascist pictures, and Harry Warner kept letting us use his radio station, KFWB, once a week. Jack wasn't quite as brave as that, but he did let me do *Life with Father.*

The fear of communism began to go around—that the Anti-Nazi League was run by Communists. There were Communists in Hollywood, and they did a lot of the work. But if you were a premature anti-fascist, you were in trouble eventually because the war hadn't broken out and here you were being politically active. When I was working on the picture [*The Women*] with Scott Fitzgerald around '38 or '39, a congressman named Martin Dies, who was head of the House Un-American Activities Committee, attacked the Hollywood Anti-Nazi League over a coast-to-coast hook-up. We were given the same time to reply, and I replied to Martin Dies. Scott and I talked over my speech before I made it. It was politically valuable for a man like Dies to point his finger at Freddie March and various Hollywood figures because he got the front page every time. McCarthy later on built up quite a reputation doing this.

Most of the producers moved out; they didn't want Martin Dies after them. But if you would have been at any of our meetings or heard our speeches, it was really good, American anti-fascism. It was a terribly unfair attack on Hollywood for political purposes. That, in a way, was Hollywood's finest hour. We were trying to prepare America for an understanding of what was going on in Germany and in Italy

"Hollywood's finest hour": Donald Ogden Stewart with Dorothy Parker, before a political benefit in Hollywood, 1936. Later, both were blacklisted.

(because Mussolini had just come in), and then the Spanish Civil War was just starting.

And so a great many of us got politically involved. All of us were eventually asked by the producers to, as they called it, "clear ourselves"—to give the names of people you'd worked with, people you knew were Communists, and so forth. Some did; some didn't. We had a lot of people like grips, electricians, and prop boys working with us, and it meant their jobs. What they wanted you to say was that you'd been duped into this Communist plot, which was a lot of nonsense.

I remember working with [the director] Leo McCarey on *Love Affair*. Leo was very great fun to be with; he just had this Catholic anti-communism thing. He almost devoted his life to destroying communism if he could. I wouldn't say he asked me to dinner or anything like that, but he "needed" me on *Love Affair*. For the protection of American ideals, there was some society they got up—John Lee Mahin, Jim McGuinness, two or three others, and Leo. And they hated our anti-Nazi guts. I think it was Leo's Catholicism. I liked the guy; he had a great sense of humor.

Keeper of the Flame [1942] is the picture that I'm proudest of having been connected with—in terms of saying the most about fascism that it was possible to say in Hollywood. It was a very good novel about the possibility of fascism in America—a dictator taking over—and I didn't change it much. We had to keep it concealed from Mr. Mayer; it wasn't what you'd call a Republican picture. There is a story that he hadn't seen *Keeper of the Flame*. The first time he saw it was in Radio City in New York, and he was so angry at the message of the picture that he got up and walked out. I can't vouch for that story, but I'd be very happy if it was true.

It was just after *Edward, My Son* [1949] that I got knocked off. They were beginning to close in on me then. We came over [to England] to see the play, and I did the screenplay. You could say that they sent me over to get away from being subpoenaed, but I did go back and wasn't subpoenaed. I don't know how close I came to it, because I came over in '51 and never went back and that was because I'd written a play called *The Kidders*, which was going to be put on over here.

There is a story about Sam Goldwyn. I was in Sam Goldwyn's office one morning, and he was furious at an actor. Sam really let go at him: "You so and so, so and so. I don't ever want to see you again—unless I need you." Now they needed me, I suppose, at least until '49. At that time I had a very good contract and it was good for two or three more years and I had been of use to them. Then, I was asked to come down and see the legal department, and they told me I had to clear myself. And I just didn't. It wasn't bravery or anything at all. I felt and still feel so very proud of those years with the Anti-Nazi League, and to say that I'd been duped into that was just not true. So that was the end of my Hollywood career.

Bibliographic Notes

Charles Bennett will prove an elusive figure if pursued in most Hollywood memoirs or general histories. Most of the principal studies of Hitchcock ignore him altogether or afford him only fleeting mention. Donald Spoto, in his revisionist *The Dark Side of Genius: The Life of Alfred Hitchcock* (Boston: Little, Brown, 1983), makes use of Bennett's perspective where convenient. Eric Rohmer and Claude Chabrol make a rare complimentary reference to Bennett, with interesting supporting detail (this is the source, for example, that attributes to Bennett the premise of *Saboteur*) in their monograph *Hitchcock: The First Forty-Four Films* (New York: Frederick Ungar, 1979). The British Film Institute pamphlet on the partnership of Sidney Gilliat and Frank Launder tends to line up with Bennett on the subject of Hitchcock, but as to their own give-and-take (they were good friends and share a credit on at least one early British talkie), they are unspecific. Bennett is noted unimportantly in Cecil B. DeMille's memoirs (it would be uncharacteristic of DeMille to cite a writer) and is overlooked in the published memos of David O. Selznick (*Memos from David O. Selznick,* edited by Rudy Behlmer. New York: Viking, 1972).

Interestingly, Jesse Lasky, Jr., whose own involvement as a co-writer with Bennett is minimized in the Bennett interview, offers a counterview in his autobiography, *Whatever Happened to Hollywood?* Whereas Bennett insists that Lasky contributed only scant dialogue to the movies for Hitchcock (in England) and DeMille (in the United States), Lasky says Bennett fell short on the actual writing. Describing a flamboyantly theatrical story conference in DeMille's office in the 1940s, Lasky offers a colorful anecdote about Bennett's ability to mesmerize directors with his storytelling. The script under discussion was for *Reap the Wild Wind*. To DeMille's delight, Bennett acted out riotous impersonations of Raymond Massey's heavy, Paulette Goddard's Florida belle,

Ray Milland's effete aristocrat, and the jaw-jutting John Wayne. Lasky adds flatly, "But too often his [Bennett's] office performances were better than the scenes themselves. The written word missed the swaggerings, struttings, eye-rollings of our spellbinding Charles. DeMille would complain that we hadn't got it on paper, quite ignoring the fact that this would have been next to impossible" (p. 217).

In the 1970s Bennett hooked up with the critic-editor Danny Peary and appeared as an essayist in several of Peary's off-beat film article anthologies. He was usually called on to critique his own work directly or obliquely. In Peary's *Close-Ups,* a volume with pieces written by a number of old-time screenwriters, Bennett comments on his relationships with Laurence Olivier and Peter Lorre. In Peary's subsequent *Cult Movies 2* (New York: Dell, 1983), sequel to an earlier book, Bennett writes about his *Curse of the Demon.* In Peary's *Omni's Screen Flights/Screen Fantasies* (Garden City, N.Y.: Double-day, 1984), he is among the stellar list of contributors discoursing on his own late-career forays into the science fiction genre.

W. R. Burnett is mentioned only in passing in the reminiscences of his principal directors, in published interviews with Howard Hawks and William Wyler, and in the autobiographies of Raoul Walsh, William Wellman, and Mervyn LeRoy. Edward G. Robinson, whose early friendship with Bennett cooled in later years, mentions the writer fondly in his autobiography, *All My Yesterdays* (New York: Hawthorn Books, 1973), a memoir that is unusually attentive to writers, perhaps because Robinson fancied himself one and per-haps because his collaborator on the book was the playwright-screenwriter Leonard Spigelgass. In his autobiography, *An Open Book,* John Huston writes at length about Burnett, about their collaboration as screenwriters, and about Burnett's merit as a novelist. They had a lifelong mutual admiration.

In his autobiography, *My First Hundred Years in Hollywood* (New York: Random House, 1964), Jack Warner, the mogul to whom Burnett devoted much of his screenwriting career, has glowing words for the hard-boiled author and contradicts him on one essential point. In his interview Burnett says Warner bought *Little Caesar* only because its protagonist hailed from Youngs-town, Ohio, boyhood home of the Warners. Warner says, on the contrary, he bought it because it was one of the few books he ever read cover to cover, for he was stuck on an overnight train without anything to read.

Burnett is most problematic when he discusses Hollywood politics or American-style Communism, a subject that became more of a bogey for him over the years. Indeed, the anti-hero of *High Sierra* (the novel, not the movie) talks with some sympathy and fascination about Communism, while a decade later the doomed Arky of his novel *Little Men, Big World* seems obsessed with expounding on the iniquity of Reds. Certainly Burnett is off when he alleges Sam Jaffe was a Communist. Although blacklisted and a pronounced Actors Equity activist, Jaffe was never a member of the Communist Party. His re-marks about the attempts of Alvah Bessie (one of the jailed Hollywood Ten) to recruit him into the Hollywood section of the Party were rebutted by Bessie

in a letter to *Film Comment:* "I believe I met him [Burnett] on one or two occasions. I cannot recall a single conversation we ever had on *any* subject. But I am certain I *never* tried to 'recruit him into the Communist Party' in the days I was doing such things forty years ago. He was scarcely the type. It was kind of him to think I was (or *say* I was) 'a pretty good guy.' How did he know?"

Ironically, although Burnett gripes about losing the sole credit on *Action in the North Atlantic,* he seems in other situations to have benefited from the largesse of Hollywood leftists, who did not regard him as a particular enemy or threat. The writer Albert Maltz (another of the Hollywood Ten) said that when he collaborated with Burnett on *This Gun for Hire,* the collaboration amounted to this: Maltz wrote the script alone; when it was completed he sent it upstairs to Burnett's office; whereupon it was returned, with Burnett's stamp of approval. They shared screenplay credit, but, according to Maltz, Burnett did not feel compelled to add a single word.

Niven Busch receives scant appraisal in the usual director autobiographies—those of King Vidor, Raoul Walsh, William Wyler, Tay Garnett, and Edward Dmytryk, all of whom were indebted to his stories—or in the memos of David O. Selznick, whose crowning effort was Busch's *Duel in the Sun.* On the other hand, Busch's version of the writing of *The Crowd Roars* is disputed by co-writer John Bright in *Cagney: The Actor as Auteur* by Patrick McGilligan (San Diego: Oak Tree, 1982), where Bright recounts his falling-out with director Howard Hawks but avers that most of the structure and dialogue of the film belong to him and his writing partner Kubec Glasmon.

The indispensable biography of **James M. Cain** is by Roy Hoopes (*Cain*), and it borrows heavily from the interview in this book to report on Cain's extensive stay in Hollywood. Although Cain's name pops up in many books about New York journalism or about *The New Yorker,* he seems to have kept a low profile as a screenwriter in Hollywood. His political activity while writing screenplays and his championing of the American Authors Authority Plan has invited more scrutiny and is examined in Nancy Lynn Schwartz's *The Hollywood Writers' Wars* and Larry Ceplair and Steven Englund's *The Inquisition in Hollywood: Politics in the Film Community, 1930–1960.*

For someone whose career as a writer spanned five decades, **Lenore Coffee** might as well have been invisible for all the attention she attracts in Hollywood histories. She is not cited in Cecil B. DeMille's autobiography nor in DeMille's brother William's, although in an interesting unauthorized account of C. B.'s relationships with his staff, particularly writers, she is included. In fact, the author Phil A. Koury (*Yes, Mr. DeMille*) notes that DeMille wanted to film Coffee's Nativity parable, *Family Portrait,* but backed off when church groups protested. Apparently, Coffee herself was unaware of this.

In published interviews director King Vidor has spoken deprecatingly of his two Coffee-scripted films for Warner Brothers, *Beyond the Forest* and *Light-*

ning Strikes Twice, indicating he was forced to accept the producer Henry Blanke's undiscriminating preference for women writers. Edward Dmytryk, who directed Coffee's version of Graham Greene's *The End of the Affair,* says in his autobiography (*It's a Hell of a Life, But Not a Bad Living* [New York: New York Times Books, 1978]) that Coffee's script was filmed as written; disputing Coffee, he says there was no rewriting in England. However, Dmytryk admits he was pressed for time in the cutting-room and therefore edited the story in a confusing fashion.

Of parenthetical interest to anyone tracing Coffee's life is the Hollywood novel, called *Reruns* (New York: Viking Press, 1981), written by her daughter Sabina Thorne.

Of **Philip Dunne**'s screenplay for *How Green Was My Valley,* the director John Ford told Peter Bogdanovich (*John Ford* [Berkeley: University of California Press, 1968]): "We stuck pretty close to it. There may have been a few things added, but that's what a director is for" (p. 80). Alternatively, in his authorized biography by Kenneth L. Geist (*Pictures Will Talk: The Life and Films of Joseph L. Mankiewicz*), the writer-director-producer Joseph L. Mankiewicz quarrels with Dunne's recollections of aspects of the three movies they collaborated on and provides details of the filming of *The Late George Apley* (1947), based on John P. Marquand's novel as dramatized by George S. Kaufman in the form of a diary; *The Ghost and Mrs. Muir* (1947), from the novel by R. A. Dick; and *Escape* (1948), an update of the 1926 John Galsworthy play.

An intimate of Nunnally Johnson's, Dunne is acknowledged in anecdotes and interviews in the three books pertaining to Johnson's life: *The Letters of Nunnally Johnson,* edited by Doris Johnson and Ellen Leventhal; *Flashback: Nora Johnson on Nunnally Johnson* by Nora Johnson; and *Screenwriter: The Life and Times of Nunnally Johnson* by Tom Stempel.

Appropriately, considering his lifelong liberal activism, Philip Dunne's own autobiography is subtitled *A Life in Movies and Politics.* His strenuous political work in Hollywood commands notice in the Nancy Schwartz history of the Guild, the Ceplair-Englund history of left-liberal agitation in the film industry, as well as in many general accounts of Hollywood ferment of the period.

Julius J. Epstein and his brother are referred to in innumerable Hollywood texts but usually as resident examples of wit and smart-aleck humor. In their respective memoirs, Bette Davis (*Mother Goddam,* by Whitney Stine with Bette Davis [New York: Hawthorn Books, 1974]) and James Cagney (*Cagney by Cagney* [New York: Doubleday, 1976]) go out of their way to pay obeisance to the Epsteins—high tribute from two normally ornery top Warners stars. Cagney, who makes a point of belittling most Warners writers in his autobiography, substantiates the Epsteins' work on *The Strawberry Blonde* and *Yankee Doodle Dandy,* two of his favorite pictures. They wrote for him "under the table" on at least one additional occasion—for *The Time of Your Life.*

Howard Koch's two books (*Casablanca: Script and Legend* and *As Time*

Goes By: Memoirs of a Writer) only serve to deepen the mystery of the writing of *Casablanca*. In his autobiography (*Starmaker* by Hal Wallis and Charles Higham [New York: Macmillan, 1980]), the producer Hal Wallis calls the Epsteins "very gifted" but contends that Koch was engaged in writing an "alternate screenplay" even when they were on the job. In her memoir (*My Story* by Ingrid Bergman and Alan Burgess [New York: Delacorte, 1980]), the actress Ingrid Bergman hints that Wallis did not cosy up to the Epsteins because they, in turn, did not get along with him. Indeed, in an unpublished portion of our interview, Julius J. Epstein made it clear that when it came to Warners producers, the Epsteins preferred the cultivated Henry Blanke.

Julius J. Epstein and Philip G. Epstein also crop up in the various chronicles of the blacklist era, for they were instrumental figures in the short-lived Committee for the First Amendment and were, for a short spell, themselves in danger of being "gray-listed."

As a solo act, Julius J. Epstein is discussed for his part in writing *Fanny* in the first volume of the writer-director-producer Josh Logan's memoirs, *Movie Stars, Real People, and Me*. Also, Epstein wound up writing the first draft of *Cross of Iron* for director Sam Peckinpah—strange bedfellows, to say the least—and the resulting embroglio is reported on in *Peckinpah: A Portrait in Montage* by Garner Simmons (Austin: University of Texas Press, 1982).

The MGM stable of directors may have been indebted to elegant writers such as **Frances Goodrich** and **Albert Hackett,** but they go unappreciated in most reminiscences. W. S. Van Dyke II, George Cukor, Rouben Mamoulian, Tay Garnett, Vincente Minnelli—each in turn submitted memoirs or published interviews without devoting much space to the Hacketts. In *Hollywood Director* by David Chierichetti (New York: Curtis Books, 1973), director Mitchell Leisen makes the rare complaint about their work, excoriating the duo for their script of *Lady in the Dark*, which was so off the mark, according to Leisen, that he had to toss it in the wastebasket and rewrite it (with the uncredited help of Catherine Turney) (pp. 195–96). (This is not an unusual boast for Leisen.) As for *It's a Wonderful Life,* Frank Capra, in his autobiography, *The Name Above the Title* (New York: Macmillan, 1971), dubs the Hacketts "perceptive, human writers." But Capra had to part ways with them, because "the Hacketts were writing some bright, sensitive scenes, but why didn't the scenes move me? I sat down and wrote some key scenes. The Hacketts melded them with their own. I had the script I wanted" (pp. 376–77). Before the Hacketts, Dalton Trumbo, Marc Connelly, and Clifford Odets had taken a crack at the Philip Van Doren Stern short story.

Incidentally, when Leo C. Rosten polled the film community in 1938 regarding the most admired screenwriters in Hollywood, the Hacketts placed among the top ten. The others were: Dudley Nichols, Robert Riskin, Donald Ogden Stewart, Claude Binyon, Ben Hecht, Lillian Hellman, John Lee Mahin, Jo Swerling, and Nunnally Johnson. The Hacketts, according to their contemporaries, were among the best-known, best-liked, and most accomplished screenwriters. They are key sources for Sheila Graham's *The Garden of Allah* and for Nancy Schwartz's history of the Guild struggle, in which they provide a non-Communist, left-wing perspective on Hollywood politics. Both books reward the reading.

For someone so patently reluctant to be interviewed on-the-record (before our session, **Norman Krasna** had written to me several times to beg off, saying he only had stupid things to utter nowadays), Norman Krasna seems ubiquitous in the memoirs of his peers. In his many books, essays, and volumes of letters, Groucho Marx refers often to Krasna, his lifelong carousing buddy and occasional collaborator. Krasna is noted in Garson Kanin's deceptively entertaining *Hollywood* and in *Hollywood Director* (the oral history of Mitchell Leisen) by David Chierichetti (New York: Curtis Books, 1973). He is observed by Josh Logan in the second installment of his recollections, *Josh: My Up and Down, In and Out Life.* (Logan, who directed two Krasna stage plays, *John Loves Mary* and *Kind Sir,* does not spare the bouquets. Of *Kind Sir,* the legit forerunner of *Indiscreet,* he writes, "It had all of the craftsmanship of the best Pinero farce—plus the charm and elegance of something by Lonsdale or Maugham.")

In Peter Bogdanovich's *Fritz Lang in America* (New York: Praeger, 1967), director Lang duly acknowledges Krasna for the inventive screen stories of *Fury* and *You and Me.* Although Lang says the *Fury* screenplay was developed largely by the writer Bartlett Cormack, elsewhere (in *The Celluloid Muse: Hollywood Directors Speak* by Charles Higham and Joel Greenberg [New York: New American Library, 1972]—which contains a lot of embellishment about *Fury* and *You and Me*) he remembers that he and Krasna also worked together on the script. Krasna himself made no such claims. In *Pictures Will Talk* by Kenneth Geist, Joseph L. Mankiewicz, then a staff producer at MGM, reserves for himself a bit of the glory for having fleshed out the story of *Fury.*

Two articles worth further reading: "I Was the Man Who Made the Starshine" by Larry Engleman in the November 1983 issue of *Los Angeles* magazine, a profile of Hubert Voight, head of the Warners publicity department during Krasna's term there in the early 1930s; and Krasna's own sardonic reflections on the making of *The Devil and Miss Jones,* published at the time of the film's release in *The New York Times* ("Some Authors Die Happy" by Norman Krasna, May 18, 1941, Drama Section); the latter is a reminder that Krasna was not always as happy with his filmed scripts as, under the influence of pragmatism and nostalgia, he later claimed to be.

Although for the most part **John Lee Mahin** managed to keep a low profile in Hollywood, he is discussed fondly in *Pappy: The Life of John Ford* by Dan Ford (Englewood Cliffs, N.J.: Prentice-Hall, 1979), and by John Huston in his autobiography, *An Open Book.* Mahin's uncredited work is intriguing. For additional information on his contribution to *Gone with the Wind, Scarlett, Rhett, and a Cast of Thousands* by Roland Flamini (New York: Macmillan, 1975) is recommended. For material on his participation in *The Wizard of Oz,* see *The Making of the Wizard of Oz* by Ajean Harmetz (New York: Knopf, 1977). In his biography (Dunne, 1980) Joseph L. Mankiewicz describes his and

Mahin's imposed ending on the original screenplay of *Woman of the Year,* the reasons behind it, and the opposition of the writers Michael Kanin and Ring Lardner, Jr., and of Katharine Hepburn.

Additionally, Mahin did work for the military during World War II that he did not care to elaborate on. Ironically, one of his last uncredited writing stints may have been for the funeral of Louis B. Mayer in 1957: Mahin was one of three former MGM stalwarts who stepped forward to concoct the eulogy delivered by Spencer Tracy. The other two were Carey Wilson and David O. Selznick.

Mahin's political troublemaking in Hollywood has proved more enticing to historians, partly because Mahin is one of the few articulate, self-avowed right wingers to have spoken out in defense of his activities. He looms in most examinations of the political strife—the Nancy Schwartz book and the Ceplair-Englund account—as one of the "Four Horsemen" of MGM, the leaders of the conservative writers who mounted an inside attack against the progressive wing, cheered on the blacklist, and in many cases individually profited by their fealty to the studios.

The career of **Richard Maibaum** is touched on in several books. In *Mank: The Wit, World, and Life of Herman Mankiewicz,* Richard Merryman offers a contrary version of the collaboration between Mankiewicz and Maibaum on the writing of *Pride of the Yankees.* The Mitchell Leisen biography by Chierichetti, *Hollywood Director,* attributes numerous production modifications to Leisen and downplays Maibaum's input as writer or producer on the five pictures on which they were associated. The writer-director Bryan Forbes recalls working with Maibaum on the Warwick films in the 1950s in *Notes for a Life* (New York: Stein and Day, 1974). *Hollywood UK: The British Film Industry in the Sixties* by Alexander Walker provides an account of Maibaum's continuing presence in England on the Bond films. And *The James Bond Films* by Steven Jay Rubin (New York: Arlington House, 1983) is a sort of unofficial record of the Bond series, with much inside dope and privy detail. Interestingly, considering Maibaum's credentials as a staunch liberal, there is a political attack from the right on the Bond themes, "Updating James Bond" by Richard Grenier, in the June 1981 issue of *Commentary.* Maibaum penned a fierce reply, but it was never published.

Casey Robinson is an aloof figure who avoided controversy (except in the case of *Casablanca*) and the publicity columns. The producer Hal Wallis hails him as "one of my favorite writers" in *Starmaker,* providing details of their long, fruitful association. Wallis verifies that Robinson did some spit-and-polish on *Casablanca* (according to the producer, Robinson built up the Paul Henreid character of the underground leader). Elsewhere, Bette Davis praises him in her autobiography, *Mother Goddam.* Robinson himself wrote about Gregory Peck for Danny Peary's *Close-Ups.* Otherwise, there is very little in the archives on this writer, whose career bridged the silents in Hollywood and the "new wave" in Australia.

The definitive reference on **Allan Scott** is Arlene Croce's marvelous paean to Astaire and Rogers, *The Fred Astaire and Ginger Rogers Book* (New York: Outerbridge and Lazard, 1972), for which Scott functioned as an interview source. The screenwriter of six Astaire-Rogers vehicles—and *Let's Dance* [1949], another Astaire trifle with Betty Hutton—is named only once in Fred Astaire's autobiography, *Steps in Time* (New York: Harper and Bros., 1959). Scott penned nostalgic profiles of Ginger Rogers and Claudette Colbert for Danny Peary's *Close-Ups*.

It may be that no one has passed through life, much less Hollywood, who was as sociable, well respected, and genuinely popular as **Donald Ogden Stewart.** Invariably, he is cited in biographies of friends and acquaintances with sparkling anecdotes of his prankish wit and imperturbable good nature. He is to be found in books about Broadway, the Algonquin Circle, New York in the 1920s, Paris in the 1920s, Hearst, Hemingway, Fitzgerald, and so on.

As a screenwriter he fared no less amiably—before the blacklist, that is. He is affectionately recalled by King Vidor in his autobiography, *A Tree is a Tree* (New York: Harcourt, Brace, 1953), by Joseph L. Mankiewicz in his *Pictures Will Talk,* and by George Cukor in his interview session with Gavin Lambert, *On Cukor* (New York: Capricorn Books, 1973). (In Higham and Greenberg's *The Celluloid Muse,* Cukor allows that, although a dozen screenwriters were enmeshed in *A Woman's Face* for Garbo, Stewart's "was the script we shot" [p. 64]. In the same volume, Lewis Milestone makes an identical claim for Stewart's involvement in the *Night of Nights* [p. 182]. Thus, Stewart was evidently one of those rare screenwriters who managed to please most directors as much as he pleased himself.)

The blacklist, for all intents and purposes, terminated Stewart's happy career. An officer of anti-fascist organizations in Hollywood, Stewart is accounted for in the Schwartz story of the emerging Guild, in the Ceplair-Englund history of Hollywood progressivism, in books about the blacklist, and in various autobiographical writings of the blacklist victims—notably Dalton Trumbo's biography (*Dalton Trumbo* by Bruce Cook) and collection of letters (*Additional Dialogue: Letters of Dalton Trumbo, 1942–1962,* ed. Helen Manfull) and Hy Kraft's neglected *On My Way to the Theatre*. He plays a role in the memorial of Garbo's principal screenwriter, Salka Viertel (*The Kindness of Strangers*), who was herself blacklisted and forced to flee to Europe, and in whose salon in Hollywood during the troubled 1930s and 1940s art and politics mingled.

Select Bibliography

Screenplays, screenwriting, and screenwriters are examined in any number of valuable books. This reading list is limited to biographies, autobiographies, career studies, or general histories of the screenwriting profession.

Abbott, George. *Mister Abbott.* New York: Random House, 1963.

Avery, Laurence G. *Dramatist in America: Letters of Maxwell Anderson, 1912–1958.* Chapel Hill: University of North Carolina Press, 1977.

Baxter, John. *The Hollywood Exiles.* New York: Taplinger, 1976.

Beach, Rex. *Personal Exposures.* New York: Harper and Bros., 1941.

Behrman, S. N. *People in a Diary: A Memoir.* Boston: Little, Brown, 1972.

Bentley, Eric, ed. *Thirty Years of Treason: Excerpts from Hearings Before the House Committee on Un-American Activities, 1938–1968.* New York: Viking, 1971.

Bercovici, Konrad. *It's the Gypsy in Me.* New York: Prentice-Hall, 1941.

Bessie, Alvah. *Inquisition in Eden.* New York: Macmillan, 1965.

Bishop, James Alonzo. *The Mark Hellinger Story.* New York: Appleton-Century-Crofts, 1952.

Blotner, Joseph. *Faulkner: A Biography.* New York: Random House, 1974.

Blotner, Joseph, ed. *Selected Letters of William Faulkner.* New York: Random House, 1977.

Brady, John. *The Craft of the Screenwriter.* New York: Simon & Schuster, 1981.

Brenman-Gibson, Margaret. *Clifford Odets, American Playwright: The Years from 1906 to 1940.* New York: Atheneum, 1981.

Brown, Geoff. *Launder and Gilliat.* London: British Film Institute, 1977.

Brown, John Mason. *The Worlds of Robert E. Sherwood: Mirror to His Times, 1896–1939.* New York: Harper & Row, 1965.

————. *The Ordeal of a Playwright: Robert E. Sherwood and the Challenge of War*. New York: Harper & Row, 1970.

Brownlow, Kevin. *The Parade's Gone By*. New York: Ballantine, 1968.

Bruccoli, Matthew Joseph. *The O'Hara Concern: A Biography of John O'Hara*. New York: Random House, 1975.

————, ed. *The Selected Letters of John O'Hara*. New York: Random House, 1978.

Burrows, Abe. *Honest, Abe*. Boston: Little, Brown, 1980.

Caspary, Vera. *The Secrets of Grown-Ups*. New York: McGraw-Hill, 1979.

Ceplair, Larry and Steven Englund. *The Inquisition in Hollywood: Politics in the Film Community, 1930–1960*. Garden City, N.Y.: Anchor Press/ Doubleday, 1980.

Coffee, Lenore. *Storyline: Recollections of a Hollywood Screenwriter*. London: Cassell and Company, 1973.

Cole, Lester. *Hollywood Red*. Palo Alto, Calif.: Ramparts Press, 1981.

Connelly, Marc. *Voices Offstage*. New York: Holt, Rinehart & Winston, 1968.

Cook, Bruce. *Dalton Trumbo*. New York: Scribner's, 1977.

————. *Brecht in Exile*. New York: Holt, Rinehart & Winston, 1982.

Corliss, Richard. *Talking Pictures: Screenwriters in the American Cinema*. Woodstock, N.Y.: The Overlook Press, 1974.

————, ed. *The Hollywood Screenwriters*. New York: Avon, 1972.

Curtis, James. *Between Flops: A Biography of Preston Sturges*. New York: Harcourt Brace Jovanovich, 1982.

Dardis, Tom. *Some Time in the Sun*. New York: Scribner's, 1976.

Dick, Bernard F. *Hellman in Hollywood*. London: Fairleigh Dickinson University Press, 1982.

Dunne, Philip. *Take Two: A Life in Movies and Politics*. San Francisco: McGraw-Hill, 1980.

Easton, Robert. *Max Brand: The Big Westerner*. Norman: University of Oklahoma Press, 1970.

Ephron, Henry. *We Thought We Could Do Anything: The Life of Screenwriters Phoebe and Henry Ephron*. New York: Norton, 1977.

Ferber, Edna. *A Peculiar Treasure*. Garden City, N.Y.: Doubleday, 1960.

————. *A Kind of Magic*. New York: Lancer, 1966.

Fethering, Doug. *The Five Lives of Ben Hecht*. London: Lester and Orpen, 1977.

Forbes, Bryan. *Notes for a Life*. London: Collins, 1974.

Fordin, Hugh. *Getting to Know Him: A Biography of Oscar Hammerstein II*. New York: Random House, 1977.

Fowler, Douglas. *S. J. Perelman*. Boston: Twayne, 1983.

Fowler, Gene. *A Solo in Tom-Toms*. New York: Viking Press, 1946.

Fowler, Will. *The Young Man from Denver*. [A biography of Gene Fowler.] Garden City, N.Y.: Doubleday, 1962.

Freedland, Michael. *Irving Berlin*. New York: Stein and Day, 1974.

Froug, William. *The Screenwriter Looks at the Screenwriter*. New York: Macmillan, 1972.

Gardner, Dorothy and Katherine Sorley Walker. *Raymond Chandler Speaking.* Boston: Houghton Mifflin, 1962.

Geist, Kenneth L. *Pictures Will Talk: The Life and Films of Joseph L. Mankiewicz.* New York: Scribner's, 1978.

Gifford, Barry and Lawrence Lee. *Saroyan.* New York: Harper & Row, 1984.

Goldman, William. *Adventures in the Screen Trade: A Personal View of Hollywood and Screenwriting.* New York: Warner Books, 1982.

Gordon, Ruth. *Myself Among Others.* New York: Atheneum, 1971.

———. *My Side: The Autobiography of Ruth Gordon.* New York: Harper & Row, 1976.

———. *An Open Book.* Garden City, N.Y.: Doubleday, 1980.

Graham, Sheila. *The Garden of Allah.* New York: Crown Publishing, 1970.

———. *The Real F. Scott Fitzgerald: Thirty-Five Years Later.* New York: Grosset and Dunlap, 1976.

Gruber, Frank. *Zane Grey.* New York and Cleveland: World Publishing, 1970.

Guiles, Fred Lawrence. *Hanging on in Paradise.* New York: McGraw-Hill, 1975.

Hart, Moss. *Act One: An Autobiography.* New York: Random House, 1959.

Hecht, Ben. *A Child of the Century.* New York: Simon & Schuster, 1954.

———. *Charlie: The Improbable Life and Times of Charles MacArthur.* New York: Harper and Bros., 1957.

Hellman, Lillian. *Three.* ["An Unfinished Woman," "Pentimento," and "Scoundrel Time."] Boston and Toronto: Little, Brown, 1979.

Hoopes, Roy. *Cain: The Biography of James M. Cain.* New York: Holt, Rinehart & Winston, 1982.

Hurst, Fannie. *Anatomy of Me: A Wonderer in Search of Herself.* Garden City, N.Y.: Doubleday, 1958.

Huston, John. *An Open Book.* New York: Alfred A. Knopf, 1980.

Johnson, Diane. *Dashiell Hammett: A Life.* New York: Random House, 1983.

Johnson, Dorris and Ellen Leventhal, eds. *The Letters of Nunnally Johnson.* New York: Alfred A. Knopf, 1981.

Johnson, Nora. *Flashback: Nora Johnson on Nunnally Johnson.* Garden City, N.Y.: Doubleday, 1979.

Kael, Pauline. *The Citizen Kane Book.* Boston: Little, Brown, 1971.

Kahn, Gordon. *Hollywood on Trial.* New York: Arno Press/The New York Times, 1972.

Kanin, Garson. *Hollywood.* New York: Viking Press, 1974.

Karr, Jean. *Zane Grey, Man of the West.* New York: Greenberg, 1949.

Kawin, Bruce. *Faulkner on Film.* New York: Ungar, 1977.

Keats, John. *You Might as Well Live: The Life and Times of Dorothy Parker.* New York: Simon & Schuster, 1970.

Koch, Howard. *Casablanca: Script and Legend.* Woodstock, N.Y.: The Overlook Press, 1973.

———. *As Time Goes By: Memoirs of a Writer.* New York: Harcourt Brace Jovanovich, 1979.

Koury, Phil A. *Yes, Mr. DeMille.* New York: Putnam, 1959.

Kraft, Hy. *On My Way to the Theatre.* New York: Macmillan, 1971.

Lardner, Jr., Ring. *The Lardners: My Family Remembered.* New York: Harper & Row, 1976.

Lasky, Jr., Jesse. *Whatever Happened to Hollywood?.* New York: Funk & Wagnalls, 1973.

Latham, Aaron. *Crazy Sundays: F. Scott Fitzgerald in Hollywood.* New York: Viking Press, 1971.

Logan, Josh. *Josh: My Up and Down, In and Out Life.* New York: Delacorte Press, 1976.

———. *Movie Stars, Real People, and Me.* New York: Delacorte Press, 1978.

Loos, Anita. *A Girl Like I.* New York: Viking Press, 1966.

———. *Kiss Hollywood Goodbye.* New York: Viking Press, 1974.

———. *Cast of Thousands.* New York: Grosset and Dunlap, 1977.

MacShane, Frank. *The Life of Raymond Chandler.* New York: Dutton, 1976.

———. *The Life of John O'Hara.* New York: Dutton, 1980.

Madsen, Axel. *Billy Wilder.* London: Secker and Warburg, 1968.

Manfull, Helen, ed. *Additional Dialogue: Letters of Dalton Trumbo, 1942–1962.* New York: M. Evans, 1970.

Marion, Frances. *Off with Their Heads: A Serio-Comic Tale of Hollywood.* New York: Macmillan, 1972.

Martin, Jay. *Nathanael West—The Art of His Life.* New York: Farrar, Strauss, and Giroux, 1970.

Marx, Samuel. *Mayer and Thalberg: The Make-Believe Saints.* New York: Random House, 1975.

——— and Jan Clayton. *Rodgers and Hart: Bewitched, Bothered, and Bedeviled: An Anecdotal Account.* New York: Putnam, 1976.

Mayer, Edwin Justus. *A Preface to Life.* New York: Boni and Liveright, 1923.

Meredith, Scott. *George S. Kaufman and His Friends.* Garden City, N.Y.: Doubleday, 1974.

Merryman, Richard. *Mank: The Wit, World, and Life of Herman Mankiewicz.* New York: William Morrow, 1978.

Meserve, Walter J. *Robert E. Sherwood: Reluctant Moralist.* New York: Pegasus, 1970.

Miller, Henry Wise. *All Our Lives: Alice Duer Miller.* New York: Coward-McCann, 1945.

Mizener, Arthur. *The Far Side of Paradise: A Biography of F. Scott Fitzgerald.* Boston: Houghton Mifflin, 1951.

Moody, Richard. *Lillian Hellman, Playwright.* New York: Pegasus, 1972.

Moreau, Genevieve. *The Restless Journey of James Agee.* New York: William Morrow and Company, 1977.

Murray, Edward. *The Cinematic Imagination: Writers and the Motion Pictures.* New York: Ungar, 1972.

Navasky, Victor. *Naming Names.* New York: Viking, 1980.

Nolan, William F. *John Huston: King Rebel.* Los Angeles: Sherbourne Press, 1965.

———. *Dashiell Hammett: A Casebook.* Santa Barbara: McNally and Loftin, 1969.

Nugent, Elliott. *Events Leading up to Comedy.* New York: Trident Press, 1965.

Partridge, Mrs. Helen. *A Lady Goes to Hollywood.* [Wife of author Larence Davis.] New York: Macmillan, 1941.

Peary, Danny, ed. *Close-Ups: The Movie Star Book.* New York: Galahad Books, 1978.

Peary, Gerald and Roger Shatzkin. *The Classic American Novel and the Movies.* New York: Frederick Ungar, 1977.

———. *The Modern American Novel and the Movies.* New York: Frederick Ungar, 1978.

Rice, Elmer L. *Minority Report: An Autobiography.* New York: Simon & Schuster, 1963.

Rinehart, Mary Roberts. *My Story.* New York: Rinehart, 1948.

Rivkin, Allen and Laura Kerr. *Hello, Hollywood.* Garden City, N.Y.: Doubleday, 1962.

Robbins, Jhan. *Front Page Marriage: Helen Hayes and Charles MacArthur.* New York: Putnam, 1982.

Rodgers, Richard. *Musical Stages: An Autobiography.* New York: Random House, 1975.

Ross, Lillian. *Picture.* New York: Avon Books, 1969.

Rosten, Leo C. *Hollywood: The Movie Colony, the Movie Makers.* New York: Harcourt Brace, 1941.

Salzman, Jack. *Albert Maltz.* Boston: Twayne, 1978.

Saroyan, William. *Places Where I've Done Time.* New York: Praeger, 1972.

———. *Sons Come and Go, Mothers Hang in Forever.* New York and San Francisco: McGraw-Hill, 1976.

———. *Obituaries.* Berkeley: Creative Arts, 1979.

Schary, Dore. *Heyday.* Boston and Toronto: Little, Brown, 1979.

Schulberg, Budd. *Moving Pictures: Memoirs of a Hollywood Prince.* New York: Stein and Day, 1981.

Schwartz, Nancy Lynn. *The Hollywood Writers' Wars.* New York: Alfred A. Knopf, 1982.

Scott Evelyn F. *Hollywood: When Silents Were Golden.* [The life of Beulah Marie Dix as chronicled by her daughter.] New York: McGraw-Hill, 1972.

Sherriff, R. C. *No Leading Lady.* London: Gollancz, 1968.

Shuman, Robert Baird. *Clifford Odets.* New York: Twayne, 1962.

Silke, James R. *Here's Looking at You, Kid.* Boston: Little, Brown, 1976.

Smith, H. Allen. *The Life and Legend of Gene Fowler.* New York: William Morrow, 1977.

Stempel, Tom. *Screenwriter: The Life and Times of Nunnally Johnson.* San Diego/London: A. S. Barnes/Tantivy Press, 1980.

Stewart, Donald Ogden. *By a Stroke of Luck!.* New York and London: Paddington Press, 1975.

Sullivan, Edward Dean. *The Fabulous Wilson Mizner.* New York: The Henkle Company, 1935.

Talbot, David and Barbara Zheutlin. *Creative Differences: Profiles of Hollywood Dissidents.* Boston: South End Press, 1978.

Teichmann, Howard. *George S. Kaufman: An Intimate Portrait.* New York: Atheneum, 1972.

Trumbo, Dalton. *The Time of the Toad.* New York: Harper & Row, 1972.

Turnbull, Andrew, ed. *The Letters of F. Scott Fitzgerald.* New York: Scribner's, 1963.

Ursini, James. *The Fabulous Life and Times of Preston Sturges: An American Dreamer.* New York: Curtis Books, 1973.

Van Gelder, Robert. *Writers and Writing.* New York: Scribner's, 1946.

Veiller, Bayard. *The Fun I've Had.* New York: Roynal and Hitchcock, 1941.

Viertel, Salka. *The Kindness of Strangers.* New York: Holt, Rinehart & Winston, 1969.

Volker, Klaus. *Brecht: A Biography.* New York: The Seabury Press, 1978.

Wallace, Edgar. *My Hollywood Diary.* London: Hutchinson and Company, 1933.

West, Jessamyn. *To See the Dream.* [An account of the filming of *Friendly Persuasion.*] New York: Harcourt Brace, 1957.

White, Sidney Howard. *Sidney Howard.* Boston: Twayne, 1977.

Wild, Max, ed. *The Wit and Wisdom of Hollywood.* New York: Atheneum, 1971.

Wilde, Meta Carpenter and Orin Borsten. *A Loving Gentleman: The Love Story of William Faulkner and Meta Carpenter.* New York: Simon & Schuster, 1976.

Zolotow, Maurice. *Billy Wilder in Hollywood.* New York: Putnam, 1977.

Notes on Interviewers

Peter Brunette teaches literature and film at George Mason University and is finishing a book on Roberto Rossellini. He directed an NEH seminar on film theory at New York University.

Tina Daniell covered the entertainment industry in Los Angeles for *The Hollywood Reporter* and *Daily Variety*. She is now a business reporter for *The Milwaukee Journal*.

Allen Eyles was the editor of *Focus on Film* and, more recently, *Films and Filming*. Nowadays he only edits the obscure *Picture House*, a magazine of British movie palace history. He was written the books *The Marx Brothers*, *The Western*, *Bogart*, and, most recently, *James Stewart*, among others. He lives with his wife and two cats on the edge of London, England.

John Gillett is one of the best-known fixtures of the British Film Institute, having worked there in various senior capacities for donkey's years. He has organized countless retrospectives for London's National Film Theatre and is always traveling to foreign archives and festivals to select movies for British screenings. He has a particular passion for Japanese cinema and his taste knows few barriers. He has written for most of the leading British film journals and many newspapers.

Joel Greenberg, a resident of Sydney, Australia, has published film history and criticism in England, Australia, and the United States and is the co-author of *Hollywood in the Forties* and *The Celluloid Muse.*

Ken Mate has written about John Ford for *The Velvet Light Trap* and is the producer of a documentary feature about the lives of the Hollywood Ten and other blacklisted film industry progressives.

Joseph McBride is an author and screenwriter whose books include *John Ford, Orson Welles, Hawks on Hawks, Filmmakers on Filmmaking,* and *High and Inside: The Complete Guide to Baseball Slang.* His scripts include the cult classic film *Rock 'n' Roll High School,* and several television specials: "Let Poland be Poland" and the American Film Institute Life Achievement Award tributes to James Stewart, Fred Astaire, Frank Capra, John Huston, and Lillian Gish, for which he has received a Writers Guild of America Award, four WGA nominations, and an Emmy nomination. He was formerly business editor and film critic for *Daily Variety* and *Variety.*

Todd McCarthy is a film critic and writer whose articles and interviews appear regularly in notable film periodicals. He is a staff reporter and movie critic for *Daily Variety* and *Variety.* He was co-editor of *Kings of the Bs* and is presently completing a biography of director Howard Hawks.

Gerald Peary teaches at Suffolk University in Boston and is a contributing editor to *American Film.* He is film critic for *Flare,* Canada's fashion magazine. His books as co-editor include *Women and the Cinema, The Classic American Novel and the Movies* and *The Modern American Novel and the Movies.*

Mark Rowland is associate editor of *Musician* magazine and a contributor to several journals on music and film. He lives in Los Angeles, where he is not writing a screenplay.

David Thomson is the author of *A Biographical Dictionary of Film, America in the Dark,* and *Overexposures,* and a regular contributor to *Film Comment.* From 1977 to 1981, he taught film at Dartmouth College, where he wrote and directed a feature film, *White Lies.* He now lives in San Francisco and has recently written a novel, *Suspects,* from Knopf.

General Index

Italic numbers indicate references to photographs.

Index of Films, Plays, and Books

Italic numbers indicate references to photographs.

Compositor: Huron Valley Graphics
Text: 10/12 Times Roman
Display: Helvetica Bold
Printer: The Murray Printing Company
Binder: The Murray Printing Company